The Institute of Chartered Accountants in England and Wales

CORPORATE REPORTING

Edition 1

Question Bank

www.icaew.com

Corporate Reporting

The Institute of Chartered Accountants in England and Wales

ISBN: 978-0-85760-749-2

First edition 2014

British Library Cataloguing-in-Publication Data
A catalogue record for this book is available from the British Library

Printed in the United Kingdom by Polestar Wheatons

Polestar Wheatons
Hennock Road
Marsh Barton
Exeter
EX2 8RP

Your learning materials are printed on paper obtained from traceable, sustainable sources.

Contents

Marking – Technical Knowledge and Skills

Marks are awarded in the Corporate Reporting paper for both technical knowledge and professional skills.

Technical knowledge and understanding

Technical knowledge and understanding will include the information in the Corporate Reporting learning materials texts for financial reporting, taxation, auditing and ethics. It may also include brought forward knowledge from professional level. Marks will be awarded for displaying this knowledge in the context of the questions. The emphasis is on the use of knowledge, rather than repetition of knowledge. Consequently, technical knowledge needs to be applied to complex scenarios in light of the specific commercial and regulatory conditions in the question and taking account of client requirements.

Professional skills

Marks will also be awarded for exercising professional skills. For a full list of these skills, with examples, you should refer to the skills grid in the Study Guide. These skills are classified under four headings:

- Assimilating and using information
- Structuring problems and solutions
- Applying judgement
- Drawing conclusions and making recommendations

Each question will require different skills. Also, the balance of marks for technical knowledge and skills is likely to vary between questions. The balance is specific to each question, hence it is difficult to generalise. However, perhaps a question that has a heavy emphasis on international financial reporting standards is likely to have a high proportion of marks for technical knowledge. Conversely, a question which requires audit judgement and analysis, rather than being dependent on ISA rules, is likely to have a high proportion of skills marks.

As another example, ethical skills will demand more than the straightforward implementation of ethical rules. Rather, they are likely to require ethical judgement to be exercised in complex scenarios, where the appropriate ethical stance may be unclear.

Mark schemes in the question bank

In the question bank that follows, the total mark for each question is analysed according to marks for technical knowledge and marks for skills. This is, however, only a general guideline. Nevertheless, it does emphasise that, while a detailed technical knowledge and understanding of the regulations is essential, it is not enough, on its own, to pass. Passing will also require the use of professional skills in using that knowledge in the context of the scenario to address the specific requirements.

Question Bank

Financial reporting questions

1 Mervyn plc

Mervyn plc manufactures electrical components for the motor trade. Mervyn is in the process of finalising its financial statements for the year ended 30 September 20X7. Due to cash flow problems Mervyn sold two pieces of its freehold land during the current financial year. The land was held in the financial statements at cost. The finance director, reviewing the draft financial statements, has asked for your advice on these sales as well as on some unusual features identified.

An extract from the statement of changes in equity in the draft financial statements shows:

	Retained earnings £'000
At 1 October 20X6	2,190
Profit for the year	1,471
Dividends paid	(515)
At 30 September 20X7	3,146

There is a note explaining that there is no 'other comprehensive income' in the statement of profit or loss and other comprehensive income as there are no gains and losses other than those recognised in profit or loss for the year.

The statement of profit or loss and other comprehensive income shows an 'exceptional' gain relating to gains on the two land bank sales:

	£'000
The Ridings	100
Hanger Hill Estate	250
	350

A contract for the sale of land at The Ridings was entered into in June 20X7 conditional upon obtaining a detailed planning consent, but only outline consent had been obtained by 30 September 20X7. Planning consent was received in October and the land sale was completed in November 20X7. Tax of £27,000 has been provided on the sale.

The sale of land at Hanger Hill to the Beauford Corp on 1 October 20X6 took place under a sale and leaseback arrangement. The terms of the lease arrangement were:

Lease term	Five years
Rentals first payable on 30 September 20X7	£80,000 per annum

On 1 October 20X6 the carrying amount of the Hanger Hill land was £900,000 and its fair value was £950,000. The first rental was paid on its due date and charged to operating expenses.

Beauford Corp is expected to take possession of this land at the conclusion of the lease.

The cumulative discount factor for a five-year annuity at 10% (the appropriate interest rate for this transaction) is 3.791.

Operating expenses include £405,000 relating to the company's defined benefit pension scheme. This figure represents the contributions paid into the scheme in the year. No other entries have been made relating to this scheme. The figures included in the draft statement of financial position represent opening balances as at 1 October 20X6:

	£'000
Pension scheme assets	2,160
Pension scheme liabilities	(2,530)
	(370)
Deferred tax asset	118
	(252)

After the year end, a report was obtained from an independent actuary. This gave valuations as at 30 September 20X7 of:

	£'000
Pension scheme assets	2,090
Pension scheme liabilities	(2,625)

Other information in the report included:

Current service cost	374
Payment out of scheme relating to employees transferring out	400
Reduction in liability relating to transfers	350
Pensions paid	220
Interest rate on high quality corporate bonds at 1 September 20X7	10%

All receipts and payments into and out of the scheme can be assumed to have occurred on 30 September 20X7.

Mervyn's accounting policy is to recognise any gains and losses on remeasurement of the defined benefit asset or liability (actuarial gains and losses) in accordance with IAS 19 *Employee Benefits* (revised 2011).

In the tax regime in which Mervyn operates, a tax deduction is allowed on payment of pension benefits. No tax deduction is allowed for contributions made to the scheme. The rate of tax applicable to 20X6, 20X7 and announced for 20X8 is 23%.

In March 20X7 a customer of Mervyn brought legal proceedings against Mervyn for alleged injury to employees and loss of business through a fault in one of Mervyn's products. In September 20X7 the case came to court but Mervyn's lawyers think that it could be a very lengthy case and believe that Mervyn will lose the case. The actual cost of damages and timing of the case are far from clear but management have made a number of estimates. They believe that the best outcome for Mervyn will be damages of £200,000 payable in one year's time. The worst possible outcome would be for the case to continue for three more years in which case the estimate of damages and costs is £1,500,000 payable in three years' time. A further estimate, between these two extremes, is that damages of £800,000 will be payable in two years' time. Management's estimates of probabilities are best outcome 25%, worst case outcome 15% and middle ground outcome 60%. No provision nor any disclosure has been made for this court case in the financial statements.

Mervyn has a new arrangement with one particular customer that Mervyn will hold the goods that it sells until such time as the customer needs them. The customer is invoiced for the goods when they are ready for delivery, but they are held until the customer needs them. The accountant of Mervyn has not been recognising the revenue on these sales until the delivery has taken place to the customer. At 30 September 20X7, there were goods with a selling price of £138,000 and cost of £99,000 which had not yet been delivered to the customer. These goods had been included at cost when the inventory count took place.

The company granted share appreciation rights (SARs) to its employees on 1 October 20X5 based on ten thousand shares. The SARs provide employees at the date the rights are exercised with the right to receive cash equal to the appreciation in the company's share price since the grant date. The rights vested on 30 September 20X7 and payment was made on schedule on 1 November 20X7. The fair value of the SARs per share at 30 September 20X6 was £6, at 30 September 20X7 was £8 and at 1 November 20X7 was £9. The company has recognised a liability for the SARs as at 30 September 20X6 based upon IFRS 2 *Share-based Payment* but the liability was stated at the same amount at 30 September 20X7.

If any figures are to be discounted a rate of 10% per annum should be used.

Requirement

Explain how each of the above transactions should be treated in the financial statements for the year ended 30 September 20X7 and prepare a statement of amended profit for the year ended 30 September 20X7. **(30 marks)**

2   Biohealth

Biohealth is a small biotechnology research and healthcare products group listed in the UK reporting to 31 December 20X7.

The finance director was assisted in prior years by a very able financial assistant (Eileen) who has since left the company shortly before the year-end. A suitable replacement has not yet been recruited. The finance director relied on his financial assistant to process the more technical journals in respect of development costs, associate investments and share-based payments. The finance director has contacted your firm outlining the accounting services required to finalise the draft financial statements. Your manager has forwarded the details of the request and has asked you to undertake the necessary calculations and outline the journal adjustments required. The finance director has provided your manager with draft financial statements which will need to be adjusted as appropriate for the following issues.

Research and development

"We have commenced developing a couple of new products this year – Sorpandex and Bimoranol. The only thing I have done so far is to include every element of the costs which are detailed below within development assets. Eileen, our former financial assistant, used to make adjustments to expense some of the spending based on the information provided by the development, production, sales and marketing teams. I have enclosed the completed Product Development Information Requests which Eileen used to use. I'm very confident you won't need to make any adjustment to reduce our profits. Roy, who completed the technical feasibility section, is an eternal pessimist. I can get him to write something more upbeat about Sorpandex if it turns out to be critical to the Proposed Bonus Scheme. Please could you calculate any adjustments you think are necessary?"

Sorpandex	Product development information request
Product name:	Sorpandex – generic oral pain relief drug for arthritis sufferers. Development focused on much cheaper production using microwave chemistry.
Salary costs:	£567,200 in 20X7
Consumables:	£829,700 in 20X7
Capital goods: (specify life/salvage)	£433,000 (Microwave upgrade at the start of the year – we had to replace the old microwave with this more powerful one needed for production of Sorpandex). Useful life of five years. Nil salvage value.
Technical feasibility review:	We are not close to achieving Good Production Practice standards necessary to progress to commercial production – current microwave technology (we have the best microwave available) can't consistently ensure full reaction of the compounds. Any organic reaction alternative is too expensive to consider. We need microwave technology to improve before we can progress.
Forward view:	Microwave technology and application are new in this area – we will continue seeking to understand why the microwave results are inconsistent and see if it's possible to produce a microwave that solves our problem. The current microwave can usefully be applied elsewhere in the research facility.
	We can't sell the research to anyone without the technology to apply it.
Product market prospects:	This drug should do very well – we can sell it cheaper than any rival drug on the market. We anticipate profits of £0.9m p.a. once established in the marketplace based on expected sales and estimated unit production costs.
Resource support:	The successful development hinges on a more sophisticated microwave being developed. The project has a remaining budget of £3.762m which should easily cover this cost.
	Total expected future costs are £3.117m (including an estimated microwave cost of £0.75m).

Bimoranol	Product development information request
Product name:	Bimoranol – a new steroidal anti-inflammatory drug
Salary costs:	£988,300 in 20X7
Consumables:	£764,200 in 20X7
Capital goods: (specify life/salvage)	£nil
Technical feasibility review:	Full technical testing has been undertaken – proposed production complies with Good Production Practice standards. All trials are proving successful. Technical testing was concluded at the end of December 20X6.
Forward view:	This product development is advancing better than expected and we are ahead of schedule with no problems expected to be encountered.
	We could sell the development as it stands, but would do better to aim for producing the drug in-house.
Product market prospects:	The fact that the drug has shown itself to reduce side-effects means it will gain a reasonable market share. Forecast sales estimates and in-house production still estimate annual recurring profits of around £1.1m p.a. once the product is established.
Resource support:	The project has a remaining budget of £3.787m which should easily cover this cost.
	Total expected future costs are now estimated at £2.876m.

Associate investment

"We acquired a further 20% stake in Laboratory Science Services on 1 November 20X7 taking our holding to 40%. They supply some of the specialist equipment we rely on in our research. This gives us the influence to help shape their production programme and board representation. We didn't get any dividends, but the profits are healthy. Eileen left a Due Diligence file with numbers for the deal which is shown below. I've included the numbers to 31 December 20X7 – the year-end results – in the schedule."

Statement of financial position – Laboratory Science Services

	01-Nov-X7 Book value £'000	01-Nov-X7 Fair value £'000	31-Dec-X7 Book value £'000	31-Dec-X7 Fair value £'000
Property, plant and equipment	4,287.4	4,287.4	4,147.9	4,147.9
Investments	854.7	1,142.2	854.7	1,142.2
Non-current assets	5,142.1	5,429.6	5,002.6	5,290.1
Inventory	854.0	854.0	1,021.6	1,021.6
Receivables	456.9	456.9	519.9	519.9
Cash and equivalents	2,754.5	2,754.5	2,998.6	2,998.6
Current assets	4,065.4	4,065.4	4,540.1	4,540.1
Total assets	**9,207.5**	**9,495.0**	**9,542.7**	**9,830.2**
Payables and other liabilities	876.3	876.3	866.2	866.2
Short-term debt	67.0	67.0	42.8	42.8
Current liabilities	943.3	943.3	909.0	909.0
Long-term debt	500.0	500.0	500.0	500.0
Deferred tax	675.3	456.4	541.3	322.4
Non-current liabilities	1,175.3	956.4	1,041.3	822.4
Share capital	623.0	623.0	623.0	623.0
Reserves	6,465.9	6,972.3	6,969.4	7,475.8
Equity	7,088.9	7,595.3	7,592.4	8,098.8
Total liabilities and equity	**9,207.5**	**9,495.0**	**9,542.7**	**9,830.2**

Statement of profit or loss and other comprehensive income

	10 months to 01-Nov-X7 £'000	12 months to 31-Dec-X7 £'000
Revenue	10,365.3	12,645.7
Cost of sales	5,349.7	6,522.1
Selling, general and admin	1,294.6	1,563.9
Operating profit	3,721.0	4,559.7
Net financial expense	354.0	456.0
Profit before tax	3,367.0	4,103.7
Taxes	1,111.1	1,344.3
Profit after tax	2,255.9	2,759.4

"Eileen also drafted a detailed addition to our accounting policy on equity method investments, which states:

"Biohealth's policy is to account for significant influence through successive share purchases under full application of IFRS 3. This alternative calculates goodwill at each purchase stage, and any existing available-for-sale reserve is reversed in equity, restating the investment to cost. The share of net assets arising from prior purchases is then re-valued to fair value at the date that significant influence is achieved, with a corresponding entry directly to equity reserves.

The deal was done in cash for a total of £1,238,500, so I have added this to the 'Associate Investments' line. I haven't done anything with the £645,800 that's sitting in the 'available-for-sale Investments' line – the original cost of the first 20% of Laboratory Science Services that we purchased a few years ago. The shares aren't traded so we couldn't adjust to fair value. I have a schedule which shows the positive goodwill relating to the original purchase was £128,300. I've made no other entries regarding the investment. Please could you calculate the required adjustments?"

Impairment of the generic drugs division

"On 12 November 20X7, the FDA (Food and Drug Administration – the US regulator) suspended our licence to produce and sell Panthraximin in the US due to a breach of Good Distribution Practices. Panthraximin is produced by our Generic Drugs Division, and was one of their key products. At 31 December 20X7, the carrying amount of the combined net assets of the Generic Drugs Division was estimated at £295.8m. This is detailed in the schedule below prepared by Eileen before her departure. No impairment losses had previously been recognised."

Statement of financial position at 31 December 20X7 – Generic Drugs Division

	Book value £'000	Comments
Property, plant and equipment	188,200	Depreciated cost
Acquired intangibles	16,700	Amortised cost – patents and licence
Allocated goodwill	27,900	From acquisition
Non-current assets	232,800	
Inventory	64,900	Carried below fair value
Receivables	35,800	At fair value
Cash and equivalents	6,100	At fair value
Current assets	106,800	
Total assets	339,600	
Payables and other liabilities	43,800	At fair value
Total liabilities	43,800	
Net assets	295,800	

"We decided to sell some of the specialist assets and redeploy the rest elsewhere within the Generic Drugs Division. We got our bankers to produce a valuation of the Generic Drugs Division – they estimate the division could be sold for £250m, leaving us with £242m after fees and other costs.

Eileen also prepared a schedule of the estimated net cash inflows for the Generic Drugs Division (taking into account sale or redeployment of the assets making the Panthraximin drug, and the impact of ceasing Panthraximin production). The summary page is extracted below. The appropriate risk-adjusted pre-tax discount rate was determined to be 9.5% for the valuation in use of the cash-generating unit."

Estimated pre-tax cash flows for Generic Drugs Division (revised)

Year		£'000
1	Year-end cash flow – 31 Dec 20X8	21,200
2	Year-end cash flow – 31 Dec 20X9	22,025
3	Year-end cash flow – 31 Dec 20Y0	23,210
4	Year-end cash flow – 31 Dec 20Y1	24,122
5	Each year end thereafter – no growth	24,900
	Pre-tax discount rate	9.5%

"Please can you assess whether any impairment adjustment is necessary to the cash-generating unit, and calculate the adjustment to the relevant asset headings if there is an impairment?

"On 18 December 20X7 we issued redundancy notices to a number of employees involved in the production of Panthraximin whom we couldn't usefully redeploy elsewhere within the business. We will terminate their employment from 31 March 20X8, at which time the redundancy payments of £1.2m will be settled. I haven't done anything about these costs as yet."

Proposed bonus scheme

We are proposing to introduce a new bonus scheme for directors for each of the following year ends, 31 December 20X6, 20X7 and 20X8. For the directors to be eligible, the underlying net profit after tax should show an increase for each of the three year ends and will be payable at the end of 20X8. Underlying profit for the years ended 31 December 20X6 and 20X7 were £2,643,000 and £2,663,000, respectively.

I asked Eileen before she left, to assess whether we were going to achieve this target. She said that the definition of underlying profit excluded the impairment and redundancies, as well as the charge for the bonus itself, but would be affected by other adjustments you need to make.

Biohealth engaged the services of VS a management consultant. However Biohealth was short of cash and agreed that Biohealth would pay VS in the form of shares (nominal value £1). The agreement began on 1 January 20X7 and was initially for a two year period. Biohealth has agreed to issue 10,000 ordinary shares every six months in exchange for 400 hours of management consultancy services over each six month period.

The hourly rate charged by VS on 1 January 20X7 was £100 per hour but this is increased by 10% on 1 July 20X7 and will increase by a further 10% on 1 July 20X8. The market value of Biohealth's shares at 1 January 20X7 was £6 per share.

Manager's request

Your manager has asked you to prepare a memorandum clearly showing:

- The journal adjustments required to the draft financial statements
- Any assumptions you have made
- An explanation of any judgements you have made, and
- All necessary workings to support your journal entries

The manager has also asked you to comment on whether the conditions under the proposed bonus scheme will be satisfied leading to a bonus being paid.

Requirement

Respond to the manager's request.   **(30 marks)**

3 Longwood

The Longwood Group is a listed European entity specialising in high grade alloy production for civil aviation, military and specialist engineering applications. On 1 January 20X7, Longwood completed the acquisition of a private company, Portobello Alloys, to strengthen its product offering in high-performance electro-magnetic alloys.

The total price paid to acquire the entire share capital of Portobello Alloys was £57m in cash paid on the deal date, along with a further £10m in deferred cash and 5m shares in The Longwood Group, both to be paid or issued in three years' time. The share price of The Longwood Group was £1.88 at 1 January 20X7, but rose to £2.04 shortly after the acquisition was completed. The best estimate of the share price on the transfer date in three years is £2.25. The appropriate discount rate for deferred consideration is 10%.

Longwood paid its bankers and lawyers fees of £0.8m in connection with the deal. Longwood estimates that £0.2m of the finance department costs relate to time spent on the acquisition by the Finance Director and his team.

Below is the draft 'deal-date' statement of financial position of Portobello Alloys. You may assume the carrying amounts of assets and liabilities are equal to their fair values, except as indicated in the information that follows.

Portobello Alloys – Statement of financial position at 1 January 20X7

	Carrying amount £m
Property, plant and equipment	18.92
Development asset	0.00
Available-for-sale investments	4.37
Deferred tax asset	0.77
Non-current assets	24.06
Inventory	7.33
Accounts receivable and prepayments	4.17
Cash and equivalents	4.22
Current assets	15.72
TOTAL ASSETS	39.78
Long-term debt	16.34
Post-retirement liability	0.37
Deferred tax liability	1.86
Non-current liabilities	18.57
Accounts payable and accruals	7.91
Current portion of long-term debt	3.40
Current liabilities	11.31
Share capital	2.50
Share premium	1.20
Retained earnings	6.20
Equity	9.90
TOTAL LIABILITIES AND EQUITY	39.78

Both Longwood and Portobello report to 31 December each year. The Board has asked your firm to examine the deferred tax implications of various areas relating to the acquisition.

Research and development

Portobello Alloys applied a policy of expensing all development expenditure as incurred. Longwood's policy is to capitalise development cost as an intangible asset under IAS 38. The carrying amount of the development asset in the deal-date statement of financial position was £0m. The fair value of the development asset was actually £5.26m at the deal date. None of this development asset will be amortised over the next year.

Property, plant and equipment

Portobello's premises are located on a prime piece of commercial real-estate. The surveyors have indicated that the land is worth £2.73m in excess of its carrying amount in the financial statements of the company. The Longwood Group has no intention of selling the property as, if it changed location, they could lose some of the key staff. Longwood's policy is to carry assets at depreciated cost, and it does not revalue any assets on a regular basis.

Retirement benefit obligation

Portobello operates a defined benefit plan for its key research and production employees. The plan asset manager has made some bad equity investments over the years, and the plan is in deficit by £1.65m. Portobello only recognised a liability of £0.37m in its financial statements. The local tax authorities grant tax relief on the cash contribution into the plan.

Tax losses

Portobello made a disastrous foray into supplying specialist alloys to a now defunct electronics business, Electrotech. It set up a special division, took on new premises and staff, and spent a lot of money on joint development with its client. Electrotech promptly went into liquidation. Portobello incurred total tax losses of £7.40m over the two years that it was involved with Electrotech – it has now paid all the redundancy costs, sold all the assets and closed the division. To date, Portobello Alloys has only relieved £1.20m of the losses. The revised forecast numbers for Portobello's performance post-acquisition suggest it will be able to relieve the balance of losses in the next couple of years (see below). Up to the date of the deal, the management forecasts used to calculate the deferred tax in the financial statements had only anticipated relieving £2.20m of the losses, as indicated in the schedule below.

Profit forecasts for tax loss utilisation

	20X7 £m	20X8 £m	Total £m
Forecast taxable profit – original	0.98	1.22	2.20
Forecast taxable profit – revised	1.90	4.74	6.64

Enacted tax rates

Deferred taxes in the deal-date statement of financial position extracted above were calculated using a tax rate of 30%. However, the corporate tax rate for Portobello has been enacted to fall to 23% for the period after 1 January 20X7. A schedule of the composition of the deferred tax assets and liabilities included in the deal-date statement of financial position is shown below.

Deferred tax schedule

	Carrying amount £m	Tax base £m	Temporary difference £m	Deferred tax 30% £m
Property, plant and equipment	18.92	13.78	(5.14)	(1.54)
Available-for-sale investments	4.37	3.30	(1.07)	(0.32)
Post-retirement liability	(0.37)	0.00	0.37	0.11
Unrelieved tax losses – recognised	0.00	2.20	2.20	0.66
				(1.09)
Deferred tax liability				(1.86)
Deferred tax asset				0.77
				(1.09)

The finance director has asked you to produce the following information:

(a) Calculate the adjustment required to the deferred tax figures in the financial statements of Portobello Alloys solely in respect of the change in enacted tax rates and draft the required journal.

(b) Calculate the adjustment required to the deferred tax asset relating to unrecognised tax losses in Portobello's financial statements resulting from the revised estimates of profitability over the next two years. You should provide a draft correcting journal.

(c) Calculate the deferred tax effect of the consolidation adjustments in respect of:

- Fair value adjustments to property, plant and equipment
- Fair value adjustments to the development asset
- Fair value adjustments to the post-retirement liability

(d) Calculate the goodwill arising in the consolidated financial statements in respect of this acquisition.

(e) Explain the deferred tax treatment of goodwill under two possible deal structures for the acquisition of Portobello Alloys:

- As the acquisition actually took place, with the purchase of the shares of Portobello Alloys,

- Under an alternative structure, with the purchase of the assets and liabilities of Portobello Alloys instead, which would have granted tax relief charged over 15 years on the straight-line basis on purchased goodwill.

Requirement

Prepare the information required by the finance director.   **(30 marks)**

4   Talbot plc

Talbot plc (Talbot) is a glass recycling company, whose shares are quoted on AIM. You are the company's financial controller, and the year end is 30 April 20X4.

Demand for glass recycling has expanded rapidly in the UK, and accordingly Talbot has grown organically in its home market. Recycling is also becoming more popular overseas, as companies become more aware of their responsibilities to stakeholders. Flask Co (Flask), a recycling company operating in Ruritania, has achieved substantial growth in recent years and John Goddard, the Chief Executive of Talbot, saw it as a target for acquisition.

Accordingly, on 1 May 20X3, Talbot acquired 75% of the issued ordinary share capital of Flask for 240 million Ruritanian Kromits (K). The retained earnings of Flask at that date were 160 million Kromits.

It is now 15 June 20X4. You have received the following email from the finance director of Talbot.

To: Group Financial Controller
From: Finance Director
Date: 15 June 20X4
Subject: Acquisition of Flask Co

Please find attached the separate financial statements of Talbot plc and Flask Co (see **Appendix 1**). I also attach some notes relating to the acquisition; some of this information has come from the Chief Accountant of Flask. The notes are contained in **Appendix 2**.

John Goddard is a little concerned that the performance of Flask Co has failed to meet his expectations. He was wondering if there was a way to minimise disclosure about its results, or, failing that, whether there could be a way that the favourable movement in exchange rates might be used to show these results in the best possible light.

I therefore need you to prepare a report containing the following information:

- An explanation of the required financial reporting treatment of Flask Co.

- A draft of the consolidated financial statements, together with supporting workings. Only the statement of profit or loss (as far as profit after tax) is needed at this stage.

Assume the tax figures are correct for the purposes of your report.

Requirement

Prepare the report required by the finance director of Talbot plc.   **(30 marks)**

Appendix 1 – Separate financial statements

Statement of financial position at 30 April 20X4

	Talbot £m	Flask Km
Property, plant and equipment	594	292
Investment in Flask	96	–
Loan to Flask	10	–
Current assets	710	204
	1,410	496
Equity		
Ordinary shares of £1/K1	120	64
Share premium account	100	40
Retained earnings	720	190
	940	294
Non-current liabilities	60	82
Current liabilities	410	120
	1,410	496

Statements of profit or loss for year ended 30 April 20X4

	Talbot £m	Flask Km
Revenue	400	284
Cost of sales	(240)	(192)
Gross profit	160	92
Distribution and administrative expenses	(60)	(40)
Profit from operations	100	52
Interest receivable	8	–
Interest payable	–	(4)
Profit before taxation	108	48
Income tax expense	(40)	(18)
Profit after taxation	68	30

Appendix 2 – Notes

(a) As you know, under revised IFRS 3 *Business Combinations* we may now value the non-controlling interest at acquisition at fair value. The fair value of the non-controlling interest of Flask at acquisition was 76 million Kromits.

(b) Goodwill is reviewed for impairment annually. At 30 April 20X4, the impairment loss in respect of recognised goodwill (group plus non-controlling interest) was K11.2m.

(c) During the financial year Flask has purchased raw materials from Talbot and denominated the purchase in Kromits in its financial records. The details of the transaction are set out below:

	Date of transaction	Selling price £m	Talbot's margin on selling price
Raw materials	1 February 20X4	12	20%

At the year-end, half of the raw materials purchased were still in the inventory of Flask. The intragroup transactions have not been eliminated from the financial statements and the goods were recorded by Flask at the exchange rate ruling on 1 February 20X4. A payment of £12 million was made to Talbot when the exchange rate was 2.2 Kromits to £1. Any exchange gain or loss arising on the transaction is still held in the current liabilities of Flask.

(d) Flask has not revalued its assets or issued any share capital since its acquisition by Talbot.

(e) Talbot had made an interest free loan to Flask of £10 million on 1 May 20X3. The loan was repaid on 30 May 20X4. Flask had included the loan in non-current liabilities and had recorded it at the exchange rate at 1 May 20X3.

(f) The fair value of the net assets of Flask at the date of acquisition is to be assumed to be the same as the carrying amount.

(g) Talbot has paid a dividend of £16 million during the financial year.

(h) The functional currency of Flask is the Kromit.

(i) The following exchange rates are relevant to the financial statements:

	Kromits to £
30 April/1 May 20X3	2.5
1 November 20X3	2.6
1 February 20X4	2.0
30 April 20X4	2.1
Average rate for year to 30 April 20X4	2.0

5 MaxiMart plc

MaxiMart plc operates a national chain of supermarkets. You are Vimal Subramanian, the Assistant Financial Controller, and the accounting year-end is 30 September 20X1.

It is now 15 November 20X1 and the company's auditors are currently engaged in their work. Jane Lewis, the Financial Controller, is shortly to go into a meeting with the audit engagement partner, Roger MacIntyre, to discuss some unresolved issues relating to employee remuneration, hedging and the customer reward card. To save her time, she wants you to prepare a memorandum detailing the correct financial reporting treatment. She has sent you the following e-mail, in which she explains the issues.

From: jlewis@maximart.com

To: vsubramanian@maximart.com

Date: 15 November 20X1

Subject: Financial statements of MaxiMart

I am pleased you can help me out with the information for my forthcoming meeting with Roger MacIntyre – as you know, I have been tied up with other work, and have not had time to look into these outstanding issues.

As you will see (**Exhibit 1**) the principal issues concern remuneration:

Historically we have had a problem with high staff turnover due to low salaries and having to work evenings and weekends. To encourage better staff retention, we introduced a share option scheme. Details of the scheme are given in **Exhibit 1**. I need you to show how the share option scheme should be dealt with in the financial statements of MaxiMart for the year ended 30 September 20X1.

Exhibit 1 also has details of the company pension scheme, which was introduced a few years ago to encourage management trainees to stay with us. Since many of our rivals no longer provide defined benefit schemes, this gives MaxiMart an edge. It would help in the meeting if I could show Roger MacIntyre the relevant extracts from the financial statements. You will need to show the amounts to be recognised in the statement of profit or loss and other comprehensive income of MaxiMart for the year ended 30 September 20X1 and in the statement of financial position at that date so far as the information permits, in accordance with IAS 19 *Employee Benefits* (revised 2011). You should also include the notes, breaking down the defined benefit pension charge to profit or loss, other comprehensive income, net pension asset/liability at the year end and changes in the present value of pension obligation and the fair value of plan assets.

There will be a deferred tax effect arising from the pension plan, but we will deal with that on a later occasion, as there isn't time before the meeting.

I also attach details of three further issues (**Exhibit 2**). The first relates to our Reward Card. I believe there is an IFRIC relevant to the treatment of these schemes, but I can't remember exactly what it says. The second issue is a futures contract. It would be good if you could explain how we should treat this and show the double entry. The third issue is a proposed dividend – we need to know if the proposed treatment is correct.

Please draft a memorandum showing the appropriate treatment of these transactions together with explanations and any necessary workings.

Requirement

Prepare the memorandum required by Jane Lewis.   **(30 marks)**

Exhibit 1: Staff remuneration

Share options

On 1 October 20X0, the board decided to award share options to all 1,000 employees provided they remained in employment for five years. At 1 October 20X0, 20% of employees were expected to leave over the vesting period to 30 September 20X5 and as at 30 September 20X1, this expectation had risen to 25%. The fair value of these options at 1 October 20X0 was £2 and this had risen to £3 by 30 September 20X1. The number of options per employee is conditional on the average profit before any expense for share options over the five years commencing 1 October 20X0 as follows:

Average profit	Number of options per employee
From £1m up to £1.2m	100
Above £1.2m up to £1.4m	120
Above £1.4m up to £1.6m	140
Above £1.6m up to £1.8m	160
Above £1.8m	180

Profit before share option expense for the year ended 30 September 20X1 was £0.9m and profit for the following four years was forecast to rise by £0.2m a year. The awarding of the options was also conditional on the share price reaching at least £8 per share by 30 September 20X5. The share price at 30 September 20X1 was £6.

Pension scheme

MaxiMart set up a funded defined benefit pension plan for management-track employees three years ago. The plan provides a pension based on $1/80^{th}$ of the final salary for each year worked for the company, subject to a minimum employment period of eight years.

The following information has been provided by the actuary for the year ended 30 September 20X1:

(a) The present value in terms of future pensions from employee service during the year is £90,000. This has been determined using the projected unit credit method.

(b) The present value of the obligation to provide benefits to current and former employees has been calculated as £2,410,000 at 30 September 20X1 and the fair value of plan assets was £2,370,000 at the same date.

(c) The interest rate on high quality corporate bonds relevant to the year was 5%.

The following has been extracted from the financial records:

(a) The present value of the defined benefit obligation was £2,200,000 at 30 September 20X0 and the fair value of the plan assets was £2,300,000 at the same date.

(b) Pensions paid to former employees during the year amounted to £60,000.

(c) Contributions paid into the plan during the year as decided by the actuary were £68,000.

    With effect from 1 October 20X0, the company amended the plan to increase pension entitlement for employees. The additional cost of the improvement in benefits was calculated by the actuary to be approximately £100,000 at 1 October 20X0. The present value of the plan liability at 30 September 20X1 correctly reflects the impact of this increase.

(d) The company recognises gains and losses on remeasurement of the defined benefit asset or liability (actuarial gains and losses) in accordance with IAS 19 *Employee Benefits* (revised 2011).

(e) Pension payments and the contributions into the plan were paid on 30 September 20X1.

Exhibit 2: Other transactions

Reward card

MaxiMart offers its customers a reward card which awards customers points based on money spent. These points may be redeemed as money off future purchases from MaxiMart or as free/discounted goods from other retailers. Revenue from food sales for the year ended 30 September 20X1 amounted to £100m. At the year end, it is estimated that there are reward points worth £5m arising from this revenue which are eligible for redemption. Based on past experience, it is estimated that only about two in five customers are likely to redeem their points.

Futures contract

MaxiMart entered into a futures contract during the year to hedge a forecast sale in the year ended 30 September 20X2. The futures contract was designated and documented as a cash flow hedge. At 30 September 20X1, had the forecast sale occurred, the company would have suffered a loss of £1.9m and the futures contract was standing at a gain of £2m. No accounting entries have been made to record the futures contract.

Proposed dividend

The company has a good relationship with its shareholders and employees. It has adopted a strategy of gradually increasing its dividend payments over the years. On 1 November 20X1, the board proposed a dividend of 5p per share for the year ended 30 September 20X1. The shareholders will approve the dividend along with the financial statements at the general meeting on 1 December 20X1 and the dividend will be paid on 14 December 20X1. The directors feel that the dividend should be accrued in the financial statements for the year ended 30 September 20X1 as a 'valid expectation' has been created.

6 Icicle plc

Icicle plc is an AIM listed company that manufactures satellite navigation equipment for cars. You are Dean Claire, a chartered accountant working on a six-month contract at Icicle.

Jacqueline Hyde, Icicle's chief executive, has asked you to advise the company on deferred tax issues in relation to the year ended 31 March 20X9. This is because the finance director has suffered a long term illness and is unable to work at present.

Jacqueline provides you with a file (**Exhibit 1**) prepared by a member of the finance department, which contains a number of transactions that have financial reporting implications, including deferred tax issues.

Jacqueline also provides you with extracts from the draft financial statements for the year ended 31 March 20X9 (**Exhibit 2**). No adjustments in respect of deferred tax have been made in these draft extracts.

She asks you to prepare a briefing note which provides explanations and calculations of the financial reporting implications, including deferred taxation, for each of the transactions in the file (**Exhibit 1**) on the consolidated financial statements for the year ended 31 March 20X9. Also, Jacqueline asks you to redraft the extracts provided (**Exhibit 2**), providing a comprehensive summary of the transactions leading to the revised figures. She requests that you then calculate the consolidated basic earnings per share.

Jacqueline has asked you to use the working assumption that Icicle will continue to pay corporation tax at the current rate of 23%.

Requirement

Prepare the briefing note requested by Jacqueline Hyde. **(30 marks)**

Exhibit 1 – Deferred tax issues identified by accounts department

1 **Non-current assets**

At 1 April 20X8 Icicle owned factory equipment that was acquired on a variety of dates, and qualifies for capital allowances for tax purposes at 20% reducing balance per annum from 1 April 20X8. On this date, the equipment had a carrying amount of £6.4 million and a tax base of £3.4 million. The original cost of the equipment was £9.6 million, and none of the equipment is more than four years old at 1 April 20X8. On 1 October 20X8 Icicle purchased additional factory equipment for £2.2 million. Icicle has depreciated all factory equipment on a straight-line basis over five years. The factory equipment is the only asset category on which deferred tax was recognised in the financial statements for the year ended 31 March 20X8.

In addition, Icicle purchased land which cost £5.8 million on 1 April 20X5. The land was revalued to £15 million at 31 March 20X9, representing its fair value at that date. A surplus of £9.2 million was credited to other comprehensive income.

The factory equipment and the land are the only tangible non-current assets owned by Icicle.

2 Acquisition of a subsidiary

On 1 January 20X9 Icicle acquired 100% of the ordinary shares of Snowball Ltd for £4 million cash. At the acquisition date, Snowball had net assets with a carrying amount of £2.6 million in the statement of financial position, which is the same as the tax base. The board of Icicle believes these net assets have a fair value of £3.4 million. The difference is due to the valuation of an intangible asset which the board have concluded has an indefinite life. Impairment tests have been completed which demonstrate no change is required to the carrying amount of any intangibles.

Icicle has sold goods to Snowball for a number of years prior to acquisition. In the year ended 31 March 20X9, Icicle generated revenues of £1.5 million from Snowball, of which 80% occurred after 1 January 20X9.

Icicle has a mark up on cost of 25%. At 31 March 20X9 Snowball has inventory purchased from Icicle for £600,000. No adjustment in respect of this inventory has been made in the draft extracts **(Exhibit 2)**.

Snowball has provided audited financial statements for the three months ended 31 March 20X9 which disclose an after-tax profit of £200,000 which has been included in the draft extracts **(Exhibit 2)**. Icicle has not prepared consolidated financial statements previously.

3 Warranty claim

In April 20X8 Icicle introduced a satellite navigation system for bicycles, which it sells with a 36-month warranty. There were 100,000 units sold in the year ended 31 March 20X9 at an average sales price of £60. The board is unsure how many claims will be made in respect of the warranty, due to its recent launch. However the production department has estimated there will be product returns in relation to these sales of 5,000, 8,000 and 7,000 units respectively in the three years ending 31 March 20Y0, 20Y1 and 20Y2, at an average repair cost of £25 per unit.

Early discussions with the tax authorities suggest that these warranty claims will only be allowed for tax purposes when the repairs take place. This is because Icicle has no history of such claims and therefore cannot make any credible estimate of cost.

No provision has been made for these warranties in the draft financial statements for the year ended 31 March 20X9.

The pre-tax annual rate of interest that reflects the time value of money and the risks relating to the project is 10%.

4 Tax losses

Icicle has only been trading for a few years, and has not made any taxable profits to date. The directors are now highly confident of being able to utilise carried forward trading tax losses of £3.9 million at 1 April 20X9 against future taxable trading profits. Profits chargeable to corporation tax are anticipated to be at least £5 million in the year ending 31 March 20Y0, after breaking even for tax purposes in the year ended 31 March 20X9. No provision for deferred tax has been made in the financial statements for the year ended 31 March 20X8 in respect of these trading tax losses.

Exhibit 2 – Icicle plc, draft extracts from the financial statements for year ended 31 March 20X9

Statement of profit or loss and other comprehensive income for year ended 31 March 20X9

	£'000
Profit before tax	1,830
Income tax expense (excluding deferred tax)	0
Profit for the year	1,830
Other comprehensive income	
Gains on property revaluation	9,200
Total comprehensive income for the year	11,030

Statement of financial position at 31 March 20X9

Equity

	£'000
Ordinary shares of 50 pence each	1,000
Share premium account	6,800
Retained earnings	1,040
Revaluation reserve	9,200
Total equity	18,040

7 Flynt plc

You are Miles Goodwin, the newly-appointed financial controller of Flynt plc, a company that manufactures electronic components for the computer industry. You receive the following email from Andrea Ward, the CEO of Flynt.

To: Miles.Goodwin@flynt.co.uk
From: Andrea.Ward@flynt.co.uk
Subject: Finalisation of consolidated financial statements for year ended 31 May 20X6

Miles, I know you have just joined us, but I would be grateful if you could look at the impact of some issues that were left unresolved by your predecessor, Shane Ponting (**Exhibit 1**). I have been very busy recently and have not had the chance to look at these issues myself.

I would like you to redraft the consolidated statement of profit or loss and other comprehensive income. I attach a draft for you to work from (**Exhibit 2**). Please explain the reasoning for any adjustments you make, as I would like a greater understanding of the impact of these issues on our post-tax profits. You should also give journal entries.

I have a meeting with the board shortly, and we are concerned about earnings per share (EPS).

I would therefore be grateful if you would also calculate the basic and diluted EPS for the year ended 31 May 20X6 and the diluted EPS if applicable.

At this stage do not worry about any adjustments to the current or deferred tax charge; just assume an effective rate of 23%.

Requirement

Draft a reply to the email from Andrea Ward. **(30 marks)**

Exhibit 1: Consolidated financial statements for year ended 31 May 20X6: Unresolved issues – arising from notes prepared by Shane Ponting

Share option scheme

On 1 September 20X5 the board approved a share option scheme for 20 senior executives. On that date each executive was granted options over 10,000 shares at an exercise price of £39 per share, which was the market price at 1 September 20X5. Each option gives the rights to one share. The options vest on 1 September 20X9 subject to the following conditions:

(a) Each executive remains in the employment of Flynt until 1 September 20X9; and
(b) The share price of Flynt has increased by at least 50% at 1 September 20X9.

The fair value of an option was estimated to be £12.60 at 1 September 20X5 and £19.40 at 31 May 20X6.

This is the first time that Flynt has operated such a scheme. As there is no cash cost to the company, I have not made any adjustments to the financial statements. The share price of Flynt at 31 May 20X6 was £52 and the average share price for the nine months to 31 May 20X6 was £48.

At 31 May 20X6 there were still 19 executives in the scheme, but I anticipate there will only be 16 still employed by 1 September 20X9.

Lease of surplus machinery

On 1 June 20X5 Flynt leased some surplus machinery to Prior plc, an unrelated company, on the following terms:

Lease term and remaining useful life of machinery	5 years	
Carrying amount and fair value of machinery at 31 May 20X5	£612,100	
Annual instalment payable in arrears	£150,000	
Interest rate implicit in lease	10% per annum	
Residual value guaranteed by Prior plc	£61,000	
Expected residual value at 31 May 20Y0	£70,000	
Initial direct costs incurred by Flynt	£1,000	

I have treated the agreement as an operating lease and recognised lease rental income of £150,000. I have also charged depreciation of £122,420 and written off the direct costs incurred to profit or loss.

Acquisition of Dipper plc

On 1 December 20X5 Flynt purchased 100% of the ordinary shares of Dipper plc for a consideration of £6.4 million when Dipper had net assets with a fair value of £4.9 million including a deficit on a defined benefit pension scheme of £0.4 million. Goodwill of £1.5 million therefore arose on acquisition. The consideration given was 150,000 ordinary shares in Flynt. This was the first equity issue for a number of years. There were 1.4 million ordinary shares in issue on 31 May 20X5.

Flynt operates a defined contribution scheme, and I am unfamiliar with how to deal with Dipper's defined benefit scheme.

We obtained the following figures from Dipper's actuaries at the acquisition date:

Fair value of scheme assets	£2.2 million
Present value of pension obligations	£2.6 million
Estimated service cost from 1 December 20X5 to 31 May 20X6	£560,000
Interest rate on high quality corporate bonds	5% per annum
Discount rate for scheme obligations	4% per annum

The total contributions paid into the scheme by Dipper from the acquisition date to 31 May 20X6 were £480,000, and I have charged this sum to operating costs. I have had a letter from Dipper's pension fund advising me that they have paid out £450,000 to pensioners in the same period. I have not adjusted the deficit in the statement of financial position.

Dipper recognises remeasurement (actuarial) gains and losses immediately in accordance with IAS 19 *Employee Benefits* (revised 2011). I intend to continue to apply IAS 19 in the group financial statements but I do not know how to calculate the remeasurement gain or loss.

I have been advised by the scheme actuary that at 31 May 20X6 the fair value of the pension assets was £2.08 million and the present value of pension obligations was £2.75 million at that date.

We conducted an impairment review of goodwill at the end of our accounting period and estimated that goodwill arising on the acquisition of Dipper was worth £1.1 million. I have therefore debited £400,000 to other comprehensive income. No other adjustments were required to goodwill.

Exhibit 2: Draft consolidated statement of profit or loss and other comprehensive income for year ended 31 May 20X6

	20X6	20X5
	£'000	£'000
Revenue	14,725	13,330
Cost of sales	(7,450)	(7,560)
Gross profit	7,275	5,770
Operating costs	(3,296)	(3,007)
Other operating income	150	–
Operating profit	4,129	2,763
Investment income	39	32
Finance costs	(452)	(468)
Profit before tax	3,716	2,327
Income tax expense	(1,003)	(628)
Profit after tax	2,713	1,699
Other comprehensive income		
Goodwill impairment	(400)	–
Total comprehensive income for the year	2,313	1,699

Note: All calculations should be to the nearest £'000

8 Gustavo plc

You are Anita Hadjivassili, the recently appointed financial controller at Gustavo plc, a manufacturer of sports equipment. During the year ended 30 September 20X6, Gustavo has sold and purchased shares respectively in two companies, Taricco Ltd and Arismendi Inc.

You have just received the following email from the CEO, Antonio Bloom.

To: Anita Hadjivassili
From: Antonio Bloom
Subject: Draft Financial Statements for the Gustavo group

I attach extracts from the draft financial statements for the year ended 30 September 20X6 (**Exhibit 1**). I know you are still unfamiliar with Gustavo's business, so I have also attached some file notes prepared by your predecessor (**Exhibit 2**).

I would like you to prepare the draft consolidated statement of profit or loss and other comprehensive income for the year ended 30 September 20X6 including other comprehensive income, as I need to present it at the next board meeting. Please provide briefing notes to explain the impact of the share transactions (**Exhibit 2**) on the consolidated statement of profit or loss and other comprehensive income. Please show separately the profit attributable to the non-controlling interest.

I would also like you to advise on the impact that any future changes in exchange rates will have on the consolidated statement of financial position.

In addition, we have a potential problem with one of our credit customers defaulting on payment (**Exhibit 3**). I have heard that the rules on revenue recognition are about to change to allow us to take account of credit risk. I would like some advice on the existing rules and whether we can apply the amended rules.

Ignore any further income tax or deferred tax adjustments.

Requirement

Respond to Antonio's email.   **(30 marks)**

Exhibit 1: Extracts from the draft financial statements for year ended 30 September 20X6

	Gustavo	Taricco	Arismendi
	£'000	£'000	Kr000
Revenue	35,660	28,944	48,166
Cost of sales	(21,230)	(22,164)	(30,924)
Gross profit	14,430	6,780	17,242
Operating costs	(5,130)	(4,956)	(9,876)
Profit from operations	9,300	1,824	7,366
Investment income	580	108	–
Finance costs	(2,450)	(660)	(1,456)
Profit before taxation	7,430	1,272	5,910
Income tax expense	(2,458)	(360)	(2,240)
Profit for the year	4,972	912	3,670
Retained earnings			
At 1 October 20X5	11,720	4,824	14,846
Profit for the year	4,972	912	3,670
Dividends paid (1 July)	(3,000)	(600)	–
At 30 September 20X6	13,692	5,136	18,516

Other financial information

	£'000	£'000	Kr000
Ordinary share capital (shares of £1/Kr1)	10,000	2,000	5,000

Profits arise evenly throughout the year for all three companies.

Exhibit 2: File notes for key issues in year

Taricco

Gustavo bought 1.5 million ordinary shares in Taricco Ltd on 1 January 20X2 for £15 million when Taricco had retained earnings of £2.4 million. The proportion of net assets method was used to value the non-controlling interest as the acquisition occurred before IFRS 3 was revised. At the acquisition date the fair value of Taricco's net assets was equal to the carrying amount.

Prior to 1 October 20X5 there had been goodwill impairments in relation to Taricco of £2.5 million. There have been no changes in share capital or other reserves since acquisition.

On 1 April 20X6 Gustavo sold 800,000 shares in Taricco for £19.8 million. Gustavo continues to be represented by two directors on Taricco's board to oversee its remaining interest in the company. (Taricco's board consists of eight directors.) The only entry in Gustavo's financial statements regarding the sale has been to credit a suspense account with the sale proceeds.

It was estimated at 1 April 20X6 that Gustavo's remaining shares in Taricco had a fair value of £8.2 million.

Arismendi

On 1 January 20X6 Gustavo bought 4 million shares in Arismendi Inc, a company located overseas, (where the local currency is the Kr) for Kr75.6 million (£12.6 million). Professional fees relating to the acquisition were £400,000, and these have been added to the cost of the investment.

At 1 January 20X6 Arismendi owned property which had a fair value of Kr14.4 million (£2.4 million) in excess of its carrying amount. This property had a remaining life of 8 years at this date.

Gustavo would like to adopt the fair value method to measure the non-controlling interest. At 1 January 20X6 the market price of Arismendi's shares was Kr12 each.

An impairment review of goodwill took place at 30 September 20X6, and no impairment was deemed necessary.

Exchange rates which may be relevant are:

1 January 20X6	£1: Kr6
Average Jan-Sep	£1: Kr5
30 September 20X6	£1: Kr4

Exhibit 3: Impaired receivable

Gustavo has entered into a contract with Bravo Ltd, a retail chain, to provide sports equipment at a value of £200,000. The terms are that payment is due one month after the sale of the goods. On the basis of experience with other contractors with similar characteristics, Gustavo considers that there is a 5% risk that the customer will not pay the amount due after the goods have been delivered and the property transferred. Gustavo subsequently felt that the financial condition of the customer has deteriorated and that the trade receivable is further impaired by £20,000.

We would like to know how the above transaction would be treated in subsequent financial statements under IAS 18 and also whether there would be any difference in treatment if the collectability of the debt is taken into account, as was proposed a few years ago.

A discount rate of 4% should be used in any calculations.

9 Inca Ltd

Inca Ltd supplies specialist plant and machinery to the oil drilling industry. On 1 May 20X0 Inca acquired 80% of Excelsior Inc, a company based in Ruritania, where the currency is the CU.

You are Frank Painter, a chartered accountant employed on a temporary contract following the retirement of the Inca finance director. You have been asked to assist the managing director in finalising the financial statements of Excelsior and the Inca group for the year ended 30 April 20X1.

Both Inca and Excelsior prepare their financial statements using IFRS. You receive the following email from the managing director of Inca.

Email

From: Inca MD
Subject: Finalising Financial Statements
To: Frank Painter
Date: 25 July 20X1

Acquisition of Excelsior

Excelsior is the first subsidiary that Inca has acquired, and so I would be grateful for some advice in relation to the consolidated financial statements and also in finalising the financial statements of Excelsior.

The cost of the investment in Excelsior was CU120 million, and at 1 May 20X0 Excelsior had retained earnings of CU64 million. There were no fair value adjustments to the net assets of Excelsior. Inca uses the proportion of net assets method to value non controlling interest.

Assistance needed

I wish to show your findings to my fellow board members, as they are concerned about Excelsior's effect on the consolidated financial statements. I have not told them that I have asked for your input as I would like to make a favourable impression in terms of my accounting knowledge.

I have provided you with the draft statements of financial position for both companies **(Exhibit 1)**. I have also provided some exchange rates **(Exhibit 2)**. The accountant at Excelsior is unqualified. He has identified a number of outstanding financial reporting issues **(Exhibit 3)**.

I have heard that there is an option of valuing non-controlling interests at fair value, rather than using the proportion of net assets method, as we do. The fair value of the non-controlling interest in Excelsior is CU20 million. I understand that using this method would change the figures for goodwill and perhaps the exchange difference relating to goodwill.

Please prepare a working paper for me which comprises:

* An explanation of the appropriate financial reporting treatment for each of the issues identified by the Excelsior accountant **(Exhibit 3)**; and

* The consolidated statement of financial position of Inca at 30 April 20X1, assuming there are no adjustments to the individual company financial statements other than those you have proposed.

* A calculation of goodwill assuming that Inca values the non-controlling interest in Excelsior at its fair value of CU20 million.

Do not tell anyone else that you are preparing this working paper for me. In return I will ensure that you are given a permanent contract in the Inca group. In order to save costs I am not intending to replace the Inca finance director as I can do this role myself with your help.

Requirements

Prepare the working paper requested by the managing director.

In addition to the working paper, explain any ethical concerns that you have, as Frank Painter, in relation to the managing director's email, and set out the actions you intend to take.   **(30 marks)**

Note: Ignore any UK current tax implications

Exhibit 1 - Draft statements of financial position at 30 April 20X1

Non-current assets	Inca £m	Excelsior CU'm
Investment in Excelsior	24.0	–
Property, plant and equipment	32.4	64.0
Intangible assets	12.4	7.0
Total non-current assets	68.8	71.0
Current assets		
Inventories	9.8	16.6
Trade receivables	17.4	35.2
Cash	1.6	12.8
Total current assets	28.8	64.6
Total assets	97.6	135.6
Equity and liabilities		
Share capital £1/CU1	4.0	10.0
Share premium account	12.0	16.0
Retained earnings	41.6	48.0
Non-current liabilities		
Deferred tax	12.0	4.4
Loans	5.8	48.0
Current liabilities	22.2	9.2
Total equity and liabilities	97.6	135.6

Exhibit 2 – Exchange rates

	£1 = CU
1 May 20X0	5.0
Average for year	4.8
30 April 20X1	4.5

	US$1 = CU
1 May 20X0	3.2
Average for year	3.0
30 April 20X1	2.8

Exhibit 3 Excelsior – Outstanding financial reporting issues prepared by Excelsior accountant

Excelsior's draft statement of profit or loss and other comprehensive income shows an after-tax loss of CU16 million for the year ended 30 April 20X1. The current tax has been correctly calculated by our tax advisers. However, I am not familiar with deferred tax and some of the more complex financial reporting rules and the following matters are outstanding:

1   At 1 May 20X0 there was a deferred tax liability of CU4.4 million in the statement of financial position and no adjustments have been made to this figure in the draft financial statements at 30 April 20X1. This deferred tax provision was solely in relation to the differences between the carrying amount of property, plant and equipment and the tax base.

The carrying amount of property, plant and equipment on 1 May 20X0 was CU60 million, compared with its tax base of CU38 million. At 30 April 20X1 these figures were CU64 million and CU36 million respectively.

Companies in Ruritania pay tax at a flat rate of 20%. This rate is not expected to change in future years.

2   In the year ended 30 April 20X1 Excelsior capitalised development costs of CU7 million. These costs are likely to be amortised over four years from 1 May 20X2.

Under Ruritanian tax law such costs are deductible when incurred.

3   The tax trading loss carried forward in respect of the year ended 30 April 20X1 is CU16 million. Excelsior has reliable budgets for a taxable profit of CU5 million for each of the next two financial years, but it has no accurate budgets beyond that date. Tax losses can be carried forward indefinitely under Ruritanian tax law.

4   On 1 May 20X0 Excelsior issued a 5% bond to American financial institutions. The bond had a nominal value of US$16 million and is repayable on 30 April 20X3. The bond was issued at a discount of US$1 million, and is redeemable at a premium over nominal value of US$1.79 million.

Interest of US$800,000 is paid every twelve months commencing 30 April 20X1. The implicit interest rate on the bond is approximately 10.91%.

The loan has been translated on 1 May 20X0 and the interest paid in relation to the bond has been charged to profit or loss. This sum was CU2.24 million (US$800,000 × 2.8) but no other adjustments have been made.

According to Ruritanian tax law, the only tax deduction in respect of the bond is for nominal interest which is tax deductible when paid. Debits and credits relating to discounts and premiums are not tax deductible.

5   On 1 April 20X1 Excelsior made a loan of CU2 million to one of the directors of the company, who also happens to be a prominent politician. I do not expect any of this sum to be recoverable, but it would be politically embarrassing to disclose this in the financial statements. The loan has been included in trade receivables and no adjustments have been made. On the grounds of materiality, the board is very keen to exclude any reference to the loan.

10   Aytace plc

Aytace plc is the parent company of a group that operates golf courses in Europe. It has had investments in a number of 100% owned subsidiaries for many years, as well as owning 40% of the share capital in Xema Limited since 20X0.

You are Frank Brown, a Chartered Accountant. You have recently taken up temporary employment with Aytace while the financial controller, Meg Blake, is on maternity leave.

You receive the following email from the finance director, Willem Zhang.

To: Frank Brown

From: Willem Zhang

Subject: Draft consolidated statement of profit or loss and other comprehensive income for the year ended 31 May 20X3

Prior to maternity leave, Meg prepared a first draft consolidated statement of profit or loss and other comprehensive income and has noted some outstanding matters relating to transactions in the year **(Exhibit 1)**.

Please prepare a working paper which comprises:

•   Advice, with explanations and relevant calculations, on the appropriate financial reporting treatment of the outstanding matters highlighted by Meg in Exhibit 1.

•   A revised consolidated statement of profit or loss and other comprehensive income, showing clearly the financial reporting adjustments you have proposed.

Ignore any tax consequences arising from the outstanding matters, as these will be finalised by our tax advisers.

Requirement

Prepare the working paper requested by the finance director.   **(30 marks)**

Exhibit 1: Briefing notes prepared by Meg Blake for year ended 31 May 20X3.

Aytace Group – Draft consolidated statement of profit or loss and other comprehensive income for the year ended 31 May 20X3

	£'000	Notes
Revenue	14,450	(i)
Operating costs	(9,830)	(i)(ii)
Operating profit	4,620	
Income from associate	867	(iv)
Other investment income	310	
Finance costs	(1,320)	
Profit before tax	4,477	
Tax	(1,220)	
Profit for the year	3,257	

Notes on outstanding matters:

I have not had sufficient time to look into the following matters because of my personal circumstances.

(i) **Golf tournament**

On 1 December 20X2 Aytace won the tender to host an annual international golf tournament for each of the next four years. The first golf tournament will take place in September 20X3.

The tender process commenced on 5 August 20X2 and the tender was submitted on 8 November 20X2. Internal management time costs of £1.2 million were incurred in relation to the tender submission. These costs were capitalised and are being amortised from 1 December 20X2 over a four-year period. Therefore £150,000 (6/48 × £1.2 million) has been recognised in profit or loss as an operating cost for the year ended 31 May 20X3.

A separate contract was subsequently signed on 1 February 20X3 with a satellite television company for the exclusive rights to broadcast the tournament. The contract fee is £4.8 million for the whole four years of the tournament. The broadcaster made an advance payment of £1.0 million to Aytace on 1 May 20X3. This amount was initially credited to deferred income. I then decided to recognise revenue on the satellite television contract evenly over a four-year period from 1 February 20X3. An amount of £400,000 (£4.8 million × 4/48) is therefore recognised as revenue in profit or loss for the year ended 31 May 20X3.

(ii) **Defined benefit pension scheme**

Aytace operates a defined benefit pension scheme. Employees are not required to make any contributions into the scheme. Aytace recognises remeasurement (actuarial) gains and losses immediately through other comprehensive income in accordance with IAS 19 *Employee Benefits* (revised 2011).

The scheme assets had a fair value of £12.2 million and £13.5 million at 31 May 20X2 and 31 May 20X3 respectively. Scheme obligations had a present value of £18.0 million and £19.8 million at 31 May 20X2 and 31 May 20X3 respectively.

At 1 June 20X2 the interest rate on high quality corporate bonds was 6%.

In the year ended 31 May 20X3, employer contributions paid into the scheme were £0.9 million, and pensions paid by the scheme during the year amounted to £1.1 million. These payments took place on 31 May 20X3. The service cost for the year ended 31 May 20X3 was £1.2 million.

Aytace decided to improve the pension benefit at 1 June 20X2 for staff who will have worked at least five years for the company at the date the benefit is claimed. The scheme actuary calculated the additional benefit obligation in present value terms to be £400,000.

The only entry in the financial statements in respect of the year ended 31 May 20X3 was to recognise in profit or loss the contributions paid to the scheme by Aytace, with no adjustment to the scheme obligations in the statement of financial position.

(iii) **Holiday pay**

The salaried employees of Aytace are entitled to 25 days paid leave each year. The entitlement accrues evenly over the year and unused leave may be carried forward for one year. The holiday year is the same as the financial year. At 31 May 20X3, Aytace has 900 salaried employees and the average unused holiday entitlement is three days per employee. 5% of employees leave without taking their entitlement and there is no cash payment when an employee leaves in respect of holiday entitlement. There are 255 working days in the year and the total annual salary cost is £19 million. No adjustment has been made in the financial statements for the above and there was no opening accrual required for holiday entitlement.

(iv) **Investment in Xema**

On 1 January 20X0, Aytace bought 40% of the issued ordinary share capital of Xema Ltd, a sportswear company, for £2.3 million. Aytace has had significant influence over Xema since this date and has used the equity method to account for the investment.

At 1 January 20X0, Xema had an issued ordinary share capital of 1 million £1 ordinary shares and retained earnings of £3.4 million. There has been no change to Xema's issued share capital since 1 January 20X0. At 31 May 20X2 retained earnings were £4.8 million. Xema's statement of profit or loss for the year ended 31 May 20X3 was as follows:

	£'000
Revenue	5,400
Operating costs	(3,600)
Operating profit	1,800
Other investment income	240
Finance costs	(720)
Profit before tax	1,320
Tax	(300)
Profit for the year	1,020

On 1 September 20X2 Aytace bought the remaining 60% of Xema's ordinary share capital for £12.4 million, at which date its original 40% shareholding was valued at £3.8 million. There were no material differences between carrying amounts and fair values of the identifiable net assets of Xema at 1 September 20X2.

I recognised the investment in Xema using the equity method and credited £867,000 to profit or loss (profit for the year of £1.02 million × 3/12 × 40% plus £1.02 million × 9/12 × 100%).

(v) **Executive and employee incentive schemes**

Aytace introduced two incentive schemes on 1 June 20X2. No entries have been made in relation to either of these schemes in the financial statements for the year ended 31 May 20X3.

The first incentive scheme is for executives. Aytace granted 100,000 share options to each of five directors. Each option gives the right to buy one ordinary share in Aytace for £6.40 at the vesting date of 31 May 20X5. In order for the options to vest, Aytace's share price must rise by a minimum of 35% from the market price on 1 June 20X2 of £6.40 per share. In addition, for a director's options to vest, he/she must still hold office at 31 May 20X5.

Aytace's share price was only £5.80 at 31 May 20X3, and I am not confident that we will achieve the required price increase of 35% by the vesting date. The fair value of a share option at 1 June 20X2 was estimated to be £2.70, but this had fallen to £1.90 by 31 May 20X3.

Most of the board has been with Aytace for a number of years, and none has left in the last twelve months. I would anticipate only one director leaving prior to the vesting date.

The second incentive scheme is an employee scheme in the form of share appreciation rights for senior managers. The vesting date is 31 May 20X5, and managers must be still in employment at that date.

There are 60 managers eligible for the scheme, each of whom has appreciation rights over 4,000 shares. Under the scheme each manager will receive a cash amount equal to the fair value of the rights over each share. I anticipate 50 of the managers being in the scheme at 31 May 20X5. The fair value of the rights was £2.85 per share at 1 June 20X2 and £2.28 per share at 31 May 20X3.

11 Razak plc

Razak plc is a listed parent company. During the year ended 30 September 20X2 Razak plc increased its shareholding in its only equity investment, Assulin Ltd.

Razak publishes magazines in the UK. You are Kay Norton, a chartered accountant and a member of the Razak financial reporting team. You report to the Razak group finance director, Andrew Nezranah, who is also a chartered accountant.

You receive the following email:

To: Kay Norton
From: Andrew Nezranah
Date: 29 October 20X2

I have recently joined the board and I am preparing for our annual update presentation to our bank.

As part of this update, I have been asked to present the bank with draft consolidated financial statements for the year ended 30 September 20X2. I appreciate that there will be tax issues to finalise at a later stage, but the bank has said that it is not interested in these at present.

For a number of years Razak plc held 15% of the ordinary share capital of Assulin, a paper pulp manufacturer. On 31 March 20X2 this shareholding was increased to 80%, as we wanted to secure continuity of supply in relation to paper pulp. Further details of this transaction can be found in **Exhibit 1**.

Razak plc's draft financial statements at 30 September 20X2 are summarised in **Exhibit 2**.

In addition I have some concerns about Razak plc's purchase of a bond in Imposter plc (**Exhibit 3**).

The directors are proposing to introduce a pension plan for next year (**Exhibit 4**) and are perhaps unclear on how to account for it.

Please would you:

- Provide explanations of how the increase in the stake in Assulin will be treated in Razak's consolidated financial statements;

- Explain any adjustments needed to account for the purchase of the Imposter bond in Razak's consolidated financial statements and evaluate any ethical issues arising from this matter;

- Prepare Razak's consolidated statement of financial position at 30 September 20X2 after making all relevant adjustments; and

- Explain how the proposed pension plan would be accounted for in the financial statements.

Requirement

Reply to Andrew's email.   **(30 marks)**

Exhibit 1 – Shareholding in Assulin

In 20W4 (eight years ago), Razak plc bought 75,000 shares in Assulin for £6 each. The shares were classified as available-for-sale. At 30 September 20X1, the shares had a fair value of £16 each, and a cumulative increase in fair value of £750,000 had been recognised in other comprehensive income and was held in equity. In Razak plc's draft statement of financial position, the increase in the share valuation has also been included in the investment in Assulin.

On 31 March 20X2 a further 325,000 shares in Assulin were purchased for £25 each. This sum has been added to the investment in Assulin.

In addition to the cash consideration of £25 per share, Razak plc agreed to pay a further £6 per share on 31 March 20X4, subject to a condition that Assulin's management team, each of whom owned shares in Assulin, remain with the company to that date. It is considered to be highly probable that this condition will be met. No adjustments for a contingent payment have been included in Razak's financial statements. Razak has a cost of capital of 9%.

On 31 March 20X2, the fair value of an Assulin share was estimated to be £20. Razak has decided to use the fair value (full goodwill) method to measure non-controlling interest.

The statements of financial position of Assulin at 30 September 20X2 and 31 March 20X2 were as follows:

	30 September 20X2 £'000	31 March 20X2 £'000
Non-current assets		
Property, plant and equipment	3,460	3,210
Current assets		
Inventories	610	580
Receivables	400	280
Cash at bank	70	90
Total assets	4,540	4,160
Equity		
£1 ordinary shares	500	500
Retained earnings	2,740	2,540
Non-current liabilities		
Loan from Razak plc	800	800
Current liabilities		
Trade payables	290	240
Tax payable	210	80
Total equity and liabilities	4,540	4,160

Included in Assulin's non-current assets is a property which had a carrying amount of £1.2 million at 31 March 20X2. This property was estimated to have a fair value of £2.6 million at this date, and a remaining useful life of five years.

Exhibit 2 – Draft statement of financial position for Razak plc at 30 September 20X2

	£'000
Non-current assets	
Property, plant and equipment	6,000
Investment in Assulin	9,325
Loan to Assulin	800
Other financial assets	1,308
	17,433
Current assets	
Inventories	1,140
Receivables	960
	2,100
Total assets	19,533
Equity	
£1 ordinary shares	2,800
Share premium account	7,400
Retained earnings	2,510
Available-for-sale reserve	750
	13,460
Non-current liabilities	2,788
Current liabilities	
Bank overdraft	1,220
Trade payables	865
Tax payable	1,200
	3,285
Total equity and liabilities	19,533

Exhibit 3 – Imposter bond

Razak plc purchased a 6% bond in Imposter plc on 1 October 20X1 (the issue date) at par for £1.2 million. The interest is payable annually in arrears. The bond is redeemable on 30 September 20X4 for £1.575 million. It is currently recognised in 'other financial assets' in the draft statement of financial position at amortised cost, and has been classified as 'held-to-maturity'. The bond has an effective annual rate of interest of 15%.

After paying the interest on its due date of 30 September 20X2, Imposter went into administration in early October 20X2. It is estimated that only 40% of the maturity value will be repaid on the original repayment date of 30 September 20X4. No further interest will be paid.

The annual market interest rate on a similar two-year, zero-coupon bond is 15% at 30 September 20X2.

The chief executive of Razak plc is also a director of Imposter and has a 5% shareholding in Imposter. The chief executive authorised the purchase of the bond. There is no record of this matter in the board minutes.

Exhibit 4 – Proposed pension plan

The directors of Razak are considering setting up a pension plan in the next accounting period with the following characteristics:

(i)   The pension liabilities would be fully insured and indexation of future liabilities will be limited up to and including the funds available in a special trust account set up for the plan, which is not at the disposal of Razak.

(ii)   The trust account will be built up by the insurance company from the surplus yield on investments.

(iii)   The pension plan will be an average pay plan in respect of which the entity pays insurance premiums to a third party insurance company to fund the plan.

(iv)   Every year 1% of the pension fund will be built up and employees will pay a contribution of 4% of their salary, with the employer paying the balance of the contribution.

(v)   If an employee leaves Razak and transfers the pension to another fund, Razak will be liable for, or is refunded the difference between the benefits the employee is entitled to and the insurance premiums paid.

In the light of the above, the directors believe that the plan will qualify as a defined contribution plan under IAS 19 *Employee Benefits* rather than a defined benefit plan, and will be accounted for accordingly.

12   Melton plc

Melton plc ('Melton') owns a number of subsidiaries that operate high quality coffee bars.

You are a recently appointed investment analyst for a major investment bank that owns 6% of the issued equity of Melton. You have been asked to analyse the profitability, cash flows and investor ratios of Melton. You need to prepare notes for a meeting with the investment team to determine whether the investment bank should consider disposing of its investment.

One of your colleagues has left you a note of background information concerning Melton (**Exhibit 1**) and some financial information (**Exhibit 2**).

Your meeting notes should:

(a)   Evaluate the investment team member's comment (Exhibit 1 point (viii)), explaining the usefulness and limitations of diluted earnings per share information to investors.

(b)   Analyse the profitability, cash flow and investor ratios of Melton plc, calculating additional relevant ratios to assist in your analysis. Your notes should identify and justify matters that you consider require further investigation.

(c)   Explain the validity or otherwise of your colleague's statement that Melton plc is unable to pay a dividend because of the debit balance on consolidated retained earnings (Exhibit 1, point (vii).

(d)   Discuss the reporting implications of the issue raised in the director's comment in Exhibit 1, point (ix).

Requirement

Prepare the meeting notes for the investment team   **(30 marks)**

Exhibit 1: Note on background information for Melton

(i)   Melton has a reputation for depreciating its assets more slowly than others in the sector.

(ii) The strategy of the group is to fund new outlet capital expenditure from existing operating cash flows without the need to raise new debt.

(iii) Like for like revenue growth in the sector is estimated at 4.1% pa.

(iv) Grow 'outlet profits' (gross profits) as a percentage of outlet revenue year on year.

(v) Increase promotional and advertising spend on new outlets to encourage strong initial sales.

(vi) Management are accused of concentrating on new outlet openings to the detriment of existing outlets.

(vii) Melton is unable to pay dividends as the company has a debit balance on its consolidated retained earnings.

(viii) One member of the investment team has questioned the usefulness of diluted earnings per share, which, he believes, 'adds in unnecessary complications that may never happen'.

(ix) Melton acquired 8,000 out of the 10,000 shares of R. T. Café Ltd, which operates a chain of cafés offering simple food and a good but limited range of coffees. Mr Bean, one of the directors of Melton, has stated the following:

'While R. T. Café Ltd is profitable, long-term it is not a good fit with the image we are trying to portray'. I suggest we dispose 2,000 of our shares in this subsidiary in January 20X8. Preliminary enquiries suggest that we could make a profit of £500,000, which would be a nice boost to earnings per share for next year.'

Exhibit 2: Financial information

Melton plc: Consolidated statement of profit or loss for the year ended 30 September

	20X7	20X6
	£'000	£'000
Revenue	37,780	29,170
Cost of sales	(28,340)	(22,080)
Gross profit	9,440	7,090
Administrative expenses	(6,240)	(4,480)
Profit from operations	3,200	2,610
Finance costs	(410)	(420)
Profit before taxation	2,790	2,190
Tax	(610)	(460)
Profit for the year	2,180	1,730
Earnings per share – basic	26.8p	21.3p
Earnings per share – diluted	21.2p	19.2p

No dividends have been paid or proposed in 20X6 and 20X7.

Melton plc: Consolidated statement of cash flows for the year ended 30 September

	20X7		20X6	
	£'000	£'000	£'000	£'000
Cash flows from operating activities				
Cash generated from operations (Note)		6,450		4,950
Interest paid		(410)		(440)
Tax paid		(320)		(260)
Net cash from operating activities		5,720		4,250
Cash flows from investing activities				
Purchase of non-current assets	(5,970)		(5,790)	
Proceeds on sale of non-current assets	20		30	
Net cash used in investing activities		(5,950)		(5,760)
Cash flows from financing activities				
Proceeds of share issue	240		20	
Borrowings	650		2,000	
Net cash from financing activities		890		2,020
Net increase in cash and cash equivalents		660		510

	20X7	20X6
Cash and cash equivalents brought forward	2,480	1,970
Cash and cash equivalents carried forward	3,140	2,480

Note: Reconciliation of profit before tax to cash generated from operations for the year ended 30 September

	20X7 £'000	20X6 £'000
Profit before tax	2,790	2,190
Finance cost	410	420
Depreciation and amortisation	3,060	2,210
Loss on disposal of non-current assets	30	10
(Increase)/decrease in inventories	(40)	10
(Increase) in receivables	(250)	(20)
Increase in trade payables	450	130
Cash generated from operations	6,450	4,950

Analysis of revenue, outlet profits and new outlet openings for the year ended 30 September

30 new outlets were opened during the year ended 30 September 20X7 to bring the total to 115.

	20X7 £'000	20X6 £'000
Revenue per outlet		
Outlets open at 30 September 20X6	354	343
Outlets opened in current financial year	258	–
Gross profit per outlet		
Outlets open at 30 September 20X6	87	83
Outlets opened in current financial year	69	–

Additional information

	20X7	20X6
Gross margin	25.0%	24.3%
Gearing (net debt/equity)	35.2%	44.4%
Current ratio	0.56:1	0.48:1
Trade payables payment period	86 days	103 days
Return on capital employed (ROCE)	20.0%	19.1%
Cash return on capital employed (CROCE)	40.2%	36.3%
Revenue per employee (£'000)	41.1	37.9
Earnings before interest, tax, depreciation and amortisation (EBITDA) (£'000)	6,260	4,820
Non-current asset turnover	1.68 times	1.49 times
Share price (at 30 September)	302p	290p

13 Ultratherma

Asha Kapoor and Hugh Evans were refrigeration engineers who were made redundant in 20X3. Whilst working together they had often discussed the idea of setting up on their own. They believed that there was a niche in the market for the manufacture of low temperature digital thermometers. Following their redundancy, they agreed to attempt to put their idea into practice.

They prepared a business plan which showed that after start-up losses the business would be profitable. They estimated that they would need £700,000 to finance the business. They presented their plan to the bank which agreed to provide an overdraft facility of £350,000 for two years on condition that they raised share capital of £350,000.

A company, Ultratherma, was formed and commenced trading on 1 July 20X4. It was financed by the issue of 200,000 £1 shares fully paid at par value to Asha and Hugh and 150,000 shares at par value to their relatives and friends.

The accounts for the period to 31 March are set out below.

Statements of profit or loss for the period ending 31 March

	20X5 £	20X6 £
Revenue	609,000	1,099,000
Cost of sales	505,574	886,340
Gross profit	103,426	212,660
Administrative expense	30,200	36,100
Selling expenses	72,980	78,736
Operating profit	246	97,824
Interest expense	7,844	36,910
(Loss)/profit before tax	(7,598)	60,914
Taxation	–	13,274
(Loss)/profit after tax	(7,598)	47,640

Statements of financial position as at 31 March

	20X5 Cost £	20X5 Dep'n £	20X5 £	20X6 Cost £	20X6 Dep'n £	20X6 £
Assets						
Non current assets						
Premises	210,000	3,200	206,800	210,000	6,400	203,600
Machinery	175,000	17,500	157,500	245,000	42,000	203,000
Office furniture	7,000	1,400	5,600	10,500	3,500	7,000
Motor vehicles	42,000	7,874	34,126	42,000	18,374	23,626
			404,026			437,226
Current assets						
Inventories		95,550			276,750	
Trade receivables		302,400			381,078	
Prepaid expenses		–			17,500	
Cash		–			2,506	
			397,950			677,834
			801,976			1,115,060
Equity and liabilities						
Share capital			350,000			350,000
Accumulated profits (losses)			(7,958)			40,042
Shareholders' interests			342,042			390,042
Non-current liabilities						
Deferred income:						
grants			36,000		32,000	
deferred tax			–		1,572	
						33,572
Current liabilities						
Trade payables		186,890			251,350	
Accrued expenses		87,550			51,924	
Taxation		–			11,702	
Bank overdraft		149,134			376,470	
			423,574			691,446
			801,976			1,115,060

Note. Agreed credit terms were 90 days for customers and suppliers.

In April 20X5 Asha and Hugh presented their first period's draft accounts to the bank. At the meeting the bank manager produced ratios which he used to analyse the year's results during their discussion.

The ratios prepared by the bank for 20X5 were as follows.

Profitability

Gross profit %	17.00%
Operating profit %	0.04%
Profit before tax %	(1.25%)
Profit after tax %	(1.25%)
Return on share capital and reserves	(2.22%)
Net asset turnover	1.78

Liquidity

Current ratio	0.94
Liquid ratio	0.71
Collection period (days)	136
Inventory period (days) based on cost of sales	52
Payment period (days) based on purchases	85

Leverage

Total liabilities/tangible net worth	1.24
Bank debt/tangible net worth	0.43
Profit cover for interest	0.03

It was agreed that Asha and Hugh would discuss the position with the bank in May 20X6. At that meeting they proposed to request a restructuring of the bank facility to take the form of a term loan of £400,000 repayable over three years. They were intending to suggest a repayment schedule of £200,000, £100,000 and £100,000 on 31 March 20X7, 31 March 20X8 and 31 March 20X9 respectively.

They produced projected statements of profit or loss and statements of financial position for three years as follows.

	20X7	20X8	20X9
	£'000	£'000	£'000
Revenue	1,340	1,500	1,920
Cost of sales	1,090	1,200	1,520
Gross profit	250	300	400
Administrative expenses	36	40	42
Selling expenses	74	80	84
Operating profit	140	180	274
Interest expense	54	28	10
Profit before tax	86	152	264
Taxation	18	40	66
Profit after tax	68	112	198

	20X7		20X8		20X9	
	£'000	£'000	£'000	£'000	£'000	£'000
Assets						
Non-current assets		460		460		460
Current assets						
Inventory	240		340		380	
Trade receivables	290		252		400	
Prepaid expenses	20		20		20	
		550		612		800
		1,010		1,072		1,260
Equity and liabilities						
Equity						
Share capital		350		350		350
Accumulated profit b/f		40		108		220
Retained profit for year		68		112		198
Total equity		458		570		768
Non-current liabilities						
Term loan	200		100		–	
Deferred tax	10		18		28	
Deferred income	28		24		20	
		238		142		48
Current liabilities						
Trade payables	280		300		360	
Accrued expenses	16		18		20	
Taxation	8		32		54	
Bank overdraft	10		10		10	
		314		360		444
		1,010		1,072		1,260

ICAEW

Asha and Hugh's request

You are an ICAEW Chartered Accountant and you act as the business adviser for Asha and Hugh who have asked you to assist them in drafting a report to the bank, requesting the restructuring of the bank facility. The report to the bank is to be presented in two sections and should:

1   Analyse the company's performance in the two periods from incorporation to 31 March 20X5 and from 1 April 20X5 to 31 March 20X6.

2   Make the case for the request for restructuring of the bank's facility, supported by the projected accounts.

Requirement

Respond to Asha and Hugh's request by:

*   Drafting the first section of the report on the company's performance in the two periods from incorporation to 31 March 20X6 that Asha and Hugh are to present to the bank. In so doing you should analyse and evaluate the company's profitiability, liquidity, gearing, and cash generatin

*   Drafting a report to Asha and Hugh analysing and evaluating the financial information iin the projected accounts and evaluating their request for a restructuring of the bank facility.   **(30 marks)**

14   Aroma

Jo West owned a highly successful technology business which she sold five years ago for £20 million. She then set up an investment entity that invests primarily in smaller private businesses in need of short to medium term funding. Jo West sits on the board as a non-executive director of a number of the entities that her business has invested in and is often able to offer valuable business advice to these entities, especially in the area of research and development activities. You are Lois Mortimer, a member of Jo West's investment management team.

Jo West has been approached by the managing director of Aroma, a small private entity looking for investment; she has asked you, as a member of her investment management team, to produce a report analysing the financial performance of Aroma for the year ended 30 June 20X1 and its financial position at that date. Your report should contain a recommendation as to whether she should consider this investment further.

Jo West has sent you the following email:

From:	jowest@westinvestments.com
To:	loismortimer@westinvestments.com
Date:	31 August 20X1
Subject:	Financial performance of Aroma

Thank you for agreeing to do this report for me. I've got hold of some extracts from Aroma's financial statements (**Exhibit 1**).

Some background detail for you:

Aroma has been trading for more than ten years manufacturing and selling its own branded perfumes, lotions and candles to the public in its 15 retail stores and to other larger retailing entities. Revenue and profits have been steady over the last ten years. However 18 months ago, the newly appointed sales director saw an opportunity to sell the products online. Using long term funding, she therefore set up an online shop. The online shop has been operating successfully for the last 14 months. The sales director also used her prior contacts to secure a lucrative deal with a boutique hotel chain for Aroma to manufacture products for the hotel, which carry the hotel chain name and logo.   The contract was set up on 1 January 20X1.

The managing director of Aroma now believes that the business could take advantage of further sales opportunities and does not wish to lose the momentum created by the sales director. The bank that currently provides both the long-term loan and an overdraft facility has rejected Aroma''s request for additional funds on the basis that there are insufficient assets to offer as security (the existing funding is secured on Aroma's property, plant and equipment).

Exhibit 1: Financial statements extracts

Statement of profit or loss for the year ended 30 June

	20X1 £'000	20X0 £'000
Revenue	6,000	3,700
Cost of sales	(4,083)	(2,590)
Gross profit	1,917	1,110
Administrative expenses	(870)	(413)
Distribution costs	(464)	(356)
Finance costs	(43)	(34)
Profit before tax	540	307
Income tax expense	(135)	(80)
Profit for the year	405	227

The revenues and profits of the three business segments for the year ended 30 June 20X1 were:

	Retail operations £'000	Online store £'000 £'000	Hotel contract
Revenues	4,004	1,096	900
Gross profit	1,200	330 387	
Profit before tax	320	138	82

The online store earned a negligible amount of revenue and profit in the year ended 30 June 20X0.

Statement of financial position as at 30 June

	20X1 £'000	20X0 £'000
ASSETS		
Non-current assets		
Property, plant and equipment	380	400
Intangible assets – development costs	20	10
	400	410
Current assets		
Inventories	1,260	1,180
Receivables	455	310
Cash and cash equivalents	–	42
	1,715	1,532
Total assets	2,115	1,942
EQUITY AND LIABILITIES		
Equity		
Share capital (£1 equity shares)	550	550
Retained earnings	722	610
Total equity	1,272	1,160
Non-current liabilities		
Long-term borrowings	412	404
Current liabilities		
Payables	363	378
Short-term borrowings (overdraft)	68	–
	431	378
Total liabilities	843	782
Total equity and liabilities	2,115	1,942

Requirement

Prepare the report required by Jo West.   **(30 marks)**

15 Kenyon

You work for a team of investment analysts at Inver Bank.

Kenyon plc, a listed entity, operates a number of bottling plants. The entity's business consists primarily of contract work for regular customers. Revenue from existing contracts has increased in the year and in November 20X0 Kenyon plc secured a new contract with a high profile drinks company. Kenyon plc paid a dividend of £100 million during the year ended 31 October 20X1.

Gary Watson, a client, recently received the latest published financial statements of Kenyon plc and was impressed by the level of profitability and the dividend paid. He was also impressed with the fact that the share price had increased from £2.80 per share on 31 October 20X0 to £4.90 on 31 October 20X1. Gary Watson is now considering acquiring some of Kenyon plc's shares and has asked for your advice in an email:

'I am interested in your views on whether it is worth investing in Kenyon plc. It would be useful in making my decision if you could produce a report which:

(a) Analyses the financial performance of Kenyon plc for the year to 31 October 20X1 and its financial position at that date and discusses whether or not it is a good investment at this time.

(b) (i) Shows the best and worst case potential impact of the contingent liability on Kenyon plc's profitability and investment potential.

(ii) Discusses any further information I may need to access regarding the contingent liability in advance of making a final investment decision.'

You have obtained the financial statements of Kenyon plc (**Exhibit 1**), together with some further information (**Exhibit 2**)

Exhibit 1: Financial statements

Kenyon plc
Statements of financial position as at 31 October

	20X1 £m	20X0 £m
ASSETS		
Non-current assets		
Property, plant and equipment	381	346
Investment in associate (Note 1)	56	–
	437	346
Current assets		
Inventories	86	40
Receivables	72	48
Cash and cash equivalents	3	60
	161	148
Total assets	598	494
EQUITY AND LIABILITIES		
Equity		
Share capital (50 cent shares)	150	150
Share premium	50	50
Retained reserves	265	223
Total equity	465	423
Non-current liabilities		
Pension liability (Note 2)	38	5
Current liabilities		
Trade and other payables	95	66
Total liabilities	133	71
Total equity and liabilities	598	494

Kenyon plc

Statements of profit or loss and other comprehensive income for the year ended 31 October

	20X1 £m	20X0 £m
Revenue	663	463
Cost of sales	(395)	(315)
Gross profit	268	148
Distribution costs	(27)	(20)
Administrative expenses	(28)	(17)
Share of profit of associate (note 1)	7	–
Investment income	1	6
Profit before tax	221	117
Income tax expense	(45)	(24)
Profit for the year	176	93
Other comprehensive income (not re-classified to P/L):		
Remeasurement loss on pension assets and liabilities (Note 2)	(48)	(10)
Tax effect of other comprehensive income	14	2
Other comprehensive income for the year, net of tax	(34)	(8)
Total comprehensive income	142	85

Exhibit 2: Additional information

(a) **Investment in associate**

Kenyon plc acquired 40% of AB, its associate on 1 April 20X1 for £49 million.

(b) **Pension liability**

The actuary has provided the valuations of pension assets and liabilities as at 31 October 20X1 in the financial statements. However, as yet the actuary has not informed Kenyon plc of the contribution level required for the year to 31 October 20X2.

(c) **Contingent liability**

The notes to the financial statements include details of a contingent liability of £10 million. On 5 October 20X1, Kenyon plc suffered a chemical leak at one of the bottling plants and there is currently an investigation into the potential damage this caused to a nearby river and surrounding area. The investigation is at an early stage and it is not yet clear whether Kenyon plc was negligent. As stated in the notes to the financial statements Kenyon plc's lawyers have intimated that, in their opinion, Kenyon plc is likely to lose the case. No obligation has been recorded because the amount of potential damages could not be measured with sufficient reliability at the year-end. However, the lawyers have given a range of possible estimates of between £7 million and £13 million. The case is due to be decided by 31 October 20X2.

Requirement

Prepare the report required by Gary Watson.

(30 marks)

16 Johnson Telecom

Johnson Telecom plc ('Johnson') is a telecommunications consultancy company delivering telecoms support to businesses across Europe. Johnson's treasury department uses financial instruments for both speculative and hedging purposes. The company has an accounting year end of 31 December. The company's financial statements show the following financial instruments:

Extracts from financial statements at 31 December

	20X6 £'000	Draft 20X7 £'000
Financial assets		
Investments in equity	485	321
Derivatives	98	102
Debt investments	143	143
	726	566
Financial liabilities		
Loan note	2,000	2,000
	2,000	2,000

You are Poppy Posgen, a newly qualified audit senior at Beckett & Co, Chartered Accountants, and you are assigned to the statutory audit of Johnson for the year ended 31 December 20X7. You have received the following email from your manager, Annette Douglas.

Date:	7 February 20X8
From:	Annette Douglas <a.douglas@beckett.co.uk>
To:	Poppy Posgen <p.posgen@beckett.co.uk>
Subject:	20X7 Financial Statements

Attachments: *Market information*

Poppy,

Following our meeting yesterday, I would like you to review the way Johnson have accounted for a number of financial instruments. As you know, the Financial Director, who has prepared the supporting documentation, is on sick leave at the moment and is not expected to return to work until after the financial statements are published. The Financial Controller has provided all the information she can find, but lacks the background knowledge on these financial instruments.

I have attached below the notes that the audit junior has taken in relation to the financial instruments. Bear in mind that planning materiality for the financial statements as a whole is £80,000, and we have set a lower performance materiality level for investments at 20% of planning materiality.

Investments in equity

The £485,000 balance at 31 December 20X6 represents two small investments in UK equity shares. Johnson has held the investment in Cole for a number of years, and sold it on 14 August 20X7 for £242,000. The investment in International Energy plc was acquired on 1 November 20X6. Both Cole plc and International Energy plc are listed companies.

	Historical cost £'000	Valuation at 31 December 20X6 £'000	Draft at 31 December 20X7 £'000
Cole plc (50,000 shares)	163	230	–
Roulers plc (16,000 shares)	–	–	93
International Energy plc (30,000 shares)	270	255	228
	433	485	321

The investments in both Cole plc and International Energy plc are designated as available for sale. In previous years, any fair value gains or losses have been taken to the AFS reserve.

A new investment of 16,000 shares (out of a total of 50,000 shares) in Routers plc was made on 8 November 20X7. In the Financial Director's absence, the Financial Controller could not find supporting documents for the investment.

According to the *Financial Times* on that date, the bid-offer spread was £5.80-£5.83 at acquisition. The Directors explained to me that this investment is a short-term investment and is held for trading, with the aim of generating a profit if the price changes. As a result, it was designated as at fair value through profit or loss.

The journal entries in respect of the disposal of Cole plc and the acquisition of the new investment in Routers plc are shown in Attachment 2.

Derivatives

The balance comprises two derivatives:

(i) **Put option**

There is a put option to hedge against a fall in the share price of the 30,000 shares in International Energy. The put was purchased on 1 January 20X7 at £2 per option and is exercisable at £9.00 until 31 December 20X8.

In the absence of the Financial Director, who prepared the documentation to support this hedge, the documentation cannot be found. The option is accounted for using hedge accounting.

The Directors are unfamiliar with the hedge accounting rules and have asked us to outline the hedging principles, and explain how fair value hedge accounting changes the way the investment and option are accounted for.

They have also asked us to provide suitable documentation to support the fair value hedge. As the original documentation has been lost, the Directors have suggested they may backdate the documentation as 1 January 20X7.

(ii) **Interest rate swap**

The interest rate swap is a five-year variable-to-fixed interest rate swap to hedge the interest rate risk of the loan note liability. The swap was entered into on 30 November 20X6. In the financial statements for the year ended 31 December 20X6, the swap was recorded at a fair value of £38,000. The swap was designated as a hedge at inception and the hedging documentation was reviewed by the audit team as part of last year's statutory audit.

The company applies cash flow hedge accounting to this swap. The Financial Director has prepared a note on the accounting treatment of the interest rate swap (see Attachment 5).

The terms of the swap:

- £2 million notional amount
- Pay 7% fixed, receive variable at LIBOR
- Semi annual payments

The fair value of the swap at 31 December 20X7, based on current LIBOR rates, is £30,000.

Debt investments

The debt investment is a four-year quoted bond in Spence and May plc acquired on 1 January 20X6 and classified as held to maturity. Half of the holding was sold on the last day of this year for £83,000.

Terms:

- Acquired at nominal value of £140,000
- Redemption at premium of £10,000 on 31 December 20X9
- Coupon 10% pa, payable six-monthly in arrears (5% per six-month period)
- Effective interest rate is 11.79% per annum (5.73% per six-month period)

Loan note

The loan note was issued at nominal value on 31 December 20X6 and is a five-year note at LIBOR with semi annual payments. Issue and redemption of the loan is at the nominal value of £2m. The variable interest rate payments are hedged by the interest rate swap referred to in the Derivatives section above.

Actions

I need you to:

- Evaluate the accounting treatment adopted in the draft financial statements for the above financial instruments, showing any journal entries where relevant. Explain any audit adjustments required.

- Draft a summary of the hedge accounting rules and hedging principles as requested by the Directors, along with a sample hedging documentation. Explain separately how we should approach the Directors' proposal to use hedging documentation prepared by us to support the put option.

- Identify and explain five key risks that arise from the derivatives trading activities, and the internal controls that should be in place to mitigate these risks.

- Identify and explain any additional audit evidence the audit team will need to obtain with regards to the financial instruments.

Attachments

Attachment 1: Market information as at 31 December 20X7

Share prices

	Day's close £	Mid market £	Bid £	Offer £
International Energy plc	7.70	7.62	7.60	7.64
Routers plc	5.84	5.86	5.85	5.88

Put option

	Fair value of option (per share)
31 December 20X6	£2
31 December 20X7	£2.40

Attachment 2: Journal entries in respect of investments

Cole plc

	£'000	£'000
Dr Cash	242	
Cr Investment		230
Cr Profit or loss		12

Being the disposal of the investment in Cole plc

Routers plc

	£'000	£'000
Dr Investment	93.28	
Cr Cash		93.28

Being acquisition of investment in Routers plc

Attachment 3: Bloomberg market data

	LIBOR
31 December 20X6	7%
30 June 20X7	7.5%
31 December 20X7	7.5%

Attachment 4: Supporting workings for Spence and May bonds

The amortised cost is calculated every 6 months in line with the frequency of the coupon payments

Period ended	Opening balance £	Interest at 5.73% £	Cash flow (5% × 140,000) £	Closing balance £
30 June 20X6	140,000	8,022	−7,000	141,022
31 Dec 20X6	141,022	8,081	−7,000	142,103
30 June 20X7	142,103	8,143	−7,000	143,246
31 Dec 20X7	143,246	8,208	−7,000	144,454

Journal entries in respect of the bonds

		£'000	£'000
Dr	Debt investment	1.2	
Dr	Cash	7.0	
Cr	Interest income		8.2

Being re-measurement of amortised cost at 31 December 20X7

- De-recognise 50% of the amortised cost of the investment holding
- Resulting gain of £10,773 is recognised in profit or loss

		£'000	£'000
Dr	Cash	83	
Cr	Debt investment		83

Being year-end disposal of 50% of holding

Attachment 5: Accounting note on the loan and interest rate swap

Loan note and interest rate swap

- The interest rate swap (IRS) provides a cash flow hedge against the interest payments on the loan note

- Hedge accounting is permitted as:

    - The hedge is a perfect hedge as all terms match (currency, maturity, nominal amount)
    - Documentation has been in place since inception

- The amortised cost of the loan will remain at £2m as the loan issue and redemption are both at par

- The entries through the year are as follows:

    - The £150,000 variable rate interest for 12 months to 31 Dec 20X7 is charged to profit or loss and accrued until payment is made (£2m × 7.5%)

    - The net settlement on the interest rate swap is £10,000 ((7.5% – 7%) × £2m). This is received from the swap bank as a cash settlement and reduces the £150,000 variable rate interest expense on the loan note to £140,000, being the fixed rate cost

    - The £8,000 change in the fair value of the swap is released from equity (other componenets of equity). This represents the settlement of £10,000 less the unwinding of the discounting in the future swap settlements

		£'000	£'000
Dr	Profit or loss – Interest expense	150	
Cr	Interest accrual		150
Dr	Interest accrual	150	
Cr	Cash		150
Dr	Cash	10	
Cr	Profit or loss – Interest expense		10
Dr	Equity	8	
Cr	Derivative asset		8

Requirement

Prepare a memorandum giving the information required by Annette Douglas. **(40 marks)**

17 Biltmore

The Biltmore group, a property business which came into being on 1 January 20X8, owns a number of investment properties. The parent company, Biltmore plc, and the other members of the group, had no connection before that date.

The directors of Biltmore plc have a reputation for adopting aggressive accounting practices. At the audit planning meeting, the need for professional scepticism was highlighted. Materiality for the financial statements as a whole is set at 1% of the group's total assets. Total group assets at the year end is £2,423 million.

You are Jane Smith, a senior in James & Co, an accounting firm. David Williams, the audit partner, has sent you the following email.

To: Jane Smith
From: David Williams, Audit Partner
Date: 5 February 20X9
Subject: Investment properties owned by Biltmore group

Following our earlier discussion, I would like you to prepare a report on the investment properties owned by the various members of the Biltmore Group at 31 December 20X8. Details of the investments are in an Appendix. As you know, this is a complex area of the audit. The valuation of investment properties was identified as an area where there is a particular risk of material misstatement.

All the detailed audit fieldwork has been completed, but the financial statements have yet to be finalised and agreed by the board of directors, and the auditor's report is still under consideration.

On thing I'm particularly concerned about is the misclassification of assets. As we have seen throughout this audit, the directors are very reluctant to make adjustments to reclassify such assets, arguing that 'you'd end up with the same total assets figure anyway.'

Your report should cover the following:

- The appropriate treatment of each investment property in the consolidated financial statements of the Biltmore Group as at 31 December 20X8, with justifications in each case.

- A calculation of the adjustments that would have to be made to the figures in the draft financial statements in order to show the corrected figures relating to investment properties in the consolidated financial statements.

- A summary and explanation of the impact on our auditor's report if the directors refuse to put through the reclassification adjustments, setting out the reasons for your conclusion.

Appendix: Details of Biltmore investments

The draft financial statements are as follows:

Summarised statements of comprehensive income for the year ended 31 December 20X8

	Biltmore plc £m	Subone plc £m	Subtoo plc £m
Revenues			
Rental income	500	–	300
Gains on investment properties	100	80	50
Operating costs			
Depreciation of property	(2)	–	(1)
Administration	(12)	(8)	(9)
Finance costs	(140)	(50)	(25)
Net profit	446	22	315

Summarised statements of financial position as at 31 December 20X8

	Biltmore plc £m	Subone plc £m	Subtoo plc £m
Property, plant and equipment (excluding investment properties)	38	–	19
Investment properties	1,000	850	510
Investments	2,000	–	–
	3,038	850	529
Current assets	3	2	1
	3,041	852	530
Equity	1,539	351	279
Non-current liabilities	1,500	500	250
Current liabilities	2	1	1
	3,041	852	530

All of the property, plant and equipment is in the form of land and buildings. All of these were professionally revalued as at the date of Biltmore plc's investment in the group members.

Biltmore plc owns 100% of the share capital of Subone plc and 80% of Subtoo plc.

All companies show all of their investment properties at fair value, unless otherwise stated.

All properties have an estimated useful life of twenty years.

The following information relates to the properties classed as investment properties in the draft statement of financial position of the group members:

Biltmore plc	Present carrying amount £m

Harmony Tower 3 – a medium-sized office block in London's Docklands

This property was purchased in February 20X8 for £200 million. The directors have decided to leave this property valued at cost because they do not believe that they can measure its fair value reliably.

Harmony Tower 3 is flanked by two identical buildings, neither of which is owned by any member of the Biltmore Group. The owner of neighbouring Harmony Tower 2 sold the property on the open market in December 20X8 for £150 million. The owner of Harmony Tower 1 has put the property on the market for £160 million. — 200

Grove Place – an office block in Birmingham City Centre

This property had a fair value of £220 million on 1 January 20X8. During the year Biltmore plc spent £30 million on a major programme of improvement and refurbishment and capitalised these costs.

The latest valuation report, dated December 20X8, suggests that the property's fair value remains at £220 million. — 250

Head office – upper floors

Biltmore plc's head office is a 12-floor office block. The company occupies the bottom four floors and has left the top eight floors vacant. The directors claim that they intend to hold these vacant floors for their "investment potential" and are not actively seeking a tenant or buyer. An architect's report on the building states that it would be difficult to remodel the building so as to let or sell the upper floors to a third party.

The upper floors are recognised in the financial statements at £100 million.

The fair value attributed to the upper floors on 1 January 20X8 was £80 million. — 100

Biltmore plc	Present carrying amount £m

Northwest Forward – a mixed retail and office complex in Lancaster

This complex had a fair value of £240 million on 1 January 20X8.

Biltmore plc rents out 99% of the floor space in this development, but occupies a small suite of management offices on the site. The complex cannot be sold separately.

300

Buy-to-let portfolio – Teesside

Biltmore plc owns a large number of flats and houses in the Northeast of England. These had a fair value of £150 million as at 1 January 20X8.

There was a downturn in house market prices in that region at the end of January 20X9. The portfolio's value was estimated at £120 million at that time.

150

Essex Mall

Subone plc's principal asset is the site of Essex Mall, which is presently under construction. This will be a major shopping development and all of the units in the mall are under contract to retail chains, with leases commencing from the estimated completion date of 1 September 20X9. Subone plc intends to sell the development once it is completed.

The cost of the site and building work as at 1 January 20X8 was £600 million. A further £170 million was spent on the work done during the year ended 31 December 20X8.

The directors of Subone plc believe that the property has a fair value of £850 million in its present state.

850

Subone plc's head office

Subone plc occupies a prestigious London office block which is leased from Subtoo plc on a 20-year lease.

The property had a fair value of £120 million on 1 January 20X8.

150

Coventry building

Subtoo plc owns a building in Coventry.

Subtoo plc commenced development of the Coventry building in March 20X8 with a view to resale. At that time its fair value was £345 million. The property remains on the market as at the present date. There have been several expressions of interest, but no formal offers.

360

Requirement

Prepare the report required by the audit partner.

(40 marks)

18 Button Bathrooms

Button Bathrooms Ltd (BB) is a retailer of bathroom fittings and accessories. You are a senior in Rudd & Radcliffe LLP, the auditors of BB.

The meeting

You have been called to a meeting with the engagement partner, Carol Ying, in respect of the audit of BB's financial statements for the year ended 30 June 20X1. Carol opened the meeting. "I would like you to act as senior on the BB audit. In the past year there have been some significant changes in BB's business model and in its accounting and internal control systems. As a consequence, I believe there is greater control risk than in previous years. In addition, the company is seeking an AIM listing in 20X2 and the board is very keen to present the company's performance as favourably as possible.

"I realise that you are new to this client, so I have provided some background notes about the company and the changes that have occurred this year (**Exhibit 1**). Especially note BB's new, and very successful, e-commerce activity and the defined benefit pension scheme. I have also provided you with the draft management accounts (**Exhibit 2**).

"I have some particular concerns about the revenue recognition procedures that BB has adopted since installing its new information systems. An audit junior has provided some notes from a preliminary audit visit (**Exhibit 3**), but he did not have time to follow up on these matters.

"I am due to meet the finance director of BB next week and I would like you to provide briefing notes for me which:

(i)   With respect to each of the matters raised by the audit junior (**Exhibit 3**):

      –   Explain the financial reporting issues that arise and show any adjustments that will be required to the draft management accounts; and

      –   Describe the key audit risks and the related audit procedures that we should carry out.

(ii)   Other than the issues raised by the audit junior, set out the audit risks which arise in respect of the new e-commerce activities of BB, including those relating to SupportTech, and explain how we should address these in our audit procedures.

(iii)   Outline the audit issues we will need to consider regarding the outsourcing of the payables ledger function. Details are provided below. You do not need to refer to any general issues relating to SupportTech that you have already referred to in (ii).

"Please ignore any tax issues."

Requirement

Respond to the instructions of Carol Ying.   **(40 marks)**

Exhibit 1 – Background details and recent changes

History

BB was established twenty three years ago as an upmarket retailer of bathroom fittings and accessories. By 20W9 (two years ago) it was operating from 30 showrooms. Of these, 20 large showrooms sold BB's full product range and it offered a service to design, supply and install bathrooms in customers' houses. Products sold included baths, showers, toilets, taps, washbasins and bathroom accessories. The other 10 smaller showrooms sold only bathroom accessories, a distinctive BB product range including towels, bathrobes, lighting and decorative items.

Competition and reorganisation

By 20W9 competition from comparable retailers, combined with the recession, forced BB to reconsider its business model. The board believed that the company's overheads were too high. As a consequence, between 1 July 20X0 and 31 December 20X0, BB closed the ten smaller showrooms and ceased selling its bathroom accessories range from the other 20 showrooms.

New e-commerce activity

BB decided to adopt an e-commerce business model for sales of all products in its range, including bathroom accessories, and it commenced the development of a website on 1 July 20X0. The website was completed and ready for use by 31 December 20X0. It enables customers to design their own bathrooms on-line, select the required products and pay in advance, also on-line. The total cost of website development in the year ended 30 June 20X1 was £1 million. This was capitalised and is to be written off over five years.

After initial development, the operation of the website, including collection of payments from customers, was outsourced to an external service provider, SupportTech plc. BB receives the cash from SupportTech each month after deduction of a service charge fee.

The selling prices of products have been reduced by approximately 10% for on-line sales, compared with the showroom prices.

Inventories of a wide range of products were previously stored in four regional warehouses. Customer orders for less popular items, not in inventory, needed to be ordered by BB, which sometimes caused delays of up to four weeks. From 1 January 20X1 the range and the value of inventories held were significantly reduced.

Goods sold via the website are all ordered from the manufacturer automatically after the information is input by the customer. Distribution of goods to the customer is outsourced by BB to a third party courier.

Costs of reorganisation, including redundancies (but excluding website development costs), in the year to 30 June 20X1 amounted to £1.5 million. Further costs of £1 million are to be paid in August 20X1 as a result of the reorganisation.

There have been problems with the new business model including high returns of goods from customers compared with those sold through showrooms. There have also been errors in goods delivered arising from customers' misunderstanding of the website.

Outsourcing of payables ledger function

Last year's audit identified a number of control issues with respect to payables and in the first half of this year staff turnover in this department was high. Following the success of the outsourcing of on-line sales to SupportTech management decided to outsource the payables ledger function too. Staff were told of the decision including details of redundancies on 1 April 20X1. SupportTech took over responsibility for the payables ledger from 1 May 20X1. Details of the way in which the system works are as follows:

- Purchase orders are raised by BB and a delivery note is signed on receipt of the goods

- SupportTech is sent soft copies of the purchase orders and the signed delivery notes

- SupportTech receives invoices from suppliers directly and matches them to the purchase order and delivery note

- The Finance Director of BB receives a schedule detailing all the payments to be made for a given month one week before SupportTech processes the payments. This must be authorised by the Finance Director before the payments are processed

- A portal has been set up which allows the Finance Director to interrogate purchase ledger accounts held by SupportTech. The system does not allow the Finance Director to update or revise the accounts.

Exhibit 2 – Draft management accounts – statement of profit or loss and other comprehensive income

Years to 30 June	20X1 £'000	20X0 £'000
Revenue		
– Showrooms	30,000	60,000
– On-line sales	33,000	–
Cost of sales	(49,000)	(42,000)
Gross profit	14,000	18,000
Less		
Administration expenses	(5,000)	(5,000)
Distribution costs	(5,000)	(6,000)
Marketing costs for website	(1,000)	–
Website development cost – amortisation	(100)	–
Reorganisation costs	(1,500)	–
SupportTech fees	(1,800)	–
Premises costs	(2,500)	(3,000)
Pension contributions	(192)	–
Profit on sale of eight small showrooms	4,000	–
Profit	908	4,000

All products sold from showrooms make a gross margin of 30% on selling price.

Exhibit 3 – Notes on matters arising during interim audit – A. Junior

(1) Customers ordering on-line pay in full at the time of ordering. BB recognises revenue when the cash is received from SupportTech. I am concerned about revenue recognition and in particular cut-off, but I did not have a chance to look at this more closely.

(2) A New Year promotion was held for showroom sales on 1 January 20X1. Any customers placing an order for a complete bathroom suite were given two years' interest free credit provided a 10% deposit was paid. Delivery of the suites was guaranteed by the end of March 20X1. The promotion was very successful and the total value of sales made to customers under this offer was £520,000. I

have confirmed that this amount has been recorded in sales and have traced a number of orders through the sales system as part of my sales testing work. No cut-off issues were identified. I was told by the Finance Director that BB's own incremental borrowing rate is 7% but that of its customers is 10% but I don't understand the relevance of this information.

(3)   The ten small showrooms were closed down between 1 July 20X0 and 31 December 20X0. However, two of these (Bradford and Leeds) were still not sold by 30 June 20X1. These two showrooms are disclosed in the BB statement of financial position as property, plant and equipment at their carrying amounts of £1 million each. The Leeds site was acquired by BB fairly recently and is stated at cost less depreciation. The Bradford site was revalued on 30 June 20X0 from its carrying amount of £700,000 to £1 million. The original cost of the Bradford site was £900,000.

A contract was agreed in June 20X1 for the sale of the Bradford showroom for £1.15 million, with the sale to be completed in September 20X1. The Leeds showroom is being advertised, but there is currently no buyer identified.

(4)   I am unclear about what audit procedures should be carried out with respect to the website development costs and how these should be treated in the financial statements.

(5)   Button Bathrooms started a defined benefit pension scheme on 1 July 20X0. I have obtained the following information at 30 June 20X1:

	£000
Present value of obligation	249.6
Fair value of plan assets	240
Current service cost for the year	211.2
Contributions paid	192
Interest cost on obligation for the year	38.4
Interest on plan assets for the year	19.2

The only entry which has been made in respect of this is the recognition of the contributions paid as an expense in the statement of profit or loss and other comprehensive income. I have agreed these payments to the cash book and bank statement. However, I am not sure whether the other information is relevant and whether I should have performed any other audit procedures.

19   Hillhire

You are an audit senior with Barber and Kennedy, a firm of chartered accountants. Peter Lanning, one of the firm's audit managers, has just been assigned to the audit of Hillhire plc after the previous audit manager was signed off sick. Peter has given you some notes made by the previous manager at the initial audit planning meeting, along with some other information, and he has given you the following instructions:

"I would like you to assist me in the audit planning and first I would like you to prepare a memorandum which identifies the key audit risks relating to Hillhire's financial statements for the year ended 31 March 20X8. You should also outline the main audit procedures that we should carry out in respect of these matters and, where appropriate, state the correct financial reporting treatment including journals for any potential adjustments that you identify at this stage.

It appears that major issues to consider include a discontinued activity, the acquisition of Loucamion SA, the company's recent use of financial instruments for hedging purposes and the proposal to introduce a major new system.

In addition, the company has granted share options to senior employees as an incentive. These have not been accounted for in the current financial statements.

The financial controller has argued that the share options granted are not an expense and therefore they have not been reflected in the financial statements. He is saying that even if they were to be accounted for as an expense, they do not yet vest as the vesting period is three years.

You are given relevant information in Exhibit 4.

You should review all of the information to hand and identify any required adjustments and any other considerations associated with the audit in terms of audit risk, ethics and our own practice management, that should be addressed before commencing the detailed audit work."

Requirement

Draft the memorandum requested by the audit manager. **(40 marks)**

Exhibit 1 – Extracts from draft financial statements

Statement of profit or loss and other comprehensive income for the year ended 31 March

	20X8 Draft		20X7 Audited	
	£'000	£'000	£'000	£'000
Revenue		283,670		257,850
Cost of sales		(187,220)		(167,900)
Gross profit		96,450		89,950
Administrative expenses (excluding amortisation)	(35,020)		(34,610)	
Amortisation	(1,960)		(970)	
Total administrative expenses		(36,980)		(35,580)
Profit from operations		59,470		54,370
Finance costs		(17,750)		(15,910)
Profit before tax		41,720		38,460
Taxation		(10,090)		(9,270)
Profit for the year from continuing operations		31,630		29,190
Loss for the year from discontinued operations		(4,390)		–
Profit for the year		27,240		29,190

Statement of financial position at 31 March

	20X8 Draft		20X7 Audited	
	£'000	£'000	£'000	£'000
Assets				
Non-current assets				
Goodwill		12,000		5,000
Other intangible assets		40,680		28,740
Property, plant and equipment		452,130		434,510
Financial non-current assets		10,260		6,130
		515,070		474,380
Current assets				
Inventories	4,280		3,820	
Receivables	86,430		78,160	
Cash and cash equivalents	19,540		15,910	
		110,250		97,890
Non-current assets held for sale		40,130		–
Total assets		665,450		572,270
Equity and liabilities				
Equity				
Share capital		10,900		10,900
Share premium		63,250		63,250
Revaluation surplus		30,900		30,900
Hedging reserve		(5,040)		–
Retained earnings		110,370		85,030
		210,380		190,080
Non-current liabilities				
Long term borrowings		382,340		313,100
Deferred tax liabilities		22,290		19,740
		404,630		332,840
Current liabilities				
Bank overdraft		11,160		10,270
Trade and other payables		32,810		33,950
Tax liabilities		6,470		5,130
		50,440		49,350
Total equity and liabilities		665,450		572,270

Exhibit 2 – Notes taken by previous audit manager at planning meeting

Hillhire plc is a long-established company that has grown rapidly, both organically and by acquisition over the last ten years. It hires out commercial vehicles using a large network of depots throughout the United Kingdom and also in Europe through a number of wholly owned subsidiaries.

The company's management has announced that 15 of its less profitable depots are to be sold off. Each depot is viewed as a cash generating unit in its own right. The depots that are for sale are clustered in Scotland and the decision to sell them is part of a strategic decision to withdraw from this area. The results of these depots have been disclosed separately as discontinued operations in the draft statement of profit or loss and other comprehensive income. The announcement was made on 1 January 20X8 and management's intentions were minuted in the board minutes. Marketing of the depot is not due to start until May or June 20X8 as Hillhire is yet to find alternative storage for the vehicles currently stored in these depots which it is intending to relocate to other parts of the business. At 1 January the carrying value of the depots was £44,520,000. They have been classified as held for sale at a fair value less costs to sell of £40,130,000. At 1 January the depots had a remaining useful life of 25 years. The loss on the discontinued operations of £4,390,000 is only the loss on the classification of the depots to assets held for sale.

On 1 April 20X7 Hillhire acquired 100% of the share capital of a competitor company, Loucamion SA, based in France. The functional currency of Loucamion is the Euro. The main reason for the acquisition was the perceived value of the customer relationships built up by Loucamion in its local market. Assets and liabilities recognised at the date of acquisition included £4,000,000 in respect of customer lists. Confidentiality agreements prohibit Loucamion from selling or exchanging information about its customers on the list. At 1 April 20X7 the useful life of the list was estimated to be 10 years and the intangible asset has been amortised on this basis.

A loan note was issued at nominal value on 1 April 20X7 and is included in the statement of financial position. It is a five year note at LIBOR plus 2%. Issue and redemption of the loan is at nominal value of £200 million. The variable interest rate payments are hedged by an interest rate swap (see below).

The company has entered into a five year interest rate swap on 1 April 20X7 for a notional amount of £200 million to hedge the interest rate risk of the loan note liability. A swap agreement has been signed whereby Hillhire plc will pay a fixed rate of 8% to a counterparty on this amount and the counterparty will pay LIBOR plus 2% to Hillhire plc. Payments are semi-annual. This swap was designated as a cash flow hedge on 1 May 20X7and the directors of Hillhire plc believe that it is effective as such. The change in fair value up to the year end has been disclosed as other comprehensive income and accumulated in equity. However no adjustment has been made for interest for the six months to 31 March 20X8.

LIBOR rates are as follows:

1 April 20X7	7%
30 September 20X7	7.5%
31 March 20X8	7.5%

Exhibit 3 – Email from Alison Ritchie, partner responsible for Technology Risk Services in Barber and Kennedy

Date:	10 April 20X8
From:	Alison Ritchie <a.ritchie@barberkennedy.com>
To:	Peter Lanning <p.lanning@ barberkennedy.com>
Subject:	Hillhire

I understand that you are now managing the audit of Hillhire plc. You should be aware that my team has been approached to tender for a one-off assurance assignment for this client. This would involve a review of risks and advice on controls in Hillhire's new online booking system, which has been piloted in 20 of their UK depots since 2 January 20X8, prior to a planned national launch later in the year.

At present, each depot operates its own bookings. Customers who wish to hire a vehicle must contact the nearest depot directly and make a booking by telephone. Transactions are logged on a networked PC system that operates independently within each branch. Every evening, this information is uploaded to the head office's computer system. Head office then processes credit card payments due from personal customers and invoices business customers using information supplied by the depots.

The new system provides a centralised booking system via the company's website. Customers can make a booking online rather than by telephone. If the vehicle type required by the customer is unavailable at that depot, the system can arrange to have a vehicle transferred from another depot provided the distance is not too great. All transactions are processed by the new system immediately, thereby accelerating the billing process.

Now that the system has been piloted, it will be extended to all depots. This will require a central register to be compiled for all vehicles held at every branch. The standing data for business customers will also have to be transferred to the new system.

It would be useful to discuss this at the earliest opportunity.

Exhibit 4 – Details of share option scheme

On 1 April 20X7, 100 share options have been granted to each of the top senior 50 employees.

The options vest after three years on condition that the employees remain in the employment of Hillhire; the directors believe that 10% of senior employees will leave during the three-year period. The scheme is not expected to be available to new employees.

Employing a binomial lattice model gives a fair value for the option on grant date of £10 and a value of £8 at the year-end.

20 Hopper Wholesale

You are an audit senior in a firm of accountants. You receive the following voicemail message from one of the audit managers in your office.

'I need some help urgently with one of our clients, Hopper Wholesale Ltd. Hopper is an unquoted company that supplies retailers with basic goods such as sugar, salt and similar items. It buys goods in bulk and packages them in its own factory using simple packets bearing the 'Hopper Value' label. Draft financial statements show revenue of £21.4 million, profit before tax of £2.75 million and total assets of £65 million.

Callum the senior on the audit is unwell and is likely to be off for the rest of the week. The final audit meeting for the reporting period to 31 December 20X8 is scheduled for the day after tomorrow. I have reviewed the audit file and have identified a number of areas where audit procedures are incomplete. I will email you a summary of these including some background information (**Exhibit 1**). I have spoken to the junior staff on the audit and they have confirmed that these are areas where they have little experience and require some guidance. I would like you to prepare a summary of audit procedures for each of the outstanding matters. I would also like you to explain the key audit issues which need to be addressed in each case – this will help the juniors to gain a better understanding of their work.

One more point. The directors of Hopper Wholesale Ltd are interested in sustainability reporting and are proposing to include social and environmental information in their financial statements. They would like us to clarify whether they are required to publish this information. Please outline the current situation so that I can pass on the information to them. If they do include social and environmental information they would like us to produce a verification report. I will email you a copy of the statements they are planning to make. (**Exhibit 2**). We have not been involved in this type of work before so I would like you to outline the evidence which we should be able to obtain in order to verify these statements and any difficulties we may experience in validating the information. You should also indicate any professional issues that we need to consider if we accept this work.

Thanks for your help on this.'

Requirement

Respond to the audit manager's voicemail. **(40 marks)**

Exhibit 1

Hopper Wholesale Ltd – Audit – 31 December 20X8

Manager's review notes: Summary of outstanding matters

1   **Inventory**

In September 20X8 the company took delivery of 30,000 tonnes of flour from a former competitor who was going out of business. Normally Hopper would not carry this level of inventory of an individual line, representing a nine month supply at normal rates of consumption, however the competitor was selling at a 10% discount to open market prices. Hopper paid £4,500,000 for the flour. At the time sales budgets suggested that 10,000 tonnes would be sold at a profit by 31 December 20X8, which has proved to be the case and that the remaining 20,000 tonnes would be sold steadily throughout the first half of 20X9.

The directors were concerned that the market price for flour can be volatile and so they took steps to protect the company by entering into an agreement with a third party, Sweetcall, a food manufacturer, under which Hopper has the right to sell 20,000 tonnes at the end of June 20X9 at an agreed price of £140 per tonne. Hopper paid £250,000 for this option and this amount is recognised in the statement of financial position within sundry receivables. If the price of flour falls then the company will be able to retain their competitive advantage by selling the bulk consignment to Sweetcall and replacing their own inventory with purchases on the open market. The price of flour at 31 December had fallen to substantially less than £140 per tonne and Sweetcall has offered £400,000 to Hopper to cancel the option.

Audit procedures completed

The quantity of flour inventory has been established by attendance at the inventory count.

Inventory has been valued at the lower of cost and net realisable value. Satisfactory audit procedures have been carried out in this respect.

2   **Financial assets**

The company has made a number of investments in shares in listed companies. These have been recognised in non-current assets at £3.25 million. They have been classified as at 'fair value through profit or loss' and are disclosed in a note to the financial statements as 'held for trading'. A gain has been recognised in profit or loss of £515,000 in respect of these investments.

Audit procedures completed

The only audit procedure performed is reperformance of the calculation of the gain recognised in profit or loss.

3   **Receivable**

The statement of financial position shows a receivable balance of £50,000. This amount is owed to Hopper Wholesale Ltd by Bourne Ltd, a company which is controlled by Hopper's managing director, Jack Maddison. We have been told that it is due to be repaid within the next 12 months. No information about this transaction is provided in the notes to the financial statements.

Audit procedures completed

A written representation has been obtained confirming the amount and that the company is controlled by Jack Maddison.

4   **Share option scheme**

On 1 January 20X8, Hopper Wholesale Ltd gave 100 employees 500 share options each which vest on 31 December 20X9. The options are dependent on the employees working for the entity until the vesting date. During 20X8, five employees left and Hopper Wholesale Ltd anticipates that in total 10% of the current employees will leave over the two-year period, including the five employees who left during 20X8. The fair value of the options has been estimated as follows:

1 January 20X8	£12
31 December 20X8	£14
31 December 20X9	£15

The share options have been recorded in the financial statements as an expense in profit or loss and a credit to non-current liabilities of £700,000 (100 × 500 × 14).

Audit procedures completed

Agreed number of employees in the scheme to details set out in the contract.

The fair value of the share options has been confirmed with management.

The adjustment required has been recalculated and agreed to the client's calculation.

Exhibit 2

Social and environmental report – suggested assertions

1   We do not use suppliers who use child labour
2   All our staff are paid at least 10% above the minimum wage
3   We have reduced staff sickness to the rate of 2.4% calendar days
4   We have reduced the tonnage of waste sent to landfill by 10%
5   Through enhanced health and safety procedures, industrial accidents have been reduced by 40%.

21   Lyght plc

The accounting firm for which you work, Budd & Cherry, is a five partner firm of chartered accountants in general practice. It has 30 staff and it generated fee income last year of £5.2 million.

Budd & Cherry has recently gained a new client, Lyght plc (Lyght), as a result of a competitive tender. The formalities connected with appointment as auditor, including communication with the previous auditor, have been completed. The tender was for the audit work, but there is a strong possibility that Budd & Cherry may also be appointed to carry out the tax work and some advisory work for Lyght. Gary Orton has been appointed as manager on the Lyght audit for the year to 30 April 20X8 and you are the senior. Gary calls you into his office and explains the situation:

"Lyght is by far the largest company that our firm has gained as a client so it's really important that we do a good job and impress the board – not least because, if we are given the tax and advisory work, our expected total fees from Lyght will be around £500,000 next year. The previous three auditors have each lasted only three years before the audit was put out to tender by the Lyght board. I want to make sure we retain them as a long-term client. They might be looking for an AIM listing in two to three years' time and there will be major additional fees for our firm if we are appointed as their reporting accountants for that process.

At the moment we are likely to make a low recovery on the audit, as we had to make a low bid to win the work. We therefore need to carry out the audit efficiently, but also look for opportunities to sell tax and other services to the client. If I can help gain the tax and other advisory work for a client like this, I think I could be made a partner in Budd & Cherry and, as the senior, there could also be a big promotion in it for you.

Harry Roberts, our ethics partner, has some concerns over the fact that this is a large client for a firm of our size and that the audit fee is so low. He is therefore monitoring the situation. Please provide me with a memo including some notes explaining any ethical issues that should be drawn to his attention.

We are commencing the audit in a fortnight, on 25th May 20X8, and I have already been out to the client for a few days with a junior. I have provided some background notes (see **Exhibit 1**). I have also been to see the board and some matters have arisen that I have recorded in my briefing notes (see **Exhibit 2**). I would like you to explain the audit and ethical issues arising from the matters raised in the briefing notes, including the relevant audit procedures we should carry out during the audit. Where relevant, you should also describe the appropriate financial reporting treatment in each case. Please include your comments in the memo referred to above."

Requirement

Respond to the request of Gary Orton, the audit manager.   **(40 marks)**

Exhibit 1 – Background notes

Lyght plc is a family owned company which is controlled and resident in the UK. It purchases public sector assets from hospitals and from the armed forces within the EU, then sells them to governments and private sector companies, frequently in developing countries. Sales and purchases are invoiced either in sterling or in the currency of the foreign customer or supplier. The assets are those which are no longer required by the public sector bodies, but they are still serviceable. Health equipment includes expensive machinery for monitoring patients, as well as more basic nursing equipment such as beds, blankets and appliances. Lyght does not purchase weapons from the armed forces, as it has no licence to do so, but it acquires a wide variety of small and large items including vehicles, equipment, boats, tents and clothing.

Draft results for 20X8 show that Lyght plc generated revenue of £107 million from which a profit before tax of £12 million was generated. The carrying amount of its net assets at 30 April 20X8 are £36 million.

Leslie Moore is the principal shareholder of Lyght plc, with a holding of 55%. He is also Chairman of the board and the Chief Executive. His daughter, Emma Everton, is finance director and has a 15% shareholding. VenRisk, a venture capital company, has a 25% shareholding and has significant influence, with the remaining shares being held by senior management.

Exhibit 2 – Manager's briefing notes

1   Lyght has grown significantly in the last few years and is in the process of updating its IT systems with work already completed by an external contractor on the sales and purchase ledger systems including both hardware and software. The project is ongoing and the next stage is to install new, more sophisticated IT systems to monitor the flows of goods across the globe and for management accounting purposes. Lyght directors have asked our firm if we wish to tender for a small part of this work, including advice on the internal controls to be built into the new system. The total cost of the new system will be about £9 million, of which £5 million will be the costs of IT consultants' time in installation, data transfer and writing new software. Work would commence in July 20X8 and would take about a year to complete.

2   Only about £2 million of inventories (out of a total carrying amount of approximately £20 million) are held in the UK at any time. Inventories are normally shipped shortly after purchase. High value inventories usually have an identified buyer prior to purchasing them, and goods are shipped to the buyer within two months of acquisition. Smaller, low value goods are held at depots in the countries of the intended customers so they are available for prompt sale. Our appointment as auditors was only formalised after the year end and as a result we were not able to attend year-end inventory counts. I am therefore worried about how we will audit inventory. I am also worried about how inventories are going to be valued.

3   A large batch of used tyres was acquired by Lyght from an army transport depot for £1,000 in August 20X7. However, they were sold a few weeks later for £105,000 to a foreign company, Hott, in which VenRisk has a 30% equity holding giving it significant influence. Leslie Moore personally arranged the sale with the manager of the depot. An invoice has been found for £3,487 for personal gifts and entertainment for the depot manager paid for by Lyght. It also appears from a few enquiries I made that the depot manager is a cousin of Leslie Moore.

4   At the start of the year Lyght took out a ten-year non-cancellable lease on some offices that were part of a new city centre development. Lyght has been keen to upgrade its offices for a while in order to impress customers, particularly representatives of overseas governments. The lease payments, payable each year in advance, are £150,000. The present value of lease payments has been calculated at £1.1 million and has been recognised as a non-current asset and a lease liability. The non-current asset is being depreciated on a straight-line basis over ten years.

5   As a result of entering this lease management decided that the existing head office should be sold. The decision was taken on 1 January 20X8 and the draft financial statements show that the property was classified as held for sale from this date. On 1 January 20X8 the property which had been revalued in the past had a carrying amount of £2,000,000 prior to being transferred to assets held for resale. Its fair value was estimated at £1,600,000 and costs to sell of £20,000. The remaining useful life of the property at the date of reclassification was 20 years. The company is not planning to market the property until May 20X8.

6   At 30 April 20X8 an analysis of trade receivables showed the following:

	£
Boulogne SA	1,200,000
Cristina	2,000,000
Other receivables	10,800,000
	14,000,000

The amount due from Boulogne SA is denominated in Euros. All other receivables are denominated in £s.

The £2,000,000 due from Cristina represents an amount due from the government of Cristina which has been outstanding for some time. Considerable efforts by the sales director and his staff have been required to recover previous amounts owed by the government of Cristina. However the Cristina government has now agreed with Lyght that the £2 million that it owes will be paid on 1 May 20X9, together with a late payment charge, in lieu of interest, of £100,000. The effective interest rate at 30 April 20X8 is 8%.

The allowance for impairment of trade receivables is to be partly calculated using a formula to give a general allowance. The company is proposing to calculate its year end allowance for receivables as the £450,000 difference between balances owed and cash expected to be received, plus a general allowance of 5%.

22   Minnex

Minnex plc is a listed company which owns 20 department stores that are located throughout the world. There is a concentration of 12 stores in the UK, with the other stores being located in Europe, Hong Kong, Malaysia and Singapore. The company has been attracting significant comment in the financial press following its reorganisation, which has been taking place over recent months. One typical comment in today's press is:

'Minnex has had a difficult few years. The appointment of a new board last December signalled changes in Minnex's strategy, but it remains to be seen whether this will result in improved profitability. The major institutional shareholders are restless and there appears to be no honeymoon period for the new board, which is under pressure for improvements in reported profits. Given the changes this year and the scale of new financing, there is pressure on the directors to report improved profits. The company's results will be subject to close attention by analysts.'

Financial Weekly, 30 November 20X6

Company background

Minnex was founded over one hundred years ago as a small retail outlet in London. It grew substantially over a long period of time by occupying a niche market of medium-sized, up-market stores selling quality, branded goods. Each store ranges from 3,000 to 6,000 square metres, normally spread over three or four floors. Departments in most stores include clothing, electricals, perfumes and furniture.

Most goods are sourced centrally, under contracts with leading international suppliers, but store managers have autonomy to purchase some store specific goods in order to accommodate local tastes and customs.

The share price of Minnex reached a high of £8.46 in June 20X4. Disappointing results followed, however, for the year ended 31 December 20X4, which were released in April 20X5 and saw the share price fall to £7.20. A series of profit warnings in the final few months of 20X5 saw the share price fall to a low of £4.67 in November 20X5, at which point the majority of the board resigned and a new board was appointed in December 20X5.

In May 20X6, the new board engaged your firm, in an advisory capacity, to assist with the directors' strategic review. Your firm also acts as the auditors of Minnex. The first stage of the strategic review was completed in November 20X6.

You are a senior engaged in the audit of Minnex for the year to 31 December 20X6. You receive the following email from the audit manager:

Date:	30 November 20X6
From:	Eddie Futch <e.futch@rosenberg.crantz.com>
To:	T.I. Senior <t.i.senior@rosenberg.crantz.com>
Subject:	Minnex Audit

Good afternoon. We have not worked together before, but I understand from your staff appraisal that you are looking for some more challenging work to broaden your experience. I would like you to take over as senior on the Minnex audit as the current senior has just resigned. There are some interesting financial reporting, audit and advisory issues for you. Also, however, we need to use some business analysis and judgement here as the board completely changed last year, and they have had a year of operational and financial reconstruction, which is still in the process of being implemented. A lot has therefore happened in governance, operational and financial terms.

We are only at the interim audit stage, but the reporting deadlines are tight. I have set out some briefing notes below (**Exhibit 1**) on areas where I have some concern. This is partly information provided by the client and partly my own notes. As you will appreciate, we have only forecast, draft financial statements without much detail. There are a number of key transactions, explained in the briefing notes, which are yet to be decided upon by the directors, and are therefore not fully included in the forecast, draft financial statements (**Exhibit 2**). Where appropriate, adjustments will need to be made to the financial statements.

In order that I can urgently discuss these matters with the directors, I would like you to set out and explain the correct financial reporting treatment for each of the items in the briefing notes and, so far as the information permits, redraft the financial statements to include these adjustments, as I have indicated in the briefing notes. Please also calculate the basic and diluted earnings per share figures after your adjustments, as I think these are going to be key measures that will be used to judge the new directors' performance.

Also, there are some '*specific audit and advisory issues*' that I have indicated in the briefing notes, as I need to discuss these matters with the directors. I would like you to provide comments on each of these matters, as I consider these to be key issues.

Eddie.

Requirement

Draft a memorandum responding to the audit manager's email. Assume a tax rate of 23%, and that this tax rate is expected to remain unchanged in the foreseeable future. **(40 marks)**

Exhibit 1– Briefing notes

1   **The reorganisation**

As a consequence of the strategic review, the following proposals were decided:

The stores which do not earn an adequate return, measured against budget, will be closed. Nearly all of these are expected to be in the UK. Initial plans include a proposal for the closure of both stores in Scotland in order to withdraw from this region. The assets are expected to be sold to a number of different purchasers, rather than under a single contract.

The furniture departments were, in general, earning a poor return for the floor space occupied in most stores. They will be reviewed again for viability in 20X7, and the worst performing furniture sections will be closed and the floor space leased to external retailers.

New stores acquired will be much larger than the existing stores and will be located mainly in Europe. Substantial additional new financing is to be raised shortly in preparation for the new stores to be purchased in 20X7.

Minnex provided the following information from its strategic review for the two Scottish stores as part of its strategic plan to withdraw from trading in Scotland:

Location	Estimated revenue and profit for 20X6	Fair value of store on 30 November 20X6	Carrying amounts of stores at 30 November 20X6	Status at 30 November 20X6
Edinburgh	Operating profit £2m Revenue £14m	£25m	£2m	A decision on disposal will be made this week. A contract for disposal in March 20X7 has been offered for immediate signature but has not yet been agreed. If the contract is to be signed the details need to be finalised during the next two months (ie before 31 January 20X7). Estimated proceeds of sale are £24m.
Glasgow	Operating profit £nil Revenue £13m	£8m	£12m	A potential acquirer has been found, but they require a final agreement to be achieved by the end of December 20X6. The company does not currently expect to decide on the sale until January 20X7.

No adjustments have been made in the 20X6 draft financial statements for any of the above information concerning the two Scottish sites. Assuming that both sites are to close, please identify the implications of the timing of the decisions and the agreements. However, please adjust the draft financial statements assuming that the decisions and the agreements occur at the earliest opportunity.

Minnex uses the cost model in its financial statements. Cost of sales is fairly consistent at around 66% of revenue for each store.

Specific audit and advisory issues

I would like you to explain the audit tests you would carry out in respect of the two Scottish stores identified for disposal.

2 **Managerial remuneration**

In order to recruit and motivate the best available people, the remuneration committee, after much discussion, will decide tomorrow (ie 1 December 20X6) whether to issue share options to directors and senior managers. If the remuneration committee decides to award the options they will be granted immediately. The proposal is to issue 120,000 options to each of 75 directors and senior managers on 1 December 20X6. The exercise price would be £2.67 per share. A condition of the share option scheme is that recipients must remain with Minnex for at least three years after the granting date before being able to exercise their options, and they must be exercised before 1 December 20Y1. It is estimated that 80% of the current directors and managers will remain with Minnex for three years or more.

Minnex provides the following information:

	1 Dec 20X6	Average for Dec 20X6	31 Dec 20X6
Price per share	£5.00	£5.50	£6.00
Fair value of each option	£3.00	£3.40	£3.80 (assumption)

The share price of Minnex at 30 November 20X6 is £5.00.

The draft, forecast financial statements do not yet include any amounts in respect of the options. Please make adjustments to the financial statements assuming that the proposed scheme is to be agreed, in order to indicate the financial reporting consequences of the decision to the board.

The tax regime in force provides a tax deduction upon the exercise of the share options. The tax deduction is calculated based on the intrinsic value of the share options (the difference between the share price at the exercise date and the exercise price).

Specific audit and advisory issues

I have no idea how the directors calculated the fair values of the options. Please describe how the fair value of these options should be measured.

The partner in charge of this audit is planning to meet with the members of the audit committee in order to discuss matters of judgement associated with the audit. For this meeting, please identify the matters that will have to be discussed in connection with the share option scheme. Your notes should indicate the extent to which we will need to obtain written representation once all possible audit procedures have been undertaken.

3 Financing

In order to finance the acquisition of the new larger stores, Minnex raised new finance during the year using a bond issue. The company is also planning to issue further finance in the near future.

(i) Bond issue

On 1 July 20X6, Minnex issued a three-year, £100m fixed interest 7.5% bond with semi-annual interest payments. Minnex also immediately entered into an interest rate swap to pay LIBOR and to receive 7.5% with semi-annual payments. The swap terms include: £100m notional principal, a three-year term and six-monthly variable rate reset.

LIBOR has been stable at 6% since the bonds were issued, and Minnex estimates it will continue at this rate until 31 December 20X6. Interest rates are expected to fall, however, in early 20X7, and the estimated fair value of the swap asset at 31 December 20X6 before settlement is £2m, and after settlement it is £1.25m. The directors have estimated the fair value of the bond at 31 December 20X6 will be £101.25m.

Minnex wishes to designate the swap as a fair value hedge, but there is some doubt about the adequacy of the supporting documentation in respect of the effectiveness of the hedge.

A liability of £100m and the corresponding cash receipt have been recognised in the draft, forecast financial statements. The cash payment of semi-annual interest on the bond has also been included, but no other entries have been made in respect of the bond.

Audit manager's note

I have somebody else working on the tax treatment of the bond, so tax can be ignored in this case.

Specific audit and advisory issues

Please set out the future financial risks arising from this bond. Also, the directors are claiming they are setting up the swap to minimise future risks, but I would value your judgement on this assessment. Moreover, I am concerned about the adequacy of the supporting documentation in respect of the effectiveness of the hedge for the bond. Please set out the nature of the documentation we need to examine in this specific case and explain the information we should be looking for in this documentation to substantiate the effectiveness of the hedge for audit purposes. Please assume, however, that the hedge is effective when adjusting the financial statements.

(ii) Future financing choices

Loan stock

One financing option is for Minnex to issue to the public £50m of zero coupon loan stock on 1 January 20X7. This issue price is at fair value. The loan stock would be redeemable on 31 December 20Y0 at a premium of 31%.

Bank loan

The Minnex board has identified an alternative source of financing to the zero coupon loan stock. This would be a 6.5% fixed rate loan from its relationship bank amounting to £50m from 1 January 20X7, repayable on 31 December 20Y1. The bank will require us to carry out an assurance report to support this loan application. Interest is payable annually in arrears. The bank will also require a range of covenants as part of the loan agreement.

The company's view is that because they are acquiring new property, then either the loan stock or the bank loan should be low risk as the stores provide good security.

Specific audit and advisory issues

What I need from you is a comparison of the loan stock and the bank loan so we can advise Minnex on their relative merits in making their choice of financing. Please also compare the future financial reporting impact of each type of debt. The loan stock would not require us to prepare an assurance report, but the bank loan would require such a report. I would therefore also like you to prepare an initial risk assessment, which identifies and evaluates the major risks to the bank that would be likely to occur, if the bank loan method of financing takes place. This assessment should include the risks that would require further consideration for an assurance report. There are some judgement issues here, so take a close look at the draft financial statements and any other available information.

Exhibit 2 – Forecast, draft statement of profit or loss for year ending 31 December 20X6

	£m
Revenue	442
Cost of sales	(292)
Other expenses	(111)
Financing costs	(20)
Profit before tax	19
Tax	(6)
Profit after tax	13

Forecast, draft summary statement of financial position at 31 December 20X6

	£m	£m
ASSETS		
Non-current assets		
Property, plant and equipment		305
Current assets		
Inventories	81	
Trade receivables	2	
Cash and cash equivalents	115	
Total assets		198
		503
EQUITY AND LIABILITIES		
Share capital (£1 shares)	50	
Share premium	14	
Retained earnings	80	
Total equity		144
Non-current liabilities		
Long-term borrowings	196	
Deferred tax	20	
Total non-current liabilities		216
Current liabilities		
Current elements of long-term borrowings	102	
Trade payables	31	
Current tax	10	
Total current liabilities		143
Total equity and liabilities		503

23 Sunnidaze

You are Jamie Spencer, the senior in charge of the final audit work on Sunnidaze Ltd for the financial year ended 30 June 20X6.

Sunnidaze is based in Birmingham and sells and installs hot tubs, saunas and jacuzzis. It was incorporated five years ago by John and Mary Cotton, both of whom invested money they had earned in the music industry. John and Mary each own 50% of the issued share capital of Sunnidaze and are also directors. They delegate the day to day running of the company to the only other director, Arnold Murray, a more experienced businessman.

Until recently, Sunnidaze focussed on sales to wealthy individuals in its local area. Its range of products and installation expertise made it very successful and the business grew rapidly. However, in the year ended 30 June 20X5 it was less successful. Revenue fell to £4 million and the company broke even. Arnold decided to expand operations to cover the whole of England and also introduced a range of larger products suitable for spas and hotels. These changes required investment of £2 million. John and Mary were not willing to invest more money so Arnold arranged for Sunnidaze to borrow £2 million from a bank on 1 July 20X5.

Under the terms of the loan, Sunnidaze was required for the first time to have an audit and, in April 20X6, your firm was appointed as auditors for the year ended 30 June 20X6. The final audit visit commenced in September 20X6 but progressed slowly. The financial controller, Maisie Juniper, was not ready for your team and could not provide you with the information to complete the audit procedures. Your team left at the end of the scheduled audit visit with matters still outstanding.

Last week Maisie contacted you to let you know she was ready for a follow up audit visit and provided you with summary financial information (**Exhibit 1**) incorporating all audit adjustments identified at your previous visit and, in addition, two late client adjustments requested by the directors. You arranged for a junior member of staff, Sam Burrows, to visit Sunnidaze to complete the necessary audit procedures. Sam has sent you an email (**Exhibit 2**) summarising the audit procedures he has performed.

You receive a voice mail message from the Sunnidaze audit manager:

"Hello Jamie. I know you are busy at the moment but I really need to understand the status of our audit procedures on Sunnidaze. The directors have a meeting with the bank later this week and want to know whether we have any further audit adjustments and what our opinion on the financial statements will look like. They have asked me to meet with them tomorrow so I really need from you today:

- A memorandum setting out and explaining the additional audit adjustments and unresolved audit matters identified at our follow up visit, together with a brief summary of any additional audit procedures required. You should also prepare revised draft summary financial statements to the extent that the available information permits.

- Your comments on any more general concerns you have in relation to the audit as a whole including ethical issues for our firm and what our audit response to these concerns should be

- Brief notes setting out an explanation of the form of audit opinion we should give. (I have already given them a copy of the standard unmodified opinion so you need only consider whether we might modify this in some way.)

- The company is planning further expansion in the year ending 30 June 20X7. To help to fund the expansion Arnold Murray is proposing to enter in to a sale and leaseback arrangement regarding its warehouse. Details are as follows:

    - The property would be sold on 1 January 20X7 for £280,000 (the original cost was £75,000).

    - It would then be leased back on a 20 year lease at an initial rental of £32,000 per annum.

    - The sale price and the rental amount both represent market value.

    - The land element of the property is approximately ¼ of the total value

    - Sunnidaze has an incremental borrowing rate of 10% (annuity discount factor over 20 years = 8.5136).

Arnold would like me to explain to him the impact of this transaction on the financial statements for the year ended 30 June 20X7 so please draft some notes that I can refer to outlining the effects.

"I am in a meeting for the rest of the day, so please leave the information I have asked for on my desk. Please don't worry about tax as the tax department will address any issues here"

Requirement

Prepare the information requested by the audit manager.   **(40 marks)**

Exhibit 1 – Sunnidaze Ltd

Summary financial information for the year ended 30 June 20X6 prepared by Maisie Juniper

	Per trial balance £'000	Audit adjustments £'000	Late client adjustments £'000	Per draft financial statements £'000
Operating profit	651	(134)	(50)	467
Exceptional items	–		(42)	(42)
Interest payable	(100)			(100)
Profit before taxation	551	(134)	(92)	325
Taxation	–	(125)		(125)
Profit after taxation	551	(259)	(92)	200
Assets				
Property, plant and equipment	357	35		392
Intangible assets	500			500
Inventories	1,392			1,392
Trade receivables	1,629		(42)	1,587
Other current assets	40			40
Cash and cash equivalents	555			555
	4,473	35	(42)	4,466
Equity and liabilities				
Share capital	1,000			1,000
Retained earnings	551	(259)	(92)	200
Long-term borrowings	2,000			2,000
Trade and other payables	922	169	50	1,141
Tax payable	–	125		125
	4,473	35	(42)	4,466

Exhibit 2 – Email from Sam Burrows, audit junior

To:	Jamie Spencer
From:	Sam Burrows
Date:	1 November 20X6
Subject:	Sunnidaze audit for the year ended 30 June 20X6

Jamie

I have now completed as many of the outstanding audit procedures as I can. I've summarised below the procedures carried out in response to each of the points on the list of outstanding issues you gave me. Throughout my work, I used our preliminary assessment of materiality of £30,000.

1   **Ensure that all audit adjustments identified during our previous audit visit have been posted correctly by Maisie**

   Adjustments posted by Maisie all tie into our audit working papers. There is, however, one adjustment she has not booked as Arnold told her it did not relate to the year ended 30 June 20X6. We had proposed an adjustment to provide for a credit note of £10,000 issued on 15 July 20X6 to a hotel chain as a discount for purchasing ten jacuzzis. As the tenth and final jacuzzi was only delivered in July 20X6, Arnold believes that the discount arose in the year ending 30 June 20X7 rather than in 20X6 and does not plan to book this transaction until next year.

2   **Review any late adjustments made by the client**

   Maisie has made two additional adjustments. She has made an exceptional impairment of receivables of £42,000 as a health club customer has refused to pay for two luxury hot tubs. The hot tubs were supplied by DupaSpa (see note 3 below). The tubs were delivered to the health club in June 20X6 but Sunnidaze's engineer only started to install them at the end of October. It was agreed during the installation process that they were unsuitable for the selected site. However, there is disagreement over who is responsible and the customer has refused to pay and has asked Sunnidaze to remove the hot tubs as soon as possible.

Maisie has also provided for a £50,000 one-off incentive payment to Arnold. This was agreed with the shareholders as operating profit (before this payment) exceeded £450,000.

Maisie has informed me of one additional adjustment she plans to make. As in prior years, all retained earnings are to be distributed to the owners as a dividend and this needs to be reflected in the financial statements once the profit figure has been finalised.

3   **Perform work on the intangible asset**

The intangible asset represents £500,000 paid to a third party supplier, DupaSpa, on 1 July 20X1 for a ten year exclusive licence to distribute DupaSpa hot tubs in its local area. I have reviewed the agreement and reconciled the original payment to the bank statement. When Sunnidaze started in business, sales of approximately £600,000 related to products supplied by DupaSpa which generated a profit margin of 47%. In recent years, other suppliers' products have become increasingly popular but sales of DupaSpa products still generated revenue of £400,000 in the year ended 30 June 20X6.

4   **Update work on cash received from customers since the year end**

Of total trade receivables of £1,629,000 at 30 June 20X6, £1,391,000 has now been paid, £42,000 provided for (see 2 above – late client adjustment) and £10,000 is expected to be credited (see 1 above – discussion of audit adjustments). That leaves £186,000 unprovided and unpaid. I selected a sample of unpaid invoices and ensured that the product they related to was delivered before 30 June 20X6. I also enquired of Arnold and the credit controller whether there were any customer disputes or issues and was informed that all customers were expected to pay. Delays in payment were either due to delays in product installation or, where customers were local builders, delays in the collection of cash from their ultimate customers.

5   **Review of agreement for new bank loan**

I obtained and reviewed a copy of the bank loan agreement. Its key terms are as follows:

- The loan capital of £2 million is repayable in five equal annual instalments commencing on 31 December 20X6.

- Interest of 5% per annum is payable annually in arrears and an arrangement fee of £40,000 was paid when the monies were advanced on 1 July 20X5.

- There is a covenant within the agreement that operating profit for a financial year will fall no lower than £280,000. Should it do so, the bank has the power to require immediate repayment of the loan or to call on personal guarantees provided by the directors.

- Audited financial statements for each financial year must be delivered to the bank no more than 150 days after the financial year end.

6   **Review of events and results after the reporting period**

The management accounts for the three months to 30 September 20X6 show revenue of £1 million and operating profit of £50,000. These results are in line with the equivalent prior year period, although below budget. The cash balance at 30 September 20X6 was £600,000. The directors' latest forecast of revenue for the year ending 30 June 20X7 remains in line with their budget of £7 million, which was a 25% increase on the previous year. They anticipate an operating profit of £750,000 for the year ending 30 June 20X7. Maisie has told me in confidence that she believes this budget is extremely optimistic.

My review of post year end board minutes revealed only one item of interest. John and Mary Cotton are keen to sell their shareholding in the company and have already entered into discussions with a number of investors. The minutes indicate that the budget is forming the basis for negotiations on the valuation of the shares.

24 Tydaway

You are Gerry Melville, an audit senior in A&B Partners LLP. Today you receive a voice mail message from your manager, Mary Cunningham:

"Hello Gerry. I'd like you to help me to plan our audit of Tydaway Ltd for the year ending 31 July 20X1. In particular, the inventory section of our audit did not go well last year.

"Tydaway is a long-standing audit client of A&B Partners and has for many years manufactured metal filing cabinets at its factory in South London. On 30 September 20X0, Tydaway acquired a division of a competitor's business which produces high-quality wooden office furniture. This business, now known as Woodtydy, continues to operate from a factory in North London as a division of Tydaway. It continues to maintain its own separate accounting records and its results have not yet been incorporated in Tydaway's monthly management accounts.

"I've left on your desk extracts from Tydaway's most recently available management accounts which are for the 10 months ended 31 May 20X1 (**Exhibit 1**), notes from last year's audit file on inventory valuation (**Exhibit 2**) and information on Woodtydy's inventory supplied by the Woodtydy financial controller (**Exhibit 3**).

"Tydaway's annual inventory count took place on 30 June 20X1 (a month before the year-end) and it was attended by audit assistant, Dani Ford. Dani's inventory count notes are also on your desk (**Exhibit 4**). As Dani is on study leave from next week, it's important that you raise any questions with her as soon as possible.

"What I need you to do is:

(i)   Review Dani's inventory count notes (**Exhibit 4**) and prepare a list of issues and queries for her to address before she goes on study leave. Your list should include brief explanations of the points raised so that Dani understands why any additional information is required; and

(ii)   For each of the relevant financial statement assertions in respect of inventory:

* Highlight any particular concerns or issues which you have identified from your review of Exhibits 1, 2 and 3; and

* Prepare a summary of the key audit procedures we will need to perform to ensure that we have adequate audit assurance on inventory.

"Assume that audit planning materiality is £40,000 as in the prior year.

We have also been asked to give our client some accounting advice. Tydaway is finding the market for the metals required to make the filing cabinets increasingly competitive. As a result it has been looking for new suppliers and has identified one in China. Tydaway is to be invoiced by the Chinese company in US dollars (as this is the functional currency of the Chinese company). On 15 July 20X1 the company intends to enter into a contract with the Chinese company to purchase metals with a contract price of $500,000. This is a large order but it has been made in the light of the lead time for transporting the raw materials. The metal will be delivered to Tydaway on 15 December 20X1 and payment will be made on that date.

The directors are concerned about the impact of foreign exchange risk and are considering whether to enter into a forward contract on 15 July 20X1 to purchase $500,000 on 15 December 20X1. They have asked me to meet them next week to discuss their options. I would like you to prepare some information that I can refer to in my meeting as follows:

* Set out, using journal entries, the impact of this contract on the financial statements for the years ending 31 July 20X1 and 31 July 20X2 under each of the following scenarios:

  – There is no hedging arrangement put in place.

  – Tydaway enters into the forward contract, but does not satisfy the conditions for hedge accounting.

  – Tydaway enters into the forward contract, satisfies the conditions for hedge accounting and chooses fair value hedge accounting.

  – Tydaway enters into the forward contract, satisfies the conditions for hedge accounting and chooses cash flow hedge accounting.

- Explain and compare the financial reporting treatment for the four scenarios above.

I do not require you to consider the tax implications of these issues and I do not require you to list hedging accounting conditions.

I have made some additional notes and working assumptions for you to use (**Exhibit 5**).

We also need to consider the implications for our forthcoming audit. If hedge accounting is used certain documentation must be kept. Please provide a list of the documentation we would be expecting to see.

"I look forward to reviewing your work later today."

Requirement

Respond to Mary Cunningham's instructions.

(Assume that today is 5 July 20X1).   (**40 marks**)

Exhibit 1 – Extracts from Tydaway Ltd management accounts for the 10 months to 31 May 20X1

Statement of profit or loss and other comprehensive income

	10 months to 31 May		
	20X1	20X0	
	£'000	£'000	Notes
Revenue generated by South London factory			
External customers	4,282	5,912	
Sales to Woodtydy	135	–	1
	4,417	5,912	
South London factory costs			
Raw materials at standard cost	2,431	3,197	
Purchase price variances	296	(10)	2
Other purchase costs, including freight	77	45	
Movement in inventory at standard cost	(99)	20	
Total raw material cost of goods sold	2,705	3,252	
Movement in inventory provision	–	5	
Labour	873	869	
Overheads and delivery costs	345	354	
Total factory cost of goods sold	3,923	4,480	
Margin as a percentage of total revenue	11%	24%	

Statement of financial position	31 May	31 May	
	20X1	20X0	
	£'000	£'000	
Inventory analysis			
Raw materials	340	270	3
Raw material element of work-in-progress	131	157	
Raw material element of finished goods	55	–	4
	526	427	
Inventory provision	(20)	(20)	
	506	407	

Notes:

1   Represents goods sold to Woodtydy in the period since Tydaway acquired the division on 30 September 20X0.

2   Purchase price variances are adverse in the period ended 31 May 20X1 as a result of an unexpected increase in the price of steel. In addition, normal bulk discounts were unavailable on components bought at short notice to fulfil a major order which was shipped in May 20X1 and gave rise to a one-off adverse price variance of £25,000.

3   Raw material inventory has increased as a result of a slow-down in customer orders. During June 20X0, certain components were purchased in bulk in anticipation of orders which have not materialised. Of these purchases, components costing approximately £60,000 remain in inventory at 31 May 20X1.

4   Finished goods held in inventory represent the cost of goods produced for Swishman plc, a customer which ordered customised products in its corporate colours for a major office refurbishment. Swishman has recently experienced financial difficulties and has cancelled its order, leaving Tydaway with a number of finished cabinets already painted in Swishman's specified colours. It is possible that these cabinets can be used to fulfil other orders, but they will need to be stripped and repainted at a total cost of around £10,000. A legal claim for £30,000 has already been made against Swishman for breach of contract. Swishman has offered £6,000 in full and final settlement of the liability.

Exhibit 2 – Notes on inventory valuation from prior year audit file for Tydaway

- Raw materials are valued at standard cost. Standard costs are reviewed and updated on the first day of each financial year and are then left unchanged throughout the year. Historically, our audit testing on the valuation of a sample of items has led us to conclude that standard costs generally represent a reasonable approximation to the actual cost of purchase.

- Standard costs include an uplift of 1.5% of the material cost to cover freight and other purchase costs.

- Inventories of finished goods are typically very low as all goods are shipped to the customer as soon as they are complete.

- Work in progress (WIP) is valued initially at the standard cost of its raw material components. An adjustment is made at the year end (for statutory accounts purposes only) to include in inventory an appropriate percentage of labour and factory overhead, calculated as follows:

$$\frac{\text{Units in WIP} \times 50\%}{\text{Total units produced in the year}} \times (\text{Total factory labour} + \text{factory overhead})$$

   *WIP is on average 50% complete

- Provision is made for any obsolete raw materials. No provision is required against finished goods or WIP as filing cabinets are typically built to order for specific customers.

Exhibit 3 – Information on Woodtydy's inventory supplied by Woodtydy financial controller

1   At 31 May 20X1, the Woodtydy business had total inventory as analysed below:

	£'000
Raw materials	230
Work in progress	120
Finished goods	159
	509
Provision	(58)
	451

2   Raw materials are valued at the latest invoice price.

3   Each customer order is recorded on a separate job card. As materials are allocated to an order, they are booked out of raw materials and booked on the job card at the latest invoice price. The time spent on the job is then recorded on the card and a cost of £30 per hour is included in inventory to reflect the cost of direct labour and factory overhead. At the period end, the job cards are sorted into complete and incomplete items and recorded as finished goods or work in progress as appropriate.

4   Provision is made on a line-by-line basis for any items which are obsolete, slow-moving or can only be sold for less than cost.

Exhibit 4 – Notes on inventory count attendance prepared by Dani Ford

I attended an inventory count at Tydaway's South London factory on 30 June 20X1. As no inventory count is planned at 31 July, the inventory quantities from this count will be posted to the book inventory records and updated for purchases and sales made in the last month of the financial year.

The count was well organised and all counters were briefed beforehand. Counters worked in teams of two, with one counting and the other recording the quantity counted and comparing it to the quantity shown on the book inventory system, as supplied on the printed inventory list prepared beforehand.

Where the quantity counted differed by more than 10% from that on the system, a second count was performed by a team from another area of the warehouse.

I performed independent counts on a sample of 25 types of raw material, noting the following differences:

(i) Quantities of smaller components were estimated by weighing a sample of ten to 20 items and comparing their weight to the weight of the total inventory of that item in order to estimate the overall quantity. When we performed our own tests, we noted differences of up to 5% in quantity for such items. This does not appear unreasonable given the estimation involved.

(ii) All tins of paint and chemicals were treated as full tins although some of them were only partly full. From a discussion with the inventory controller this is unlikely to have resulted in any material overstatement of inventory.

(iii) Two differences were noted in samples taken from the mezzanine area of the stores. In both cases, the counters had recorded a count which agreed with the quantity on the system whereas our count showed less in one case and more in the other. Our counts were agreed with the counters and the inventory sheets were updated to record the correct quantities.

I performed counts on a sample of five types of work in progress. All counts were accurate.

I inspected the despatch areas, noting that there were no shipments in progress during the count. In the goods received area, I noted a large consignment of filing cabinet drawers which had not been counted. From a discussion with the inventory controller, these drawers had just been returned from a subcontractor who finishes the premium range to a high standard. They will be booked back into WIP after the count is complete.

Exhibit 5

Proposed contract with China

Hedging

Tydaway is considering two alternatives:

(i) Do not hedge and therefore accept any consequent exchange rate risks.

(ii) Enter into a foreign exchange forward contract on 15 July 20X1 to purchase $500,000 on 15 December 20X1.

At 15 July 20X1, the spot exchange rate is expected to be £1=$1.6108.

At 15 July 20X1, the 5-month forward rate is also expected to be £1=$1.6108. The forward rate contract will have a zero fair value at 15 July 20X1.

At 15 July 20X1, the contract with China would be a firm commitment and, if Tydaway decides to enter into the forward contract at that date, it is unsure whether it would be better to treat it as a fair value hedge or as a cash flow hedge for financial reporting purposes. However, it may be that Tydaway cannot satisfy the hedge accounting conditions, although it is hoped it will be able to do so.

Working assumptions

For illustrative purposes I would like you to adopt the following working assumptions as one possible scenario of future exchange rate movements:

At 31 July 20X1
  Spot   £1=$1.5108
  Fair value of forward contract   £20,544 positive (ie in favour of Tydaway)

At 15 December 20X1
  Spot   £1=$1.4108
  Fair value of forward contract   £43,994 positive (ie in favour of Tydaway)

25 Wadi Investments

The Wadi Investments Group invests in capital markets and real estate primarily in the Indian subcontinent and Asia. Your firm is responsible for the audit of Wadi Investments and the consolidated financial statements. The audit has already commenced but you have been asked to join the team as the manager is concerned that there is not the appropriate level of expertise in the current team. You have been sent the following email from your manager.

To: APerdan@ABCAccountants
From: TFlode@ABCAccountants
Date: 30 July 20X9

Subject: Audit of the financial statements for the year ended 30 June 20X9

Amar,

I am very glad that you are joining the audit as things have not been going well. I have had a fairly inexperienced team and I am concerned about some of the work which has been prepared to date. We are responsible for both the parent company audit and the audit of the group. Work has already started on the audit of the parent company. I have briefly reviewed most of the working papers produced to date but have not been able to look at them in detail. My review has raised a number of concerns which I would like you to address in a report which I can use to evaluate how to approach the remaining audit work. I have listed my concerns below and have attached a number of other relevant documents including relevant exchange rates (**Attachment 2**). I have confirmed the exchange rates myself so you should use these in any calculations.

Audit of the parent: Wadi Investments

Acquisition of Strobosch

We have been told that Wadi purchased an 80% subsidiary on 1 January 20X9. It is an investment company based in Ruritania and its functional currency is the Ruritanian Rand (RR). Some work has been done on the investment in the parent's statement of financial position but from my review of the audit assistant's working paper (**Attachment 1**) a number of significant issues have not been addressed. Please identify these including any audit adjustments that may be required. You should also review the work performed by the junior and list any additional procedures which are needed.

Investment property

The group carries all land and buildings, including investment property, at fair value. On 15 March 20X9 the head office building in London was vacated and is to be leased out for the next five years to a company outside the Wadi Group. The building originally cost £90m back on 3 April 20X6 and as at the next valuation on 30 June 20X7 it was valued at £112m. Its fair value at 15 March 20X9 was £124m and at 30 June 20X9 is £128m.The depreciation policy for buildings is straight line over 50 years, measured to the nearest month. Our audit work to date shows that the asset has been included in property, plant and equipment in the year end statement of financial position but any further work on this issue is outstanding. Please can you set out how to account for the change in the use of this asset and outline the audit adjustments required. You should also list the audit procedures which should be performed.

Audit of Wadi Investments Group

This is still at the planning stage and there are a number of issues which I would like your help with.

- The Strobosch audit is being conducted by a local firm, Kale & Co. I am familiar with the firm and its practices and am confident that they will do a professional job. However, I need to communicate with them and will have to draft a letter of instruction. Please draw up a checklist of the points which I need to include so that I can ensure that all necessary matters are covered.

- At a recent meeting with the finance director of Wadi, he mentioned that the investment in Strobosch was financed by a number of Ruritanian Rand loans in order to hedge the foreign currency exposure and that hedging provisions are to be adopted. Total exchange losses on the loans for the six months to 30 June 20X9 are £36m. He also mentioned a loan made to Strobosch on 1 January 20X9 to assist with expansion plans. Further details regarding the net investment in Strobosch and the loan to Strobosch are attached (**Attachment 3**). Please identify the audit and financial reporting issues that we will need to consider.

Requirement

Respond to the manager's instructions. **(40 marks)**

Attachment 1 – Audit assistant's working paper for the acquisition of Strobosch

Client: Wadi Investments
Year end: 30 June 20X9
Prepared by: Sam Brown

Investment in Strobosch

	£m
Cash paid on 1 January 20X9	675
8% debentures	360
Costs	18
	1,053

Analysis of costs

	£m
Costs of internal merger and Acquisitions team at Wadi Investments	2
Issue costs of debentures	6
Legal costs (RR23m × 0.45)	10
	18

Note: I have been told that the IRR on the debentures is 4.42% per six month period but I am not sure what the relevance of this is. Interest on the debentures is paid every six months.

Work performed

1 Agreed cash paid to bank statement.
2 Agreed £360m debentures to matching liability in the statement of financial position.
3 Obtained a schedule of the breakdown of costs.
4 Cast total and agreed spot rate.

Attachment 2 – Exchange rates

The following exchange rates should be used for the preparation of the 20X9 financial statements.

Date	RR: £
1 January 20X9	1: 0.45
30 June 20X9	1: 0.47
Average for six months to 30 June X9	1: 0.46

RR = Ruritanian Rand

Attachment 3 – Hedge of net investment

Extract from the financial statements of Strobosch as at 30 June 20X9

	Draft RR (millions)
Property, plant & equipment	389
Investment property	1,453
Financial assets	659
Current assets	124
Total assets	2,625
Share capital	300
Retained earnings	1,720
	2,020
Non-current liabilities	518
Current liabilities	87
Total liabilities and equity	2,625

- Retained earnings at acquisition were RR 1,440m and the fair value of net assets at acquisition was RR 1,865m
- The long-term liabilities of Strobosch include RR 444m in respect of a five-year interest free loan of £200m made by Wadi on 1 January 20X9

26 Poe, Whitman and Co

You are an audit senior with Poe, Whitman and Co, a firm of chartered accountants. Upon returning to the office this week from vacation, you find the following email in your in-box from Margaret Fleming, one of your firm's audit managers.

Date: 2 April 20X7
From: Margaret Fleming <m.fleming@poe.whitman.com>
To: Audit Senior <a.senior@poe.whitman.com>
Subject: Commedia Ltd

Attachments: Commedia background notes; email from Bob Kerouac

I hope you had a good holiday. As you may know I have recently been given managerial responsibility for the firm's new audit client Commedia Ltd, and I understand that you will be the senior on the group's audit for the year ended 28 February 20X7. We have only recently been appointed auditor following the unexpected resignation of the previous auditor just two weeks ago.

Please could you consider the practical and ethical issues specifically in connection with our late appointment and the steps we should take to ensure that these issues do not affect the performance of our duties as the group's auditor.

Please also summarise for me the relevant audit procedures and our reporting responsibilities which arise from the Commedia engagement being a new audit for Poe, Whitman and Co.

I have also attached to this email some notes on the Commedia group, **(attachment 1)**.

In addition to providing some background information on the group, the notes also include information on some specific events that occurred within the group during the year. I would like you to identify the audit risks relating to these events and draft the audit procedures required to mitigate them.

Finally, I attach an email I received last week from Bob Kerouac **(attachment 2)**, requesting advice on some financial reporting matters. Please draft a response in note form for me to use at the meeting I have arranged with Bob for next week.

Margaret

Requirement

Respond to the email from your audit manager. **(30 marks)**

Attachment 1 to email – Commedia group background notes

Commedia Ltd ('Commedia')

Commedia is an independent television production company with annual revenues last year of approximately £60m. The company's creative team develops ideas for television programmes, which are then 'pitched' to one or more of the television broadcasting companies within the UK. If the pitch is successful, the programme is commissioned by the broadcaster and then made by Commedia to an agreed budget.

During the year, a number of Commedia's customers changed the terms of some of their commissions from a 'funded' to a 'licensed' basis.

Funded commissions

The broadcaster is responsible for funding the entire production budget (which includes an agreed management fee for Commedia) in monthly instalments as the production progresses. Upon delivery of the programme to the broadcaster, all future rights to exploit the programme are signed over to the broadcaster.

Licensed commissions

Under these arrangements, Commedia is paid an agreed amount, in full, upon delivery of the programme. The broadcaster acquires the rights to broadcast the programme an agreed number of times, with Commedia retaining all residual rights to future exploitation of the programme. The price paid by the broadcaster for a licensed commission is 25% to 30% lower than that for the equivalent funded commission. Where the cost of making the programme exceeds the value of the licensed commission payment, the difference is carried forward as an intangible asset by Commedia to write off against future revenues arising from the residual rights held.

At the start of this accounting period, 1 March 20X6, Commedia had two wholly-owned subsidiaries, Scherzo Ltd and Riso Ltd. The subsidiaries were set up by Commedia Ltd many years ago. All three companies have the same 28 February year end and they are all audited by your firm.

Scherzo Ltd ('Scherzo')

Scherzo is a concert and events promotion company. The company stages major popular and classical music concerts throughout the year, which are held principally in open-air venues.

Disposal of shareholding

On 30 April 20X6, Commedia disposed of 70% of its shareholding in Scherzo to that company's management team for a possible total sum of £20m. £15m of this total was paid in cash on completion of the sale, with the remainder to be paid 15 months later, contingent on the profit of the company for the year ended 28 February 20X7. Scherzo has also appointed your audit firm as its auditor. Extracts from the terms of the sale of shares in Scherzo are set out below.

Extracts from contract for sale of shares in Scherzo Ltd

(a) The completion date for the disposal of the shares was 30 April 20X6

(b) Total possible consideration for the shares is £20m, split as follows:

- £15m payable on completion

- £5m payable on 31 July 20X7 if the pre-tax profit of the company for the year ended 28 February 20X7 is at least £5m

- If the pre-tax profit for the year ended 28 February 20X7 is below £3m, no further consideration is payable

- For pre-tax profit between £3m and £5m, the further consideration payable is calculated as follows:

    Further consideration = £5m × (pre-tax profit less £3m)/£2m

(c) Pre-tax profit for the purpose of this contract is defined as 'Profit before tax per the company's audited financial statements excluding the following items:

- Total directors' emoluments in excess of £350,000

- Exceptional items (ie items of income and expense of such materiality that IAS 1 requires their nature and amount to be disclosed separately)'

'Rock in the Park' concert

Scherzo was responsible again this year for 'Rock in the Park', a major outdoor series of popular music concerts spanning three days in July 20X6. On the evening of the third day, part of the stage collapsed causing injury to some members of the stage crew and audience. The incident also led to the cancellation of the rest of the concert, including the performance scheduled for the event's most well known performer. Scherzo had sub-contracted the erection and maintenance of the stage to another company, Highstand Limited.

The directors of Scherzo have included a provision in the year-end financial statements of £2m. This is to allow for the cost of refunding all monies received from the sale of tickets to the concerts, and to recognise the cost of personal injury claims received by the company as at the year end.

Riso Ltd ('Riso')

Riso's sole activity is the operation of a large television studio which it hires out to customers for the production of television programmes. The television studio is based in a former glass bottle factory and is occupied by Riso under a ten-year lease, originally taken out on 1 March 20X3. The studio is hired out to Commedia (on an arm's length basis) approximately 30% of the time for the filming of its own commissions. For the remaining 70% of the time the studio was, until recently, hired out to two different broadcast companies, each for the production of their own competing daytime television drama serial.

During the year ended 28 February 20X7, one of these broadcasters announced that, due to poor viewing figures, it would no longer be making a drama serial. Riso has spent the last three months looking for an alternative customer, but has so far been unsuccessful. The directors of Riso are aware that there is currently surplus capacity in UK-based studio facilities, due to a reduction in UK-produced programmes. This reduction has been brought about by an increase in programmes imported from overseas and reduced TV advertising budgets.

The directors of Riso have produced a forecast of future pre-tax cash-flows for the company as follows:

Year ending 28 February	£'000 inflow/(outflow)
20X8	(100)
20X9	(50)
20Y0	900
20Y1	1,375
20Y2	1,495
20Y3	1,695

Riso made an initial £8m investment in the television production equipment required for its studio on 1 March 20X3. No further capital expenditure is likely to be required for the foreseeable future. The company expects the equipment to have an expected useful life of ten years at which point its disposal value is estimated to be £2m. Riso depreciates the equipment on a straight-line basis. The carrying amount of the company's other assets and liabilities at 28 February 20X7, was £250,000.

Attachment 2

Copy of email from Bob Kerouac

Date: 26 March 20X7
From: Bob Kerouac <bkerouac@commediagroup.com>
To: Margaret Fleming <m.fleming@poe.whitman.com>
Subject: Year end financial statements

Margaret,

It was good to meet you recently. Further to our scheduled meeting in two weeks' time, there are some matters in connection with the current year financial statements that I want to discuss with you. I hope that when we meet you can provide me with advice on their appropriate treatment in the financial statements for the year ended 28 February 20X7. The matters are as follows:

(1) Disposal of our majority holding of shares in Scherzo: as you know, we sold the majority of our shares held in this company during the year. I would be grateful if you could provide me with some advice on how to account for this disposal in Commedia's own financial statements for the year; and also how the remaining investment in Scherzo is now to be treated in the group's consolidated financial statements.

(2) Treatment of the television production equipment in Riso: as you are aware, we have recently lost a major contract in this company due to cancellation by our customer of their daytime TV drama serial. This has given rise to a loss in the company this year, and will mean future losses if an alternative customer cannot be found. I am unsure how, if at all, this affects the value and presentation of the equipment in the financial statements of Riso. I am particularly concerned as we recently had the equipment externally valued at a figure of £4m. Please could you clarify this issue for me, indicating what adjustments, if any, are required to ensure proper presentation in the financial statements for the year. I am unsure whether this is of use to you, but the pre-tax annual rate of return that the market would expect from this type of investment is 10%.

27 Pottington Printers

You are a senior working for the newly-appointed auditors of Pottington Printers Ltd (hereafter PP), a private company that has traditionally sold printers for PCs.

As part of the audit planning procedures for the accounting year ended 31 March 20X3, the assignment partner, Alice Kumar, has asked you to accompany her to a meeting with the finance director, Sydney Slytherin.

The finance director outlined the situation as follows:

"PP has been in decline but, on 30 March 20X0, we signed a five-year contract with a company in the Far East, Mitzuki, to be its exclusive retailers in the UK of a machine which acts as a compact wireless printer, scanner and photocopier. This Mitzuki model is now the only product we sell. While there are other models on the market, the Mitzuki machine sells for only £480, which is only two-thirds of the price of comparable machines sold by our major competitors. We have targeted a niche market of small businesses, which have restricted office space. We sold 150,000 machines this year. This represents a good level of growth for us: we sold 125,000 machines last year and 80,000 machines in 20X1.

"Frankly, we have had some problems with reliability but we got round these with our guarantee which applies within three years of purchase. Under this we have a four hour call-out service, whereby we agree to have a repair engineer with the customer within four hours of notification of a fault. It is costing us a fortune, but there is no other way we can sell these machines, and they have only been costing us £320 each up to now under the terms of the contract. Mitzuki gives us only a one year guarantee, but we would lose our customers if that was all we were to provide for them. As it is, we keep our customers because our rivals charge their customers £50 a year for that type of service support after the one-year guarantee period.

"We are expanding sales enormously, and we hope to get an Alternative Investment Market listing next year to raise substantial new equity capital, so we need to show significant profit growth. We also need to ensure that our annual report looks good and would like an assurance from you that our audit report will be clean.

"We are concerned about what will happen at the end of the five year contract with Mitzuki. If the contract is renewed, we think the price we're charged will increase significantly. Therefore over the last year we've started buying more and more machines and stockpiling them, so that we can buy as many as possible before the contract runs out. So far Mitzuki haven't queried what we're up to. We invested heavily in training costs for our repair engineers at the beginning of the contract spending £5 million, and this will prove useful experience compared to our competitors. We do, however, have a high staff turnover for engineers, which loses us valuable experience every year."

Following the meeting you receive the following memorandum from Alice Kumar.

MEMO

To   A Senior
From   Alice Kumar (partner)
Date   9 April 20X3
Subject   Pottington Printers audit

The assignment manager is ill at the moment, so meanwhile I would like you to report directly to me.

I would like you to provide me with a memorandum, summarising the key audit and financial reporting issues that have arisen from:

- Our meeting with the finance director
- The audit issues raised by junior staff
- The draft financial statements

Please indicate what you suggest we should do about these matters.

I would also like you to redraft the financial statements to the extent that the available information permits at this stage.

Alice Kumar
Partner

Audit issues

Junior audit staff have provided you with the following information on issues which have arisen in the first week of the audit of PP. Draft financial statements have also been prepared (see **Exhibit**).

(1)   The inventory count revealed 5,000 machines which are not capable of being repaired at the customers' premises. They have therefore been returned to PP's warehouse by service engineers and a replacement machine provided to the customers in question. These machines are included in inventories at their original cost price. It is estimated that repair costs for each machine will amount to £180 after which the machines will be suitable for resale to new customers at £460.

(2)   Training costs have been capitalised and depreciated over the period of the Mitzuki contract. Thus, for example, costs incurred in the first year of the contract (year ended 31 March 20X1) are being depreciated over five years. Depreciation is recognised as an operating cost.

(3)   It has been discovered that another company in the UK has started to sell Mitzuki machines, which have been imported from the US in breach of Mitzuki's agreement with its US retailers. Lawyers for PP have contended that litigation is likely to be successful and have estimated damages in favour of PP at £4 million. PP made a prudent estimate of £2 million and this has been included in profit for the year to 31 March 20X3.

(4)   On 1 January 20X3 the company took out a loan of £20 million. Under the conditions of the loan no interest would accrue in the first two years. For the following two years interest would be paid at 12% per year before being redeemed at par on 1 January 20X7. No interest has been charged by PP in respect of this loan in the current year, as no interest was paid under its terms.

Exhibit – Draft financial statements

Statements of profit or loss and other comprehensive income for the years ended 31 March

	Draft 20X3 £m	20X2 £m
Revenue	72	60
Cost of sales	(45)	(40)
Gross profit	27	20
Operating costs	(17)	(16)
Litigation claim	2	–
Operating profit	12	4
Interest payable	(1)	(1)
Profit before taxation	11	3
Taxation	(2)	(1)
Profit for the year	9	2

Dividends of £1m were paid in 20X3; none were paid in 20X2.

Statements of financial position at 31 March

	Draft 20X3 £m	Draft 20X3 £m	20X2 £m	20X2 £m
Non-current assets				
Land and buildings		10		10
Training costs		2		3
Inventories	67		10	
Receivables	10		9	
		77		19
Total assets		89		32
Share capital: £1 shares		5		5
Retained earnings		14		6
		19		11
Non-current liabilities		32		12
Current liabilities				
Trade payables	15		5	
Overdraft	23		4	
		38		9
Total equity and liabilities		89		32

Requirement

Prepare the information requested by the engagement partner.   **(30 marks)**

28 Precision Garage Access

Precision Garage Access plc (PGA) is a listed company which manufactures and installs garage doors for private residences. You are a senior working for PGA's auditors and are currently supervising the planning and interim audit work for the year ending 30 September 20X6. You are also carrying out a review of the interim financial statements for the nine months to 30 June 20X6.

As part of the planning process, an audit junior, Claire Chalker, has completed some initial analytical procedures on the management accounts for the nine months ended 30 June 20X6. She has provided some background information (**Exhibit 1**) and set out some basic financial data and notes (**Exhibit 2**). She does not however have the experience to analyse this data in order to identify audit risks.

The engagement manager, Gary Megg, reviewed Claire's work and sent you the following email:

To: A. Senior
From: Gary Megg, Engagement Manager
Date: 26 July 20X6
Subject: PGA audit

I have been through the notes prepared by Claire. I think she has highlighted some interesting points, but she has not really analysed the data in any depth or identified key audit issues. There appear to be some financial reporting issues arising from her work which may require adjustment to the management accounts.

Prior to our audit planning meeting next week I would like you to:

- Carry out revised analytical procedures using Claire's data and other information provided. This work should:

    - Identify any unusual patterns and trends in the data which may require further investigation. Show supporting calculations (where appropriate assume 360 days in a year for the purpose of computing any ratios); and

    - Outline the audit risks that arise from the patterns and trends identified in the analytical procedures and set out the audit procedures you would carry out.

- Set out the financial reporting issues that arise from the above audit work with respect to the interim financial statements for the nine months ended 30 June 20X6 and are expected to arise for the year ending 30 September 20X6. I do not require any detailed disclosure requirements. I do not require you to consider tax, or deferred tax, implications at this stage.

There is one further matter which I would like you to look at. I have just received an email from David May, the finance director of PGA. The board has acknowledged that the company is experiencing difficulties retaining key staff. This is particularly the case with senior and middle management. Whilst a bonus scheme has been introduced this year in place of a pay rise (see Claire's notes below) the directors realise that they need to encourage individuals to commit to the company longer-term. David has come up with a proposal for a share based bonus scheme but is concerned about its effects on future profits. I have attached his email which provides details of the scheme and the information he requires (**Exhibit 3**). I would like you to produce the information he has requested so that I can forward it on to him. Please use his working assumptions. I think that his predicted share price increases may be optimistic in the current climate but I can discuss this with him at a later date.

Many thanks,

Gary

Requirement

Respond to the engagement manager's instructions.   **(30 marks)**

Exhibit 1 – Background information prepared by Claire Chalker

PGA makes and installs two types of garage doors:

- Manually operated wooden doors – the "Monty". The list price of the Monty was increased by 5% on 1 October 20X5 to £840 each, including installation.

- An electrically operated set of metal doors with a motor – the "Gold". The list price of the Gold was increased by 5% on 1 October 20X5 to £2,520 each, including installation.

Nearly all doors are made to order.

Each of the two types of door is made on a separate production line at PGA's factory in the South of England. Production equipment is specialised and highly specific to each of the separate production processes.

PGA makes about 70% of its sales of both products in Germany and France where it has a network of sales offices. All selling prices are set at 1 October each year. Prices for overseas markets are fixed in euro at this time, at the equivalent of £ sterling prices.

The company has had a difficult trading year so far, due to the general economic downturn. The trading performance in the year ending 30 September 20X6 is thus expected to be weaker than in the previous year.

In previous years, approximately equal quantities of Gold and Monty doors have been sold. However, sales of the Gold have suffered particularly badly this year, as customers appear unwilling to spend large sums on their garage doors in the recession. Sales of Gold doors are not expected to increase in the foreseeable future.

Customers are either individual householders or small building companies. Discounts may be given to building companies for large orders but PGA sales staff have stated that door prices to individual customers are never discounted.

Exhibit 2 – Financial data and notes prepared by Claire Chalker

Management accounts – Statements of profit or loss and other comprehensive income

	Notes	Draft 9 months to 30 June 20X6 £'000	9 months to 30 June 20X5 £'000	Year ended 30 Sept 20X5 £'000
Revenue:	1			
Monty		7,500	9,600	10,400
Gold		14,000	28,800	31,200
Cost of sales:	2			
Monty		(6,700)	(7,800)	(9,200)
Gold		(15,500)	(23,400)	(27,600)
Gross profit/(loss)		(700)	7,200	4,800
Fixed administrative and distribution costs		(1,200)	(1,200)	(1,600)
Exceptional item				
Staff bonus scheme	3	(450)	–	–
Profit/(loss) before tax		(2,350)	6,000	3,200
Income tax expense		–	(1,680)	(900)
Profit/(loss) for the period		(2,350)	4,320	2,300

Management accounts – Extracts from statements of financial position

	Notes	At 30 June 20X6 £'000	At 30 June 20X5 £'000	At 30 Sept 20X5 £'000
Current assets				
Inventories	4	3,500	3,500	1,200
Trade receivables	4	2,400	4,300	1,000

Notes:

1   **Revenue**

Inventory records show the number of doors sold as:

	9 months to 30 June 20X6	9 months to 30 June 20X5	Year ended 30 Sept 20X5
Monty	9,000	12,000	13,000
Gold	6,000	12,000	13,000

Sales volumes in the final quarter of the year ending 30 September 20X6 are expected to be the same as the final quarter of the year ended 30 September 20X5 for both the Monty and the Gold.

Revenue from garage doors is recognised when they are delivered to a customer's house. Revenue from installation is recognised when the contract is completed to the customer's satisfaction.

2   **Cost of sales**

The production process for the Gold is technologically advanced, so annual budgeted fixed production costs of £12 million are expected. For the Monty, annual budgeted fixed production costs are £4 million. These fixed costs have not changed for some years and are incurred evenly over the year, with an equal amount being recognised in each quarter. The variable cost per unit for each product is budgeted at 50% of selling price.

3   **Staff bonus**

As a result of the recession, there was a zero general pay increase for employees. However, a bonus scheme was introduced under which a payment to employees of £600,000 will be made for the full year if revenue for the year ending 30 September 20X6 exceeds £26 million.

4   **Inventories and receivables**

Inventories consist mainly of partly-made doors. There is little finished inventory as doors are normally made to order.

Sales are normally on 30 day credit terms.

Exhibit 3 – Extract of email from David May: share based bonus scheme

To tie in middle and senior managers to the company, a bonus would be given to existing managers after three years of continued employment from 1 October 20X6, on which date the scheme would commence. If these employees leave before 30 September 20X9 they will receive no bonus. Also, however, I want to link the bonus to company performance – which I think is best achieved by basing it on share price.

The proposal is to either: (A) issue 600 shares; or (B) pay a bonus equivalent to the value of 600 shares at the date of redemption for each existing manager. The amount would only be given in either case after three years' service. Those managers joining after 1 October in any year would not qualify for the scheme in that year.

The problem is that these managers would probably stay for three years to receive the bonus and then leave. My idea is – and this is the clever part – to have the same bonus scheme every year so, whenever managers leave, they would be giving up a large sum in bonuses that have not vested.

Using proposal (A) as an example, if we start the scheme on 1 October 20X6, each eligible manager will receive 600 PGA ordinary shares on 30 September 20X9. There would then be another scheme on 1 October 20X7 for 600 shares which would vest on 30 September 20Y0 (ie three years later), and the same again in each future year. The same rolling system would apply if we decide to go with proposal B instead.

My working assumptions are:

•   The PGA share price will be £8 on 1 October 20X6 and increase by 25% in the first year and then 20% per annum thereafter (our future order book looks strong and I believe that there are signs that we are coming out of the recession);

•   There are 80 eligible managers now. It is assumed that ten managers (all of whom are currently in employment) will leave during each year and ten managers will join;

- The fair value of the share based cash settled instrument is equal to the share price.

Information required

I would like the following information:

1 Using my working assumptions, prepare a computation of the effect on profit of this scheme for each of the years ending 30 September 20X7, 20X8 and 20X9 under the following alternative assumptions:

- Proposal A – the bonus is given in the form of 600 PGA shares per manager each year; or

- Proposal B – the bonus is paid in cash as an amount equivalent to 600 PGA shares per manager each year.

2 An explanation of why the impact on profit may vary:

- From year to year for each proposal;
- Between the two proposals.

29 Tawkcom

You are the senior responsible for the audit fieldwork at Tawkcom Ltd, the UK trading subsidiary of Colltawk plc, a major international telecommunications group, listed on the London Stock Exchange. Tawkcom provides data and communication services to commercial and public organisations. These services utilise Tawkcom's UK-wide fibre optic network, a valuable and unique asset built up over many years.

You are currently completing the final audit of Tawkcom for the year ended 30 September 20X9. The audit has not gone smoothly and reporting to the group audit team is overdue. The most significant incomplete area of audit procedures is the work on property, plant and equipment (PPE), which has been allocated to a junior member of your team, Jo Carter. You are due to meet the audit manager, Jan Pickering, this evening to discuss progress on this work.

Jan has just left you this voicemail:

"The Colltawk group financial statements are due to be signed off early next week and I'm very worried about the work we have left to do on Tawkcom. PPE is a key audit area for this business and Jo is likely to require detailed guidance if she is to complete the procedures satisfactorily. I know you've been very busy but I need you to look today at what she's done so far (**Exhibit 1**), both to identify any unresolved audit or financial reporting issues and to determine what audit procedures we have left to do.

"I've sent you some extracts from the group audit instructions (**Exhibit 2**) so you can take these into account in determining the required audit procedures.

"Please come to the meeting this evening prepared for a detailed discussion. You will need to prepare the following documents for the meeting:

- Notes explaining any financial reporting and audit issues you have identified from your review of Jo's work to date (**Exhibit 1**);

- A list of the additional steps we will need to perform to complete our audit procedures on PPE, both for group reporting and to support our opinion on the statutory financial statements of Tawkcom;

- A summary identifying where the group audit team may provide useful evidence in completing the audit of PPE."

Requirement

Prepare the documents Jan has asked you to bring to this evening's meeting.   **(30 marks)**

Exhibit 1 – PPE work papers prepared by Jo Carter

Summary of balances

The group reporting pack for Tawkcom at 30 September 20X9 includes the following schedule. All balances and movements have been agreed to the register of PPE and to the schedules used for detailed testing.

	Freehold land and buildings £'000	Leasehold improvements £'000	Network assets £'000	Fixtures and equipment £'000	Investment property £'000	Total £'000
Cost/valuation						
Brought forward at 1 October 20X8	32,000	4,160	162,831	19,255	0	218,246
Additions	0	3,409	34,391	2,406	0	40,206
Disposals	(6,550)	(102)	0	(508)	0	(7,160)
Transfer from assets held for sale	0	0	0	0	3,936	3,936
Carried forward at 30 September 20X9	25,450	7,467	197,222	21,153	3,936	255,228
Accumulated depreciation						
Brought forward at 1 October 20X8	476	882	38,697	14,577	0	54,632
Charge for the year	0	298	2,875	4,051	0	7,224
Disposals	(95)	(98)	0	(129)	0	(322)
Carried forward at 30 September 20X9	381	1,082	41,572	18,499	0	61,534
Carrying amount at 30 September 20X9	25,069	6,385	155,650	2,654	3,936	193,694

Summary of procedures performed

Opening balances

Opening balances have been agreed to prior year signed financial statements with the exception of the opening cost for Network assets. This is greater than the balance shown in the prior year financial statements by £1.3 million due to an audit adjustment to remove from non-current asset additions the cost of certain repairs to and maintenance on the fibre optic network. This was recognised in the financial statements but not reflected in the register of PPE or in the group reporting pack, as it was not considered material for group purposes.

Additions

A sample of additions was selected for each category of PPE using group materiality of £4 million to determine the sample size. Each item in the sample was physically inspected where possible, verified as a capital item and, where appropriate, agreed to a third party invoice. Further information is provided below:

Leasehold improvements

Tawkcom has one leasehold property, its head office building. This building is leased under a 20 year operating lease, expiring in 20Z5. During the year ended 30 September 20X9, Tawkcom completed a major refurbishment programme to update and improve all office accommodation.

Network assets

Additions comprise new fibre optic cable laid to extend network coverage or to connect a particular customer to the network. Tawkcom's own staff perform much of the work and additions could not therefore be agreed to third party invoices. Instead they were agreed to project sheets detailing the material, labour and overhead costs incurred on each stretch of cable.

Additions are higher than in the prior year as group management instructed the local finance director to increase the day rates used for staff time so they were consistent with the rates used to compute charges to external customers. A rough calculation indicates that the increase in rates has increased additions to network assets by around £5 million.

Physical inspection of the network assets was not possible as the fibre optic cabling is laid underground.

Disposals

There were only three significant disposals in the year ended 30 September 20X9.

1   In June 20X9, Tawkcom disposed of office equipment with a cost of £332,000 to AR Hughes Ltd. The accounting assistant informed me that this company is owned by friends of Max Dudley, Tawkcom's finance director. The group finance director approved the disposal. The accumulated depreciation of £62,000 was correctly removed from the register of PPE. There were no proceeds and a loss of £270,000 was included within the statement of profit or loss and other comprhehensive income.

2   In September 20X9, the company's freehold property in Scotland, Glasgow House, was sold to LJ Finance plc, a finance company owned by the bank for the Colltawk group. The group finance team arranged this transaction and local management has limited information. Tawkcom is still occupying the building as it has been leased back from LJ Finance under a 20-year lease, which can be extended to 50 years at Colltawk's option. An external valuer revalued Glasgow House at 30 September 20X7, along with the company's other freehold properties. Its value of £5.8 million was agreed to the prior year audit work papers. The valuation and associated accumulated depreciation were correctly removed from the register of PPE, cash proceeds of £7 million were vouched to the bank account on 30 September 20X9 and the gain of £1,295,000 was agreed to the statement of profit or loss and other comprhehensive income.

3   Tawkcom disposed of land for £1,500,000 recognising a profit on disposal in profit or loss of £750,000. The contract was entered into on 31 July 20X9 conditional upon detailed planning approval being granted. By 30 September 20X9 outline planning consent only had been granted. Full planning consent was received on 20 October and the sale was completed on 30 October 20X9.

Sale proceeds were agreed to the cash book and bank statement. The cost of land was correctly removed from the register of PPE and the profit on disposal correctly calculated.

Transfer from assets held for sale

In the financial statements for the year ended 30 September 20X8, a freehold property, surplus to Tawkcom's requirements, was transferred out of PPE and shown separately as a non-current asset held for sale. Our prior year audit files concluded that this treatment was correct on the basis that the property was being actively marketed and a sale at its carrying amount of £3.9 million was considered imminent.

This sale was not concluded and management has now decided to retain the property for the time being until the property market has improved. To generate some return from the property, management intends to divide the property into small office units which it will rent out as office space under short-term rental agreements. In order to make this more attractive to prospective tenants, Tawkcom will provide services such as telecommunications, reception, secretarial support and meeting rooms. As the property is now being held for its investment potential, it has been transferred back into PPE and designated as an investment property.

Depreciation charge for the year

The Tawkcom financial statements for the year ended 30 September 20X8 disclose the following depreciation policy:

Depreciation is charged so as to write off the cost or valuation of assets over the following periods:

Freehold buildings	50 years
Leasehold improvements	20 years (the minimum term of the lease)
Network assets	20 years
Fixtures and equipment	3–10 years

For each category of asset, an expectation for the depreciation charge for the year ended was formed using the above rates and taking into account the timing of additions and disposals.

The following points were noted:

1. No depreciation has been charged on freehold buildings as these properties are carried at valuations which the finance director believes reflect their market value at the reporting date and the buildings are maintained to a high standard.

2. The depreciation charge for network assets is considerably lower than expected. This is as a result of a group wide review of useful lives conducted by head office. This review concluded that the life of network assets is greater than 20 years and a revised useful life of 22 years has been applied to all such assets. Calculations of the revised carrying amounts for a sample of assets were reviewed and verified as accurately reflecting for each asset the unexpired portion of a 22-year life.

Exhibit 2 – Extracts from the Group audit instructions for the Colltawk plc group for the year ended 30 September 20X9

Risk of fraud and misstatement

The following key risks have been identified and should be considered by all subsidiary audit teams:

1. The group has banking covenants on long-term bank loans requiring it to maintain a certain ratio of non-current assets to net borrowings (defined as bank borrowings and lease creditors less cash). As a result, management may have an incentive to overstate non-current assets or to understate net borrowings.

2. Subsidiary management participates in the group's bonus scheme. The level of bonus to be paid depends on the performance both of the individual subsidiary and of the group as a whole. Management may therefore have an incentive to overstate profit either at a subsidiary or group level.

Materiality and reporting of misstatements

Pre-tax materiality for the Colltawk group audit is £4 million. All individual misstatements over £200,000 should be reported to the group audit team.

30 Expando Ltd

You are a supervisor in the audit department of Jones & Co. You are currently in charge of the audit of Expando Ltd (Expando), a private limited company which imports and retails consumer electronic equipment. Expando's year-end is 30 June 20X7. Today you are in the office when you receive the following email from the audit senior who is working for you on the audit of Expando:

Email

To: Audit Supervisor
From: Audit Senior

As you are aware we are nearing the completion of the audit of Expando Ltd, however, there are a number of outstanding issues which need to be addressed. I have summarised these in an attachment (**Attachment 1**). Unfortunately I am not sure how these should be dealt with in the financial statements so I have not been able to revise the draft financial statements provided by the client (**Attachments 2 and 3**). The audit partner has specifically requested a set of revised financial statements as he wants to take them to the meeting with Expando's FD tomorrow. I am also unclear whether these issues have any implications for our remaining audit procedures. I was hoping that you may be able to help me as follows:

1. Explain the financial reporting treatment of the outstanding issues
2. Complete the draft statement of profit or loss and other comprehensive income, statement of changes in equity and statement of financial position where indicated and make any appropriate adjustments and corrections
3. List any additional audit procedures which I need to do

A couple of final points. I have found a list of procedures performed by the auditors of Titch (see point 5 below). I am not quite sure what to do with these. Shouldn't we do the audit of Titch?

The client has a member of the accounts department who is due to go on maternity leave in three months time. I have been asked if we can provide temporary help to cover for their absence. Can we do this?

Attachment 1

Notes of outstanding issues

1   With the exception of the property referred to in note 4, below, all of Expando's trading premises are held on short leases, and are not shown on the statement of financial position. The land recorded on the statement of financial position refers to the storage facility in Northern England. This is not depreciated. During the year it was revalued upwards, by £1 million, to £5 million. The valuation was commissioned in the early summer of 20X6, to support the company's fundraising.

2   New finance was taken out on 1 July 20X6, in the form of an issue of a £2 million debenture loan. Issue costs were £150,000. The coupon rate on the debenture is 3%. Its terms provide that it was issued at par but that it will be redeemed at a premium. The overall effective interest rate for Expando is 7%.

3   On 1 September 20X6, Expando acquired the business of Minnisculio, a small competitor, for £250,000. The acquisition was structured as a purchase of trade and assets, with £20,000 allocated to inventories and the balance to goodwill. Expando has not conducted an impairment review in respect of goodwill as there is no indication of circumstances which would give rise to an impairment.

4   Prior to the acquisition by Expando of its trade and assets, Minnisculio had negotiated the acquisition of new freehold premises, to be acquired on 1 October 20X6 for a consideration of £125,000. The asset was estimated to have a useful life of 20 years and a policy of straight-line depreciation was to be adopted. These premises were, however, surplus to requirements after Minnisculio's business had been acquired by Expando. On 31 March 20X7 the management took the decision to sell the premises at which date the fair value less costs to sell amounted to £115,000.

5   On 1 October 20X6, Expando acquired 25% of Titch Ltd, for a consideration of £400,000. Titch is co-owned by three other UK companies, each of which holds 25% of its shares. Unfortunately, due to unforeseen events which are not expected to be repeated, Titch made a trading loss for its year ended 30 September 20X7 of £350,000. The results of Titch have not been reflected in Expando's draft financial statements with the exception of the tax effect which has been dealt with by the tax department.

6   The tax impact of the above is being dealt with by the tax department.

Attachment 2

Summary draft statement of profit or loss and other comprehensive income and statement of changes in equity

Year ended	30 June 20X7 (draft) £'000	30 June 20X6 (audited) £'000
Revenue	4,430	3,660
Less: Operating expenses	(3,620)	(2,990)
Operating profit	810	670
Interest payable – note 2 above	(260)	(200)
Profit before tax	550	470
Taxation	(91)	(141)
Profit for the year	459	329
Other comprehensive income:		
Gain on property revaluation	1,000	–
Total comprehensive income for the year	1,459	329

Statement of changes in equity 30 June 20X7 (extract)	Retained earnings £'000	Revaluation surplus £'000
Balance at 1 July 20X6	713	–
Total comprehensive income for the year	459	1,000
Balance at 30 June 20X7	1,172	1,000

Summary draft statement of financial position

Period end date	30 June 20X7 (draft) £'000	30 June 20X6 (audited) £'000
Non-current assets		
Land	5,000	4,000
Premises – note 4 above	125	–
Plant and machinery	2	2
Investments – notes 3, 5 above	650	–
Current assets	2,155	520
Current liabilities		
Taxation	(91)	(141)
Other	(300)	(149)
Non-current liabilities		
6% bank loan	(3,333)	(3,333)
3% debenture – note 2 above	(1,850)	–
Deferred tax	to be completed	–
Net assets	to be completed	899
Share capital	86	86
Share premium	100	100
Revaluation surplus – note 1 above	1,000	–
Retained earnings	1,172	713
Equity	2,358	899

Requirement

Respond to the audit senior's email. Assume that the tax figures will be audited by your firm's tax audit specialists, so you can ignore tax (including deferred tax) for now. **(30 marks)**

31 Netus UK Ltd

You are a senior on a large team which is planning for the audit of Netus UK Ltd, a media company, for the year ending 30 September 20X9. Netus UK is a wholly owned subsidiary of an Australian parent company, Netus Oceania (also audited by your firm), and contributes a very substantial proportion of the revenue and profit reported by the Netus Oceania Group. Your team is required to report to your firm's Australian office in Perth on the results of Netus UK and also to report on Netus UK's statutory UK accounts. Netus Oceania is planning to raise additional capital from shareholders and the deadlines for group reporting are very tight. Your firm is required to provide the final report to the Perth office by 16 October 20X9.

You receive an email from the manager with overall responsibility for the Netus UK audit, Louise Manning:

To: A. Senior
From: L. Manning
Subject: Netus UK audit planning
Date: 20 July 20X9

Welcome to the Netus team. As you know, we have a large team assigned as this is a very significant client. I'm asking each team member to take responsibility for a particular section of our work and to prepare a detailed audit plan, setting out the procedures to be performed at both our interim visit in August and our final audit visit in October. Materiality for planning purposes has been set at £1.5 million.

You will be responsible for staff costs and the assets and liabilities related to staff costs in the statement of financial position. Attached to this email is an extract from Netus UK's June 20X9 management accounts (**Exhibit 1**) showing the items for which I wish you to take responsibility.

Staff costs were audited using only substantive testing for the year ended 30 September 20X8, but Netus UK's Finance Director, Harry Dalton, is very keen for us to rely on internal controls wherever possible for this year's audit. I have attached an email from him (**Exhibit 2**) which includes details of the company's own controls assessment in the payroll area. I'm hoping that this controls assessment will be of reasonable quality as Mary Fox, one of the assistants on our team, tells me it was prepared by her boyfriend, Mark Young, who used to work for our firm.

I need you to send me the following planning documentation so that I can complete the overall planning file for this audit and submit it for manager review. Apart from item (iv), your responses should concentrate solely on the audit of staff costs and related assets and liabilities in the statement of financial position. You do not need to consider any corporation tax or deferred tax balances.

Planning documentation required

(i) Your comments on the design of the payroll controls and the extent to which you believe these controls will be effective in reducing, to an acceptable level, the risk that the financial statements will be materially misstated. Your comments should identify clearly, with reasons, any specific areas where controls appear inadequate and any risks associated with staff costs which are not covered in the company's assessment of controls.

(ii) Briefing notes for Harry Dalton so he understands what entries he needs to make to account correctly for pension costs and where he can obtain any additional information necessary.

(iii) A schedule summarising the audit procedures you believe we should complete at our interim audit visit and the procedures which we will need to perform at our final visit in October. As time is extremely limited during the final audit, the procedures to be performed during the October visit should be kept to a minimum. For the audit procedures on controls, please explain and summarise each step of our approach. I do not need detailed tests of each control at this stage. For the substantive procedures, please be specific about the procedures you plan to perform on each relevant balance.

(iv) Your comments on any other matters, including ethical issues, you think we should take into account in planning our audit procedures more generally or any concerns you have as a result of the information you have been given.

I look forward to receiving your audit planning.

Louise

Requirement

Respond to Louise Manning's email.   **(30 marks)**

Exhibit 1

Extract from Netus UK's management accounts for the nine months ended 30 June 20X9

Summary of staff costs reflected in the statement of profit or loss and other comprehensive income for the 9 months to 30 June 20X9

	Cost of sales £000	Distribution costs £000	Administrative expenses £000	Total 9 months to 30 June 20X9 £000	Total 9 months to 30 June 20X8 £000
Payroll	78,301	40,815	33,974	153,090	141,496
Pension cost	10,487	5,466	4,550	20,503	12,634
Temporary staff	5,690	0	2,451	8,141	1,065
Employee expenses	341	287	2,074	2,702	2,396
Total staff costs	94,819	46,568	43,049	184,436	157,591

Summary of staff cost related balances in the statement of financial position at 30 June 20X9

	30 June 20X9 £000	30 June 20X8 £000
Current liabilities		
Employment taxes	6,903	6,287
Employer's pension contributions payable	2,397	1,484
Accruals		
Temporary staff	204	119
Commission payable on June sales	454	429

Note:

For management accounting purposes, pension costs comprise only employer contributions payable to Netus UK's defined benefit pension scheme. The rate of employer contribution increased from 10% of pensionable salary to 15% of pensionable salary with effect from 1 October 20X8 following an actuarial valuation which showed a significant deficit.

Exhibit 2

To: L. Manning
From: H.Dalton@Netus.com
Subject: Audit planning
Date: 17 July 20X9

Hi Louise

Following our planning meeting last week, I attach a copy of the controls documentation for the payroll cycle. This documentation was completed by our new financial controller, Mark Young, and is part of a large project instigated by our parent company to document controls in all areas. This project has taken up a huge amount of my team's time for little, if any, obvious benefit. I'm encouraged therefore that you may be able to put it to use in your audit.

You already have our management accounts for the period ended 30 June 20X9 which have been prepared on the same basis as last year's group reporting. As you know, the group head office has never required us to include adjustments for the pension scheme deficit. I've just received instructions from head office which state that, for this year's group reporting, they want full compliance with IFRS and will not be making central adjustments for our pension scheme. I'm going to need your help in calculating the necessary entries as I have no real experience of accounting for pension schemes and you've always helped me with the entries for our statutory accounts.

As you know, we have one UK defined benefit pension scheme open to all employees. Head office has told me that I should recognise the actuarial gains and losses immediately.

I look forward to receiving your advice on these matters and to discussing your detailed audit plan.

Regards

Harry

Attachment

Background

Netus UK has around 5,000 permanent employees, 1,000 of whom are remunerated on an hourly basis. A time sheet system records time for hourly paid staff and overtime for those salaried staff who are entitled to overtime payments. The company runs a single computerised payroll system covering both hourly paid and salaried staff and all staff are paid monthly. Each staff member is allocated to one of the company's 80 departments, which range in size from three to 400 employees.

Internal controls

Control objectives	Controls
Only valid payroll costs are recorded and paid.	1 Payroll summary is authorised by the FD before payment.
	2 Hours recorded by hourly paid staff are taken directly from time-recording system.
	3 All new staff are authorised by departmental heads.
	4 Departmental heads review payroll costs for their departments and would raise queries if there were unexpected costs.
All payroll costs are recorded in the correct period.	5 Hours recorded by hourly paid staff are taken directly from time-recording system, so hours worked in the period cannot be missed.
	6 FD's review of monthly management accounts would identify a missed payroll journal.
	7 The nominal ledger journal is posted automatically from the payroll system to the ledger when the payroll is prepared five days before each month end.
	8 Departmental heads review payroll costs for their departments and would raise queries if the costs were not as expected.
Payroll costs are recorded accurately at the appropriate rates.	9 Rates of pay for hourly paid and salaried staff are agreed annually. They are input to the payroll system by the payroll clerk and checked by the departmental heads. Changes to the rates are made by the payroll clerk only when she has written authority from a departmental head.
	10 Rates of pay for new staff are authorised by the departmental head and detailed on the new joiners form used by the payroll clerk to update the system.
Payroll related liabilities are recorded accurately in the accounts.	11 Monthly payroll is always paid on the last working day of each month so no accruals are generally necessary.
	12 Employment tax liabilities are reconciled to the payroll summary at each month end.

32 Dormro

You are Bernie Eters, an audit assistant manager working for FG Chartered Accountants. The audit engagement manager in charge of the Dormro Ltd and Dormro group audit gives you the following briefing:

"This audit is turning into a nightmare and I need your assistance today. The Dormro finance director has just informed me that Dormro acquired an investment in Klip Inc., an overseas company resident in Harwan, on 31 January 20X2, which is not included in the consolidation schedules. Klip is audited by a local Harwanian auditor.

"I am also unhappy about the level of detailed testing carried out by our audit senior. I have provided you with the following relevant work papers:

Exhibit 1	Extract from Dormro audit planning memorandum
Exhibit 2	Consolidation schedule, notes and outstanding audit procedures
Exhibit 3	Information concerning the acquisition of Klip provided by Dormro finance director; statement of financial position for Klip; and audit clearance from Klip auditors in Harwan.

"I have a meeting with the audit partner tomorrow and I need to inform her of any issues relating to the group financial statements and to provide a detailed summary of the progress of our work. Please review all the information provided and prepare a work paper which:

- Identifies and explains any known and potential issues which you believe may give rise to material audit adjustments or significant audit risks in the group financial statements, and

- Outlines, for each issue, the additional audit procedures, if any, required to enable us to sign our audit opinion on the group financial statements.

"Also, please include in your work paper a revised consolidated statement of financial position for the year ended 30 April 20X2, which includes the overseas subsidiary, Klip."

Requirement

Prepare the work paper requested by the audit engagement manager.   **(40 marks)**

Exhibit 1 – Extract from Dormro audit planning memorandum for year ended 30 April 20X2

Group planning materiality has been set at £250,000.

Dormro has two wholly-owned UK subsidiaries; Secure Ltd and CAM Ltd.

Secure was set up several years ago and supplies security surveillance systems.

CAM, is a specialist supplier of security cameras and was acquired by Dormro on 31 October 20X1. CAM is a growing business with profitable public sector contracts.

The UK companies have a 30 April year end and FG audit all the UK companies.

Exhibit 2 – Dormro: consolidation schedules for the year ended 30 April 20X2

Statement of financial position

ASSETS	Dormro £'000	Secure £'000	CAM £'000	Adjustments £'000	Notes	Group £'000
Non-current assets						
Property, plant and equipment	45	2,181	788			3,014
Goodwill	–	–	–	9,490	1	6,251
				(3,239)	2	
Investments	10,180	–	15	(10,010)	1	185
Current assets						
Inventories	–	3,380	2,947			6,327
Trade receivables		4,292	4,849			9,141
Intercompany receivables	2,045	–	1,474	(3,519)	3	–
Cash and cash equivalents	567	(706)	382			243
Total assets	12,837	9,147	10,455	(7,278)		25,161
EQUITY AND LIABILITIES						
Equity						
Share capital	200	10	510	(520)	1	200
Retained earnings at 1 May 20X1	4,523	973	1,758	(1,758)	2	5,496
Profit/(loss) for the year	54	(867)	2,962	(100)	3	568
				(1,481)	2	
Non-current liabilities						
Long-term borrowings	8,000	–	–		4	8,000
Current liabilities						
Trade and other payables	37	5,702	4,513			10,252
Intercompany payables	–	3,329	90	(3,419)	3	–
Current tax payable	23	–	622			645
Total equity and liabilities	12,837	9,147	10,455	(7,278)		25,161

Statement of profit or loss

	Dormro £'000	Secure £'000	CAM £'000	Adjustments £'000	Notes	Group £'000
Revenue	767	23,407	28,097	(14,049)	2	37,455
				(767)	3	
Cost of sales	–	(19,703)	(19,455)	9,727	2	(29,431)
				767	3	
Administrative expenses	(740)	(4,532)	(4,688)	(100)	3	(6,949)
				2,344	2	
Finance income/(cost)	50	(39)	31	(15)	2	27
Profit/(loss)before tax	77	(867)	3,985	(2,093)		1,102
Income tax expense	(23)	–	(1,023)	512	2	(534)
Profit/(loss) for the year	54	(867)	2,962	(1,581)		568

Notes on adjustments

1   This adjustment eliminates investments in the subsidiary companies Secure and CAM. The equivalent adjustment in the prior year was £10,000 and related to the elimination of share capital in Secure. The increase in the current year is due to the acquisition of CAM for £10 million which I have agreed to the bank statement. Also £170,000 was paid to acquire the shares in Klip and there is an investment of £15,000 held by CAM both of which are below the materiality level.

2   This adjustment removes from the statement of profit or loss half of CAM's results as the subsidiary was acquired on 31 October 20X1. In addition, all pre-acquisition retained earnings have been eliminated and treated as part of the goodwill calculation.

3   These adjustments eliminate intercompany balances and management charges from Dormro to its subsidiaries. The difference of £100,000 between the receivables and payables has been written off to profit or loss and is concerning a dispute between Secure and CAM.

4   This loan was taken out by Dormro on 1 May 20X1. I have agreed the balance to the loan agreement, noting capital repayable over 8 years in equal annual instalments commencing 1 May 20X2 and an effective interest rate of 6.68%. An arrangement fee of £200,000 has been expensed to profit or loss and interest is payable at 6% annually in arrears. An adjustment is required to accrue for interest of £480,000.

Outstanding audit procedures

I have reconciled all balances from the consolidation schedules to the audit work papers for each company, noting no exceptions. The following procedures are outstanding:

Secure:

Review of the directors' assessment of the company's ability to continue as a going concern given the loss for the year, the overdraft balance and the company's reliance on loans from other group companies.

CAM:

Final conclusion on the adequacy of the inventory obsolescence provision. CAM has applied the group accounting policy in determining its provision, but this is based on historical sales. Given the technical issues with the product range, I am concerned that the calculated provision may be understated by around £220,000.

Audit procedures on the provision for warranty costs of £205,000 (20X1: £275,000). Management have failed to supply any supporting documentation for this provision.

Secure and CAM:

Receipt of bank confirmation letters and confirmation of balances due to other group companies

Exhibit 3 – Information concerning the acquisition of Klip provided by Dormro finance director

On 31 January 20X2, Dormro paid H$918,000 (£170,000) to acquire 90% of the issued ordinary share capital of Klip which trades in Harwan where the currency is the Harwan ($H). Klip makes security cameras and is a supplier company to CAM. There were no adjustments to the fair value of the net assets acquired except that inventory required a write down of H$1,000,000. None of this inventory had been sold at the year end.

Dormro measures non-controlling interest using the proportion of net assets method. The rate of exchange at 30 April 20X2 was H$ 4.2 = £1 and the average rate for the three months to 30 April 20X2 was H$4.8 = £1.

Klip – Statement of financial position as at 30 April 20X2

	H$'000
ASSETS	
Non-current assets	
Property, plant and equipment	1,940
Current assets	
Inventories	2,100
Trade receivables	600
Cash and cash equivalents	40
Total assets	**4,680**
EQUITY AND LIABILITIES	
Equity	
Share capital	200
Retained earnings at 1 May 20X1	1,200
Profit for the year	500
Non-current liabilities	
Long-term borrowings	1,400
Current liabilities	
Trade and other payables	1,380
Total equity and liabilities	**4,680**

Clearance from Harwanian auditors of Klip

From: Mersander Partners, Harwan
Date: 26 July 20X2
Subject: Audit of Klip for the year ended 30 April 20X2
To: Finance director, Dormro, United Kingdom

We have performed an audit of the accompanying reporting package of Klip for the year ended 30 April 20X2 in accordance with Harwanian Standards on Auditing and using materiality specified by you of £250,000. The reporting package has been prepared in accordance with group accounting policies as notified by Dormro. Where no group policy has been notified, the reporting package has been prepared using accounting policies consistent with those adopted in previous years.

The net profit for the year increased by 10% compared to the previous year. This is due to a decrease in inventory obsolescence provisions when the group accounting policy was applied.

There is no outstanding audit work which would affect our opinion and there are no uncorrected audit adjustments.

In our opinion, the reporting package of the entity has been prepared in all material respects in accordance with group accounting policies and presents fairly the results of Klip for the year ended 30 April 20X2 and its financial position as at that date.

Mersander Partners

33 Kime

Kime plc is in the property industry, operating in both the commercial and private housing sectors. Kime uses the cost model for measuring its property portfolio in its financial statements and has a 30 June year end.

You are Jo Ng, Kime's recently appointed financial controller. Your role is to prepare the financial statements for the year ended 30 June 20X2 before the auditors start work next week. The finance director has supplied you with some work papers containing a trial balance and outstanding issues **(Exhibit 1)** which have been prepared by a junior assistant. The finance director gives you the following instructions:

"The auditors are due to start their audit work on Monday and I would like to be aware of any contentious financial reporting issues before they arrive.

"Review the outstanding issues identified by the junior assistant (Exhibit 1) and explain the potentially contentious financial reporting issues. Determine any adjustments you consider necessary and explain the impact of your adjustments on the financial statements, identifying any alternative accounting treatments. The board of directors has indicated that accounting policies should be selected which maximise the profit in the current year.

"Using the trial balance and after making adjustments for matters arising from your review of the outstanding issues (Exhibit 1) prepare a draft statement of financial position and statement of comprehensive income.

Requirement

Respond to the finance director's instructions. **(30 marks)**

Exhibit 1 – Work papers prepared by the junior assistant

Trial balance at 30 June 20X2

	Notes	£m Dr	£m Cr
Land	1	30.5	
Buildings – cost		132.7	
Buildings – accumulated depreciation			82.5
Plant and equipment – cost		120.0	
Plant and equipment – accumulated depreciation			22.8
Trade receivables	2	174.5	
Cash and cash equivalents		183.1	
Ordinary share capital (£1 shares)			100.0
Share premium			84.0
Retained earnings at 1 July 20X1			102.0
Long-term borrowings			80.0
Deferred tax liability at 1 July 20X1	3		33.0
Trade and other payables			54.9
Sales			549.8
Operating costs		322.4	
Distribution costs		60.3	
Administrative expenses		80.7	
Finance costs		4.8	
		1,109.0	1,109.0

Notes and outstanding issues

1 **Freehold land and buildings – at 30 June 20X2**

	Land £m	Buildings £m	Total £m
Cost:			
At 1 July 20X1	34.0	118.4	152.4
Additions	–	26.8	26.8
Disposals	(3.5)	(12.5)	(16.0)
At 30 June 20X2	30.5	132.7	163.2
Accumulated depreciation:			
At 1 July 20X1	–	84.8	84.8
Charge for the year	–	5.9	5.9
Disposals	–	(8.2)	(8.2)
At 30 June 20X2	–	82.5	82.5
Carrying amount:			
At 30 June 20X2	30.5	50.2	80.7
At 30 June 20X1	34.0	33.6	67.6

The accounting policy states that land is not depreciated and all buildings are depreciated over their expected useful life of 50 years with no residual value.

Additions – total £26.8 million

The additions comprise two major commercial property projects: (These are the first construction projects undertaken by Kime for a number of years):

- *Renovation of Ferris Street property (£8.8 million)*

  Kime commenced this renovation during the year ended 30 June 20X2. The budgeted cost of this project is £15 million, of which £12 million (80%) has been designated as capital expenditure by the project manager. The remaining £3 million is charged in the budget as repairs and maintenance cost.

In the year ended 30 June 20X2, the company incurred costs of £11 million on the project. Therefore I have capitalised 80% of the cost incurred in line with the original budget.

- *Construction of a sports stadium in London (£18 million)*

    On 1 July 20X1, Kime began constructing a sports stadium for a local authority, which was expected to take 20 months to complete. Kime agreed a total contract price of £34 million. Total contract costs were expected to be £16 million, however costs incurred at 30 June 20X2 are £18 million and these have been capitalised in the year ended 30 June 20X2. Reliable estimates of costs to complete the project have been certified by the company's own surveyor to be £4.5 million. He has also provided a value of work completed to date of £23.8 million.

    In the year ended 30 June 20X2, Kime raised invoices totaling £17 million to the local authority and recognised this amount in revenue for the year. The local authority had paid all outstanding invoices by 30 June 20X2.

Disposals

Kime disposed of two properties during the year:

Property	Cost of land £m	Cost of buildings £m	Accumulated depreciation at disposal date £m
FX House	2.0	8.0	4.2
Estate agency buildings	1.5	4.5	4.0
Total	3.5	12.5	8.2

FX House

This property was leased to a third party under an agreement signed on 1 January 20X2. This is a 40-year lease and the title to both the land and buildings transfers to the lessee at zero cost at the end of the lease term. The annual rental is £2 million payable in advance. The present value on 1 January 20X2 of the future lease payments discounted at the interest rate of 10% implicit in the lease was £21.5 million, which clearly exceeds the carrying amount at the date of disposal and the lease is therefore a finance lease.

I have derecognised the property and recognised a loss on disposal equal to the carrying amount of £5.8 million in administrative expenses for the year ended 30 June 20X2. The first annual lease payment received on 1 January 20X2 has been credited to finance costs for the year ended 30 June 20X2.

Estate agency buildings

Due to the recession Kime has reconsidered its business model and closed down its high street estate agencies buildings from which it operated its private housing business. The estate agencies business is now operated entirely on-line.

In May 20X2 a contract for the sale of these buildings, including land was agreed for a price of £10 million, with the sale to be completed in September 20X2. A gain has been recognised in administrative expenses in profit or loss of £8 million and a receivable of £10 million in trade receivables.

2   **Trade receivables and forward contract**

Included in trade receivables is an amount due from a customer located abroad in Ruritania. The amount (R$60.48 million) was initially recognised on 1 April 20X2 when the spot exchange rate was £1 = R$5.6.

At 30 June 20X2, the exchange rate was £1 = R$5.0. No adjustment has been made to the trade receivable since it was initially recognised.

Given the size of the exposure, the company entered into a forward contract, at the same time as the receivable was initially recognised on 1 April 20X2, in order to protect cash flows from fluctuations in the exchange rate. The forward contract is to sell R$60.48 million and the arrangement satisfies the necessary criteria to be accounted for as a hedge.

At 30 June 20X2, the loss in fair value of the forward contract was £1.5 million. The company elected to designate the spot element of the hedge as the hedging relationship. The difference between the change in fair value of the receivable and the change in fair value of the forward contract since inception is the interest element of the forward contract.

3 **Current and deferred taxation**

I have not yet made any adjustments for deferred or current taxation, but have been told to make the following assumptions:

- The tax rate is 24%.

- Taxable profits are calculated on the same basis as IFRS profits except for temporary differences arising on plant and equipment.

- The deferred tax temporary taxable differences are £14 million at 30 June 20X2 after the effects of accounting for depreciation on plant and equipment only. No tax relief is available on freehold buildings and land.

34 Thyme

Assume the current date is August 20X2. The firm of chartered accountants that you work for as an audit senior, has been appointed as auditors of Thyme Ltd, a distributor and adviser on business software and IT solutions. Thyme is a wholly owned subsidiary of a US parent company, Utah Inc, which is also audited by your firm. You are currently working on the audit of Thyme's financial statements for the year ended 30 September 20X2. Thyme contributes a very substantial proportion of the revenue and profit reported by the Utah group. Your firm is required to report to its US office on the results of Thyme and also to report on Thyme's individual company financial statements.

You receive the following instructions from the audit manager with overall responsibility for the Thyme audit:

"I'm asking each team member to take responsibility for a particular section of our work and to prepare a detailed audit plan, setting out the work to be performed. Materiality for planning purposes has been set at £500,000.

"You will be responsible for staff costs in the statement of profit or loss and staff cost payables and accruals in the statement of financial position. An audit junior, Tina Jie, has provided some financial data and preliminary analytical procedures using the June 20X2 management accounts (**Exhibit 1**). She has performed some preliminary analytical procedures, but does not have enough experience to identify audit risks.

"Thyme's financial controller, Jon Dillan, has told me that the previous auditors relied on internal controls for the audit of staff costs, supplemented by analytical procedures work. Jon, who is Tina Jie's boyfriend, used to work for our firm. He is hoping to become the Thyme finance director, a post which is currently vacant. I have forwarded you an email from him (**Exhibit 2**) which includes two attachments:

Attachment 1: Details of the employee incentive schemes and;

Attachment 2: A summary of key internal payroll controls.

"I would like you to prepare an audit work paper in which you:

- Explain the correct financial reporting treatment for employee incentive schemes set out in Jon's email (Exhibit 2, Attachment 1) showing, where appropriate, calculations and correcting journal adjustments. You do not need to consider any corporation tax or deferred tax balances.

- Perform relevant analytical procedures for staff costs based on the information available, identifying any unusual patterns and trends and outlining the audit risks which arise from your work.

- Evaluate the summary of key internal payroll controls prepared by Jon Dillan. Identify any areas where controls appear inadequate and any further risks associated with staff costs not covered by these controls (Exhibit 2, Attachment 2). Determine the extent of reliance that can be placed on these controls in reducing the risk that the financial statements will be materially misstated.

"I would also like your comments on any ethical issues or concerns you have arising from the information you have received."

Requirement

Respond to the audit manager's instructions.   (30 marks)

Exhibit 1 – Financial data and analytical review – prepared by Tina Jie, audit junior

Management accounts – statements of profit or loss

	9 months to 30 June 20X2 £'000	9 months to 30 June 20X1 £'000	Year ended 30 September 20X1 £'000
Revenue	21,500	28,400	31,600
Cost of sales	(1,505)	(2,700)	(2,920)
Gross profit	19,995	25,700	28,680
Operating expenses (other than staff costs)	(520)	(520)	(690)
Staff costs			
Directors' salaries (Note 1)	(700)	(600)	(800)
Payroll (Note 2)	(15,300)	(14,150)	(18,860)
Pension costs (Note 3)	(2,050)	–	–
Temporary staff (Note 4)	(815)	(105)	(110)
Employee expenses	(270)	(240)	(250)
Operating profit	340	10,085	7,970

Analytical procedures

1   Directors' salaries have increased because a bonus payment of £100,000 has been accrued. The bonus is payable if operating profit, before charging the bonus, is greater than £300,000 for the year. Jon says it is fairly certain that this bonus will be paid and has therefore accrued all of the £100,000 payable to the directors.

2   The payroll cost for the nine months to 30 June 20X2 has increased by £1,150,000. This is because an additional 25 employees joined on 5 July 20X1 increasing the number of employees from 500 to 525. Also a staff bonus has been accrued of £450,000.

3   Pension costs comprise employer contributions paid to Thyme's defined benefit pension scheme. The scheme, which is open to all employees, was introduced in July 20X1. Jon has informed me that the parent company actuaries have all the details and the £2,050,000 agrees to their instructions. I have agreed this amount to the bank statement.

4   Temporary staff are paid on a commission basis. Jon has told me that there will be no further temporary staff costs in the three months to 30 September 20X2. This is a quiet time in the industry and revenue is expected to be the same in the final quarter to 30 September 20X2 as it was in the quarter to 30 September 20X1.

Exhibit 2 – Email and attachments 1 and 2

To: Audit manager
From: J.Dillon@Thyme.com
Subject: Audit planning
Date: 15 August 20X2

I have attached details of the employee incentive schemes (Attachment 1). I have not made any entries in the financial statements in respect of these schemes other than to accrue the staff bonus of £450,000. I would be grateful if you would provide me with the journal entries that I need to account correctly for these schemes.

Following our planning meeting last week, I attach a summary of key internal payroll controls (attachment 2). I prepared this document as part of a large project instigated by our parent company to document controls in all areas. This project has taken up a huge amount of my time for little, if any, obvious benefit. I'm encouraged therefore that you will be able to put it to use in your audit and pass on the cost saving to Thyme in a reduced audit fee. This will obviously improve my chances of a permanent appointment as FD.

I look forward to receiving your advice on these matters and to discussing your detailed audit plan.

Regards

Jon

Attachment 1 Employee incentive schemes

Thyme has introduced two incentive schemes. On 1 October 20X1 all of the 500 employees of Thyme (excluding directors) accepted a 10% reduction in their basic pay in exchange for being eligible for both of the following incentive schemes:

1   **Staff bonus scheme**

A bonus scheme was introduced under which a payment to employees of £600,000 will be made for the full year if revenue for the year ending 30 September 20X2 exceeds £26 million.

2   **Share appreciation rights**

On 1 October 20X1 Thyme introduced an employee incentive scheme in the form of share appreciation rights for employees. These are based on the shares of the US parent company for employees. The vesting date is 30 September 20X4, and employees must be still in employment at that date.

There are 500 employees eligible for the scheme, each of whom has appreciation rights over 4,000 shares. Under the scheme, each employee will receive a cash amount equal to the fair value of the rights over each share. I anticipate 450 of the employees being in the scheme at 30 September 20X4. The fair value of the rights was £2.85 per share at 1 October 20X1 and expected to be £2.28 per share at 30 September 20X2.

Attachment 2 – A summary of key internal payroll controls

Thyme has around 500 permanent employees, 100 of whom are remunerated on an hourly basis. A timesheet system records time and overtime for staff who are entitled to overtime payments. The company runs a computerised payroll system covering all staff who are paid monthly. Each staff member is allocated to one of the company's eight departments, which range in size from three to 100 employees.

Control objectives	Controls	
Only valid payroll costs are recorded and paid.	1	Payroll summary is authorised by the financial controller before payment.
	2	Hours recorded are taken directly from time-recording system.
	3	All new staff are authorised by departmental heads.
	4	Departmental heads review payroll costs for their departments and raise queries if there were unexpected costs.
All payroll costs are recorded in the correct period.	5	Hours recorded are taken directly from time-recording system, so hours worked in the period cannot be missed.
	6	Review of monthly management accounts would identify a missed payroll journal.
	7	The nominal ledger journal is posted automatically from the payroll system to the ledger when the payroll is prepared five days before each month end.
	8	Departmental heads review payroll costs for their departments and raise queries if the costs were not as expected.
Payroll costs are recorded accurately at the appropriate rates.	9	Rates of pay are agreed annually. They are input to the payroll system by the payroll clerk and checked by the departmental heads. Changes to the rates are made by the payroll clerk only when written authority received from a departmental head.
	10	Rates of pay for new staff are authorised by the departmental head and detailed on the new joiners form used by the payroll clerk to update the system.
Payroll related liabilities are recorded accurately in the accounts.	11	Monthly payroll is always paid on the last working day of each month so no accruals are generally necessary.
	12	Employment tax liabilities are reconciled to the payroll summary at each month end.

Answer Bank

1 Mervyn plc

Marking guide

			Marks
		Technical	Skills
(a)	Explanations:		
	Sale of land: The Ridings/Event after reporting period	1	1
	Sale of land: Hanger Hill/sale and leaseback	2	2
	Pensions	2	2
	Provision	1	2
	Revenue	2	–
	Share appreciation rights	2	
(b)	Adjusted profit calculations:		
	Elimination of gain on sale of The Ridings	1	–
	Sale and leaseback	2	2
	Pensions	2	3
	Provision	1	–
	SARs	3	2
	Revenue	1	–
	Closing inventories	1	–
	Quality of discussion	–	2
Total marks		21	16

Maximum   30

For more guidance on how skills are tested and rewarded, please refer to the section at the start of this question bank.

(a) **Sale of land: The Ridings**

This sale and profit earned have been treated as an adjusting event after the reporting period. This appears to contravene IAS 10 *Events After the Reporting Period*. The completion of the sale in November does not give evidence of circumstances as at the reporting date. This would only have been the case if the contract in existence at 30 September had been unconditional, or if the condition, that is, detailed planning consent, had been met by the year-end.

The gain, and associated tax effect, should be eliminated from the financial statements, to be recognised in the following accounting period.

The land probably met the criteria to be classed as 'held for sale' under IFRS 5 *Non-current Assets Held for Sale and Discontinued Operations* at the year-end. However, this has no profit impact as IFRS 5 only requires recognition of a loss when fair value less costs to sell is below book value, which is clearly not the case here.

The transaction may be disclosed in the notes as a non-adjusting event after the reporting period if considered material to the user.

Sale of land: Hanger Hill

IAS 17 *Leases* requires sale and leaseback transactions to be treated according to their substance, which may differ from their legal form.

The first consideration is whether a sale has taken place. In this case, the lease is clearly an operating lease, as it is short-term and the lease payments are significantly less than the fair value of the asset. It is therefore appropriate to derecognise the asset but the true nature of the profit must be established.

According to IAS 17, the excess of fair value over the carrying amount of the asset is a normal profit and should be recognised immediately in profit or loss. Any excess profit, here £200,000 (W1) should be deferred and amortised over the period the asset is expected to be used, and therefore eliminated from the profit or loss for the year at the point of the sale and leaseback contract.

IAS 17 does not provide guidance as to how the excess profit should be amortised. There are two possible methods.

One is to spread the gain of £200,000 over the life of the lease on a straight line basis. This gives an annual credit of £40,000 to profit or loss for the year (200,000 ÷ 5). The balance of £160,000 is deferred income and recognised as a liability.

The other method looks at the substance of the arrangement. It treats the excess profit as a loan paid back through higher lease rentals. Under IAS 39 *Financial Instruments: Recognition and Measurement* the lease rentals must be split between the amount deemed to be a genuine lease rental and the amount deemed to be a repayment of the loan.

The appropriate treatment here is (see (W1) for detailed calculations):

		£	
Loan repayment :	Capital	33,000	
	Interest	20,000	Correct to charge
∴ Lease rental		27,000	to profit or loss
Total rental paid		80,000	

The capital repayment element must be eliminated from the profit or loss and offset against the loan.

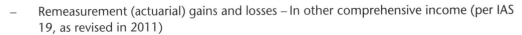

Tutorial note:

Either method of recognising the amortised profit is acceptable. The amended profit computation in (ii) below uses figures from the first method, giving the second method based on IAS 39 as an alternative.

Pensions

The contributions paid have been charged to profit or loss in contravention of IAS 19 *Employee Benefits*.

Under IAS 19, the following must be done:

- Actuarial valuations of assets and liabilities revised at the year-end

- All gains and losses recognised:

    - Current service cost

    - Transfers } In profit or loss

    - Interest on net defined asset/liability

    - Remeasurement (actuarial) gains and losses – In other comprehensive income (per IAS 19, as revised in 2011)

Deferred tax must also be recognised. The deferred tax is calculated as the difference between the IAS 19 net defined benefit liability less its tax base (ie nil as no tax deduction is allowed until the pension payments are made). IAS 12 *Income Taxes* requires deferred tax relating to items charged or credited to other comprehensive income to be recognised in other comprehensive income hence the amount of the deferred tax movement relating to the actuarial losses charged directly to OCI must be split out and credited directly to OCI.

Provision

According to IAS 37 *Provisions, Contingent Liabilities and Contingent Assets* a provision shall be recognised when:

- An entity has a present obligation as a result of a past event

- It is probable that an outflow of resources embodying economic benefits will be required to settle the obligation; and

- A reliable estimate can be made of the amount of the obligation.

If these conditions are met then a provision must be recognised.

The assessment of a provision for a legal claim is always a difficult area as it will be based upon the evidence available but it could also be argued that any provision or disclosure could be prejudicial to the court case itself.

In this case it would appear that the lawyers and management are fairly certain that damages and costs will be payable. The problem is the amount of any provision to be made. As there is a timescale involved here then the first stage will be to calculate the present value of each of the outcomes. Management have also assigned probabilities to each of the three possible outcomes so a further decision must be made as to whether to calculate an expected value or take the value of the most likely outcome. IAS 37 states that where a single obligation is being measured the individual most likely outcome may be the best estimate of the liability. Although in some circumstances the range of outcomes may mean that a higher figure is required.

Outcome	£'000	Discount factor @ 10%	Present value £'000	Probability	Expected Value £'000
Best	200	$1/1.10$	182	25%	46
Most likely	800	$1/1.10^2$	661	60%	397
Worst	1,500	$1/1.10^3$	1,127	15%	169
					612

IAS 37 requires the estimated value of the provision to be the amount that the entity would rationally pay to settle the obligation. The directors are likely to want as low a provision as possible they are likely to prefer the expected value of £612,000. However, this is a single event, and IAS 37 requires £661,000 as the most likely outcome or £612,000.

Bill and hold sales

When a buyer requests that the delivery of goods purchased does not take place immediately even though the buyer takes legal title of the goods and pays for them such arrangements are commonly referred to as "bill and hold" sales. Revenue from such sales should be recognised when the buyer takes title to the goods provided that:

- It is probable that delivery will take place
- The goods are available and ready for delivery at the time that title passes
- The buyer specifies the deferred delivery arrangements, and
- Payment is under the usual terms of the seller.

In this case it would appear that these sales are bill and hold sales. There is an established relationship with the customer and the arrangement has taken place during the year. Therefore the revenue should be recognised when the title to the goods passes to the buyer which will be when the goods are ready for delivery and the buyer has been invoiced. Therefore the goods must be removed from closing inventories in the statement of financial position at their cost price of £99,000, with a corresponding increase in cost of sales, and the additional revenue for the year to 30 September 20X7 must be recognised in the profit or loss for the year.

Share appreciation rights

The granting of share appreciation rights is a cash settled share based payment transaction as defined by IFRS 2 *Share based payment*. IFRS 2 requires these to be measured at the fair value of the liability to pay cash. The liability should be re-measured at each reporting date and at the date of settlement. Any changes in fair value should be recognised in profit or loss for the period.

However, the company has not remeasured the liability since 30 September 20X6. Because IFRS 2 requires the expense and the related liability to be recognised over the two-year vesting period, the rights should be measured as follows:

	£'000
At 30 September 20X6: (£6 × 10,000 × ½)	30
At 30 September 20X7 (£8 × 10,000)	80
At 1 November 20X7 (settlement date) (£9 × 10,000)	90

Therefore at 30 September 20X7 the liability should be re-measured to £80,000 and an expense of £50,000 should be recognised in profit or loss for the year.

The additional expense of £10 million resulting from the remeasurement at the settlement date is not included in the financial statements for the year ended 30 September 20X7, but is recognised the following year.

(b) **Amended profit**

	£'000
Profit for the year – per question	1,471
Eliminate net gain on sale – The Ridings (100 – 27)	(73)
Eliminate gain on sale in excess of fair value – Hanger Hill Estate (W1)	(200)
Portion of gain credited to P/L (200,000 ÷ 5) (W1)	40
Pension contributions	405
Current service cost	(374)
Interest on obligation (W2)	(253)
Interest on plan assets (W2)	216
Transfers (400,000 – 350,000)	(50)
Share appreciation rights	(50)
Deferred tax on pension obligation (W3)	(20)
Provision for damages for court case (see above)	(661)
Additional revenue from bill and hold sales	138
Reduction in closing inventories	(99)
Amended profit for the year	490

Alternative calculation – IAS 39 method for sale and leaseback:

	£'000
Profit for the year – per question	1,471
Eliminate net gain on sale – The Ridings (100 – 27)	(73)
Eliminate gain on sale in excess of fair value – Hanger Hill Estate (W1)	(200)
Rental element treated as capital repayment (W1)	33
Pension contributions	405
Current service cost	(374)
Interest cost	(253)
Interest on plan assets	216
Share appreciation rights	(50)
Transfers (400,000 – 350,000)	(50)
Deferred tax on pension obligation (W3)	(20)
Provision for damages for court case (see above)	(661)
Additional revenue from bill and hold sales	138
Reduction in closing inventories	(99)
Amended profit for the year	483

WORKINGS

1   Sale and leaseback (Hanger Hill Estate)

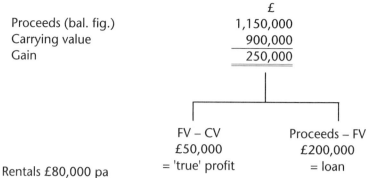

	£
Proceeds (bal. fig.)	1,150,000
Carrying value	900,000
Gain	250,000

FV – CV
£50,000
= 'true' profit

Proceeds – FV
£200,000
= loan

Rentals £80,000 pa

For alternative IAS 39 method only:

Loan repayment: repayment × 3.791 = £200,000

$$\text{Repayment} = \frac{200,000}{3.791}$$

= £53,000 (rounded)

Interest
200,000 ×
10% = 20,000

Capital
= 33,000

Remaining £27,000 (£80,000 – £53,000) represents operating lease rental.

2   Pension scheme

	Pension scheme assets £'000	Pension scheme liabilities £'000
At 1 October 20X6	2,160	2,530
Interest cost (10% × 2,530,000)		253
Interest on plan assets (10% × 2,160,000)	216	
Current service cost		374
Contributions	405	
Transfers	(400)	(350)
Pensions paid	(220)	(220)
∴ Loss on remeasurement through other comprehensive income*	(71)	38
At 30 September 20X7	2,090	2,625

*Note. IAS 19 (revised) stipulates that remeasurement losses **must** be recognised in other comprehensive income in the period in which they arise.

3   Deferred tax on pension liability

	£'000
Net pension liability (2,625 – 2,090)	(535)
Tax base (no deduction until benefits paid)	(0)
	(535)
Deferred tax asset @ 23%	123
Deferred tax asset b/f	(118)
	5
Credited to OCI re losses ((38,000 + £71,000) × 23%)	(25)
∴ Charge to profit or loss for the year	(20)

2 Biohealth

	Marks	
	Technical	Skills
Development expenditure	4	3
Associate investment	4	4
Impairment loss	4	5
Share-based payment transaction	3	3
	15	15
Development data discussion	2	3
Total marks	17	18
Maximum		30

For more guidance on how skills are tested and rewarded, please refer to the section at the start of this question bank.

MEMO

To	Client Manager
From	Client Senior
Date	X – X – XX
Subject	Financial statements of Biohealth year ended 31 December 20X7

As requested here are all the relevant journals to be applied to the draft financial statements for the year ending 31 December 20X7.

Required journal summary

	Dr £'000	Cr £'000	Profits £'000
Draft underlying profit			2,663.0
WORKINGS			
1 Sorpandex development costs			
Research and development expense	1,396.9		(1,396.9)
Development assets		1,396.9	
PPE cost (new microwave)	433.0		
Development assets		433.0	
Research and development expenses	86.6		(86.6)
PPE depreciation (Charge for the year)		86.6	
2 Bimoranol development costs			
No adjustment	0.0	0.0	
3 Transfer of original 20% purchase			
Associate investments	645.8		
Available-for-sale investments		645.8	
4 Existing holding step-up to fair value			
Associate investments	873.3		
Equity reserves		873.3	
5 Associate negative goodwill on current purchase			
Associate investments	280.6		
Associate income		280.6	280.6
6 Associate share of net income			
Associate investments	201.4		
Associate income		201.4	201.4

		Dr £'000	Cr £'000	Profits £'000
7	Generic Drugs Division impairment			
	Impairment charge (separate disclosure)	41,300.0		
	Goodwill		27,900.0	
	PPE		12,307.9	
	Acquired intangibles		1,092.1	
8	Redundancy provision			
	Redundancy costs	1,200.0		
	Redundancy provision		1,200.0	
	Revised underlying profit			1,661.5
	Prior year figure			2,643.0
	Proposed bonus scheme terms breached			Yes

Development expenditure

Development expenditure is only capitalised under IAS 38 *Intangible Assets* when certain criteria demonstrating the existence of future economic benefits are met. If these are not met at the year-end in relation to the two new projects, all expenditure must be written-off as an expense on a project by project basis.

WORKINGS

1   **Sorpandex**

The development appears to clearly fail capitalisation criteria as outlined in IAS 38. Technical feasibility is not reasonably assured. The salary and consumables costs will need to be expensed. The microwave, however, can be used elsewhere in the business and should be capitalised into PPE (not the development asset) and depreciated over its useful life. I have assumed a full year's charge in the first year.

	£'000
Reverse costs to be expensed (£567,200 + 829,700)	1,396.9
Initial cost of new microwave	433.0
Residual value	0.0
Depreciable amount	433.0
Useful economic life (years)	5.0
Annual charge	86.6

2   **Bimoranol**

The costs of this development appear to meet the IAS 38 criteria from the start of the year and all costs can be capitalised into the development asset – no adjustment required.

	£'000
Salary costs to capitalise	988.3
Consumables to capitalise	764.2
Total	1,752.5

The development expenditure relating to the drugs in commercial production should begin to be amortised over its expected useful life to a nil residual value as of the date when it is 'available for use', ie when commercial production starts.

3   **Investment in associate**

The increased investment in Laboratory Science Services on 1 November 20X7 changes the status of the investment from available-for-sale to an associate accounted for under the equity method. The intended accounting policy states that the investment is to be initially recognised at current fair value (full application of IFRS 3). This will require the original cost held in Available-for-Sale investments to be transferred to Associate investments, and then revalued at the fair value of assets at the date that significant influence is achieved.

4 Existing holding revaluation

	£'000
Original cost	645.8
Fair value of net assets acquired	
20% × 7,595.3	1,519.1
Step-up – to equity reserves	873.3

The goodwill on the current purchase needs to be calculated. Since the goodwill on the current purchase is negative, it needs to be credited to profit or loss for the current year.

5 Goodwill calculation

	£'000
Fair value of consideration	1,238.5
Fair value of net assets acquired	
20% × 7,595.3	1,519.1
Goodwill	(280.6)

Finally, Biohealth needs to incorporate its share of the post-acquisition net income of the Associate into the investment in the statement of financial position and recognise this amount in profit or loss for the year.

6 Associate share of net income

	£'000
Share of post-acquisition profits	
40% × (2,759.4 – 2,255.9)	201.4

Tutorial note:

Although the accounting policy states that the goodwill is calculated at each purchase stage, there is some ambiguity in the standard. It is recognised that this area is unclear, and omitting this step would be a legitimate alternative.

7 Impairment loss

The loss of the licence to produce Panthraximin necessitates an impairment review of the Generic Drugs Division as a cash-generating unit. Under impairment testing, the carrying value of the assets of the cash-generating unit cannot exceed the higher of the fair value less costs to achieve sale and the value-in-use valuation based on discounted cash flows. Calculation of the value in use is presented below.

Year			Discount factor	Present value
		£'000		£'000
1	Year-end cash flow – 31 Dec 20X8	21,200	0.9132	19,360
2	Year-end cash flow – 31 Dec 20X9	22,025	0.8340	18,369
3	Year-end cash flow – 31 Dec 20Y0	23,210	0.7617	17,679
4	Year-end cash flow – 31 Dec 20Y1	24,122	0.6956	16,779
5	Each year end thereafter – no growth	24,900	7.3218	182,313
				254,500

This can then be used to calculate the impairment by taking the higher of this value-in-use (£254.5m) and the fair value less costs to achieve the sale (given as £242m).

	£'000	£'000
Higher of sale value/value in use		254,500
Carrying amount		295,800
Impairment loss		41,300
Goodwill impairment	27,900.0	
PPE impairment (pro-rated)	12,307.9	
Intangibles impairment (pro-rated)	1,092.1	
		41,300

The impairment loss should be recognised first against the goodwill of £27.9m with the remaining amounts to be allocated against the other non-monetary assets of the unit pro-rata, but not so as to reduce any asset below its fair value less costs to sell (or value in use if determinable).

This precludes any impairment being allocated against inventory, and it has therefore been pro-rated against PPE and intangibles.

	£'000
Goodwill impairment	27,900.0
PPE impairment (pro-rated)	
(41,300 – 27,900) × 188,200/(188,200 + 16,700)	12,307.9
Intangibles impairment (pro-rated)	
(41,300 – 27,900) × 16,700/(188,200 + 16,700)	1,092.1
	41,300.0

IAS 36.76 states that the carrying amount of a cash generating unit should not include the carrying amount of any recognised liability, unless the recoverable amount of the cash generating unit cannot be determined without consideration of this liability. This is assumed to be the case here, because the division would be sold as a whole and the buyer would assume the liabilities. Otherwise, the recoverable amount of the division would be compared with the carrying amount of its gross assets: £339.6m.

8 Termination benefits

A provision should be made for the £1.2m of redundancy payments as the issue of redundancy notices in December demonstrates commitment to discontinue the production of Panthraximin. This is a termination benefit under IAS 19 *Employee Benefits* and should be disclosed as such.

9 Services of management consultant

This is a share-based payment transaction with a third party where it is possible to measure reliably the fair value of the services received. Therefore it is this fair value which is both the cost of the services in profit or loss and the amount by which equity will increase.

			£	No. shares	Value/share (for info only) £
Y/e 31 December 20X7	=	400 hours × £100	40,000	10,000	4.00
		400 hours × £110	44,000	10,000	4.40
			84,000	20,000	

The double entry required in 20X7 is:

	£	£
DEBIT Expenses	£84,000	
CREDIT Share capital		£20,000
CREDIT Share premium (bal)		£64,000

Product development and bonus: judgements made

Development expenditure is only capitalised under IAS 38 *Intangible Assets* when criteria demonstrating the existence of future economic benefits are met. The criteria require the reporting entity to demonstrate all of the following:

- Technical feasibility of completing the intangible asset so that it will be available for use or sale.

- Intention to complete the intangible asset and intention and ability to use or sell it.

- How the intangible asset will generate probable future economic benefits. Among other things, the entity can demonstrate the existence of a market for the output of the intangible asset or the intangible asset itself or, if it is to be used internally, the usefulness of the intangible asset.

- Availability of adequate technical, financial and other resources to complete the development and to use or sell the intangible asset.

- Ability to measure reliably the expenditure attributable to the intangible asset during its development.

Some of these criteria require judgement rather than being matters of fact. If the costs being considered for capitalisation are deferred, the impact on profit, and hence bonus, will be favourable.

3 Longwood

	Marks	
	Technical	*Skills*
Change in tax rate	4	4
Revised tax losses adjustment	3	5
Fair value adjustments	4	3
Goodwill calculation	4	3
Deferred taxes, goodwill and share versus asset deals	4	4
Total marks	19	19

Maximum	30

For more guidance on how skills are tested and rewarded, please refer to the section at the start of this question bank.

(a) **Change of tax rate**

Per IAS 12 *Income Taxes*, the tax rate to be used is that expected to apply when the asset is realised or the liability settled, based upon laws already enacted or substantively enacted by the year end.

The deferred tax assets and liabilities therefore need to be measured using the enacted rate for 20X7 of 23%, rather than 30%.

The net change in the carrying amount of the deferred tax assets and liabilities (£0.22m, as shown in the table below) arising from a change in rates will normally need to be taken to profit or loss for the year of Portobello Alloys. However, this will not be the case where it relates to a transaction or event which is recognised in equity (in the same or a different period), when the resulting deferred tax is also included in 'other comprehensive income'. This is the case for the available-for-sale investments (but not the retirement obligation, where the changes in value are taken through profit or loss under the corridor method).

The schedule below calculates the adjustments to the deferred tax assets and liabilities by reworking the temporary differences at the new rate.

Deferred tax schedule (in £m)

	at 30%	*at 23%*	*Adjustment*
Property, plant and equipment	(1.54)	(1.18)	0.31
Available-for-sale investments	(0.32)	(0.25)	0.06
Post-retirement liability	0.11	0.09	(0.02)
Unrelieved tax losses – recognised	0.66	0.51	(0.13)
	(1.09)	(0.83)	0.22
Deferred tax liability	(1.86)	(1.43)	0.37
Deferred tax asset	0.77	0.60	(0.15)
	(1.09)	(0.84)	0.22

The resultant adjustments are:

	Dr	*Cr*
	£m	*£m*
Deferred tax asset		0.15
Deferred tax liability	0.37	
Tax charge – profit or loss		0.16
Equity – available-for-sale investments		0.06

(b) **Deferred tax asset recognition for losses**

The increased forecast profitability may allow Portobello Alloys to recognise a deferred tax asset in respect of all the thus-far unrecognised unrelieved tax losses incurred. However, there is a risk that no losses will be available to carry forward. This will be the case if there is a major change in the nature and conduct of the trade post-acquisition. The amount of unrecognised losses is shown below.

Tax losses working

	£m
Total losses for tax purposes	7.40
Already utilised	(1.20)
Remaining	6.20
Recognised	(2.20)
Unrecognised	4.00

The analysis of the adjustment between current and non-current deferred taxes can be derived from the profit forecast as below.

Profit forecasts for tax loss utilisation

	20X7 £m	20X8 £m	Total £m
Forecast taxable profit – original	0.98	1.22	2.20
Forecast taxable profit – revised	1.90	4.74	6.64
Additional taxable profits	0.92	3.52	4.44
Additional recoverable losses	0.92	3.08	4.00
Addition to deferred tax asset at 23%	0.21	0.71	0.92

Note that the additional recoverable losses for 20X8 are restricted to £3.08m (rather than being equal to the additional taxable profits of £3.52m) since the total of unrecognised losses is only £4.00m.

Note that the change in the deferred tax asset must be recognised in profit or loss:

	Dr £m	Cr £m
Deferred tax asset	0.92	
Tax charge – profit or loss		0.92

(c) **Deferred taxes on fair value adjustments**

These adjustments will arise as consolidation adjustments rather than in the financial statements of Portobello Alloys.

The deferred tax adjustment in respect of the PPE should be to equity since the underlying revaluation on land will be recognised through equity in the revaluation reserve. The land will not be depreciated, and the deferred tax on the temporary difference will only crystallise when the land is sold. It is clear that there is no intention to sell the property in the current horizon.

The required adjustments to the deferred tax assets and liabilities are summarised in the table below.

	Fair value £m	Carrying amount £m	Temporary difference £m	Deferred tax at 23% £m
Property, plant and equipment	21.65	18.92	(2.73)	(0.63)
Development asset	5.26	0.00	(5.26)	(1.21)
Post-retirement liability	(1.65)	(0.37)	1.28	0.29
	25.26	18.55	(6.71)	(1.55)
Deferred tax liability				(1.84)
Deferred tax asset				0.29
				(1.55)

The resulting consolidation adjustment is

	Dr £m	Cr £m
Deferred tax asset	0.29	
Deferred tax liability		1.84
Goodwill adjustment	1.55	

(d) Goodwill calculation

The first step is to determine the fair value of the consideration.

Deferred consideration must be measured at its fair value at the date that the consideration is recognised in the acquirer's financial statements, usually the acquisition date. The fair value depends on the form of the deferred consideration.

Where the deferred consideration is in the form of equity shares:

- Fair value is measured at the date the consideration is recognised, usually the acquisition date. Consequently, the share price used must be £1.88.

Where the deferred consideration is payable in cash:

- Fair value is measured at the present value of the amount payable, hence the present value of the £10m cash.

Under IFRS 3 (revised) all acquisition-related costs must be written off as incurred. They are not included in the consideration transferred.

Fair value of consideration

	£m
Cash payment	57.00
Deferred equity consideration (5m × £1.88)	9.40
Deferred cash consideration (£10m/1.1^3)	7.51
	73.91

The value of the net assets acquired needs to be adjusted for the changes to reflect the fair value of PPE, the development asset, the pension and deferred taxes as shown below.

Fair value of net assets acquired

	£m
Book value per statement of financial position provided	9.90
Fair value adjustment to PPE	2.73
Fair value adjustment to development asset	5.26
Fair value adjustment to pension liability	(1.28)
Deferred tax – rate change	0.22
Deferred tax – tax losses (0.21 + 0.71)	0.92
Deferred tax – fair value adjustments (0.29 – 1.84)	(1.55)
	16.20

The resulting fair value of goodwill, on which no deferred tax is applicable is:

	£m
Fair value of consideration	73.91
Fair value of net assets acquired	(16.20)
Goodwill	57.73

(e) Deferred taxes and goodwill

Goodwill and share acquisitions

When an entity purchases the shares in a target and gains control, IFRS 3 requires that consolidated financial statements are produced and the target is introduced at fair value, including any attributable goodwill.

The goodwill arising in this manner does not appear in any of the companies' individual financial statements, but arises as a consolidation adjustment in the consolidated financial statements.

Tax authorities look at the individual financial statements of the companies within the group and tax the individual entities. As such, no goodwill is recognised for tax purposes. The individual financial statements of the buyer will simply reflect an investment in shares in its statement of financial position, not the subsidiary assets, liabilities or goodwill.

Under IAS 12 *Income Taxes*, a deferred tax liability or asset should be recognised for all taxable and deductible temporary differences, unless they arise from (inter alia) goodwill arising in a business combination. As such, no deferred tax is recognised.

Goodwill and asset acquisitions

The essential difference here is that the buyer has not purchased shares, but the assets and liabilities of the target. The assets and liabilities are measured and introduced at fair value, including any purchased goodwill. These are introduced directly into the individual financial statements of the buyer.

It is this goodwill that the tax authorities will recognise as a purchased asset and on which they may charge tax.

As tax relief is permitted over 15 years but goodwill is not amortised, then the tax base and the accounting base are not the same, therefore a taxable temporary difference arises and deferred tax recognised.

4 Talbot plc

Report on the required treatment of Flask Co in the consolidated financial statements of Talbot plc

Prepared by: Group Financial Controller

Date: 20 June 20X4

Introduction

This report sets out the appropriate treatment of Flask Co, together with the draft consolidated financial statements of the Talbot Group. In addition, it indicates any further narrative and numerical disclosures that may be required and other matters to consider.

Required treatment of Flask Co

Talbot acquired 75% of the issued ordinary share capital of Flask on 1 May 20X3. Following **IFRS 10** *Consolidated Financial Statements*, unless there are strong indications to the contrary, ownership of more than half the voting power of an entity indicates **control** of that entity. (Even an entity which does not own a majority of the voting power of another entity may sometimes control it.) IFRS 10 states that an investor **controls** an investee if and only if it has all of the following.

(i) **Power** over the investee
(ii) Exposure, or rights, to **variable returns** from its involvement with the investee, and
(iii) The **ability to use its power** over the investee to affect the amount of the investor's returns

Voting rights are the most straightforward indicator of power, and there is nothing to suggest that criteria (ii) and (iii) do not apply.

This means that **Flask is a subsidiary, and must be consolidated** from the date of acquisition.

It is not possible to choose to present the movement in exchange rates in a favourable light. The rules of **IAS 21** *The Effects of Changes in Foreign Exchange Rates* apply. This standard specifies how the foreign subsidiary's financial statements are to be translated and how its results and financial position are to be included in the consolidated financial statements of the parent.

Talbot is incorporated and operates in the UK. Its functional currency, that is the primary economic currency in which it operates, is sterling (£). This is also almost certainly its presentation currency, as its financial statements are issued in sterling.

Flask is incorporated in Ruritania, and its functional currency is the Kromit. In order to consolidate its financial statements, they must be **translated into sterling**, being the presentationa currency of the group:

1   Translate assets and liabilities at the closing rate at the year end (K2.1 to £1)

2   Translate equity (share capital and reserves) on acquisition at the exchange rate on the acquisition date (K2.5 to £1)

3   Translate income and expenses at the average rate for the year (K2 to £1)

4   Present resulting exchange differences as a separate component of equity

5   IAS 21 states that goodwill should be treated as an asset of Flask and translated at the closing rate

Intra-group balances and transactions will need to be **eliminated.**

Draft consolidated financial statements

Note: Workings are shown in the Appendix to this report.

Talbot

Consolidated statement of financial position at 30 April 20X4

	£m
Assets	
Property, plant and equipment (594 + 139)	733
Goodwill (W4)	19
Current assets (710 + 97.2 – 1.2) (W8)	806
	1,558
Equity and liabilities	
Equity attributable to owners of the parent:	
Share capital	120
Share premium	100
Retained earnings (W5)	726
Translation reserve (W9)	18
	964
Non-controlling interest (W6)	39
	1,003
Non-current liabilities (60 + 37.1 – 10)	87
Current liabilities (410 + 58)	468
	1,558

Talbot

Consolidated statement of profit or loss and other comprehensive income for the year ended 30 April 20X4

	£m
Revenue (400 + 142 – 12)	530
Cost of sales (240 + 96 – 12 + 1.2) (W8)	(325)
Gross profit	205
Distribution costs and administrative expenses (60 + 20)	(80)
Impairment of goodwill (W4)	(5)
Finance costs	(2)
Interest receivable	8
Exchange gains (W7)	1
Profit before tax	127
Income tax expense (40 + 9)	(49)
Profit for the year	78
Profit attributable to	
Owners of the parent	75
Non-controlling interests ((25% × 15.8 (W3)) – 1.4 (W4))	3
	78

Appendix: Workings for consolidated financial statements

1 **Group structure**

1 May 20X3	Talbot	75%
	Flask	

Cost	= 240m Kromits
Pre acqn. reserves	= 160m Kromits

2 **Translation of statement of financial position**

	Km	Rate	£m
Property, plant and equipment	292.0	2.1	139.0
Current assets	204.0	2.1	97.2
	496.0		236.2
Share capital	64.0	2.5	25.6
Share premium	40.0	2.5	16.0
Retained earnings:			
Pre-acquisition	160.0	2.5	64.0
	264.0		105.6
Post–acquisition: 30 + (4 – 2.4) (W7)	31.6	2.0	15.8
	295.6		121.4
Translation reserve	–	Balancing figure	19.4
	295.6		140.8
Non-current liabilities (82 – 4 (W7))	78.0	2.1	37.1
Current liabilities (120 + 2.4 (W7))	122.4	2.1	58.3
	496.0		236.2

3 **Translation of statement of profit or loss and other comprehensive income**

	Km	Rate	£m
Revenue	284.0	2	142.0
Cost of sales	(192.0)	2	(96.0)
Gross profit	92.0	2	46.0
Distribution and administrative expenses	(40.0)	2	(20.0)
Interest payable	(4.0)	2	(2.0)
Exchange gain (4 – 2.4) (W7)	1.6	2	0.8
Profit before tax	49.6	2	24.8
Income tax expense	(18.0)	2	(9.0)
Profit for the year	31.6	2	15.8

4 Goodwill

	Group Km	Km	NCI Km	Rate	Group £m	NCI £m	Total £m
Consideration transferred/FV NCI		240.0	76.0				
Less fair value of net assets acquired							
Share capital	64						
Share premium	40						
Retained earnings	160						
	264						
Group/NCI share (75%/25%)		(198.0)	(66.0)				
		42.0	10.0	2.5	16.8	4.0	20.8
Impairment losses (11.2 × 75%/25%)		(8.4)	(2.8)	2.1	(4.0)	(1.4)	(5.4)
FX gain (75%/25%*)		–	–		3.0	1.0	4.0
		33.6	7.2	2.1	15.8	3.6	19.4

*Note: The foreign exchange gain has been split between the parent and NCI using ownership percentage. It would also be correct, and come to the same total for goodwill, to use the actual values of group and NCI share of goodwill to apportion the FX gain. If it was done in this way, the figures for group and NCI share of goodwill would be £16m and £3.4m respectively.

5 Retained earnings

	£m
Talbot	720.0
Flask (75% × 15.8 (W2))	11.8
Provision for unrealised profit (W8)	(1.2)
Impairment of goodwill (W4)	(4.0)
	726.6

6 Non-controlling interest

	£m
Non-controlling interest share of net assets (25% × 140.8 (W2))	35.2
NCI share of goodwill (W4)	3.6
	38.8

7 Exchange gains and losses in the accounts of Flask

Loan from Talbot (non-current liabilities)

	Km
At 1 May 20X3 (£10 million × 2.5)	25.0
At 30 April 20X4 (£10 million × 2.1)	(21.0)
Gain	4.0

Inter-company purchases (current liabilities)

	Km
Purchase of goods from Talbot (£12 million × 2)	24.0
Payment made (£12 million × 2.2)	(26.4)
Loss	(2.4)

Exchange differences in statement of profit or loss and other comprehensive income (retranslated to sterling)

	£m
Gain on loan (4 ÷ 2)	2.0
Loss on current liability/purchases (2.4 ÷ 2)	(1.2)
	0.8

8 Provision for unrealised profit

	£m
Sale by parent to subsidiary (£12 million × 20% × ½)	1.2

9 Translation reserve

	£m	£m
Opening net assets at closing rate (W2) 264 @ 2.1	125.7	
Less opening net assets at opening rate (W2) 264 @ 2.5	(105.6)	
		20.1
Reported profit at closing rate (W3) 31.6 @ 2.1	15.1	
Reported profit at average rate (W3) 31.6 @ 2	(15.8)	
		(0.7)
Gain on translation of Flask		19.4
Group (75%)		14.6
Exchange gain on retranslation of goodwill (W4)		3.0
		17.6

5 MaxiMart plc

			Marks
	Technical	Skills	
(1) Share option scheme	4	3	
(2) Pension scheme	8	6	
(3) Reward card	3	2	
(4) Futures contract	3	2	
(5) Proposed dividend	3	2	
Total marks	21	15	
Maximum			30

For more guidance on how skills are tested and rewarded, please refer to the section at the start of this question bank.

MEMO

To: Jane Lewis
From: Vimal Subramanian
Date: 15 November 20X1

Transactions of MaxiMart

1 Share options awarded

This is an equity-settled share-based payment. An expense should be recorded in profit or loss, spread over the vesting period of five years with a corresponding increase in equity.

Each option should be measured at the fair value at the grant date ie £2. The year end estimate of total leavers over the five year vesting period (25%) should be removed in the calculation of the expense as they will never be able to exercise their share options.

There are two other vesting criteria here:

(a) The average profit which should be taken into account because it is a performance criterion. The average profit for the next five years is £1.3m ([£0.9m + £1.1m + £1.3m + £1.5m + £1.7m]/five years), resulting in 120 options per employee.

(b) The share price which should not be taken into account because it is a market condition which is already factored into the fair value. So the fact that the share price target of £8 has not been met by the year end does not need to be taken into account.

The expense and the corresponding increase in equity for the year ended 30 September 20X1 is calculated as follows:

= 1,000 employees × 75% employees remaining × 120 options × £2 FV × 1/5 vested
= £36,000

2   Pension scheme

Statement of financial position as at 30 september 20X1 (extract)

	30 September 20X1 £'000	30 September 20X0 £'000
Non-current assets		
Defined benefit pension plan	–	100
Non-current liabilities		
Defined benefit pension plan	40	–

Statement of profit or loss and other comprehensive income for the year ended 30 September 20X1 (extracts)

	£'000
Profit or loss	
Defined benefit expense	185
Other comprehensive income	
Actuarial gain on defined benefit obligation	(30)
Return on plan assets (excluding amounts in net interest)	53
Net remeasurement loss	(23)

Note: IAS 19 (revised 2011) requires remeasurement gains and losses to be recognised in other comprehensive income.

Notes to the financial statements

Defined benefit plan: amounts recognised in the statement of financial position

	30 September 20X1 £'000	30 September 20X0 £'000
Present value of defined benefit obligation	2,410	2,200
Fair value of plan assets	(2,370)	(2,300)
	40	(100)

Defined benefit expense recognised in profit or loss for the year ended 30 September 20X1

	£'000
Current service cost	90
Net interest on the net defined benefit asset (115 – 110)	(5)
Past service cost	100
	185

Changes in the present value of the defined benefit obligation

	£'000
Opening defined benefit obligation at 1 October 20X0	2,200
Past service cost	100
Interest on obligation (2,200 × 5%)	110
Current service cost	90
Benefits paid	(60)
Remeasurement gain through OCI (balancing figure)	(30)
Closing defined benefit obligation at 30 September 20X1	2,410

Changes in the fair value of plan assets

	£'000
Opening fair value of plan assets at 1 October 20X0	2,300
Interest on plan assets (2,300 × 5%)	115
Contributions	68
Benefits paid	(60)
Remeasurement loss through OCI (balancing figure)	(53)
Closing fair value of plan assets at 30 September 20X1	2,370

3 Reward card

IFRIC 13 *Customer Loyalty Programmes* requires that reward points are treated as a separate component of the sale. They should be measured at the fair value to the customer (effectively the amount for which they could be sold separately). This amount should be deferred and recognised in revenue when the reward points are redeemed.

In substance, customers are implicitly paying for the reward points they receive when they buy other goods and services and hence some of that revenue should be allocated to the points.

Here, total reward points have a face value of £5m at the year end but only two in five customers are expected to redeem their points, giving a value of £2m (ie £5m × 2/5). Effectively MaxiMart has sold goods worth £102m (ie £100m + £2m) for a consideration of £100m. Thus allocating the £2m between the two elements would mean that £98.04m (£100m/£102m × £100m) would be allocated to food revenue and the balance of £1.96m (£2m/£102m × £100m) to the reward points. £98.04m would be recognised as revenue in year ended 30 September 20X1 and £1.96m would be deferred in the statement of financial position until the reward points are redeemed.

4 Futures contract

The loss on the forecast sale should not be accounted for as the sale has not yet taken place. However, the gain on the future should be accounted for under IAS 39. Hedge accounting can be applied because the hedge has fallen within the required 80 – 125% effectiveness range (2/1.9 = 105%).

The double entry required is:

DEBIT	Financial asset (future)	£2m
CREDIT	Retained earnings (with effective portion)	£1.9m
CREDIT	Profit or loss (with ineffective portion)	£0.1m

5 Proposed dividend

The dividend was proposed after the end of the reporting period and therefore IAS 10 *Events After the Reporting Period* applies. This prohibits the recognition of proposed equity dividends unless these are declared before the end of the reporting period. The directors did not have an obligation to pay the dividend at 30 September 20X1 and therefore there cannot be a liability. The directors seem to be arguing that their past record creates a constructive obligation as defined by IAS 37 *Provisions, Contingent Liabilities and Contingent Assets*. A constructive obligation may exist as a result of the proposal of the dividend, but this had not arisen at the end of the reporting period.

Although the proposed dividend is not recognised it was approved before the financial statements were authorised for issue and should be disclosed in the notes to the financial statements.

6 Icicle plc

Scenario

The candidate is reporting to the chief executive of a plc regarding the financial reporting implications including deferred taxation of a number of financial reporting transactions. The candidate is also asked to revise draft extracts from the financial statements and calculate the consolidated EPS. The company is preparing consolidated financial statements for the first time and the candidate needs to identify the additional adjustments arising from intra group trading. The acquisition of the subsidiary also gives rise to deferred taxation implications on consolidation. In addition there are some transactions which require adjustment in both the parent company and the group financial statements and which will also therefore impact on the EPS.

Marks

		Technical	Skills	
1	Explanations and calculations of deferred tax implications of: Non current assets Factory equipment		1	Clear and concise notes written in appropriate style responding to chief executive
	Land	4	2	Distinguish between temporary and non temporary timing differences
	Acquisition of subsidiary	4	2	Appreciate the different status of companies / groups for tax and financial reporting purposes
				Identify additional adjustments required for consolidation
	Warranty	3	1	Evaluate the appropriateness of a warranty provision making recommendations regarding financial reporting treatment
	Tax losses	2	1	Distinguish between temporary and non temporary timing differences
				Appreciate the different status of companies / groups for tax and financial reporting purposes
2	Redraft financial statement extracts, providing a comprehensive summary of transactions	6	4	Link brought forward deferred tax position to issues in the file to redraft extracts
				Prepare a table in clear form
3	Calculate the consolidated EPS	1	1	Identify which adjustments to make to calculate consolidated EPS
	Total marks	20	12	
	Maximum		30	

For more guidance on how skills are tested and rewarded, please refer to the section at the start of this question bank.

MEMO

To: Jacqueline Hyde
From: Dean Claire
Subject: Deferred Tax and Group Issues relating to Icicle plc

1 (a) **Factory Equipment Depreciation**

The deferred tax position is determined by comparing the carrying amount of equipment to its tax base.

	Tax base £'000	Carrying amount £'000
Balance at 1/4/X8	3,400	6,400
Additions	2,200	2,200
Accounting depreciation (£9.6m × 20% + £2.2m × 20% × 6/12)		(2,140)
Tax depreciation (£5.6m × 20%)	(1,120)	
Balance at 31/3/X9	4,480	6,460

There is therefore a taxable temporary difference of £1.98m (£6.46m – £4.48m) and a deferred tax liability of £455,400 (£1.98m × 23%) in respect of this equipment. This compares to an opening deferred tax liability of £690,000 (23% × (£6.4m – £3.4m)). A credit of £234,600 is therefore taken to the statement of profit or loss and other comprehensive income to reflect the reduction in the deferred tax provision.

Dr   Deferred tax liability   £234,600

Cr   Tax expense   £234,600

(b)   **Land revaluation**

The carrying amount of the asset at 31 March 20X9 was £15m, compared to the tax base of £5.8m giving a taxable temporary difference of £9.2m. This applies whether recovery is through sale or future use.

The deferred tax liability is £9.2m × 23% which is £2.116m.

This is recognised as 'other comprehensive income' in the statement of profit or loss and other comprehensive income.

£9.2m is added to the cost of the asset and £7.084m (£9.2m – £2.116m) to revaluation reserve.

Dr   Revaluation reserve   £2.116 million

Cr   Deferred tax liability   £2.116 million

IAS 16 requires a prospective adjustment in respect of the revaluation.

2   **Acquisition of Snowball Ltd**

A deferred tax liability will arise in respect of the fair value adjustment of Snowball's assets. This gives a taxable temporary difference of £800,000, on which deferred tax at 23% of £184,000 arises. This deferred tax decreases the net assets of Snowball in the consolidated statement of financial position, and as a consequence, increases goodwill.

Dr   Goodwill   £184,000

Cr   Deferred taxation liability   £184,000

Goodwill is calculated as follows:

	£'000
Fair value of consideration	4,000
Fair value of net assets acquired	(3,400)
Deferred tax on fair value adjustment	184
Goodwill	784

Goodwill must be reviewed for impairment at 31 March 20X9.

An adjustment is required for unrealised profits in closing inventories, calculated as £120,000 (£600,000 × 25/125). This will increase cost of sales in the statement of profit or loss and other comprehensive income and decrease retained earnings and inventories in the statement of financial position.

Dr   Cost of sales   £120,000

Cr   Inventories   £120,000

A deferred tax asset arises in relation to these unrealised profits. This is because companies are taxed, rather than groups, and so Icicle will have to pay tax in relation to the goods sold to Snowball that are still held within the group at the statement of financial position date. The deductible temporary difference is £120,000, and a deferred tax asset of £27,600. This deferred tax asset would be recognised in the financial statements of Snowball.

Dr   Deferred tax asset   £27,600

Cr   Tax expense   £27,600

3   **Provision for warranty claim**

Under IAS 37, a provision should be created for the present value of the expected liability. Although there is some uncertainly about the accuracy of the calculations by the production department, this does not prevent a provision being calculated as it would appear that the provision can be calculated with reasonable certainty. The figure for inclusion at 31 March 20X9 is therefore £410,400 (see table below). This should also be charged against profit for the year to 31 March 20X9.

Expected repairs in year to 31 March	£'000
20Y0	113.6 (5,000 × £25/1.1)
20Y1	165.3 (8,000 × £25/1.1²)
20Y2	131.5 (7,000 × £25/1.1³)
Total	410.4

Because the above provision will not be deductible for tax purposes until the repairs take place, a deductible temporary difference arises for the £410,400. This in turn gives rise to a deferred tax asset of £94,392.

Dr	Deferred tax asset	£94,392	
Cr	Tax expense		£94,392

4 Losses

The brought forward losses can be offset against future trading profits, but a deferred tax asset can only be recognised to the extent that it can be offset against future taxable profits of the company. Assuming that the directors' optimism in Icicle's future profitability is correct, then a deferred tax asset can be created of £897,000 (£3.9m × 23%). This will also be credited against profit.

Dr	Deferred tax asset	£897,000	
Cr	Tax expense		£897,000

Summary of transactions

Debit/(credit) Calculations to nearest £1,000

Impact on:		Consolidated Statement of Financial Position					Statement of comprehensive income		
	Warranty provision	Inventories	Goodwill	Rev. surplus	Deferred tax liability	Deferred tax asset	Profit before tax	Tax expense	Other Comp. Income
(1) Deferred taxation on Equipment					235			(235)	
(1) Revaluation				2,116	(2,116)				(2,116)
(2) FV Adjustment – Snowball			184		(184)				
(2) Unrealised profit in Inventory		(120)					120		
(2) Inventories						28		(28)	
(3) Provision	(410)					94	410	(94)	
(4) Losses						897		(897)	
Total								530	(1,254)

Debit/(credit) to nearest £1,000

Statement of profit or loss and other comprehensive income for year ended 31 March 20X9

	Draft	Tax expense	Revaluation	Snowball acquisition	Warranty	Revised
Profit before tax	1,830			(120)	(410)	1,300
Income tax credit	0	1,254				1,254
Profit for the year	1,830					2,554
Other comprehensive income						
Gains on property revaluation	9,200		(2,116)			7,084
Total comprehensive income for the year	11,030					9,638

Statement of financial position at 31 March 20X9

Equity	Draft	Adjustments	Revised
Ordinary shares of 50 pence each	1,000		1,000
Share premium account	6,800		6,800
Retained earnings	1,040	+1,254–120–410	1,764
Revaluation reserve	9,200	–2,116	7,084
Total equity	18,040		16,648

EPS Calculation

Earnings per share is based on the group profit for the year of £2.554 million, divided by the number of ordinary shares of 2 million. This gives an EPS figure of 127.7 pence per share.

Please contact me if you need any further information.

7 Flynt plc

Scenario

The candidate is in the role of a newly appointed financial controller who is asked to produce journals and adjust a consolidated statement of comprehensive incomestatement of profit or loss and other comprehensive income in respect of three technical issues: share options, defined benefit scheme and lease of surplus machinery. The candidate is also asked to calculate the EPS and diluted EPS taking into account the adjustments to the consolidated statement of comprehensive incomestatement of profit or loss and other comprehensive income.

Marking guide

Marks

		Technical	Skills	
1	Redraft consolidated statement of profit or loss and other comprehensive income	20	8	Identify the treatment of share options is incorrect
				Evaluate the lease to determine correct accounting treatment
				Appreciate impact on different elements of the statement of profit or loss and other comprehensive income
				Explain the difference between defined contribution and benefit schemes
				Calculate the figures for the defined benefit scheme in accordance with IAS 19 (revised)
				Show journal entries for the above adjustments.
				Produce revised statement of profit or loss and other comprehensive income in an appropriate format
2	Calculate EPS and diluted EPS where appropriate	5	2	Summarise the impact of adjustments on EPS and diluted EPS where appropriate
				Identify the impact of adjustments on EPS
	Total marks	25	10	
	Maximum		30	

For more guidance on how skills are tested and rewarded, please refer to the section at the start of this question bank.

To: Andrea.Ward@flynt.co.uk
From: Miles.Goodwin@flynt.co.uk

Re: Finalisation of financial statements for year ended 31 May 20X6

I would respond to your email as follows:

Share Option Scheme

Shane Ponting's treatment of the option scheme is incorrect. IFRS 2 *Share-Based Payment* should have been applied as follows:

The fair value of the options at the grant date should be treated as an expense in profit or loss and spread over the vesting period, which is from the grant date until the date the scheme conditions vest.

The scheme conditions are both market and non-market based, as they are impacted by both the share price and continuing employment.

The fact that the share price has increased since the grant date is ignored when determining the charge to profit or loss. This is because market based conditions are embedded in the fair value calculations.

The continuing employment condition should be based on the best estimates at the statement of financial position date, which in this case is for 16 executives to be employed at the vesting date.

The journal entry is as follows:

DEBIT	Profit or loss	£378,000	
CREDIT	Equity (retained earnings)		£378,000

The charge to profit or loss is therefore £378,000 ($10,000 \times 16 \times £12.60 \times \frac{1}{4} \times 9/12$). This will reduce profit after tax and therefore EPS.

In addition this sum is also credited in the statement of financial position to equity. IFRS 2 does not state where in equity this entry should arise, and many companies add it to retained earnings.

When calculating diluted EPS it will normally be necessary to take into consideration the number of 'free' shares being allocated to executives assuming the whole scheme will vest. Also, normally, there is an adjustment to be made to the option exercise price in terms of the remaining IFRS 2 cost to be expensed in future (per IAS 33 example 5A). However in the case of Flynt there is a share price condition to be satisfied, in addition to the mere passage of time. There are therefore performance based share options and, in accordance with para 48 of IAS 33, these should be treated as contingently issuable shares.

Para 54 of IAS 33 therefore applies which states that "the calculation of diluted EPS is based on the number of ordinary shares that would be issued if the market price at the end of the reporting period were the market price at the end of the contingency period". In the case of Flynt, to satisfy this contingency the price would need to rise to £58.5 (ie £39 × 150%). At the period end it is only £52, so in accordance with para 54 there is no dilution.

Lease of machinery

Shane Ponting's analysis of the agreement as an operating lease is incorrect. This would appear to be a finance lease because:

(a)   The lease term and useful life of the asset are the same

(b)   The present value of the lease payments received, plus the residual value guaranteed by Prior plc come to £607,000 (appendix 2), which is almost all of the fair value of the machinery.

The asset should therefore be derecognised and a receivable created. This is called the net investment in the lease. The direct costs incurred should be included in the initial measurement of the finance lease receivable and will therefore be recognised in profit or loss over the lease term as part of interest receivable.

The rental income of £150,000 is removed from profit or loss. Interest receivable of £61,000 is credited to profit or loss (appendix 3).

Because the machinery is being derecognised the depreciation charge should be added back to profit.

Overall the reclassification of the lease to a finance lease will increase EPS.

In the statement of financial position at 31 May 20X6 there will be a receivable of £524,000 (appendix 3) which should be analysed between amounts due in less than and more than one year.

Journal entries are as follows:

DEBIT	Depreciation provision	£122,000	
CREDIT	Profit or loss		£122,000

Being removal of the depreciation charge

DEBIT	Net investment in lease	£1,000	
CREDIT	Profit or loss		£1,000

Being adjustment re-allocation of direct costs

DEBIT	Profit or loss	£150,000	
CREDIT	Net investment in the lease		£150,000

Being removal of rental income

DEBIT	Net investment in the lease	£61,000	
CREDIT	Profit or loss		£61,000

Being interest income

Dipper Pension Scheme

The accounting treatment for a defined benefit scheme is considerably different to that of a defined contribution scheme. It is therefore necessary to remove the charge of £480,000 made by Shane Ponting and replace it with the following.

The profit or loss charge is split into two elements:

(a) Service cost: This is the pension earned by the employees of Dipper in the year, and is an operating cost. This means that operating costs will rise by a net £80,000 after deducting the contributions paid into the scheme that have been incorrectly charged by Shane Ponting.

(b) Net interest on the net defined benefit liability. This in turn consists of two elements:

    (i) Interest on plan assets:. This works out as £55,000 (5% × £2.2 million × 6/12). IAS 19 does not specify where this should appear in the statement of profit or loss and other comprehensive income. I have treated it as investment income but it would not be incorrect to offset it against operating costs.

    (ii) Interest on obligation: This is the unwinding of the present value of the pension liability due to employees who are one year closer to retirement at the end of the accounting period. A charge of £65,000 (5% × £2.6 million × 6/12) should therefore be made in profit or loss. Because it relates to a present value, I have added this to finance costs, but once again IAS 19 is silent on the issue.

The net charge to profit or loss is thus £(65,000 − £55,000) = £10m

The actuarial difference reflects that some of the above figures are estimates, and also the increase in the net liability in the pension fund to £670,000 (£2.75m − £2.08m). This net liability will appear in the statement of financial position as a liability.

Per appendix 4 there is a net remeasurement loss of £180,000. IAS 19 requires immediate recognition of this in other comprehensive income.

Journal entries are as follows:

DEBIT	Profit or loss	£560,000	
CREDIT	Pension obligation		£560,000

Being recognition of service costs

DEBIT	Pension asset	£480,000	
CREDIT	Profit or loss		£480,000

Being contributions paid into the scheme

DEBIT	Interest on assets	£55,000	
CREDIT	Profit or loss		£55,000

Being recognition of interest on assets

DEBIT	Profit or loss	£65,000	
CREDIT	Pension obligation		£65,000

Being recognition of interest on obligation

DEBIT	Other comprehensive income	£205,000	
CREDIT	Pension asset		£205,000

Being recognition of remeasurement loss on pension asset

DEBIT	Pension obligation	£25,000	
CREDIT	Other comprehensive income		£25,000

Being recognition of gain on pension obligation

Goodwill impairment

The goodwill impairment should be charged to profit or loss rather than other comprehensive income. The entries to correct are:

DEBIT	Profit or loss	£400,000	
CREDIT	Other comprehensive income		£400,000

Being correct treatment of goodwill

This will impact on EPS.

Summary of adjustments

As a result of these adjustments EPS has increased from £1.21 to £1.50 per share from the previous year.

Appendices

Appendix 1

Flynt plc: Revised statement of profit or loss and other comprehensive income for year ended 31 May 20X6

	20X6	Options	Lease	Pension	Goodwill	Total
	£'000	£'000	£'000	£'000	£'000	£'000
Revenue	14,725					14,725
Cost of sales	(7,450)					(7,450)
Gross profit	7,275					7,275
Operating costs	(3,296)	(378)	122+1	(80)		(3,631)
Goodwill impairment					(400)	(400)
Other operating income	150		(150)			0
Operating profit	4,129					3,244
Investment income	39		61			100
Finance costs	(452)			(10)		(462)
Profit before tax	3,716					2,882
Taxation at 23%	(1,003)					(663)
Profit after tax	2,713					2,219
Other comprehensive income						
Remeasurement loss on pension				(180)		(180)
Goodwill impairment	(400)				400	0
	2,313					2,039

Appendix 2: PV of lease agreement at 10%

	Cash Flow	PV
Year	£'000	£'000
1	150	136
2	150	124
3	150	113
4	150	103
5	211	131
5 Unguaranteed	9	6
Total		613

Fair value plus the direct costs is equal to the net investment in the lease

£612,100 + 1,000 = 613,100

Appendix 3: Net investment in lease

	Bal b/f £'000	Interest income £'000	Instalment £'000	At 31 May £'000
1 June 20X5	613	61	(150)	524
1 June 20X6	524	52	(150)	426

Appendix 4: Pension Calculations

	Asset £'000	Obligation £'000
Balance at Acquisition	2,200	2,600
Interest on assets	55	
Unwinding of discount (interest on liability)		65
Service cost		560
Contributions	480	
Pension Paid	(450)	(450)
Expected closing bal	2,285	2,775
Actual closing balance	2,080	2,750
Difference on remeasurement through OCI	(205)	25
Net actuarial loss	(180)	

Appendix 5: Basic EPS

	20X6 £'000	20X5 £'000
Profit after tax	2,219	1,699
Shares at start and end of year (000s)	*1,475	1,400
Basic EPS	£1.50	£1.21

*6/12 × 1,400,000 =   700,000
6/12 × 1,550,000 =   775,000
           1,475,000

As reported above, there is a share price condition to be satisfied, in addition to the mere passage of time. There are therefore performance based share options and, in accordance with para 48 of IAS 33, these should be treated as contingently issuable shares. Para 54 of IAS 33 therefore applies and there should therefore be no dilution.

8 Gustavo plc

Scenario

The candidate is in the role of a newly appointed financial controller of a company called Gustavo who is asked to prepare a draft consolidated statement of comprehensive income statement of profit or loss and other comprehensive income incorporating the results of two subsidiaries. The company has sold and purchased shares in the subsidiaries during the year.

The sale of shares in its UK subsidiary called Taricco involves the candidate recognising that the investment should be consolidated as a subsidiary for the six months until the date of disposal takes place. On sale of the shares the investment decreases to 35% and is therefore a partial disposal. Candidates need to recognise that because Gustavo has the ability to appoint directors to the board this is a strong indication that Taricco would be treated as an associate for the remaining six months of the year.

The acquisition of shares is an investment in 80% of the share capital of an overseas company. The investment is made on 1 January and therefore should be treated as a subsidiary from that date.

The candidate is specifically asked to explain the impact on the consolidated statement of comprehensive income statement of profit or loss and other comprehensive income and to show separately the impact on the non controlling interest and the impact of future changes in exchange rates on the consolidated statement of financial position. The candidate must also deal with issues involving revenue recognition.

Marks

	Technical	Skills	
Prepare the draft consolidated statement of profit or loss and other comprehensive income for the year ended 30 September 20X6 including other comprehensive income showing separately the profit attributable to the non-controlling interest Prepare briefing notes to explain the impact of the share transactions (Exhibit 2) on the consolidated statement of profit or loss and other comprehensive income	21	6	Use the information in Exhibit 2 to determine the appropriate method of consolidation for Taricco and Arismendi Prepare consolidated financial statements from those of individual companies Present information suitable for presentation to board Explain and calculate the appropriate adjustments to the statement of profit or loss and other comprehensive income Apply recent changes to group accounting standards to the given scenario Appreciate that the two investments have different impacts on statement of profit or loss and other comprehensive income Identify the impact of goodwill adjustment on non controlling interest
Advise on the impact that any future changes in exchange rates will have on the consolidated statement of financial position	4	3	Apply IFRS to explain impact of exchange rates to future profits
Advise on how to account for the impaired receivable under current IAS 18 rules, and show what effect taking account of credit risk would have.	3	2	Apply the current rules and identify the impact of any potential changes, showing an awareness of current issues.
Total marks	28	11	
Maximum		30	

For more guidance on how skills are tested and rewarded, please refer to the section at the start of this question bank.

To: Antonio Bloom
From: Anita Hadjivassili
Subject: Gustavo plc financial statements

I attach the draft consolidated statement of profit or loss and other comprehensive income for the year ended 30 September 20X6, the explanations you requested, and supporting workings.

Gustavo plc: Consolidated statement of profit or loss and other comprehensive income for year ended 30 September 20X6

	£'000
Revenue	57,357
Cost of sales	(37,221)
Gross profit	20,136
Operating costs	(9,489)
Gain on sale of subsidiary	13,340
Profit from operations	23,987
Share of profit of associate	160
Investment income	424
Finance costs	(2,998)
Profit before taxation	21,573
Income tax expense	(2,974)
Profit for the year	18,599

	£'000
Other comprehensive income	
Exchange differences on translating foreign operations	7,369
(Restatement of goodwill 4,370	
Exchange gain in year 2,999)	
Total comprehensive income for the year	25,968
Profit attributable to:	
Non controlling interests (W9)	170
Owners of parent company	18,429
	18,599
Total comprehensive income	
Attributable to:	
Non controlling interests (W9)	1,474
Owners of parent company	5,895
	7,369

Supporting Notes (Requirement 2)

1 **Taricco Limited**

Taricco is treated as a subsidiary for the six months until disposal takes place. This is because Gustavo has a 75% stake in the company until that date. Upon the sale of the shares on 1 April 20X6 the investment decreases to 35%. Because Gustavo still has the ability to appoint directors to the board Taricco should be treated as an associate, and the equity accounting method used for the last six months of the year.

The non-controlling interest (NCI) have a 25% share of profit of Taricco for the first six months of the year until disposal takes place.

A gain on disposal arises of £13.34 million in the statement of profit or loss and other comprehensive income. The dividend received by Gustavo from Taricco of £210,000 should be eliminated on consolidation, as it is replaced by share of Taricco's profits. As the dividend is paid after the disposal of the majority stake in Taricco it is not deducted from the net asset total at disposal.

It should be noted that in future years Taricco will make less of a contribution to group profit due to the reduction in the investment.

2 **Arismendi Inc**

Gustavo acquired an 80% stake in Arismendi, and so the investment should be treated as a subsidiary from 1 January 20X6.

The acquisition fees of £400,000 have been incorrectly treated, and should be expensed in profit or loss in the year of purchase.

The results of Arismendi are translated into sterling at the average rate for the nine months post acquisition in the statement of profit or loss and other comprehensive income.

The impact that any future changes in exchange rates will have on the consolidated statement of financial position (Requirement 3)

An exchange difference will arise each year, due to the movement in exchange rates from each statement of financial position date in relation to net assets, and also because the profits in the statement of profit or loss and other comprehensive income will be retranslated from the average to the closing rate in the statement of financial position. This gives a gain on translation of £2.999 million, and is taken to other comprehensive income, and 20% is allocated to the NCI, representing their share of Arismendi.

The cost of the investment is restated each year for consolidation purposes to take into consideration the movement in exchange rates.

As a consequence goodwill is restated at the year end to take into account the change in exchange rates, as it is deemed to be an asset of the subsidiary.

As a consequence goodwill has increased from £8.739 million to £13.109 million (W7). This is taken to other comprehensive income in the statement of profit or loss and other comprehensive income, and 20% is allocated to the NCI, representing their share of Arismendi.

WORKINGS

(W1)	Gustavo £'000	Taricco 6 months £'000	Arismendi 9 months £'000	Adjust £'000	Total £'000
Revenue	35,660	14,472	7,225		57,357
Cost of sales	–21,230	–11,082	–4,639		–37,221
Depreciation (£14.4m/8 years × 9/12)/5			–270		
Operating costs	–5,130	–2,478	–1,481		–9,489
Acquisition fees	–400				
Gain on disposal (W4)				13,340	13,340
Share of associate's profit (W6)				160	160
Investment income	580	54	–	–210	424
Interest paid	–2,450	–330 –218			–2,998
Income tax expense	–2,458	–180	–336		–2,974
PAT	*4,572	456	281	13,290	18,599

*As originally stated £4,972,000 less acquisition fees £400,000

(W2) Net Assets of Taricco

	On disposal £'000	At acquisition £'000
Share capital	2,000	2,000
Retained earnings b/f	4,824	2,400
Profits to disposal (6 months)	456	
Dividend paid	0	
Total	7,280	4,400

(W3) Goodwill

	Taricco £'000
Cost to parent	15,000
NCI at acquisition (25%)	1,100
Less: Net assets	–4,400
Goodwill	11,700
Impairment	–2,500
Goodwill at disposal	9,200

(W4) Gain on sale of Taricco shares

	£'000
Proceeds	19,800
FV of interest retained	8,200
NCI at disposal (W5)	1,820
	29,820
NA at disposal (W2)	–7,280
Goodwill at disposal (W3)	–9,200
Gain on disposal	13,340

(W5) NCI at disposal

	£'000
At acquisition	1,100
Up to disposal (25% × (4,824 – 2,400)) + 114 (W9)	720
At disposal	1,820

(W6) Share of profits of associate
Taricco
35% × PAT × 6/12   160

(W7) Goodwill of Arismendi	KR'000	£'000 1.1.X6 (Kr 6)	£'000 30.9.X6 (Kr 4)
Cost of investment	75,600	12,600	18,900
NCI at acquisition			
12Kr × 5,000 shares × 20%	12,000	2,000	3,000
	87,600	14,600	21,900

Net assets at Acquisition
Share capital	5,000		
Retained earnings	14,846		
Three months to 1 January 20X6			
3,670 × 3/12	918		
Fair value adjustment			
£2.4m × Kr 6	14,400		

	35,164	5,861	8,791
Goodwill	52,436	8,739	13,109
Increase to other comprehensive income			4,370

(W8) Exchange difference arising in Arismendi

	£'000	£'000
Net assets at acquisition		
Kr 35,164 @ closing rate 4Kr : £1	8,791	
Kr 35,164 @ acquisition rate 6Kr : £1	5,861	
		2,930
Nine months profit to 30.9.X6		
Kr 3,670 per question × 9/12 = 2,753 – *1,350 = 1,403 @ closing rate Kr4:£1	350	
Kr 3,670 per question × 9/12 = 2,753 – *1,350 = 1,403 @ average rate Kr5:£1	281	
		69
		2,999

*depreciation on FV adjustment ((14,400/8) × 9/12)

(W9)

	£'000
Non controlling interests	
Taricco	
456 × 25%	114
Arismendi	
281 × 20%	56
Share of goodwill restatement for Arismendi	
4,370 × 20%	874
Share of exchange difference	
2,999 × 20%	600
	1,644

3   **Bravo Ltd**

IAS 18 treatment

Under IAS 18, revenue of £200,000 would be recognised on the sale of the sports equipment and a trade receivable of £200,000 set up. The trade receivable would be reviewed periodically for impairment, and the deteriorating financial situation of the customer would be seen as an indicator of impairment. An impairment of £20,000 would be recognised. However, no recognition would be made, under current rules of the 5% risk that the customer would default. This is not 5% of the revenue – if it were, a receivables expense of £10,000 would be required – but a 5% risk that none of the revenue can be collected, for which current standards make no arrangements.

Taking account of credit risk

If credit risk were taken into account in the recognition of revenue, the amount recognised on the sale would be reduced by the 5% likelihood of default, meaning that only 95% of the revenue, ie £190,000 would be recognised. The impairment of £20,000 would still be recognised as an expense, not as a reduction in revenue.

The current rules do not take account of credit risk, and an earlier proposal to include it was not accepted in the latest Exposure Draft on revenue recognition.

9 Inca Ltd

Scenario

This was the single silo corporate reporting question and included ethical issues. The scenario was a company supplying plant and machinery to the oil drilling industry. At the beginning of the year it acquired an 80% interest in an overseas subsidiary. The candidate was employed on a temporary contract, reporting to the managing director. There was some concern about the impact of the new subsidiary on the statement of financial position, and there were some outstanding financial reporting issues, particularly with regard to deferred tax. The accountant had identified five particular matters that needed to be resolved: accelerated capital allowances on PPE; developments costs; tax trading losses; a foreign currency loan which required correct treatment by considering both IAS 21 and IAS 39; and a loan to a director. Candidates were provided with a draft statement of financial position for the parent and the overseas subsidiary.

Candidates were required firstly, to explain the correct financial reporting treatment for each of the five issues identified; secondly, to prepare the consolidated statement of financial position; thirdly to show the difference between the two permitted methods of calculating non-controlling interest and fourthly as a separate requirement, to highlight any ethical concerns and actions with respect to the email from the MD.

Marking guide

		Marks		
		Technical	Skills	
(a)	An explanation of the appropriate financial reporting treatment for each of the issues identified by the Excelsior accountant (Exhibit 3); and	15	4	Communicate in an appropriate manner to given audience
				Query the validity of the budgets to determine the future available profits for the set off of losses
(b)	The consolidated statement of financial position of Inca at 30 April 20X1, assuming there are no adjustments to the individual company financial statements other than those you have proposed.			Identify the incorrect treatment of the loan interest and the loan translation
				Identify no deferred tax adjustment required for the loan interest
				Recommend an appropriate adjustment for the loan interest and the loan translation
				Provide financial statements in an appropriate format
(c)	A calculation of NCI at fair value	3	2	Show a clear distinction between the two methods of calculation

		Technical	Skills	
(d)	Explain any ethical concerns that you have in relation to the MD's email, and set out the potential actions you may take	2	6	Explain ethical issues and apply to scenario in relation to conflict of interest, transparency and application of IFRS.
				Link technical knowledge and ethical implications of non-disclosure of related parties
				Identify threats to independence
				Outline appropriate actions to minimise ethical threats
		—	—	Identify need for expert help
Total marks		20	12	
Maximum		30		

For more guidance on how skills are tested and rewarded, please refer to the section at the start of this question bank.

Inca plc

To: Managing Director
From: Accountant
Subject: Excelsior – Outstanding Issues

Deferred Tax

Deferred tax is calculated on all temporary timing differences, and is based on the tax rates that are expected to apply to the period when the asset is realised or liability is settled. The tax rates are those that have been enacted or substantively enacted by the end of the reporting period. In the absence of any other information to the contrary, therefore the current rate of 20% should be used.

1 Property, Plant and Equipment (PPE)

There is a temporary taxable timing difference of CU22 million (CU60million-CU38million) at 1 May 20X0. This agrees to the opening deferred tax liability of CU4.4 million shown in Excelsior's statement of financial position.

At 30 April 20X1 this has increased to CU28 million (CU64million-CU36million) and therefore the deferred tax liability in respect of PPE increases to CU5.6 million.

Therefore a deferred tax charge on the increase in the difference of CU1.2million is required. This would be charged to the statement of profit or loss and other comprehensive income of Excelsior.

2 Development Costs

There is a temporary taxable difference arising in respect of development costs because they have a carrying amount of CU7 million at 30 April 20X1 in the statement of financial position. However they have a zero tax base because they have been treated as an allowable deduction in the company's tax computation at that date.

When the development costs are amortised in the statement of profit or loss and other comprehensive income the timing difference will reverse.

This gives a deferred tax liability of CU1.4million (20% × CU7million) and a charge to the profit or loss.

3 Tax Losses

A deferred tax asset arises because the tax losses can be used to reduce future tax payments when being offset against future taxable profits.

However, the amount of the deductible difference should be restricted to the extent that future taxable profit will be available against which the losses can be used. This is an application of the prudence principle.

As such, the deferred tax asset should be recognised on the budgeted profit of CU5 million for the next two financial years only.

Therefore, the deferred tax asset would be CU2 million (20% × (CU5 million × 2)). This will be a credit to profit or loss.

Given the inexperience of the company accountant, the validity of these forecasts must be considered and verified.

4 American Loan

The loan should initially be measured at the sum received of US$15million, which at the borrowing date is CU48.0million.

Excelsior's accountant has incorrectly charged the repayment of ($800,000 × 2.8) CU 2.2 million to profit or loss. This should be reversed and replaced with the interest calculated using the amortised cost method. Therefore the interest charge for the year is US$1.6million (US$15million × 10.91%).

In Excelsior's own statement of profit or loss and other comprehensive income this could be translated at either the average or the closing rate of exchange.

I have used the average rate in my figures and this gives an interest charge of CU4.8 million (US$ 1.6 million × 3 = CU4.8 million). Therefore an adjustment to profit or loss of CU2.6 million (4.8 million less 2.2 million) is required.

No deferred tax adjustment arises as only the interest paid is tax deductible and not the discount or premium on redemption.

The loan constitutes a monetary liability, and therefore should be translated in the books of Excelsior using the closing rate of exchange between the CU and the US Dollar. The loan is US$15.8 million which gives a figure of CU44.2 million ($15.8 m × year end rate of 2.8). The loan is currently stated after the above interest correction, at CU50.6 million (CU48 million plus the adjustment for interest of CU4.8 million less interest paid of CU2.2 million) and has not yet been translated by the accountant at the year-end rate. Therefore an exchange gain of CU 6.4 million arises, and this is taken to the statement of profit or loss and other comprehensive income.

5 Director's Loan

Given the issues in terms of recoverability of the loan, it should be written off and removed from receivables. This will also result in an expense in profit or loss.

As the loan is to a director, it is likely to be treated as a related party transaction, and as such should be disclosed in the notes to the financial statements. The writing off of the loan should also be disclosed.

There are likely to be current tax implications of this loan write off and the Ruritanian tax treatment of this would need to be ascertained.

Consolidation of Subsidiary

Goodwill

As Excelsior is a subsidiary, goodwill arises at the acquisition date, and is restated at 30 April 20X1 using the exchange rate at that date. The initial recognition of goodwill does not in itself create a deferred tax consequence. This is because goodwill is only recognised in the consolidated financial statements.

The assets and liabilities of Excelsior at 30 April 20X1, after any adjustments to align IFRS and Ruritanian GAAP, should be translated using the closing rate of exchange in the consolidated statement of financial position, and at the average rate in the consolidated statement of profit or loss and other comprehensive income. Any gain or loss arising in respect of the movement in exchange rates is taken directly to equity.

Goodwill should be subject to an impairment review at the end of the first year of acquisition. This is especially important because of the post acquisition losses generated by Excelsior.

Goodwill with non-controlling interest at fair value.

If non-controlling interest in Excelsior is valued at its fair value of CU 20 million, the goodwill is CU 2 million greater, at CU 50 million, which is £11.1 million on translation. The exchange difference on translation of the goodwill remains at £1.1 million (see Working 2).

Ethical Issues

Director's Loan

The loan to the director should be investigated to see if it is legal in accordance with Ruritanian company law. It is advisable to seek expert advice on this issue.

On a separate issue it would be unethical to disregard the rules in relation to IAS 24 in respect of related party transactions. I would expect that Excelsior's auditors will insist that the transaction is disclosed in the notes to the financial statements.

The board's wish that the loan is not disclosed on the grounds of immateriality is irrelevant; materiality is determined by nature in related party transactions rather than by value.

Potential Permanent Contract

The offer of a permanent contract in return for my 'silence' in respect of the preparation of the working papers creates an improper working relationship and a threat to independent judgement. This demonstrates a lack of integrity and professional behaviour on behalf of the managing director.

Actions to be taken

Initially the issues I have should be discussed with the managing director, to make him aware of the ethical responsibilities that a Chartered Accountant must abide by.

If those discussions are fruitless, then representations should be made to Inca's audit committee, assuming that it has one.

If the above fails to resolve the issues with the managing director in a satisfactory manner then the ICAEW ethical hotline, or legal counsel, should be sought. As a last resort resignation should be considered.

Workings for adjustments to Excelsior financial statements for Exhibit3

PPE	CU'm
Carrying amount	64.0
Tax base	(36.0)
Temporary taxable difference	28.0
Tax rate	20%
Deferred tax	5.6
Provision at 1 May 20X0	4.4
Increase in provision	1.2
Development costs	
Carrying amount	7.0
Tax base	0.0
Temporary taxable difference	7.0
Tax rate	20%
Deferred tax liability	1.4

Tax losses

Deferred tax asset is restricted to the extent that probable taxable profit is available.

	CU'm
20X2 and 20X3 Expected profits	10.0
Tax rate	20%
Deferred tax asset	2.0

American loan	US$m	Rate	CU'm
Borrowed	15.0	3.2	48.0
Interest for year to income statement (10.91%)	1.6	3.0	4.8
Interest paid	(0.8)	2.8	(2.2)
Balance pre exchange adjustment			50.6
Balance at year end	15.8	2.8	44.2
Exchange gain on loan			(6.4)

Statement of Financial Position of Excelsior

Adjustment to Excelsior's financial statements for issues in Exhibit 3

	CU'm Draft	PPE	Dev Costs	Tax Loss	Interest/exchange adjustment	Director's loan	CU'm Final
Non-current assets							
PPE	64.0						64.0
Intangible assets	7.0						7.0
Total non-current assets	71.0						71.0
Current assets							
Inventories	16.6						16.6
Accounts receivable	35.2					(2.0)	33.2
Cash	12.8						12.8
Total current assets	64.6						62.6
	135.6						133.6
Equity and Liabilities							
Share capital CU1	10.0						10.0
Share premium account	16.0						16.0
Retained earnings at acq'n	64.0						64.0
Net assets at acquisition	90.0						90
Loss since acquisition	(16.0)	(1.2)	(1.4)	2.0	(2.6) 6.4	(2.0)	(14.8)
Non-current liabilities							
Deferred tax	4.4	1.2	1.4	(2.0)			5.0
Loans	48.0				2.6 (6.4)		44.2
Current liabilities	9.2						9.2
Total equity and liabilities	135.6						133.6

The subsidiary is translated at the closing rate for the assets and liabilities in the statement of financial position and average rate for loss for the year.

Statement of financial position for Excelsior

	CU'm	Rate	£m
PPE	64	4.5	14.2
Intangible assets	7	4.5	1.6
Current assets			
Inventories	16.6	4.5	3.7
Trade receivables	33.2	4.5	7.4
Cash	12.8	4.5	2.8
	133.6		29.7
Equity and liabilities			
Share capital	10	5	2.0
Share premium	16	5	3.2
Retained earnings			
Pre acquisition	64	5	12.8
Post acquisition	(14.8)	4.8	(3.1)
Translation reserve (working 1)			1.8
			16.7
Non current liabilities: Deferred tax	5	4.5	1.1
Loans	44.2	4.5	9.8
Current liabilities	9.2	4.5	2.1
	133.6		29.7

WORKING 1 – **Translation reserve**

| | | £m | £m |
			Gain/(Loss)
Opening net assets @ Closing rate	90 @ 4.5	20	
Opening net assets @ Opening rate	90 @ 5	18	2.0
Loss for the year			
@ Closing rate	(14.8) @ 4.5	(3.3)	
@ Average rate	(14.8) @ 4.8	(3.1)	(0.2)
Translation reserve for Excelsior			1.8

Inca group – Consolidated statement of financial position

	£m
PPE (32.4 + 14.2)	46.6
Goodwill (Working 2)	10.7
Intangible £(12.4 + 1.6)	14.0
	71.3
Inventories (9.8+3.7)	13.5
Trade receivables (17.4 + 7.4)	24.8
Cash (1.6 + 2.8)	4.4
	114.0
Share capital	4.0
Share premium	12.0
Retained earnings (Working 2)	41.6
NCI (Working 2)	3.4
Deferred tax (12 + 1.1)	13.1
Loans (5.8 + 9.8)	15.6
Current liabilities (22.2 + 2.1)	24.3
	114.0

WORKING 2 – **Consolidation of Excelsior**

Goodwill on consolidation

	CU'm
Consideration	120
NCI @ acquisition (90 × 20%)	18
NA: 10 + 16 + 64	(90)
Goodwill	48

	£m
48 @ Opening rate 5	9.6
48 @ Closing rate 4.5	10.7
Exchange difference on translation of goodwill	1.1

Goodwill on consolidation with NCI at fair value

	CU'm
Consideration	120
NCI @ FV	20
NA: 10 + 16 + 64	(90)
Goodwill	50

	£m
50 @ Opening rate 5	10.0
50 @ Closing rate 4.5	11.1
Exchange difference on translation of goodwill	1.1

Consolidated retained earnings

	£m
Inca – Retained earnings	41.6
Excelsior (80% × 3.1)	(2.5)
Exchange differences:	
Translation of goodwill	1.1
Group's share of exchange difference on translation of Excelsior (1.8 × 80%)	1.4
	41.6

Non-controlling interest (NCI) in consolidated statement of financial position
20% × 16.7   3.4

10   Aytace plc

Scenario

The candidate is in the role of a financial controller for Aytace plc, the parent company of a group that operates golf courses in Europe. The candidate is requested to explain the financial reporting treatment of a number of outstanding matters which include revenue recognition, defined benefit scheme, a holiday pay accrual, executive and employee incentive schemes and the piecemeal acquisition of a subsidiary. The question requires the candidate to produce a revised consolidated statement of comprehensive income statement of profit or loss and other comprehensive income.

To:	Willem Zhang
From:	Frank Brown
Subject:	Financial Reporting Issues

1   Golf Tournament

1.1   Tender Costs

Tender costs should be expensed in the year in which they were incurred, and therefore a further £1.05 million should be charged to profit or loss. This is because at the tender date there was no probable inflow of economic benefits to Aytace and therefore it would not be possible to capitalise the tender costs as an intangible asset as it is highly unlikely to satisfy the recognition criteria as an internally generated asset per IAS 38.

1.2 TV Revenues

Per IAS 18 *Revenue,* in relation to services, revenue should be recognised only when:

(i) The amount can be measured reliably

(ii) Probable economic benefits will flow to Aytace

(iii) The stage of completion at the SFP date can be reliably measured. At 31 May 20X3 Aytace had not provided any services to the broadcaster, and therefore no revenue should have been recognised.

Therefore revenue should be reduced by £400,000 (£4.8 million × 4/12 × ¼).

2 Pension Scheme

The pension expense in the statement of profit or loss and other comprehensive income consists of a number of elements.

The service cost represents the extra pension liability arising in the year from employee service in the year. It is charged to profit or loss in the year.

Pension assets are the equities, bonds and other investments in the fund, and the interest income on these is credited to profit or loss.

Scheme liabilities are the pension obligations due to current and former employees, and these are discounted by the market rate on high quality corporate bonds. The interest charge on the liability is expensed to profit or loss.

The improvement in the pension benefit should be recognised by adding £400,000 should be added to the liability immediately. Interest on this increased liability should therefore be charged to profit or loss. As the liability is increased at 1 June 20X2, an interest charge is made in relation to this increase of £24,000 (6% × £400,000).

Instead of the contributions paid into the scheme, the calculation should be as follows:

Defined benefit expense recognised in profit or loss

	£'000
Current service cost	1,200
Net interest on net defined benefit liability (732 – (1,080 + 24))	372
Past service cost	400
Total expense	1,972

IAS 19 is silent on how this expense should be charged, I have therefore charged it all to operating costs, but some companies separate out the interest costs,and take these to finance costs.

Therefore operating costs should be increased by the difference of £1,072,000 (£1,972,000 – £900,000) over the contributions paid into the scheme, which was the sum incorrectly charged to the statement of profit or loss and other comprehensive income.

Pension Scheme	FV Asset	PV Obligation
	£'000	£'000
Opening balance	12,200	18,000
Past service cost		400
Interest on plan assets	732	
Interest on obligation		1,080
Interest cost on past service cost		24
Contributions	900	
Pensions paid	(1,100)	(1,100)
Current service cost		1,200
Expected closing balance	12,732	19,604
Difference on remeasurement through OCI	768	196
Actual closing balance	13,500	19,800

The net actuarial gain of £572,000 (768,000 – 196,000), should be recognised in other comprehensive income.

The net pension obligation recognised in the statement of financial position is £6.3 million (£19.8 million – £13.5 million).

3 Holiday pay accrual

IAS 19 *Employee Benefits* requires that an accrual be made for holiday entitlement carried forward to next year.

Number of days c/fwd: $900 \times 3 \times 95\% = 2{,}565$ days

Number of working days: $900 \times 255 = 229{,}500$

$$\text{Accrual} = \frac{2{,}565}{229{,}500} \times £19m = £0.21m$$

DEBIT	Operating costs	£0.21m
CREDIT	Accruals	£0.21m

4 Investment in Xema

4.1 Accounting method to be used

Xema should be treated as an associate only up to 1 September 20X2, when control is achieved. Therefore the equity method should credit the statement of profit or loss and other comprehensive income with only £102,000 (£1.02 million × 3/12 × 40%).

For the remaining nine months of the year Xema should be consolidated using the acquisition method, and income and expenditures included in the financial statements on a line by line basis.

As Xema is 100% owned at the statement of financial position date there are no entries in respect of non-controlling interests.

4.2 Gain on increase in stake

At 1 September 20X2 the carrying amount of the stake held in Xema is £2.962 million, calculated as follows:

Original cost	2,300	
Share of profit to 31 May 20X2	560	(40% x(£4.8 million – £3.4 million))
Share of profit to 1 Sept 20X2	102	See above
	2,962	

At 1 September per IFRS 3 this should be restated to the fair value of the shares of £3.8 million.

The gain of £838,000 is recognised in the profit or loss for the year. It would most likely be shown as 'other operating income' or netted off against operating costs.

4.3 Goodwill

Goodwill only arises when control is achieved, and is therefore calculated at 1 September 20X2.

The calculation should be as follows:

	£'000
FV of original investment	3,800
Cost at 1 Sep 20X2	12,400
	16,200
Less: Net assets at fair value (W1)	6,055
Goodwill	10,145

(W1) Net assets at carrying amount/fair value:

Share capital	1,000
Retained earnings (at 31/5/20X2)	4,800
Retained earnings to 1/9/20X2 (1020 × 3/12)	255
Net assets at carrying amount/FV	**6,055**

The goodwill figure should be reviewed for impairment at 31 May 20X3.

5 Incentive schemes

5.1 Executive scheme

This is an equity settled share based payment scheme. The vesting conditions are market-based as they relate to a share price target and a non-market based condition requiring the director to still hold office at 31 May 20X5.

Because the vesting condition relates to the market price of Aytace's shares, the probability of achieving the target price by 31 May 20X5 is integrated into the fair value calculation. Therefore your concerns about not achieving the share price rise can be ignored when determining the charge to profit or loss. The non-market based condition will impact on the number of options expected to vest and as it is anticipated that one of the directors will leave by the vesting date this is taken into consideration when calculating the charge.

Per IFRS 2 the fair value of the options is spread over the vesting period of three years to 31 May 20X5.

The charge should therefore be £360,000 (£2.70 × 100,000 × 4 directors × 1/3), and the same amount should be included in equity.

5.2 Share appreciation rights

These are deemed to be cash settled share based rights because they do not involve the issue of shares. The vesting conditions are not market based, because the scheme only relates to continued employment.

Instead of recognising a credit in equity, a liability is created in the statement of financial position. The fair value of the liability is remeasured at each reporting date, and also takes into consideration the expected number of employees in the scheme at the vesting date.

The charge is therefore £152,000 (£2.28 × 4,000 × 50 × 1/3), with an equal increase in liability.

6 Revised profit figures

After taking into consideration the above adjustments my revised profit is as follows:

Consolidated statement of profit or loss and other comprehensive income for year ended 31 May 20X3

	£'000	Golf/TV £'000	Pension £'000	Holiday accrual £'000	Options £'000	Xema 9 mths £'000	Total £'000
Revenues	14,450	(400)				4,050	18,100
Operating costs	(9,830)	(1,050)	(1,97242)				
				(210)	(360)	(2,700)	
					(152)		(15,374)
Operating profit	4,620						2,726
Other operating income						838	838
Associate income	867					(765)*	102
Other investment income	310					180	490
Finance charges	(1,320)					(540)	(1,860)
Profit before taxation (ignore tax as instructed)	4,477						1,396
Other comprehensive income							
Net gain on remeasurementin year							572
Total comprehensive income for the year							2,368

Working: adjustment to income for associate

	£'000
Xema's revenue	4,050
Cpsts	(2,700)
Investment income	180
Finance costs	(540)
	990
Tax for nine months	(225)
	(765)

11 Razak plc

Scenario

The candidate is in the role of a member of the financial reporting team at Razak plc. Razak has increased its shareholding in the year in an investment, a company called Assulin. This mid-year acquisition of shares results in a change in accounting treatment of the investment from a financial asset to a subsidiary. The accounting is made further complex by a contingent payment which is to be made provided that Razak's management team remain in post.

The candidate is also asked to explain the accounting adjustments needed in respect of a bond purchased in Imposter plc. Imposter went into administration shortly after the year-end requiring a write down of the bond in Razak's financial statements. The candidate must also explain the appropriate accounting for a proposed pension plan.

The chief executive of Razak is a director of, and a minority shareholder in Imposter. The candidate is asked for the ethical implications of this scenario in the knowledge that the purchase of the bond was not recorded in the Razak board minutes.

Marking guide

	Marks		
	Technical	Skills	
Provide explanations on how the increase in the stake in Assulin will be treated in the financial statements of the Razak group	10	2	• Understand, assimilate and present information to the appropriate technical audience (the finance director)
			• Identify the step acquisition and its implications
Explain any adjustments needed to account for the purchase of the bond in Imposter plc in Razak's group financial statements and evaluate any ethical issues arising from this matter	4	5	• Appreciate that the bond has correctly been accounted for in the financial statements prior to impairment
			• Identify the need for the impairment of the bond to be adjusted in the financial statements
			• Identify self interest threat
			• Appreciate need to abide by ICAEW ethical code, establish facts, take advice
			• Apply scepticism to the extent of CEO's involvement with Imposter
			• Recommend appropriate action considering Andrew is also a chartered accountant

Prepare Razak's consolidated statement of financial position at 30 September 20X2 after making all relevant adjustments	4	5	•	Assimilate adjustments and prepare consolidated statement of financial position.
Explain how to account for the proposed pension plan	5	4	•	Apply knowledge of the distinction between defined contribution and defined benefit scheme, identifying the reality behind the form.

Total marks	23	16
Maximum	30	

For more guidance on how skills are tested and rewarded, please refer to the section at the start of this question bank.

To:	Andrew Nezranah
From:	Kay Norton
Subject:	Razak plc, Group financial statements
Date:	5 November 20X2

Explanations of how the increase in the stake in Assulin will be treated in the financial statements of Razak group.

Status as subsidiary

At 31 March 20X2 Assulin becomes a subsidiary because Razak now has a controlling stake (80%). This means that goodwill arises on the transaction and a non-controlling interest will be created in relation to the 20% of Assulin owned by minority shareholders.

Remeasurement of original investment

Per IFRS 3 the gains on the available for sale investment of £750,000 previously taken to OCI are now transferred to profit or loss.

In addition the cost of the original stake is remeasured to the fair value of £20 each immediately prior to acquisition. This gain of (£20 – £16) × 75,000) = £300,000 is added to the cost of the investment, and taken to profit or loss.

Intra group balance

The intra group loan of £800,000 is eliminated upon consolidation.

Contingent consideration

The contingent consideration should be measured at fair value (IFRS 3). A liability should be recognised to pay £1.95 million (£6 × 325,000).

However as the payment is not due for two years from the acquisition date, it should be discounted at the cost of capital of 9% to a present value of £1.641 million. This sum should be added to consideration when calculating goodwill.

This discount should be unwound for six months to the SFP date, giving a charge of £73,845 (£1.641m × 9% × 6/12) to profit or loss, and increasing the liability by the same amount.

Fair value adjustment

The assets of Assulin should be remeasured to fair value at the acquisition date as a property with a carrying amount of £1.2 million has an estimated fair value of £2.6 million, giving an increase in PPE of £1.4 million. This sum should then be depreciated over the remaining useful life of the property of five years, reducing both PPE and profits for the year by £140,000 (£1.4 million × 1/5 × 6/12).

Goodwill

The consideration for goodwill takes into account the remeasurement of the fair value of the original investment, plus the cost of the shares on 31 March 20X2, plus the fair value of the NCI. The remeasured net assets of Assulin are then deducted from this total to give a goodwill total of £8.826 million (W3).

Imposter Bond

The bond has been correctly measured at amortised cost of £1.308 million. As only 40% of the bond will be repaid at 30 September 20X4, the bond must be reviewed for impairment and adjustment of £832,000 made to impair the bond. This amount is written off to income statement (see Working 6).

Explanation of the adjustments needed to account for the purchase of the bond in Imposter and evaluation of the ethical issues.

Ethical issues

First of all, both Andrew and Kay are chartered accountants and are both therefore bound by the ICAEW ethical code.

If it was foreseeable that Imposter would be placed in administration and the bond impaired, the chief executive would be in breach of his fiduciary duty and potentially guilty of an illegal act. At worst this is a case of fraud and at best a conflict of interest. We must first ascertain the facts.

As the chief executive is a shareholder and a director of Imposter there is potentially a self-interest threat here and he may be seen to be behaving in the best interests of Imposter in preference to the best interests of the shareholders of Razak. The question to be resolved is - did the chief executive know of the financial position of Imposter at the time when the bond was issued and was there evidence at that point that the bond would or could go bad? As a member of the board this would appear highly likely.

Kay and Andrew should consider reporting the matter to the company's money laundering officer and possibly discussing their concerns with a non-executive director. Advice from ICAEW can also be taken regarding their own positions considering they are both chartered accountants.

Razak's consolidated statement of financial position at 30 September 20X2

	Razak £'000	Assulin £'000	Adjustments £'000	Consolidated	
Goodwill			8,826	8,826	Working 3
Non-current assets					
			FV adjustment		
Property, plant and equipment	6,000	3,460	1,400 – 140	10,720	
Investment in Assulin	9,325		(9,325)		
Loan to Assulin	800		(800)		
			Impairment		
Other financial assets	1,308		(832)	476	Working 6
	17,433				
Current assets					
Inventories	1,140	610		1,750	
Receivables	960	400		1,360	
Bank	0	70		70	
	2,100	1,080		3,180	
Total assets	19,533	4,540	(871)	23,202	
Equity					
£1 ordinary shares	2,800	500	(500)	2,800	
Share premium account	7,400			7,400	
			(2,740)		
Retained earnings	2,510	2,740	192	2,702	Working 5
AFS	750		(750)		
NCI			2,012	2,012	Working 4
	13,460				
Non-current liabilities					
					1641 + 74 (unwinding 6/12 months)
Contingent consideration			1,715	1,715	
Other	2,788			2,788	
Loan from Razak		800	(800)		

Current liabilities

Bank overdraft	1,220			1,220
Trade payables	865	290		1,155
Tax payable	1,200	210		1,410
	3,285	500		3,785
Total equity and liabilities	19,533	4,540	(871)	23,202

Consolidated Statement of Financial Position

	£'000
Non-current assets	
Goodwill	8,826
Property, plant and equipment	10,720
Other financial assets	476
Current assets	
Inventories	1,750
Receivables	1,360
Bank	70
Total Assets	23,202
Equity	
£1 ordinary shares	2,800
Share premium account	7,400
Retained earnings	2,702
Non-controlling interests	2,012
Non-current liabilities	
Contingent consideration	1,715
Other	2,788
Current liabilities	
Bank overdraft	1,220
Trade payables	1,155
Tax payable	1,410
Total equity and liabilities	23,202

(W1) Group Structure

Razak's shareholding has increased from 15% to 80% therefore the investment should now be accounted for as a subsidiary.

(W2) Net Assets	SFP	Acquisition
	£'000	£'000
Share Capital	500	500
Retained Earnings	2,740	2,540
Fair Value adjustment	1,400	1,400
Depreciation (six months)	(140)	
Total	4,500	4,440
Since acquisition (4,500 – 4,440)		60

(W3) Goodwill	£'000
Original cost of 15% shares in Assulin	450
Revalue 15% shareholding to £16 per share at 30 Sept 20X1 to AFS	750
Revalue 15% shareholding to £20 per share at 31 March 20X2	300
Cost of 325,000 shares at £25 per share 31 March 20X2	8,125
Contingent consideration (£6 × 325,000 DCF 9% 2 years)	1,641
NCI at acquisition 100,000 shares × £20 per share	2,000
Total	13,266
Less: Net assets at acquisition including FV adjustment (W2)	(4,440)
Goodwill at acquisition	8,826

(W4) Non-Controlling Interest	£'000
At acquisition	2,000
Profit share of Assulin since acquisition (60 × 20%)	12
Total	2,012

(W5) Reserves

	Retained earnings	AFS reserve
	£'000	£'000
Razak per draft	2,510	750
Transfer from AFS to RE	750	(750)
Revalue 15% shareholding in Assulin at 31 March 20X2 (W3)	300	
Unwinding of contingent payment	(74)	
80% of Assulin's profit since acquisition (60 × 80%)	48	
Imposter – impairment of debt	(832)	
Total	2,702	

(W6) Imposter debt write off	£'000
Cost	1,200
Interest @15%	180
Interest received @6%	(72)
Carrying amount before impairment	1,308
PV of cash flows discounted for two years	
at 15%	476
Impairment	832

Proposed pension plan

Razak wishes to account for its proposed pension plan as a defined contribution scheme, probably because the accounting is more straightforward and the risk not reflected in the figures in the financial statements. However, although the entity's proposed plan has some features in common with a defined contribution plan, it needs to be considered whether this is really the case.

With defined contribution plans, the employer (and possibly, as proposed here, current employees too) pay regular contributions into the plan of a given or 'defined' amount each year. The contributions are invested, and the size of the post-employment benefits paid to former employees depends on how well or how badly the plan's investments perform. If the investments perform well, the plan will be able to afford higher benefits than if the investments performed less well.

With defined benefit plans, the size of the post-employment benefits is determined in advance, ie the benefits are 'defined'. The employer (and possibly, as proposed here, current employees too) pay contributions into the plan, and the contributions are invested. The size of the contributions is set at an amount that is expected to earn enough investment returns to meet the obligation to pay the post-employment benefits. If, however, it becomes apparent that the assets in the fund are insufficient, the employer will be required to make additional contributions into the plan to make up the expected shortfall. On the other hand, if the fund's assets appear to be larger than they need to be, and in excess of what is required to pay the post-employment benefits, the employer may be allowed to take a 'contribution holiday' (ie stop paying in contributions for a while).

The main difference between the two types of plans lies in who bears the risk: if the employer bears the risk, even in a small way by guaranteeing or specifying the return, the plan is a defined benefit plan. A defined contribution scheme must give a benefit formula based solely on the amount of the contributions.

Razak's scheme, as currently proposed, would be a defined benefit plan. Razak, the employer, would guarantee a pension based on the average pay of the employees in the scheme. The entity's liability would not be limited to the amount of the contributions to the plan, but would be supplemented by an insurance premium which the insurance company can increase if required in order to fulfil the plan obligations. The trust fund which the insurance company builds up, is in turn dependent on the yield on investments. If the insurer has insufficient funds to pay the guaranteed pension, Razak has to make good the deficit. Indirectly, through insurance premiums, the employer bears the investment risk. The employee's contribution, on the other hand is fixed.

A further indication that Razak would bear the risk is the provision that if an employee leaves Razak and transfers the pension to another fund, Razak would be liable for, or would be refunded the difference between the benefits the employee is entitled to and the insurance premiums paid. Razak would thus have a legal or constructive obligation to make good the shortfall if the insurance company does not pay all future employee benefits relating to employee service in the current and prior periods.

In conclusion, even though the insurance company would limit some of the risk, Razak, rather than its employees, would **bear** the risk, so this would be a defined benefit plan.

12 Melton plc

Marking guide

		Technical	Skills
		Marks	
(a)	Up to 1 mark for each valid point	4	4
(b)	Appropriate ratios and comparatives	4	5
	Other points		
(c)	Up to 1 mark for each valid point	4	4
(d)	Up to 1 mark for each valid point	4	5
Available		16	18
Maximum			30

For more guidance on how skills are tested and rewarded, please refer to the section at the start of this question bank.

Notes for Meeting of Investment Team

(a) **Diluted earnings per share**

Information that helps users of financial statements make predictions of future earnings and cash flows is very useful. The diluted EPS disclosure provides additional information regarding the future of the basic EPS amount, in that it relates current earnings to a possible future capital structure.

Where financial instruments have been issued by a company which will potentially lead to the issue of further new equity shares, the earnings will be shared by more equity shares. In some cases earnings themselves will be directly affected by the issue of the shares, in other cases, they will not. The diluted EPS figure shows how the current earnings of the company, as adjusted for any profit effect of the issue of the new shares, would be diluted, or shared out amongst the future, potential new shares as well as the current shares. This gives the current shareholders an idea of the effect that these dilutive financial instruments could have on their shareholding in the future.

However, there are limitations to the use of these figures

- The diluted EPS is based upon the current earnings figure, as adjusted for any profit effect of the issue of the new shares. This earnings figure may not be relevant in future years. What is more important is the level of earnings at the time conversion actually takes place.

- Also, the calculation assumes a worst case scenario, that all potential diluting financial instruments will be exercised. It may be that future events do not unfold like this. For example, holders of convertible debt may choose to redeem rather than convert their debt or share options issued may lapse if the holders leave the company or there are adverse future movements in the share price.

The diluted EPS is therefore a 'warning' to existing shareholders about potential future events. It is not a forecast of future earnings. Shareholders often find it helpful to calculate the P/E ratio based on diluted EPS to show the potential valuation effects.

(b) **Analysis of performance of Melton plc**

Further ratios could be calculated. For example –

	20X7	20X6
Performance ratios		
Operating profit % (3,200 as % of 37,780) and (2,610 as % of 29,170)	8.5%	8.9%
Gross profit – existing outlets (87 as % of 354) and (83 as % of 343)	24.6%	24.2%
Gross profit – new outlets(69 as % of 256)	26.9%	–
Administration expenses % (6,240 as % of 37,780) and (4,480 as % of 29,170)	16.5%	15.4%
Depreciation and amortisation as % of (cost of sales + administration expenses) – (3,060 as % of (28,340 + 6,240)) and (2,210 as % of (22,080 + 4,480))	8.8%	8.3%
Cash flow and liquidity ratios		
Interest cover (3,200/410) and (2,610/420)	7.8 times	6.2 times
Cash interest cover (6,450/410) and (4,950/440)	15.7 times	11.3 times
Cash generated from operations as % of operating profit (6,450 as % of 3,200) and (4,950 as % of 2,610)	202%	190%
EBITDA/interest expense (6,260/410) and (4,820/420)	15.3 times	11.5 times
Investor ratios		
P/E ratio (302/26.8) and (290/21.3)	11.3 times	13.6 times
P/E ratio (based on diluted EPS) (302/21.2) and (290/19.2)	14.2 times	15.1 times

(Credit will be given for other ratios; the basis of the calculation should be given.)

Introduction

A first look at the information indicates that the group has grown significantly during 20X7. Revenues have increased by 29.5% ((37,780/29,170) – 1) and operating profits by 22.6% ((3,200/2,610) – 1). However, the additional information shows that there have been structural changes in the business with a 35% ((30/(115 – 30)) – 1) increase in the number of outlets that have opened. These structural changes will need to be considered in determining the performance of the business.

A review of the statement of cash flows shows strong operating cash flows. However, these cash flows are being reinvested in new outlet openings (through capital expenditure). The group's objective is to limit its new debt financing but this may be hindering the availability of distributions to investors.

Profitability

Revenue has grown by 29.5% during the year. For existing outlets (those open at 30 September 20X6) growth during the year has been 3.0% ((354/343) – 1). The real rate of growth may be lower than this as some outlets may have only been open for part of the previous year (ie 20X7 is first full year of opening).

This rate of 'organic' growth is disappointing and below the sector average of 4.1%. It may be that Melton only operates in a part of this sector which has a different growth rate that management are concentrating on new outlets.

Gross profit margins have grown year on year from 24.3% to 25.0%. However, the segmental analysis shows that gross margins from existing outlets have only improved marginally to 24.6% and the new outlets have far better gross margins at 26.7%. This could be due to:

- The locations of the new outlets in more profitable sites or
- Strong promotional activities of new outlets in their initial phase or
- Older outlets require refitting or advertising support or
- Management focusing on new outlets to the detriment of older ones

Revenue per employee has grown from £37,900 to £41,100. This is an increase of 8.4%. This is significant as wage costs will be a major cost for the business. It may be that new working practices have reduced employee numbers or that staff numbers (eg admin) do not increase linearly with the number of outlet openings.

Administration costs as a percentage of revenue have increased significantly from 15.4% to 16.5%. These costs have increased by approximately £1.8 million. The list of key issues for Melton did not mention operating costs and this may not have been the focus of management's attention. Alternatively, investment in administration may have been made with a view to further expansion.

Melton has a reputation for 'under depreciating' assets. Some support for this is indicated by the losses on disposal in both years (see statement of cash flows). The depreciation rates are inconsequential when considering the cash flow which is strong (see below). Depreciation is 8.8% of the total of costs of sales and administrative expenses but it is growing significantly (up from 8.3% and from £2.21 million to £3.06 million) and any future change in estimates could significantly affect profit.

EBITDA has improved significantly, mainly because of better absolute profit figures due to the continuing expansion. EBITDA is strong and confirms the strong cash flows (see below).

The return on capital employed (ROCE) has improved from 19.1% to 20.0% giving the indication that the overall efficiency of management in employing the resources of the group has improved. Operating cash flows are strong and net capital employed has only increased by a small amount as the capital expenditure is almost covered by the operating cash flow. Resources have been well managed. However, this should be viewed against the fact that no dividend has been paid.

Non-current asset turnover supports the assertion that management have managed the assets well. It has improved and the assets have been sweated harder.

Interest costs in the statement of profit or loss have reduced slightly (by £10,000) but the statement of cash flows shows that net debt (new borrowings less cash increase) has increased. This may be a result of the timing of the cash flows (in particular capital expenditure and new outlet openings) during the year.

Cash flow (and changes in financial position)

The improvement in ROCE is supported by the increase in the cash return on capital employed to 40.2%. As expected it is higher than traditional ROCE as that ratio takes into account depreciation and amortisation. The cash return on capital employed suggests that cash flow is strong and capital has been well managed. It appears that the objective of funding growth from existing cash flows is being achieved and this is having a positive effect on performance statistics.

This is supported by the interest cover (7.8 times), which demonstrates the strong financial position and the possibility of further growth through borrowing if necessary.

Other measures of interest are also strong – cash interest cover is 15.7 times and EBITDA/interest is 15.3 times. Both have improved as new outlet openings have improved operating cash flows whilst net debt has not changed significantly.

The cash flows show that the quality of operating profits is strong. Cash generated from operations as a percentage of profit from operations is over 200% and improving year on year. The concerns about depreciation should only improve this ratio if depreciation increased.

The current ratio is low at 0.56 times but this may not be unusual in an industry where customers will pay cash for their products and cash flow will be almost immediate. However, cash is high, and probably inventory, which may indicate a high paybles balance.

The trade payable period has fallen but the absolute amount of trade payables has increased. This will be due to the expansion of the business. Trade payables will be principally for sourcing goods and possibly lease rentals. It may be due to changes in payment patterns as the number of outlets expand.

Investor ratios

EPS has grown by 25.8% ((26.8/21.3) – 1) but diluted EPS has only increased by 10.4% ((21.2/19.2) – 1). This is potentially a concern. There appear to be some diluting instruments in issue that are having a potential adverse effect on future earnings. This could affect the future movements in market price.

The P/E ratio has fallen. This may be in line with general trends in share prices or may be as a result of investor disappointment. The company is not paying a dividend and investors may be unhappy about this. The policy of reinvestment of cash flows limits dividend payments without taking on more debt.

Further matters for investigation

- Further analysis of revenue – is there true 'like for like' growth and what was the timing of the outlet openings in the prior year?

- Locations of new outlet openings and product offerings to understand the higher margins on new against older outlets.

- Non-current asset disclosure information – to determine the depreciation and amortisation policies and quantify the potential effect of any differences from industry averages.

- Analysis of capital expenditure between expenditure on existing and new outlets to determine profile of ongoing replacement expenditure required by the business.

- Dividend policy – shareholders will undoubtedly demand a return on their investment. The operating and financial review may indicate dividend and financing policy.

- Details of future outlet openings and planned levels of capital expenditure.

- An analysis of employee numbers by function and details of any changes in working practices to understand the strong increase in revenue per employee.

- Details of administration costs changes – are there any non-recurring items disclosed in the notes or any details of costs in the Operating & Financial Review/Management Commentary?

- Details of the tax charge and the tax reconciliation should be reviewed in the notes to the financial statements to understand why it is low (21.9% (610 as % of 2,790)) and the year on year change.

- Receivables have increased significantly. As almost all sales will be for cash, this needs investigation.

- Details of the potential diluting financial instruments (terms, timing etc) that may affect future EPS.

(c) **Payment of dividend**

Distributable profits (the profits that are legally distributable to investors) are determined as the accumulated realised profits less accumulated realised losses of an entity. Generally they equate to the retained earnings of an entity.

However, the legality of a dividend distribution is determined by the distributable profits in the separate financial statements (of a single company) rather than by the consolidated retained earnings.

A company may have a debit balance on its consolidated retained earnings (for example due to losses in subsidiaries) but it may have a credit balance on its own retained earnings which would allow the payment of a dividend to the parent company's shareholders.

In addition, a public company may not make a distribution if this reduces its net assets below the total of called-up share capital and undistributable reserves. In effect any net unrealised accumulated losses must be deducted from the net realised accumulated profits.

The colleague's comment is incorrect and further investigation is needed to determine why no dividends have been paid or proposed.

(d) **Proposed sale of stake in R. T. Café**

The director proposes to sell 2,000 of Melton's 8,000 shares in R.T. Café, which has a share capital of 10,000 shares, in January 20X8. In doing so it would be selling a 20% shareholding and going from an 80% stake to a 60% stake. R. T. Café would remain a subsidiary. In substance, under IFRS 3 *Business Combinations* there would be no disposal. This is simply a transaction between group shareholders, with the parent (Melton) selling a 20% stake to the non-controlling interest.

The transaction would be dealt with by increasing the non-controlling interest in the statement of financial position, which has effectively doubled from 20% to 40% and recording an adjustment to the parent's equity.

The formula used to calculate the adjustment to equity at disposal is:

	£'000
Consideration received	X
Increase in NCI on disposal (NCI in assets at disposal date × 20%/20%]	(X)
Adjustment to parent's equity (**to be credited to group retained earnings**)	X

Since the adjustment is recognised in retained earnings rather than profit for the year, there would be no impact on earnings per share.

13 Ultratherma

Marking guide

			Marks
		Technical	*Skills*
1	Explanations and ratios:		
	Liquidity	2	1
	Profitability	2	2
	Gearing	2	2
	Cash generation	2	2
	Cash generation	2	1
	Conclusion	1	2
2	Explanations and calculations:		
	Growth	1	–
	Profitability	2	2
	Interest cover	2	3
	Working capital management	1	–
	Inventories	3	2
	Revised forcasts	3	3
	Conclusion	1	2
Total marks		24	22

Maximum 30

For more guidance on how skills are tested and rewarded, please refer to the section at the start of this question bank.

1   **Report**

To: ABC Bank
From: An Accountant on behalf of Asha Kapoor and Hugh Evans
Date: 14 June 20X6
Subject: Ultratherma trading performance for 20X5 and 20X6

This report looks at the trading performance of Ultratherma over the two full periods of trading from incorporation on 1 July 20X4: nine months to 31 March 20X5 and the year to 31 March 20X6. A detailed breakdown of ratios is given in an appendix to this report and these are generally based on the standard ratio table.

Liquidity

The current ratio has risen slightly from 0.94 to 0.98, but the quick ratio has fallen from 0.71 to 0.58 as a result of the substantial lengthening of the inventory turnover period. In addition, the overdraft has

Interestingly, Aroma is paying its suppliers more quickly in 20X1 ie taking on average 32 days as opposed to 53 days in 20X0. This seems inadvisable given that a significant overdraft has arisen in the current year. Aroma should take full advantage of the credit period offered by their suppliers. It may be that they are sourcing from a new supplier with stricter credit terms to fulfil the hotel contract.

Solvency

Even though the bank is refusing further funding, Aroma's gearing, despite a small increase in the year, remains at a manageable level (38% in the current year). Furthermore, Aroma can easily afford to pay the interest on its debt as illustrated by an interest cover of 13.6 in the current year.

Conclusion

On initial analysis, there seems to be a strong case for investing in Aroma. The business is growing and innovative having just expanded into 2 new areas with the online store and new hotel contract due to the skills of the new sales director. It is also profitable and the profitability is improving year on year. Perhaps the only concern is reliance on the overdraft but this can be resolved by improving working capital management and ensuring that the full credit period of suppliers is taken advantage of. With further new initiatives from the sales director such as new contracts with other hotel chains and further growth of online sales, there is potential for even more growth in the future.

One issue to raise, however, is whether the owner-managers are using a cash investment – and have tried to increase the overdraft – in order to pay themselves excessive dividends. However profitable the company, this needs clarification before any investment is made.

Appendix

	20X1	20X0
Return on capital employed = PBIT/(Debt + Equity – Investments)	$\dfrac{540+43}{412+68+1,272}=33.3\%$	$\dfrac{307+34}{404+1,160}-21.8\%$
Asset turnover = Revenue/total assets	$\dfrac{6,000}{2,115}=2.84$	$\dfrac{3,700}{1,942}=1.91$
Gross margin = Gross profit/revenue	$\dfrac{1,917}{6,000}=32.0\%$	$\dfrac{1,110}{3,700}=30\%$
Gross margin of retail operations	$\dfrac{1,200}{4,004}=30.0\%$	
Gross margin of online store	$\dfrac{330}{1,096}=30.1\%$	
Gross margin of hotel contract	$\dfrac{387}{900}=43\%$	
Operating profit margin = PBIT/revenue	$\dfrac{540+43}{6,000}=9.7\%$	$\dfrac{307+34}{3,700}=9.2\%$
Net margin = PBT/revenue	$\dfrac{540}{6,000}=9\%$	$\dfrac{307}{3,700}=8.3\%$
Net margin of retail operations	$\dfrac{320}{4,004}=8.0\%$	
Net margin of online store	$\dfrac{138}{1,096}=12.6\%$	
Net margin of hotel contract	$\dfrac{82}{900}=9.1\%$	
Current ratio = Current assets/current liabilities	$\dfrac{1,715}{431}=3.98$	$\dfrac{1,532}{378}=4.05$

	20X1	20X0
Quick ratio =	$\dfrac{1,715-1,260}{431}=1.06$	$\dfrac{1,532-1,180}{378}=0.93$
(Current assets – inventories)/current liabilities		
Inventory days =	$\dfrac{1,260}{4,083}\times365=113\,\text{days}$	$\dfrac{1,180}{2,590}\times365=166\,\text{days}$
(Inventories/cost of sales) × 365		
Receivable days =	$\dfrac{455}{6,000}\times365=28\,\text{days}$	$\dfrac{310}{3,700}\times365=31\,\text{days}$
(Receivables/revenue) × 365		
Payable days =	$\dfrac{363}{4,083}\times365=32\,\text{days}$	$\dfrac{378}{2,590}\times365=53\,\text{days}$
(Payables/cost of sales) × 365		
Gearing =	$\dfrac{412+68}{1,272}=38\%$	$\dfrac{404+68}{1,160}=35\%$
Debt/Equity		
Interest cover =	$\dfrac{540+43}{43}=13.6$	$\dfrac{307+34}{34}=10.0$
PBIT/interest expense		

15 Kenyon

Marking guide

	Marks	
	Technical	Skills
Financial performance discussion and ratios		
Profitability	3	4
Earnings per share	3	3
Contingent liability	2	1
Pension	1	2
Financial position discussion and ratios		
Liquidity	3	3
Working capital management	3	2
Conclusion and recommendation		
Contingent liability – impact on ratios	2	2
Contingent liability – further information	2	2
Total marks	19	19

Maximum	30

For more guidance on how skills are tested and rewarded, please refer to the section at the start of this question bank.

Report

To: Gary Watson
From: Investment Analyst
Date: X-XX-XXX
Subject: Kenyon plc

(a) **Analysis**

    Introduction

    This is an analysis of the financial performance and position of Kenyon plc (an operator of bottle plants) for the year to 31 October 20X1 in the context of whether or not it would make a good investment.

Financial performance

Kenyon plc's revenue has grown in the year by 43%. This is due to a combination of increased volume of sales to existing customers and a new contract secured at the start of the year.

This increased volume has not been at the cost of profitability, which has improved in the year with return on capital employed increasing from 26% to 48%. This is due to both **improved efficiency in using non-current assets** to generate revenue (non-current asset turnover has increased from 1.34 to 1.74) and **improved margins** (see below).

Kenyon plc's gross profit margin has improved from 32% to 40% implying an improvement in how Kenyon management is running its core operations. This could well be due to a **higher selling price** under the new contract compared to the existing contracts. Alternatively there may have been some **production efficiencies**.

The operating profit margin has improved in line with the gross margin (32% in 20X1; 24% in 20X0). However administration expenses have increased by more proportionately than other expenses or revenue implying some cost control issues with overheads.

The investment in the associate partway through the year was a **good investment**, generating a return of 12.5%, (7/56).

The investment income has declined significantly in the year in relation to the falling cash balance. The fall in the cash balance is discussed below.

The earnings per share has improved from 31 cents to 58.7 cents in line with the improved profitability above. However, although the share price has increased in absolute terms from £2.80 to £4.90, the **P/E ratio has deteriorated** from 9.03 to 8.35. This implies decreased market confidence in Kenyon plc despite its increased volume and profitability. This is likely to be for 2 main reasons:

(i)   There is a **contingent liability** relating to a court case pending against Kenyon plc as a result of a chemical leak shortly before the year end. The lawyers believe that Kenyon plc is likely to lose the case but the amount of potential damages cannot be reliably estimated. The decline in P/E ratio indicates that the market is concerned about the impact that the loss of this case could have on the future profitability of Kenyon plc. In a worst case scenario, Kenyon plc's **going concern could be called into doubt.**

(ii) The net pension liability which must relate to a defined benefit pension scheme has increased from £5m to £38m indicating a **serious deficit** in the scheme. This will undoubtedly result in increased contributions in the year ended 31 October 20X2, however, the amount is unknown. This is another uncertainty likely to have an impact on the share price.

A cash-seeking investor would have been happy with the £100m dividend paid in 20X1 (57% of profit for the year).

Financial position

There has been a significant **decline in liquidity** in the year as illustrated by the fall in the quick ratio from 1.64 to 0.79 and the fall in the cash balance from £60m to £3m. Arguably Kenyon plc were wrong to keep such a large balance of cash in 20X0 as better returns could usually be earned elsewhere. This could be the reason for the investment in the associate in 20X1 which is generating a healthy 12.5% return. Kenyon plc has also invested in non-current assets in the year which will be good for future growth.

Working capital management has deteriorated slightly. Inventory days have nearly doubled from 46 to 79 days. This could be deliberate in terms of building up inventory levels to meet increased demand from existing and new contracts. However, Kenyon plc will be incurring significant holding costs and there is a risk in light of bad publicity from the court case, that Kenyon plc will be unable to sell all of the inventory, resulting in a write down.

Receivable days have seen a slight increase from 38 days to 40 days but it seems that Kenyon plc's credit control function is working efficiently. If may be that longer than standard credit terms were awarded under the new contract.

Payable days have increased from 76 to 88 days. Whilst it is advisable to take advantage of free credit, Kenyon plc must be careful not to alienate their suppliers as it could ultimately result in **withdrawal of credit** or even supplies.

Conclusion

Kenyon plc's growth and profitability make it an attractive investment proposition. However, there are two significant uncertainties making it a risky investment:

- A pending court case which Kenyon plc is **likely to lose**
- A **large pension deficit** and future contributions to make good the deficit are uncertain

It would be advisable to wait until the amount of likely damages from the court case and the increase in contributions to the pension scheme are known before making a final decision on whether or not to invest.

(b) (i) **Best and worst case potential impact of the contingent liability**

The lawyers have estimated the potential damages as being between £7 million and £13 million. The amount cannot be measured reliably, as there is no information available as to the likelihood of either outcome. However, it might be useful to consider the best and worst case scenarios of the potential impact on selected key ratios.

The results (see appendix) can be summarised as follows:

Ratio	No liability recognised	Liability of £13m recognised	Liability of £7m recognised.
ROCE	48%	46%	47%
Operating margin	32%	30%	31%
EPS	58.7p	54.3p	56.3p

The potential effect on profitability ratios is only slight, with ROCE decreasing by 2% if the liability is £13m and only 1% if it is £7m and the operating margins showing the same variation. The fall in EPS is proportionally greater, but not such as to deter an investor. The main concern is as yet unquantifiable, and relates to the bad publicity that could arise from the negative outcome of the court case, and the potential future effect on sales.

(ii) **Further information regarding the contingent liability**

(1) The report resulting from the investigation into the potential environmental damage from the chemical spill to try and ascertain the likelihood of Kenyon plc losing the case and the **possible damages** they might have to pay

(2) Whether the chemical leak caused damage to the buildings, machinery and inventories and whether a **write down** was needed at the year end and if so, for how much

(3) How the incident has been reported in the press to ascertain the potential **damage to Kenyon plc's reputation** and subsequent **loss of business**

(4) Post year-end sales orders to ascertain **potential loss of business** as a knock-on effect from the spill

(5) Whether the plant has been repaired and is still in working order to ascertain ability to keep operating at the same capacity in the future

(6) Whether safeguards have been put in place to prevent it from happening again/in other plants

(7) Details of the length of the new contract, other contracts in place which expire soon and future contracts under negotiation?

Appendix

Key ratios (excluding potential impact of contingent liability)

All workings in £m	20X1	20X0
$\text{ROCE} = \dfrac{\text{PBIT}}{\text{Equity}+\text{debt}-\text{investments}}$	$\dfrac{221-1-7}{465+38-56}=48\%$	$\dfrac{117-6}{423+5}=26\%$

All workings in £m	20X1	20X0
Gross margin = Gross profit/revenue	268/663 = 40%	148/463 = 32%
Operating margin = Operating profit/revenue	$\dfrac{221-1-7}{663}=32\%$	$\dfrac{117-6}{463}=24\%$
EPS = Profit for year/weighted average no of equity shares (Note: 50 cent shares)	176/300 = 58.7c	93/300 = 31c
P/E ratio = Price per share/EPS	490/58.7 = 8.35	280/31 = 9.03
Non-current asset turnover = Revenue/non-current assets	663/381 = 1.74	463/346 = 1.34
Quick ratio = (Current assets – inventories)/Current liabilities	(161 – 86)/95 = 0.79	(148 – 40)/66 = 1.64
Inventory days = Inventory/cost of sales × 365	86/395 × 365 = 79 days	40/315 × 365 = 46 days
Receivable days = Receivables/revenue × 365	72/663 × 365 = 40 days	48/463 × 365 = 38 days
Payable days = Payables/cost of sales × 365	95/395 × 365 = 88 days	66/315 × 365 = 76 days

Selected key ratios (including potential impact of contingent liability)

All workings in £m	Damages of £13m	Damages of £7m
ROCE = $\dfrac{\text{PBIT}}{\text{Equity}+\text{debt}-\text{investments}}$	$\dfrac{221-1-7-13}{465-13+38-56}=46\%$	$\dfrac{221-1-7-7}{465-7+38-56}=47\%$
Operating margin = Operating profit/revenue	$\dfrac{221-1-7-13}{663}=30\%$	$\dfrac{221-1-7-7}{663}=31\%$
EPS = Profit for year/weighted average no of equity shares (Note: 50 cent shares)	176 – 13/300 = 54.3p	176 – 7/300 = 56.3p

16 Johnson Telecom

		Technical	Skills	Marks
(a)	**Treatments**			
	Disposal of Cole	1	2	
	Hedge re International Energy	2	3	
	Acquisition of Routers	1	2	
	Loan note and swap	1	1	
(b)	**Hedging**			
	Explanation of hedging principles	2	2	
	Draft hedging documentation	2	1	
	Note independence issues	1	1	
(c)	**Key risks and internal controls**			
	1 mark for each risk/control identified and explained	2	7	
(d)	**Audit evidence**			
	1 mark for each piece of evidence, maximum of	2	7	
Total marks		14	26	
Maximum				**40**

For more guidance on how skills are tested and rewarded, please refer to the section at the start of this question bank.

MEMORANDUM

To: Annette Douglas
From: Poppy Posgen
Date: 7 February 20X8
Subject: Year-end reporting of financial instruments at Johnson Telecom

Accounting treatment of financial instruments

1   **Disposal of equity investment in Cole plc**

- 50,000 shares initially recorded at cost of £163,000

- The fair value (FV) at 31 December 20X6 was £230,000, hence £67,000 gains accumulated in AFS reserve

- As the investment was classified as available-for-sale (AFS), it was correct to adjust its carrying amount to fair value at bid price at each reporting date

- The journal correctly removed the FV of the investment from the statement of financial position and recorded a gain on disposal of £12,000 (£242,000 – £230,000).

However, holding gains of £67,000 remain in the AFS reserve. These need to be reclassified from the reserve to profit or loss, giving a total profit or loss impact of £79,000 (£67,000 + £12,000).

The following journal is required to transfer the holding gains from the AFS reserve to profit or loss:

	£'000	£'000
Dr AFS reserve	67	
Cr Profit or loss		67

2   **Investment in Routers plc**

8 November 20X7

- 16,000 shares out of 50,000 shares were acquired, giving Johnson Telecom a holding of 32%. Routers plc should therefore be treated as an investment, not as a subsidiary.

- The investment in Routers plc has been recorded at the offer price of £5.83.

- Acquisition of 16,000 shares should have been initially recorded at bid price of £5.80 per share, a cost of £92,800.

- The bid-offer spread of 3p reflects the transaction cost and as the investment is classed as fair value through profit or loss, this cost of £480 should have been expensed to profit or loss for the year.

- The journal entry to adjust for the transaction cost is as follows:

	£'000	£'000
Dr Profit or loss	0.48	
Cr Investment		0.48

31 December 20X7

- In addition, as the investment is classed as at fair value through profit or loss, the investment should have been re-measured to its fair value at the year end.

- The year-end bid price is £5.85. The fair value of the investment at the year end should therefore be £93,600, with a gain of £800 being recorded in profit or loss

	£'000	£'000
Dr Investment	0.8	
Cr Profit or loss		0.8

3   **Hedged investment in International Energy plc**

Eligibility to apply special hedge accounting rules

In order to apply special hedge accounting rules, IAS 39 requires that the hedge be designated and documented at inception, and the effectiveness of the hedge to be tested at least every reporting date. As there is currently no documentation to support the hedge, Johnson will not be permitted to apply hedge accounting. IAS 39 does not permit documentation to be backdated, nor for hedge accounting to be applied retrospectively.

It is therefore incorrect to apply hedge accounting rules.

Equity investment in International Energy

- Since hedge accounting has been applied, the loss on revaluating the investment has been charged to profit or loss. Reversing hedge accounting would require an adjusting entry to transfer the loss to the AFS reserve.

- 30,000 shares measured at FV at 31 December 20X6 are valued at £255,000 (£8.50 per share), and £228,000 at 31 December 20X7 based on bid price of £7.60 per share.

- Without applying special hedge accounting rules, the loss of £27,000 is recognised in the AFS reserve in the statement of equity, as follows:

	£'000	£'000
Dr AFS Reserve	27	
Cr Investment		27

The journal required to reverse the hedge accounting is:

	£'000	£'000
Dr AFS Reserve	27	
Cr Profit or loss		27

Put options

- The put options are initially measured at cost and re-measured to fair value at each reporting date

- The original cost of the put options was £60,000 (30,000 @ £2.00). At the year end, the fair value of the options is £72,000 (30,000 @ £2.40)

- The £12,000 fair value gain is recorded in profit or loss irrespective of the application of hedge accounting rules:

	£'000	£'000
Dr Derivative asset	12	
Cr Profit or loss		12

No adjustment is required.

4 Investment in Spence & May bonds

Year-end disposal of 50% of holding

- The journal entry recording the disposal of the 50% holding neglected the gain arising from the disposal. As the supporting workings correctly calculate, the amortised cost of the debt investment sold was £72,227 (£144,454/2), giving a gain of £10,773 to be taken to the profit or loss, as follows.

		£'000	£'000
Dr	Cash	83	
Cr	Profit or loss		10.8
Cr	Debt investment		72.2

The journal entry to adjust for this error is as follows:

		£'000	£'000
Dr	Debt investment	10.8	
Cr	Profit or loss		10.8

Tainting of remaining holding

- The tainting of the remaining holding as a result of the disposal at the year end has not been recorded or considered.

- The disposal of a significant proportion of a held-to-maturity (HTM) asset before maturity results in the entire HTM category becoming tainted for the next two years.

- The remaining debt investment must be transferred from HTM to the available-for-sale category.

- This results in the remaining investment of £72,200 being fair valued to £83,000, with the corresponding gain being recognised in equity.

		£'000	£'000
Dr	Debt investment	10.8	
Cr	AFS reserve		10.8

5   Loan note and interest rate swap

- The treatment of the interest rate swap appears to be correct. However, the accounting note made no mention of the effectiveness of the swap, a factor upon which the appropriateness of hedge accounting depends. (Please see Audit evidence section below.)

Hedge accounting rules and hedging principles

Hedging principles

- The fair value of the derivative is comprised of an intrinsic value (exercise price less share price) and a time value, based on the period to expiry of the option

- Where the share price is higher than the exercise price, the intrinsic value is zero as the put option is out-of-the-money and will not be exercised

- At acquisition, the share price was £9 (30,000 shares with a total cost of £270,000). The exercise price of the put option was also £9. The intrinsic value is therefore zero

- At the year end, the fair value of an option is £2.40 representing an intrinsic value of £1.40 (£9-£7.60) and a time value of £1

- The share price has fallen by £1.40 since acquisition and this is exactly matched by the increase in the intrinsic value of the options from zero to £1.40. Hence it can be seen that the intrinsic element of the option provides a highly effective hedge for the change in fair value of the share price below £9.00

- It can be seen that the hedge constitutes a "fair value hedge" as the option is protecting against movements in the fair value of the recognised equity investments below £9

Tutorial note:

The company does not have to designate only the changes in the intrinsic value of the option as the hedging instrument: it could in fact designate the changes in the total fair value of the option as the hedging instrument instead. However, in this case the hedge would not be effective.

Fair value hedge accounting

Without applying hedge accounting, a mismatch would arise: the gain on the options and the loss on the associated investment are not recorded in the same financial statement. While the gain on the options is recorded in profit or loss, the loss on the investment is charged to other comprehensive income. Hedge accounting prevents such a mismatch.

- The derivative would be accounted for as normal, ie fair valued through profit or loss resulting in a gain of £12,000. This could be analysed as:

    - Gain on the intrinsic value change of £27,000 (90p × 30,000)
    - Loss on the time value change of £15,000 (50p × 30,000)

- The £27,000 loss arising on the FV movement in the shares would be hedged by the gain arising on the increase in the intrinsic value of the options of £27,000.

- Special hedge accounting rules would therefore require this loss on the shares to be matched in profit or loss against the gain on the intrinsic element of the options, rather than being recorded in the AFS reserve in equity.

- The net effect on profit or loss for the year would be to show a loss of £15,000, reflecting the change in the time value of the options.

Hedge documentation: International Energy plc

As discussed above, the hedging documentation cannot be prepared retrospectively. The following is therefore for reference only. We should make clear to the Directors that they must use the documentation to support the hedge in question. As stated, hedge accounting should not be applied in this case.

Hedge No.	X
Date	7 February 20X8

Risk management objective and strategy:	

The investment in the equity of International Energy plc is exposed to fluctuations in the market value. To hedge exposure of a decline in share price, management has entered into a put option over the entire holding.

Hedge type	Fair value
Hedged risk	Market risk that share price falls below £9.00

Hedged item

Investment in holding of 30,000 equity shares in International Energy plc

Hedging instrument

Put option in 30,000 equity shares in International Energy plc at an exercise price of £9.00 exercisable until 31 December 20X8

Hedge effectiveness

Monitor on a quarterly basis comparing change in intrinsic value of options to change in share price where price falls below £9.00

From an ethical perspective, the preparation of documents for financial reporting purposes on behalf of the client would constitute a self-review risk. We should explain to the client that due to our obligation to remain independent, we are unable to prepare supporting documentation for the financial statements.

<u>Risks from derivatives trading</u>

Key risks

There are a number of concerns that we should address as auditors.

- Credit risk is the risk that a customer or counterparty will not settle an obligation for full value. This risk will arise from the potential for a counterparty to default on its contractual obligations and it is limited to the positive fair value of instruments that are favourable to the company.

- Legal risk relates to losses resulting from a legal or regulatory action that invalidates or otherwise precludes performance by the end user or its counterparty under the terms of the contract or related netting agreements.

- Market risk relates to economic losses due to adverse changes in the fair value of the derivative. These movements could be in the interest rates, the foreign exchange rates or equity prices.

- Settlement risk relates to one side of a transaction settling without value being received from the counterparty.

- Solvency risk is the risk that the entity would not have the funds to honour cash outflow commitments as they fall due. It is sometimes referred to as liquidity risk. This risk may be caused by market disruptions or a credit downgrade which may cause certain sources of funding to dry up immediately.

Necessary general controls and application controls

Tutorial note

This answer assumes that a computer system is used in processing trades involving derivatives.

General controls

A number of general controls may be relevant:

- For credit risk, general controls may include ensuring that off-market derivative contracts are only entered into with counterparties from a specific list and establishing credit limits for all customers

- For legal risk, a general control may be to ensure that all transactions are reviewed by properly qualified lawyers and regulation specialists

- For market risk, a general control may be to set strict investment acceptance criteria and ensure that these are adhered to

- For settlement risk, a general control may be to set up a third party through whom settlement takes place, ensuring that the third party is instructed not to give value until value has been received

- For solvency (liquidity) risk, general controls may include having diversified funding sources, managing assets with liquidity in mind, monitoring liquidity positions, and maintaining a healthy cash and cash equivalents balance

Application controls

These include the following:

- A computer application may identify the credit risk. In this case an appropriate control may be monitoring credit exposure, limiting transactions with an identified counterparty and stopping any further risk-increasing transactions with that counterparty

- For legal risk, an application control may be for the system not to process a transaction/trade until an authorised person has signed into the system to give the authority. Such an authorised person may be different depending on the nature and type of transaction. In some cases it may be the company specialist solicitor, or the dealer's supervisor

- For market risk, an application control may be to carry out mark-to-market activity frequently and to produce timely exception management reports

- For settlement risk, an application control may be a computer settlement system refusing to release funds/assets until the counterparty's value has been received or an authorised person has confirmed to the system that there is evidence that value will be received

- For solvency risk, an application control may be that the system will produce a report for management informing management that there needs to be a specific amount of funds available on a given date to settle the trades coming in for settlement on that date.

In addition to the above, a fraud risk arises because the Financial Director – who has maintained the accounting records for the derivatives almost single-handedly – also appears to be the only person within the company familiar with the accounting treatment for the financial instruments (Including the derivatives). An effective system of internal controls will go some way to mitigate the fraud risk, but an informed management with an adequate understanding of derivatives and hedge accounting is crucial.

Audit evidence

The additional audit evidence that we will need to obtain with regards to the financial instruments includes the following:

Equity investments

- Confirmations from management regarding the basis on which the year end valuation of the equity investments were made

- Information from third-party pricing sources regarding the fair value of the investments (including details of valuation techniques, assumptions and inputs)

- Observable market prices at the year end for comparison

- Supporting documentation (board meeting minutes, accounting notes produced by the Treasury department) to support the classification of the investments in Cole plc and International Energy plc as AFS

- Details of controls that management has in place to assess the reliability of information from third-party pricing sources

- For the disposal of the investment in Cole plc, the sale agreement to support the disposal value of £242,000 and bank statement to confirm the receipt of the consideration

- For the acquisition of the investment in Routers plc, documentation (sale agreement, valuation documentation) to support the purchase price; bank statement and sale documentation to confirm the payment of the consideration.

Hedged investment in International Energy plc

- Copy of the put option agreement, and back office report confirming the processing of the put option

- Statement from the clearing agents confirming the details of the options

- Third-party pricing sources to support the fair value of the options

- (As discussed above, hedge accounting is not expected to be applied, as the hedge documentation has been lost and the criteria for hedge accounting have therefore not been met.)

Investment in Spence & May bonds

- Copy of the purchase agreement for the initial purchase of the bonds

- Board meeting minutes or internal analysis supporting the classification of the bonds as held to maturity

- Sale agreement for the disposal of the bonds during the year

- Bank statements supporting interest payments and disposal proceeds

Loan note and interest rate swap

- Copy of the loan documentation

- Copy of the interest rate swap agreement

- Counterparty and broker confirmations agreeing the details of the interest rate swap

- Copy of the hedging documentation for the files

- Supporting workings analyzing the effectiveness of the swap as a hedge, including an explanation of the method used and any assumptions made

- Bank statements showing the interest payments on the loan and the interest receipts from the swap

- Supporting documentation for the fair value of the swap at the year end (including details of the methodology used, assumptions made, and report from independent experts where relevant)

The exercise of professional scepticism will be particularly important around fair value measurements. Where the audit evidence obtained is inconsistent or incomplete, we must seek to perform further audit procedures. Further, where external experts have been consulted by the entity, the degree of reliance that can be placed on the external experts also needs to be considered.

17 Biltmore

		Technical	Skills	Marks
(a)	Treatments			
	General	1	1	
	Harmony Tower 3	2	1	
	Grove Place	2	1	
	Head office	2	1	
	Northwest Forward	1	1	
	Teesside	2	1	
	Essex Mall	1	1	
	Subone Head Office	2	1	
	Coventry Building	2	1	
(b)	Adjustments			
	1 mark for each journal entry, maximum of	4	4	
(c)	Impact on the auditor's report			
	Quantify the combined impact	2	2	
	Appropriate audit opinion and explanation, maximum of	3	1	
Total marks		24	16	
Maximum				40

For more guidance on how skills are tested and rewarded, please refer to the section at the start of this question bank.

REPORT

To: David Williams, Audit Partner
From: Jane Smith, Audit Senior
Subject: Biltmore Group – Investment properties
Date: February 20X9

As requested, I report below on the issues raised by the Biltmore Group's investment properties.

(a) Proposed treatment

Broadly, the group has not met the requirements of IAS 40 *Investment Property* in most cases. Each of those breaches has the effect of overstating profit and of overstating the value attributed to investment properties in the statement of financial position.

Harmony Tower 3

We cannot accept the directors' claim that this property must remain at cost because there is no reliable means of estimating its fair value. This is a standard office block in an area where there is a thriving market for such properties. There are observable market prices. It would be reasonable to expect this property to be valued at around £150 million because there is good evidence of that being the current market valuation.

IAS 40 states that fair value must be measured in accordance with IFRS 13 *Fair Value Measurement,* which defines fair value as:

'the price that would be received to sell an asset in an orderly transaction between market participants at the measurement date'

IFRS 13 states that entities should maximise the use of relevant **observable inputs** and minimise the use of **unobservable inputs**.

The standard establishes a three-level hierarchy for the inputs that valuation techniques use to measure fair value:

Level 1   Quoted prices (unadjusted) in active markets for identical assets or liabilities that the reporting entity can access at the measurement date

Level 2   Inputs other than quoted prices included within Level 1 that are observable for the asset or liability, either directly or indirectly, eg quoted prices for similar assets in active markets or for identical or similar assets in non-active markets or use of quoted interest rates for valuation purposes

Level 3   Unobservable inputs for the asset or liability, ie using the entity's own assumptions about market exit value.

Harmony Tower may be valued using a Level 2 input, that is, prices that are directly observable for identical buildings in an active market.

To obtain further evidence that a fair value of £150m is appropriate, the use of auditor's experts may be necessary.

Grove Place

The fair value of the property is £220 million. The £30 million spent during the year should only have been capitalised in accordance with IAS 16 if it represented an improvement in the asset – ie increased the future economic benefits rather than maintaining the asset. Evidence has shown that the refurbishment work has not created the future economic benefits. Therefore, the £250m carrying value must be written down to fair value at the year end, being £220m, with the refurbishment expense of £30 million charged to profit or loss for the year.

Head office – upper floors

This is not an investment property. Biltmore plc occupies and uses a significant part of the building and the vacant part is not capable of being leased or sold separately. The whole building will have to be treated as normal owner-occupied property.

Northwest development

Biltmore plc's use of this property is restricted to only a very small proportion, and the complex cannot be sold separately. It is therefore acceptable, under IAS 40, to treat the whole development as investment property.

Buy-to-let portfolio – Teesside

The fair value should be decided in terms of market conditions as at the year end. Thus, the company's proposed valuation of £150m is correct providing that the downturn arose after the year-end. There may be an argument for treating this downturn as a non-adjusting event after the reporting period and disclosing the change in the market value in a note to the accounts.

Essex Mall

IAS 40 states that a property which is being developed for future sale cannot qualify as an investment property. Thus, the building must be treated in accordance with IAS 2 until such time as it is ready for disposal. Its initial recognition should be at cost, but it should be written down to its net realisable value if this falls below cost.

Subone plc's head office

It is perfectly legitimate for Subtoo plc to treat this property as an investment property in its individual company financial statements because it is occupied by a third party. However, the Biltmore Group cannot treat the property as an investment property because it is owned by one group member and occupied by another. There is nothing to prevent the group from showing the property in its statement of financial position, but the revaluation gain on consolidation cannot be recognised in profit or loss for the year and must instead be recognised as other comprehensive income and accumulated in a revaluation reserve in equity. As an item of PPE, the asset must be depreciated over the duration of the lease.

Coventry development

This property ceased to be an investment property when it was placed on the market. It should have been transferred to inventory at that time at its deemed cost of £345m which is its fair value at the date of its change in use. It should be accounted for under the requirements of IAS 2 Inventories. Any subsequent downward reassessment of the sales value would cause the asset to be written down to the new net realisable value.

(b) **Required adjustments**

Harmony Tower 3

Recognise loss:

	£m	£m
Debit: Gains on investment properties	50	
Credit: Investment properties		50

Grove Place

Treat costs incurred as revenue:

	£m	£m
Debit: Repairst	30	
Credit: Investment properties		30

Head office – upper floors

Cancel gain recognised for year:

	£m	£m
Debit: Gains on investment properties	20	
Credit: Investment properties		20

Reclassify building as non-investment property:

	£m	£m
Debit: Property, plant and equipment	80	
Credit: Investment properties		80

Charge depreciation on additional non-investment property:

	£m	£m
Debit: Depreciation expense	4	
Credit: Property, plant and equipment		4

Northwest development

No adjustment required.

Buy-to-let portfolio – Teesside

No adjustment required.

Essex Mall

Cancel gain recognised for year:

	£m	£m
Debit: Gains on investment properties	80	
Credit: Investment properties		80

Reclassify development as non-investment property:

	£m	£m
Debit: Property under construction	770	
Credit: Investment properties		770

Subone plc's head office (consolidation adjustment only)

Reclassify building as non-investment property:

	£m	£m
Debit: Property, plant and equipment	150	
Credit: Investment properties		150

Charge depreciation on additional non-investment property:

	£m	£m
Debit: Depreciation expense	6	
Credit: Property, plant and equipment		6

(Book value throughout the year = £120 million, divided by 20-year life = £6 million.)

Transfer recognised gain to revaluation reserve

	£m	£m
Debit: Gains on investment properties	30	
Debit: Property, plant and equipment	6	
Credit: Revaluation reserve		36

(The additional depreciation charged to profit or loss has to be added to the recognised gain on revaluation and added back to property, plant and equipment at valuation less depreciation.)

Coventry development

Cancel the revaluation gain recognised since property became part of inventory:

	£m	£m
Debit: Gains on investment properties	15	
Credit: Investment properties		15

Transfer property to inventory:

	£m	£m
Debit: Inventory	345	
Credit: Investment properties		345

(c) **Impact on auditor's report**

If Biltmore's directors refuse to put through the reclassifying adjustments in respect of investment properties, several different accounts in the consolidated statement of financial position will be misstated as follows:

	Investment properties	PPE	Current assets	Property under construction	Total
	£m	£m	£m	£m	£m
Draft	2,360	57	6	0	2,423
Harmony Tower 3	(50)				(50)
Grove Place	(30)				(30)
Head office	(100)	76			(24)
Essex Mall	(850)			770	(80)
Subone Head Office	(150)	150			–
Coventry building	(360)		345		(15)
Revised	820	283	351	770	£2,224

In addition, the misclassification has resulted in the profit or loss account being overstated by £235m as a result of associated adjustments, as follows:

	£m
Harmony Tower 3 (fair value gain)	50
Grove Place (refurbishment costs)	30
Head office – upper floors (depreciation and fair value gain)	24
Essex Mall (fair value gain)	80
Subone plc's head office (depreciation and fair value gain)	36
Coventry (revaluation gain)	15
Total	235

The revaluation reserve is also understated by £36m.

The materiality level for the financial statements as a whole is £24m (total group assets of £2,423m × 1%). This shows clearly that the misstatements in each of the affected accounts are material. Indeed, the overstatement in investment properties alone represents 64% of the group's total assets.

Besides materiality for the financial statements as a whole, ISA 320 requires us to consider performance materiality. In particular, specific materiality levels may be set for particular account balances that could have a particular influence on users' decisions in the particular circumstances of the entity.

As Biltmore is a property business, and investment properties currently represent the largest account balance in group's statement of financial position, the investment properties account should be assigned a lower performance materiality. This makes the level of misstatement in the investment properties account even less acceptable.

Arguably, inventory and properties under construction are equally significant to the users' economic decisions. The difference between an inventory of less than £6m (current assets in the summary statement of financial position) and £345m, and indeed between properties under construction of £nil and £770m, is highly important. Left unadjusted, it could very misleading to the users of the financial statements.

Finally, assuming the directors do agree to make the remaining adjustments listed above, keeping the four properties in the investment properties account at their adjusted carrying amount simply would not make any sense from an accounting point of view. As they current stand, the properties would not be accounted for in accordance with IAS 40.

I would recommend explaining the above to the directors, so that they understand that the reclassification adjustments do have a material impact on the financial statements.

Should the directors still refuse to make the adjustments, a qualified opinion should be issued, on the basis that the misstatements over which disagreements exist are material, but not pervasive.

As a separate point, given the directors' attitude, it may be necessary to consider adjusting our materiality level, and to think about how this may impact other classes of transactions, account balances and disclosures.

18 Button Bathrooms

	Technical	Skills	
	Marks		
Financial reporting issues and key audit risks			
(1) Revenue recognition – FR and audit issues	4	6	Appreciate the revenue recognition issues that arise from the use of an outside service provider collecting cash from customer
			Understand key cut off issues that arise with outside service provider
			Split of sales made on interest free credit between revenue and finance element
(2) Reorganisation – FR and audit issues	3	4	Identify and apply held for sale and discontinued activities criteria
(3) Website development costs – FR and audit issues	2	3	Apply IAS 38 and SIC 32 in the context of BB
			Consider impairment criteria
(4) Pension	3	4	
E commerce and service provider – audit risks	3	5	Understand e-commerce audit risk in context of BB and identify audit procedures
			Understand key control risks for outside service provider using judgment as to how these may be evaluated
Outsourcing of payables ledger	1	4	
Total marks	16	26	
Maximum		40	

To:	Partner
From:	A Senior
Date:	25 July 20X1
Subject:	Button Bathrooms Audit

1 Audit junior's points

1.1 Revenue

On-line sales

The timing of receipt of cash should not determine the timing of revenue recognition. Revenue should be recognised for the sale of goods when risks and rewards pass. This would normally occur on the passing of possession of the goods (ie physical delivery).

The key audit risk is therefore that revenue is inflated as being recognised when cash is received from SupportTech rather than when the goods are delivered which may be up to 4 weeks later. This would in turn inflate profits.

A key audit risk is also cut off, as if revenue is recognised then the cost of sales should also be recognised.

There is therefore a risk that profit is significantly inflated by overstating revenue and failing to recognise any cost of sales on items paid for by customers in June. There needs to be an appropriate system for recording the delivery date in order to have control over the timing of revenue recognition and cut-off.

Similarly, there needs to be a system for recording the nature and timing of returns. If returns are significant consideration could be given to making a provision or even deferring revenue recognition until after the end of the returns period.

A key legal issue is with which party is the customer's contract. This could be SupportTech. Alternatively it may be that the contract is with BB and SupportTech is merely an agent. This could be significant in the case of default.

As goods are delivered to order there is no material issue with inventories in this respect.

Audit procedures will include:

- Examining the dates of delivery to customers of sales recognised in June 20X1

- Examining the dates of delivery to customers of sales recognised in July 20X1

- Tracing the receipt of cash recognised as revenue in June to delivery dates to ensure that recognition is not according to the cash receipt date

- Reviewing returns post year end to ensure revenue has not been inflated

- Considering the need for a returns provision by examining returns ratios over the period on line sales have been in operation.

Sales made on interest-free credit terms

The key issue here is that revenue would appear to be overstated as the full £520,000 has been recognised as sales revenue. The revenue should be recognised at the fair value of the consideration received. As an interest-free credit period has been given the revenue is effectively made up of two elements:

- The fair value of the goods sold
- Finance income

These two elements should have been accounted for separately. In order to calculate the fair value of the goods sold the future cash receipts are discounted to present value at an imputed rate of interest. The imputed rate of interest reflects the credit status of customers so in this case 10% should be used.

Revenue should be recognised as follows:

	£
Sale of goods	
Deposit (£520,000 × 10%)	52,000
Balance (468,000 × $1/1.1^2$)	386,777
	438,777
Finance income (386,777 × 10% × 6/12)	19,339

Sales revenue is currently overstated by £81,223 (520,000 – 438,777). This represents 8.9% of net profit as per the draft management accounts.

The net impact on profit is £61,884 (81,223 – 19,339). This is approximately 6.8% of the net profit as per the draft management accounts. In both cases the adjustment is likely to be material.

A receivable would also be included in the statement of financial position of £406,116 (386,777 + 19,339).

Audit procedures

Audit procedures will include the following assuming that the adjustments above are made:

- Confirm total sales made on interest free credit

- Check agreement details to confirm amount of deposit and interest free period

- Agree deposits received to cash receipts and bank statements

- Discuss with management the basis on which the 10% interest rate reflecting the credit status of customers has been calculated

- Recalculate discounting of sale proceeds

- Recalculate finance income and confirm disclosure as finance income (rather than sales revenue)

- Confirm that receivable balance is included in current assets and discuss any recoverability issues with management.

1.2 Disposal of showrooms

Held-for-sale classification

IFRS 5 requires that a non-current asset, such as BB's unsold showroom, should be classified as 'held for sale' when the company does not intend to utilise the asset as part of its on-going business but instead intends to sell it. The showroom having been closed is therefore potentially in this category. However to be classified as 'held for sale' the showroom should be available for immediate sale.

The likelihood of a sale taking place should also be considered to be highly probable and normally completed within one year of the date of its classification.

The intended sale date of the Bradford showroom is in September 20X1 and there is a contract in place. This showroom is therefore within the category of held for sale. It would therefore be reclassified as a current asset and measured at the lower of its carrying amount and its fair value less costs to sell at the date that it is deemed as held for sale. The current values will therefore need to be reassessed at this date but the sale price of £1.15 million (less selling costs) would be a guideline. The revalued amount less depreciation up to the time of the reclassification as held for sale should therefore be the amount recognised.

The Leeds showroom is more uncertain in terms of the disposal date and the level of certainty. Audit procedures should therefore review the probability of sale up to the audit completion date. In this respect, the showroom must be actively marketed for sale by BB at a price that is reasonable in relation to its current fair value. For a sale to be considered as highly probable there should be a committed plan and BB management should be actively trying to find a buyer. The mere act of advertising may not be enough in this respect and audit procedures need to obtain evidence of the likelihood of sale. If the conditions are only met after the reporting date, there should be full disclosure in the notes to the financial statements. Depreciation should cease when the held for sale criteria are satisfied.

It should be considered whether the Leeds showroom should be revalued as the company has adopted the revaluation model. However, as it was acquired 'fairly recently' the scope for revaluation is likely to be somewhat limited.

Conversely, given that trade is difficult the fair values may have fallen and the issue of impairment arises according to IAS 36. This raises the question of obtaining audit evidence in respect of whether the showrooms are cash generating units. This is the smallest identifiable group of assets that generates cash inflows that are largely independent of the cash inflows from other assets or groups of assets. Each showroom appears to meet the criterion and should be reviewed for impairment on this basis. As the showrooms have been closed they have no value in use hence the carrying amount should be compared to the fair value less costs to sell.

Discontinued operations

Separate disclosure in the statement of profit or loss and other comprehensive income as 'discontinued operations' is also required when a company discontinues a 'component' of its activities, which should have been a cash generating unit while held for use. The definition of a discontinued operation is when it is classified as 'held for sale' or when it is sold and according to IFRS 5 para 32:

(a)   Represents a separate major line of the business or geographical area of operations;

(b)   Is part of a single co-ordinated plan to dispose of a separate major line of the business or geographical area of operations; **or**

(c)   Is a subsidiary acquired exclusively with a view to resale.

Thus, in this case, IFRS 5 para 32(b) may apply as the closure is part of the single co-ordinated plan to withdraw from the showroom based accessories products market.

A component of an entity comprises operations and cash flows that can be clearly distinguished operationally, and for financial reporting purposes, from the rest of the entity and this seems likely to include each individual BB showroom given the policy of managing performance on an individual showroom basis. The question of whether the closure is a withdrawal from the market is however a question of judgment as accessories products are now being sold on-line.

Revaluation

The revaluation reserve would become realised when the asset is sold but would not be affected by being classified as held for sale. If there is an impairment charge that was a reversal of this previous revaluation then it would be a write down in the revaluation reserve rather than a charge to profit.

Audit procedures

- Review contract terms of the sale of the Bradford showroom
- Review legal and other correspondence in respect of the sale of the Bradford showroom
- Obtain an independent valuation of Bradford and Leeds sites
- Review the probability of sale of the Leeds site up to the audit completion date
- Review advertising and any correspondence in response of this
- Review reorganisation plan for evidence of a coherent and co-ordinated plan
- Review impairment procedures and calculations for compliance with IAS 36

1.3 Website development costs

Website development costs may be treated as an internally generated intangible asset according to IAS 38 if the appropriate conditions are satisfied. SIC 32 *Intangible Assets – Web Site Costs,* confirms that internal costs of the development stage of a web site are subject to IAS 38.

Conditions about feasibility have been satisfied as the site is operational. Similarly, the costs appear to be able to be measured reliably at £1 million. There may be some question over whether there are future economic benefits as while BB has made a profit this year this is only due to exceptional items. Clearly this is for the business as a whole and on-line sales are not yet established, but there is doubt over the future profitability of on-line sales and therefore whether the website development costs can be recovered and thus over whether they should be capitalised.

According to SIC 32 internal costs incurred at the operating stage of a website (ie once it is completed), should be treated as an expense.

Audit procedures

- Given the possibility of future losses the capitalised web site costs need to be reviewed for impairment

- Examine costs capitalised to ensure they are attributable to website development

- Consider any overhead allocations in capitalised costs

1.4 Defined benefit pension plan

The key audit issue here is that the defined benefit plan does not seem to have been accounted for in accordance with IAS 19 *Employee Benefits* (as revised in 2011).

The excess of liabilities over assets should be reported as a liability in the statement of financial position. This is calculated as follows:

	£000
Present value of plan obligations	249.6
Less: Fair value of plan assets	(240)
Plan deficit	9.6

Profit or loss for the year should include:

	£'000
Current service cost	211.2
Net interest on net defined benefit liability (38.4 – 19.2)	19.2
	230.4

The charge recognised in profit or loss must therefore be increased by £38,400 (230.4 – 192). This represents 4.2% of the net profit based on the draft management accounts, therefore may not be material. Materiality would need to be reassessed however on the basis of other adjustments which may be required eg on-line sales recognition. Also as it relates to pensions (which affects employees) it may be judged material in qualitative terms.

The remeasurement gain of £28,800 is then recognised in other comprehensive income (see below).

Remeasurement gain

	PV of obligation £000	Fair value of plan assets £000
B/f	–	–
Contributions paid		192
Interest on plan assets		19.2
Current service cost	211.2	
Interest cost on obligation	38.4	
Actuarial difference (bal. fig)	–	28.8
C/f	249.6	240

Audit procedures

Ask the directors to reconcile the scheme assets valuation at the scheme year end date with the fair value of the plan assets of £240,000 at 30 June 20X1.

Obtain direct confirmation of the scheme assets from the investment custodians.

Consider the extent to which it is appropriate to rely on the work of the actuary eg ascertain the qualifications and experience of the actuaries.

Through discussion with the directors and actuaries:

- Obtain a general understanding of the assumptions made
- Consider whether they are unbiased and based on market expectations at the year end
- Consider whether assumptions are consistent with other information

2 E-commerce

2.1 Audit risks arising from use of external service provider

A key risk to BB of the new e-commerce strategy is that it is using an outside service provider.

ISA 402 *Audit Considerations Relating to an Entity Using a Service Organisation* provides guidance on how auditors should carry out their responsibility to obtain sufficient appropriate audit evidence when the audit client, which is a 'user entity', relies on such services.

In the case of BB the on-line sales are clearly material to the business as they make up around half of revenue, even though they have only been launched for half a year. The service is also fundamental in being a key element of the internal control systems for BB.

ISA 402 requires the auditor to understand how the user entity uses the services of the service organisation. In the case of BB, this most significantly requires an understanding of the nature of the services provided by SupportTech; the degree of interaction between the activities of BB and SupportTech; and the nature of the relationship between the two companies, including the contractual terms.

When obtaining an understanding of internal control we should:

- Evaluate the design and implementation of controls at BB that relate to the services provided by SupportTech

- Determine whether this gives sufficient understanding of the effect of SupportTech's operations on BB's internal controls in order to provide a basis for the identification and assessment of risks of material misstatement.

If not, then we should do one or more of the following:

- Obtain a report from SupportTech's auditors

- Contact SupportTech, through BB, then visit SupportTech and perform audit procedures that will provide information about the relevant controls, or

- Use another auditor to perform procedures that will provide information about the relevant controls at SupportTech.

If proposing to visit SupportTech we should first determine whether sufficient appropriate audit evidence concerning the relevant assertions is available from records held at BB. However given the extent of SupportTech's activities this seems unlikely.

We should therefore perform further procedures including tests of controls.

Substantive procedures will include inspecting documents and records held by SupportTech (access to records held by SupportTech may be established as part of the contractual arrangement with BB). This could include the use of CAATs, if permitted by SupportTech.

Substantive procedures will also include obtaining confirmation of balances and transactions from the service organisation where the user entity maintains independent records of balances and transactions. This will include the cash balance outstanding paid by customers.

We may also perform analytical procedures on the records maintained by BB and SupportTech.

2.2 E-commerce risks

Aside from the risks that arise because BB has used an external service provider there are additional business risks that would arise from e-commerce even if it were operated internally by BB. These include:

- Risk of non-compliance with taxation, legal and other regulatory issues

- Contractual issues arising: are legally binding agreements formed over the internet?

- Risk of technological failure (crashes) resulting in business interruption

- Impact of technology on going concern assumption, extent of risk of business failure

- Loss of transaction integrity, which may be compounded by the lack of sufficient audit trail

- Security risks, such as virus attacks and the risk of frauds by customers and employees

- Improper accounting policies in respect of capitalisation of costs such as website development costs, misunderstanding of complex contractual arrangements, title transfer risks, translation of foreign currency, allowances for warranties and returns, and revenue recognition issues

- Over-reliance on e-commerce when placing significant business systems on the Internet

An entity that uses e-commerce must address the business risks arising as a result by implementing appropriate security infrastructure and related controls to ensure that the identity of customers and suppliers can be verified, the integrity of transactions can be ensured, agreement on terms of trade can be obtained, as well as payment from customers is obtained and privacy and information protection protocols are established.

When auditing an entity that uses e-commerce, the auditor must consider in particular the issues of security, transaction integrity and process alignment.

Therefore when examining the issue of security, we should carry out audit procedures to address the following:

- The use of firewalls and virus protection software

- The effective use of encryption

- Controls over the development and implementation of systems used to support e-commerce activities

- Whether security controls already in place are as effective as new technologies become available

- Whether the control environment supports the control procedures implemented

When considering transaction integrity, we need to consider the completeness, accuracy, timeliness and authorisation of the information provided for recording and processing in the financial records, by carrying out procedures to evaluate the reliability of the systems used for capturing and processing the information.

Process alignment is the way the IT systems used by entities are integrated with one another to operate effectively as one system. We need to assess the extent to which SupportTech's systems are automatically integrated with the internal systems of BB and this may affect issues such as the completeness and accuracy of transaction processing, the timing of recognition of sales and receivables, and the identification and recording of disputed transactions.

A more general business risk also exists in that e-commerce sales may merely be displacing shop sales. This may be indicated for BB by the fact that total sales in the year are similar to the previous year.

3 Outsourcing of payables ledger accounts

Audit issues

Problems have been identified with controls in the past which increases audit risk in this area. Details of these problems need to be clarified by reviewing the previous year's audit file. The current year's procedures may have to be revised to address these.

Inherent risk is increased by the fact that the company has outsourced the payables ledger part-way through the year. The transition may not have been well-managed. This risk is increased by the historic in-house control issues as there may have been errors in the information initially transferred to SupportTech.

There has been a high turnover in staff and staff continued to work for BB after redundancy notices had been issued. Disgruntled and/or inexperienced staff increases the risk of error.

We need to understand how SupportTech is being used by BB. This will include:

- The contractual terms

- The nature of the relationship and the service provided by SupportTech. The Finance Director authorises all invoices before they are paid. This means that a key control is maintained by BB, although SupportTech is responsible for processing the invoices

- Details of the information sent by BB to SupportTech and the level of detail in the schedule sent back by SupportTech for approval by the Finance Director.

Other issues

Whilst purchase orders and delivery notes are maintained by BB, invoices are sent directly to SupportTech. It is unlikely that sufficient evidence will be obtained from records maintained by BB alone. However the fact that records were maintained in-house for 10 months of the year increases this possibility.

Effectiveness of controls over access to the portal. The system should operate such that the Finance Director can view the payables accounts but not change them. If both SupportTech and BB can update balances there is an increased risk of duplication.

Results of enquiries of management eg whether management is aware of any issues eg uncorrected errors made by SupportTech.

19 Hillhire

		Marks
Requirements	*Technical*	*Skills*
Key audit risks and financial reporting treatment		
General	2	3
Discontinuation		
• Audit risk	1	2
• Financial reporting treatment	2	2
• Audit procedures	1	2
Acquisition	4	3
Swap		
• Audit risk	1	2
• Financial reporting treatment	2	2
• Audit procedures	1	2
New system	2	2
Share options	2	3
Ethical	2	2
Total marks	20	25
Maximum		40

For more guidance on how skills are tested and rewarded, please refer to the section at the start of this question bank.

To: Peter Lanning
From: A. Senior
Date: 12 April 20X8
Subject: Hillhire plc audit for the year ended 31 March 20X8

Audit risks

1   **General points**

The profit for the year of £27,240,000, after taking into account the loss for the year from discontinued operations, has decreased by 6.7%. Although this is not particularly serious in itself, management might be concerned that the shareholders will react unfavourably. We need to take particular care over any matters of accounting judgement that could have distorted the results in order to improve matters. It may be that the profit according to the draft statement of profit or loss and other comprehensive income has been overstated already in order to mitigate the effects of this decline. We will also have to pay attention to any adjustments that are proposed to the draft accounts that have the effect of increasing the reported profit.

Continuing operations

More importantly we need to check that the profit from discontinued operations has been correctly classified. Excluding the loss arising from discontinued operations, profit for the year from continuing operations has shown an increase of 8.4%. The increase in revenue for 20X8 compared to 20X7 is 10% and whereas this is not materially out of line, it would be useful to look at expenses more closely by carrying out some analytical procedures.

Cost of sales

In 20X8 cost of sales has increased by 11.5% over 20X7, compared with a 10% increase in revenue. As part of the analytical procedures we should be looking at the possibility of increases in costs which have not been reflected in higher sale prices.

Administrative expenses

In spite of the 10% increase in revenue, administrative expenses (excluding amortisation) have increased by only 1.2%. We need to look into this to ensure that expenses relating to continuing operations have not been incorrectly allocated.

Gearing and borrowing costs

The company continues to be highly geared. Indeed, a great deal of additional borrowing has been raised. There does not appear to be any particular concern about going concern issues arising from this, but we should be sceptical about any accounting practices that have the effect of smoothing profits, as well as any that have the effect of increasing reported income.

Long-term borrowings have increased by £69,240,000 or 22% whereas finance costs have increased by 11.56%. We need to look at the movement of interest rates in the period, look into the company's other borrowings and request details of finance costs reflected in the profit or loss and other comprehensive income, to establish these have been correctly calculated and accounted for. We also need to ensure that the allocation of finance costs has been correctly made and not inappropriately allocated to the discontinued operations.

It is possible that the figure for long-term borrowings could be even higher if the divested depots have borrowings which have been netted off within assets held for sale. This treatment would not be correct.

Are depots able to raise their own finance? If so their borrowings are included within total borrowings in 20X7 but it is unclear how the liabilities of depots held for sale are treated in the current year. Have they been incorrectly netted off within assets held for sale or are they listed within total liabilities? Further investigation is needed.

We should also establish when repayment of the long-term borrowings is due as it's a large amount. The company's ability to repay any borrowings due in the near future needs to be considered, as this could affect the going concern assumption.

In addition, perhaps the new borrowings were taken on mid-year so there's not a full year's finance charge, which will have implications for the future.

2 Discontinued operations risks

There is a risk that IFRS 5 *Non-current Assets Held for Sale and Discontinued Operations* has not been complied with.

Professional scepticism would identify this as a risk here especially as the directors' bias in the current year may well be to try to classify these depots as 'discontinued' as this allows them to disclose the losses separately in the hope of downplaying their significance to analysts assessing the company's future prospects.

In order to be treated as a discontinued operation the Scottish depots would have to be a component of Hillhire which:

- Represents a separate major line of business or geographical area of operations; and
- Is part of a single co-ordinated disposal plan; and
- Is either disposed of by the reporting date or classified as held for sale.

IFRS 5 defines a component of an entity as 'operations and cash flows that can be clearly distinguished operationally and for financial reporting purposes from the rest of the entity'. As each depot is viewed as a cash-generating unit the group of Scottish depots represents a component of Hillhire.

All of the depots are located in Scotland and the decision to sell is based on a strategic decision to withdraw from this part of the country. This suggests that this is a separate geographical area of operations. However further details would be required to determine what proportion of the total number of depots held is represented by the 15 being sold to assess whether this constitutes a major geographical area of operations.

The plan to dispose of the Scottish depots would appear to be a single co-ordinated disposal plan based on the information provided.

Despite meeting the first two criteria to be classified as discontinued, the Scottish depots have not been disposed of by the reporting date and do not appear to meet the definition of 'held for sale' at this date.

A disposal group is classified as held for sale only if its carrying amount will be recovered primarily through a sales transaction rather than through continuing use. The following criteria must be met in order for this to be the case:

- The depots must be available for immediate sale in their present condition. In this case the depots are not available for immediate sale as they are still in use and no alternative arrangements have been made to store the vehicles currently held at these depots.

- The sale must be 'highly probable', that is:

    - Being actively marketed at a reasonable price;

    - Changes to the plan are unlikely;

    - Management must be committed to the sale;

    - There must be an active programme to locate a buyer; and

    - The sale must be expected to be completed within one year from the date of classification

From the information currently available, whilst management appear committed to the sale, indicated by the recording of the decision in the board minutes, there is currently no active programme to locate a buyer. Marketing of the properties is not due to start until May or June of 20X8.

On this basis the Scottish depots should not be classified as either held for sale or discontinued operations and the loss for the year in respect of this group of depots should not be separated from the results of the continuing operations of the business in the statement of profit or loss and other comprehensive income.

In the statement of financial position, the depots should not have been reclassified as held for sale on 1 January 20X8 but should have been retained in property, plant and equipment and depreciated for the remainder of the year.

From the draft financial statements we can see that on transfer to held for sale, the depots have been measured at the lower of carrying amount and fair value less costs to sell. Therefore the following journals are required to reverse this transfer and record depreciation for the 3 months to 31 March 20X8:

DR Property, plant and equipment	£44,520,000	
CR Profit or loss – discontinued operations		£4,390,000
CR Assets held for sale		£40,130,000

and

DR Profit or loss	£445,200	
(44,520/25 x 3/12)		
CR Accumulated depreciation		£445,200

The carrying value of the depots at 31 March 20X8 is therefore £44,074,800 (44,520 – 445.2).

An assessment should be made to determine whether the depots have suffered an impairment. The depots are be impaired if the carrying amount is in excess of the recoverable amount, being the higher of fair value less costs to sell and value in use. The carrying amount would appear to be in excess of fair value but further information is required in order to calculate the value in use.

Audit procedures

Discuss the necessary adjustments with the directors.

Enquire of directors as to the progress of the planned sale of the depots.

Inspect board minutes and budgets and forecasts for evidence that management intend to sell the depots.

Determine the proportion of depots which the sales of the 15 Scottish depots represent in comparison to the business as a whole.

Confirm plans for moving vehicles currently held in the depots in Scotland

Obtain details and inspect correspondence with agents for evidence that the marketing of the depots is due to start in May/June only.

Ascertain how fair value was assessed and review any valuation reports prepared by independent valuers.

Agree remaining useful lives of the Scottish depots with the company's stated depreciation policy.

Discuss with the directors the extent of any impairment reviews performed by them.

Obtain details of the value in use for the Scottish depots and review the basis of these calculations.

3 **Acquisition of Loucamion**

The figure for intangibles (nearly £12 million) that appear to have been recognised on the acquisition of Loucamion is high, and there is a risk that some of the intangibles, especially any value allocated to customer relationships, may not meet the recognition criteria of IFRS 3 *Business Combinations* and IAS 38 *Intangible Assets*. The overriding requirements are that it is probable that future economic benefits will flow to the entity and that the cost can be reliably measured.

In the case of an acquisition, the key issue to determine is whether other intangibles can be identified separately from goodwill. IFRS 3 *Business Combinations* gives some illustrative examples and these include customer lists and customer contracts and the related customer relationships. For the customer lists of Loucamion to be recognised they must meet the contractual-legal criterion or the separability criterion. Loucamion does not appear to have any legal rights to protect or control the relationship it has with its customers or their loyalty therefore the lists do not satisfy the contractual-legal criterion. IFRS 3 states that a customer list acquired in a business combination does not meet the separability criterion if the terms of confidentiality or other agreements prohibit the entity from selling, leasing or otherwise exchanging information about its customers. This appears to be the case with Loucamion's customer list. On this basis the customer list should not have been recognised as a separable asset but should have been subsumed within goodwill. This error should be corrected and the amortisation charged for the year reversed as follows:

DR Goodwill £4,000,000

CR Intangible assets £3,600,000

CR Profit or loss £400,000

(4,000,000/10)

There may be unrecognised impairments of goodwill and other assets by the year-end.

The other newly acquired intangible assets may not be amortised over a realistic useful life.

It is essential we obtain details of the amortisation schedules and review these closely.

Audit procedures

Obtain a breakdown of the allocation of the purchase consideration and determine how much has been allocated to the other intangibles. Confirm that items recognised in other intangibles meet the criteria to be recognised separately.

Obtain details from the auditors of Loucamion about the nature of the customer relationships to confirm that no legal relationships exist and that the confidentiality terms are in place.

Ascertain how management have assessed the useful lives of the other intangibles for the purpose of amortisation and consider whether this is reasonable.

Ascertain how the fair values of the assets and liabilities of Loucamion were assessed and review any valuation reports prepared by independent valuers.

Obtain the consolidation schedules to review whether Loucamion has been correctly consolidated, including only post-acquisition results.

Review the disclosures relating to the acquisition to ensure that all the requirements of IFRS 3 have been met.

All relevant exchange rates should be recorded in the audit file so that we can ensure the subsidiary's financial statements are translated from its functional currency to the presentation currency of the group ie £.

We need to consider the arrangements for the audit of Loucamion. It may not be cost-effective for us to visit the company ourselves. We will need to ensure that we are satisfied by the assurances provided by any local audit firm. Presumably this will not be too great a problem because the company already has a range of operations throughout Europe.

4 **Interest rate swap**

This appears to be the first time that Hillhire has used derivatives in this way, which increases the risk that the treatment is incorrect. There is a risk that the swaps do not meet the criteria for hedge accounting as set out in IAS 39. We need to confirm that:

- The interest rate swap was designated as a hedge at inception and this strategy is fully documented

- The hedge is 'highly effective' (ie the ratio of the gain or loss on the hedging instrument compared to the loss or gain on the item being hedged is within the ratio 80% to 125%), and this is subject to continuous assessment, and

- The hedge effectiveness can be reliably measured

The condition that the hedge should be highly effective appears to be met as the hedge is a perfect match in terms of currency, maturity and nominal amount.

There is a risk that hedging may be applied from the wrong date. Whilst the interest-rate swap was acquired on 1 April 20X7 it was only designated as a hedge on 1 May 20X7. In accordance with IAS 39 hedge accounting may only be applied prospectively, from the later of the date of designation and the date that the formal documentation was prepared. We would need to check the date of the documentation but based on information currently available hedge accounting can be applied no earlier than 1 May 20X7.

These risks are exacerbated by the fact that the company is highly geared. The directors have an obvious incentive to manipulate the manner in which this swap is accounted for so as to minimise the volatility associated with any changes in interest rates or the values of any assets or liabilities.

The credit rating of the counterparty needs to be considered. The hedge will fail if the counterparty defaults. We need to seek some assurance that the counterparty is creditworthy and solvent.

The directors might be under some pressure to be optimistic in any evaluation of the swap arrangement. There is a debit balance of more than £5m on the hedging reserve that would have a material impact on reported profit if hedge accounting had to be discontinued.

Interest for the period 1 October 20X7 – 31 March 20X8 has not been accounted for.

The £9.5m (£200m × 6/12 × (7.5% + 2%)) variable interest for the six months to 31 March 20X8 is charged to profit or loss and is accrued until payment is made.

The net settlement on the interest rate swap of £1.5 m (£200m × 6/12 × (9.5%-8%) received from the swap bank as a cash settlement reduces the £9.5m variable rate interest expense to £8m. This is equivalent to the fixed rate cost (£2m × 6/12 × 8%).

The following adjustments are required:

DR Profit or loss – interest expense	£9.5m	
CR Interest accrual/cash		£9.5m
DR Cash	£1.5m	
CR Profit or loss – interest expense		£1.5m

Audit procedures

- Review board minutes documenting the decision to enter into the swap and the strategic reason for this ie to confirm that there is formal designation of the hedge

- Review and recalculate the effectiveness of the hedge.

- Check that documentation is adequate. This must include:

    – Identification of the hedging instrument ie interest rate swap

    – The hedged item or transaction ie interest payments

    – Nature of the risk being hedged ie changes in interest rates

    – Details of calculation of hedge effectiveness

    – Statement of entity's risk management objective and strategy

- Confirm date of preparation of the documentation to determine the date from which hedge accounting should be applied.

- Check that adjustments already reflected in the draft financial statements have been calculated from the correct date and that hedge accounting has not been applied retrospectively.

- Seek specific assurances about the credit rating of the counterparty to the swap.

- Confirm basis on which the fair value of the hedge has been determined and assess whether this complies with IAS 39.

- Confirm that adjustments required for interest to 31 March 20X8 as outlined above have been made.

5 **Controls review on new online ordering system**

Risk

The new system has been piloted at quite a large number of depots during the current year. There is a risk that any errors in the system will have affected the recording of transactions during the year.

This is a highly sensitive system. It raises transactions involving payments from business customers and credit card companies. It can instigate the transfer of vehicles between branches. The whole point of piloting is the recognition that new systems frequently contain errors.

Breakdowns in the system could have led to vehicles being transferred for fraudulent purposes. It is unlikely that staff would steal a commercial vehicle, but it might have been possible to "lose" a vehicle in the system and hire it out for cash. Apart from the loss of revenue, that could have led to exposure to claims if the unauthorised use meant that the company's insurance policy did not cover any claims for damages in the event of an accident.

Ideally, the pilot testing will have been controlled by a parallel run of the existing system at the branches. In practice, it is unlikely that resources would permit this to happen.

It is worrying that the company has only engaged our IT specialists at this stage. That might suggest that there was no independent, expert oversight of the piloting process or that the consultant providing any such support has been sacked or has chosen to withdraw from the engagement. At best, this suggests some recklessness in terms of the manner in which the pilot process was managed. At worst, management may be planning to implement a system that has been found to be defective.

Audit procedures

The new system needs to be documented and control risk assessed.

Management should be asked to provide detailed information about the errors that were uncovered in the course of the pilot testing and the steps that have been taken to correct them, both in terms of adjusting the system and correcting the underlying records that were affected by the errors.

The proposal to roll the system out will also have implications for future audits. We will have to take great care over the audit of the system testing phase and the implementation phase. The transfer of standing data and the reconstruction of the vehicle register should both, ideally, be checked clerically and the results retained for us to review.

6 Share options

IFRS 2 *Share-Based Payment* requires that the share options are reflected as an expense in profit or loss.

We need to assess the assumption that 10% of senior employees will leave and therefore forfeit the shares.

Assuming the forfeiture of 10% is accurate, the expenses reflected in each of the three years from 20X8 should be as follows:

Year ending		Expenses £	Cumulative expenses £
31 March 20X8	$(50 \times 100 \times 90\% \times £10 \times 1/3)$	15,000	15,000
31 March 20X9	$(50 \times 100 \times 90\% \times £10 \times 2/3) - 15,000$	15,000	30,000
31 March 20Y0	$(50 \times 100 \times 90\% \times £10) - 30,000$	15,000	45,000

The adjustment for 20X8 should be

		£	£
Dr	Profit or loss	15,000	
Cr	Equity		15,000

7 Ethical points arising

The firm needs to consider whether the potential assurance assignment relating to the new system may pose a threat to objectivity in respect of the audit.

There appear to be a number of threats:

Firstly, we need to remain vigilant to any increase in our evaluation of global inherent risk. If the company's profitability and financial position are deteriorating then management might be tempted to distort the financial statements. That will lead to an increased risk that we will be blamed for some alleged audit failure. If we see any clear evidence that the financial statements are being manipulated then we should consider resigning the appointment in order to protect our reputation.

Secondly, if our IT specialists are going to assist in the implementation of a new system we need to manage the perception that there could be a self interest threat. We might be accused of being prepared to compromise on our audit opinion in order to win this consultancy business.

Looking ahead to future years' audits, if Barber and Kennedy provide assurance relating to the controls over the system it could amount to a self-review threat, especially if in future years the firm was to place reliance on controls in gathering their audit evidence.

20 Hopper Wholesale

Marking guide

		Technical	Skills	Marks
(a)	Inventory			
	Audit issues	2	3	
	Audit procedures	2	3	
(b)	Financial assets			
	Audit issues	2	2	
	Audit procedures	2	2	
(c)	Receivable			
	Audit issues	2	1	
	Audit procedures	2	1	
(d)	Share option scheme			
	Audit issues	3	2	
	Audit procedures	2	2	
(e)	Sustainability issues (including ethics)	–	10	
Total marks		17	26	
Maximum				40

For more guidance on how skills are tested and rewarded, please refer to the section at the start of this question bank.

(a) **Inventory**

Audit issues

(i) **Materiality**

The option may be material to the statement of profit or loss and other comprehensive income as the potential gain of £150,000 represents 5.5% of profit before tax.

(ii) **Risk**

There is a risk that the option is incorrectly valued particularly as there is no directly comparable instrument being traded on the open market at the period end and that any change in value is incorrectly calculated.

If the underlying market price of flour has fallen as at 31 December 20X8 then the option's intrinsic value will increase by 20,000 multiplied by the difference between the market price of flour and the strike price of £140 per tonne.

The fair value of the option will have to be determined. From the information provided, it does not necessarily sound as if the original contract was determined by reference to a traded option that will have a standardised set of terms and conditions and that will have an open-market, observable market value. The £400,000 offered by the counterparty to the option will possibly constitute a reasonable estimate of the fair value as at the reporting date, although the amount offered could be significantly different from fair value. Sweetcall would have an incentive to offer less than the fair value in order to be released from this potential commitment, but could just as easily offer more than the fair value in order to resolve the significant uncertainty associated with the cost of having the option exercised against it in June 20X9.

The option was recorded at cost of £250,000. If the £400,000 is regarded as a fair value then the gain of £150,000 on the option would be recognised in profit or loss for the year ended 31 December 20X8. If this is not deemed suitable as a fair value then the difference between the carrying value and any assessed fair value should be included as the gain (or loss – less likely).

There is a risk that the option may be incorrectly treated as a hedging instrument.

The directors might argue that the option is a hedging instrument because it was purchased with the express intention of reducing risk arising from changes in the value of the inventory. The hedge could be described either as a fair value hedge or as a cash flow hedge. However, to account for the transaction as a hedge, the following requirements must be met:

- At inception of the hedge there is a formal designation and documentation of the hedging relationship and the entity's risk management objective and strategy for undertaking the hedge.

- The hedge is expected to be highly effective.

- The effectiveness of the hedge can be reliably assessed.

- The hedge is assessed for effectiveness on an ongoing basis.

- In respect of a cash flow hedge the forecast transaction is highly probable.

Based on the information available, it would appear not all these conditions are met, specifically that the documentation is not in place, and that the purchase was arguably opportunistic rather than a part of a coherently planned risk management strategy and so it would be inappropriate to use hedge accounting.

There is a risk that the price of flour could change in such a way that the option lost much of its value (market risk). Prices do seem to change dramatically, as evidenced by the fact that the option was purchased substantially out-of-the-money and three months later it is substantially in-the-money.

We need to consider the counterparty's ability to honour the commitment imposed by the option (credit risk). This should have been investigated before paying for the option, however even if this is the case Sweetcall's solvency will have to be reconsidered as at the reporting date.

There is a risk that any errors in the drafting of the contract could result in the option lapsing even if it would have been in Hopper's interests to exercise it (legal risk).

Disclosure may be inadequate. The option should be disclosed in accordance with IFRS 7 as a derivative financial asset.

Additional audit procedures

Review the option contract to determine that the contract exists and that the company has the rights and obligations relating to the option.

Vouch the provenance of the contract by referring to correspondence with the counterparty and any professional advisers.

Write to Sweetcall and ask for direct confirmation of the terms and conditions of the option.

Investigate whether there are any other contracts in existence which relate to this transaction.

Valuation and measurement will be a difficult area. Determine the basis on which management have valued the option eg. Black and Scholes method.

Check the accuracy of any parameters that have been input into the model, such as the volatility of flour prices, the strike price and the time left to run. Some simple sensitivity analysis would be sensible in order to assess how suitable the valuation is.

Compare the results of that calculation with the £400,000 offered by Sweetcall to cancel the contract and assess the implications of any difference.

Check the creditworthiness of Sweetcall as the option will not be worth anything if they default.

Confirm disclosures are in accordance with IFRS 7.

(b) **Financial assets**

Audit issues

(i) **Materiality**

The financial assets are material to both the statement of financial position and the statement of profit or loss and other comprehensive income. The amount recognised in non-current assets amounts to 5% of total assets. The gain amounts to 19% of profit before tax and 2.4% of revenue.

(ii) **Risk**

There is a risk that the investments have been incorrectly classified as a financial asset at fair value through profit or loss on the basis that it is held for trading. In accordance with IAS 39 *Financial Instruments: Recognition and Measurement* this categorisation is only appropriate if it is:

- Acquired principally for the purpose of selling in the near future

- Part of a portfolio of identified financial instruments that are managed together and for which there is evidence of a recent actual pattern of short-term profit taking, or

- A derivative

Whilst it is not impossible for a held for trading investment in equity to be a non-current asset, it would be more usual for such items to be current. This fact raises the risk of inappropriate disclosure.

There is a risk that the investments have been incorrectly valued. Financial assets at fair value through profit or loss should initially be measured at fair value. At the end of each reporting period the financial assets should be remeasured to fair value with any changes recognised in profit and loss. This does appear to be the treatment adopted here and is therefore correct provided that the categorisation is appropriate.

Additional audit procedures

Obtain a schedule detailing the purchase price of the individual investments and their valuation at the period end.

Agree initial recognition at fair value to the transaction price eg statements from stockbrokers.

Obtain details of any transaction costs and confirm that these have not been included in fair value but have been expensed.

Determine the means by which the period end fair values have been established. In this case shares are listed therefore there should be a quoted market price and agree to schedule.

Obtain details and review the way in which the investments are managed to determine that they are held for trading eg enquire of management of their intention to sell in the short term corroborated by a review of events after the end of the reporting period, review of portfolio for evidence of short-term trading.

Review other information eg notes of board meetings and ensure that discussion of investments is consistent with their classification as being held for the short-term.

Review the adequacy of the disclosure note in the financial statements and ensure that it is in accordance with IFRS 7 *Financial Instruments: Disclosures*.

(c) **Receivable**

Audit issues

(i) **Materiality**

The receivable represents only 0.08% of total assets and is therefore not material on a quantitative basis. However it is material due to the nature of the transaction ie on a qualitative basis, because it is a director-related transaction.

(ii) **Risk**

There is a risk of non-compliance with IAS 24 *Related Party Disclosures* due to the lack of disclosure as this transaction constitutes a related party transaction. We have been told that the receivable is due from a company which is under the control of Jack Maddison, who is Hopper's managing director. Jack Maddison is in a position to control or significantly influence both companies. The transaction may not be a normal commercial transaction and may be subject to bias. A trade receivable with credit terms of 12 months would be unusual. However, a loan with such terms would not.

Completeness is a high risk assertion. Whilst we are aware of this transaction and can confirm the details there may be other similar transactions which we are not currently aware of. Due to the nature of related party transactions they may be difficult to identify.

There is a risk that the receivable may be overstated. If there is any doubt about the recoverability of the debt then an allowance may be required.

The classification of the debt also needs to be considered. We have been told that it will be repaid within the next twelve months. If this is not genuinely the case then the asset should be disclosed as an asset recoverable after more than one year, in other words, a non-current asset.

Additional audit procedures

Discuss the transaction with Jack Maddison to establish the nature and the purpose of the transaction.

Review any documentary evidence of the transaction eg invoice or loan agreement and check the terms of the agreement, in particular the repayment terms and timing.

Review board minutes for authorisation of the transaction and any discussions regarding the purpose of the transaction and its repayment. Also review the board minutes for evidence of any other related party transactions.

Obtain evidence that Jack Maddison does control Bourne Ltd eg review of Bourne Ltd financial statements.

Review financial statements of Bourne Ltd to establish that it recognises that it has a liability to Hopper and assess the ability of the company to repay the debt.

Obtain general representation from management confirming that they have disclosed all related party transactions to us and that they are appropriately accounted for and disclosed.

Obtain further specific written representations regarding the receivable due from Bourne Ltd including details of the control which Jack Maddison has over Bourne Ltd, confirmation that management believes the debt to be recoverable and the date on which it will be repaid.

(d) **Share options**

Audit issues

(i) **Materiality**

Profits are understated by £430,000 (700 – 270). This represents 15.6% of profit before tax and is therefore material. As the share options are transactions with employees the transaction is likely to be material from a qualitative as well as from a quantitative perspective.

(ii) **Risk**

The key issue is that of inappropriate accounting treatment. In accordance with IFRS 2, Hopper Wholesale Ltd is required to recognise the remuneration expense as the services are received, based on the fair value of the share options granted.

In this case the fair value at the date the options were granted was £12. The calculation performed by the entity currently uses the fair value at the end of the reporting period of £14.

The full expense has been recognised in profit or loss in the year of issue. In accordance with IFRS 2, the cost should be recognised over the vesting period (in this case two years).

The calculation performed by Hopper Wholesale Ltd does not take in to account the number of options expected to vest but simply assumes that all will vest at the end of the period. IFRS

2 requires that the amount recognised take in to account estimates of the number of employees expected to leave.

The credit entry has been recognised as a long-term liability. This should be recognised as part of equity rather than as a liability.

The expense should have been recognised as £270,000 (100 × 500 × 90% × 12 × ½)

Additional audit procedures

Agree other contractual terms to legal document ie number of shares awarded to each employee, vesting terms and length of vesting period.

Enquire of directors regarding the numbers of employees estimated to benefit and the basis on which the 10% leaving rate has been estimated.

Compare staffing numbers to forecasts and numbers of leavers to prior years.

Confirm that £12 is the fair value at the grant date by reference to documentation supporting the fair value calculation.

Enquire of the directors as to the model used to estimate fair value. Consider whether this is in accordance with IFRS 2 (eg Black-Scholes) and that it is appropriate in the circumstances. (As the company is not listed it is unlikely that a market value for shares will be available).

Consider whether expert advice is required on the valuation.

Obtain representations from management confirming that the assumptions used are reasonable.

(e) **Social and environmental report**

Requirement to publish information

The Companies Act 2006 requires quoted companies to include information on environmental, employment and social issues as part of its business review. Quoted companies must also report on greenhouse gas emissions in their Directors' Report (from 1 October 2013). As Hopper is not a quoted company these requirements do not apply. However, companies are encouraged to provide this information voluntarily therefore increasingly its inclusion is being seen as best practice.

Assertion 1

This will be a difficult statement for us to verify for the following reasons:

- The statement is dependent on the integrity of others and we will not have access to the records of the suppliers

- There may be some flexibility in the definition of child labour eg in terms of age and potential hours worked

Possible sources of evidence would include assertions by suppliers, inspection by auditors, information available in the press.

Assertion 2

This assertion is more straightforward. The current minimum wage is set in law. A review of payroll records should be performed targeting the lower paid workers in particular and comparisons made with the minimum wage. A calculation would then be performed to ensure that the additional pay rate does equate to at least 10% of the minimum wage.

Assertion 3

Again there should be evidence to support this assertion provided adequate payroll records are maintained. Details of staff sickness rates for the current year and previous year should be obtained from payroll records. A comparison should be made and a calculation performed to confirm that rate of decrease.

Assertion 4

Our ability to verify this statement will depend on the records on waste disposal maintained by the company. For example, if disposal is conducted by a contractor, invoices for the cost of disposal would provide evidence of the volumes of waste sent to landfill. A comparison with previous years could then be made. If this is not the case, we would need to establish the basis on which the management have made this claim. Specific procedures would then depend on the source information available.

Assertion 5

The company should a maintain log of all accidents which take place in the workplace. Assuming that these records are available we should be able to compare the number of recorded accidents which took place in the current year, compare this with the number which took place in the previous year and recalculate the percentage change.

What will be more difficult to confirm is that the reduction is due to improved health and safety procedures. We may not have the expertise to determine whether procedures have improved (as opposed to simply being different) unless they have been made in response to recommendations made by experts in the health and safety field. If this is the case we would be able to confirm that procedures have been revised in accordance with those recommendations.

Professional considerations

We have not been involved in this type of work before, therefore we need to ensure that we have the relevant expertise and resources to complete this assignment. The scope of this work is not set down in statute so we would need to clarify precisely our responsibilities in an engagement letter. We also need to clarify the purpose of our report and consider issues regarding any liability that we may have to third parties. This exercise would also constitute the provision of other services, which is allowed under ethical guidance. We would need to consider the fee that we will receive and ensure that we are not economically dependent on this client.

In addition, the social and environmental report is expected to be included in the same document that contains the audited financial statements. As such, it would form part of the other information which we, as the statutory auditors, are required by ISA 720 to read to identify any material inconsistencies. If any of the proposed assertions are found to be inconsistent with the audited financial statements, and management refuses to resolve the inconsistency, we would need to consider what impact this would have on the auditor's report, and more generally, whether we should continue the audit engagement.

21 Lyght plc

Marking guide

		Technical	Skills	Marks
(a)	Concerns of ethics partner	3	5	
(b)	New IT system	4	4	
(c)	Inventories	2	3	
(d)	Sale of tyres	3	3	
(e)	Leased buildings	3	3	
(f)	Asset treated as available for sale	4	3	
(g)	Receivables	3	4	
Total marks		22	25	
Maximum				40

For more guidance on how skills are tested and rewarded, please refer to the section at the start of this question bank.

To:	Gary Orton
From:	A Senior
Date:	11 May 20X8
Subject:	Lyght plc – final and interim audit and ethical issues

1 Concerns of ethics partner

1.1 Tender and low audit fee

Obtaining an audit by tender does not, of itself, give rise to ethical concerns. Similarly, the fact that the bid was at a low price and will generate a substantial under-recovery does not constitute unethical conduct. However there are a number of other potential threats to independence.

1.1.1 Self-interest threat

One threat to independence is a 'self interest' threat. This may occur as a result of any interest of professional accountants that may conflict with their duty to report independently. In this case the threat is that the low bid may have been made in the expectation of obtaining more profitable non-audit work. As the other work has not yet been awarded, the client may pressurise us during the audit by threatening not to award us the other work. If we are awarded the work, the client may threaten during future audits to take it away from us. An alternative self-interest threat may be to 'reward' us with unduly high fees for other tax and advisory work in return for us inappropriately attesting the financial statements.

There is also a potential self-interest threat from doing inadequate amounts of audit procedures in order to reduce the under-recovery. The audit plan should clearly require sufficient, relevant and reliable audit evidence to support the audit opinion, irrespective of the fee.

1.1.2 Self-review threat

If we are successful in gaining the other work there may also be a 'self review' threat. This may occur when a judgement needs to be re-evaluated during the audit by the professional accountant who originally made that judgement.

1.1.3 Non-audit services

ES 5 sets out a clear general approach to non-audit services. Under ES 5 it would never be appropriate for the audit firm to undertake a management role.

Tax work for Lyght would normally be acceptable under ES 5, but the materiality and risks involved in the work would need to be considered on their merits.

The nature of other advisory work would also need to be considered on its merits (the potential tender for the IT work is considered below). Where there is doubt, ES 5 states that our firm should:

- Consider the impact of the provision of non-audit services

- Establish safeguards to counter any threats (which may include resignation or refusal to accept appointment as auditor or provider of the non-audit services)

- Communicate with those charged with governance

- Document the rationale for the decisions taken

According to ES 4 audit staff should not be assessed, or have their pay related to, their ability to cross-sell the firm's products. The suggestion that promotions may depend on selling the additional tax and advisory services to Lyght is ethically inappropriate.

1.2 Size of client

Lyght is a large client for a firm of our size. At the moment it appears the fees from Lyght (if we gain the tax and advisory work) will make up about 8.8% (£0.5m/(£5.2m + £0.5m)) of our firm's total fee income. This is within the bounds set by ES 4 (15% of the firm's total fee income for unlisted client companies). However if Lyght obtains a listing, our fee income would be likely to increase (eg from acting as reporting accountant) and the ethical limit according to ES 4 would fall from 15% to 10%. We are therefore likely to breach the limits at this stage.

According to ES 4, where fees amount to 5% – 10% (for listed clients) or 10% – 15% (for non-listed clients) the fact needs to be disclosed to the ethics partner and those charged with governance at the client and appropriate safeguards adopted where necessary. This may include declining some of the work.

The fee percentage limits in ES 4 are not however rigid. They are based on expected regular levels of fee income and relate to situations where a "reasonable and informed third party" might consider the firm or the engagement partner's objectivity to be impaired.

2 New IT system

2.1 Ethical issues

According to ES 5, the firm should not undertake work on computerised accounting systems on which the auditors would place significant reliance. The threat to independence in this case is one of self-review, the auditors performing services for an assurance client that directly affect the subject matter of the assurance engagement.

Auditor involvement in the design and implementation of IT systems that generate information forming part of a client's financial statements would therefore create a self-review threat. Here Budd & Cherry would only be doing part of the work. It needs to be clearly established how the work would impact upon the financial statements, as opposed to producing management information that did not feed into financial statement disclosures. (The briefing notes state that the new IT system is "to monitor the flows of goods across the globe and for management accounting purposes".)

However, where the information provided by the new IT system is likely to have a significant impact on Lyght's financial statements, then the self-review threat is likely to be too significant to allow us to provide such services. Appropriate safeguards would certainly be required, ensuring that Lyght:

- Acknowledges its responsibility for establishing and monitoring the system of internal controls;

- Makes all management decisions with respect to the design and implementation process;

- Evaluates the adequacy and results of the design and implementation of the system;

- Is responsible for the operation of the system (hardware or software) and the data used or generated by the system.

Additionally the non-assurance services should be provided only by personnel not involved in the financial statement audit engagement and with different reporting lines within the firm.

Nevertheless in spite of the safeguards, the self-review threat may still be considered to be so great that we should not tender for this work.

2.2 Audit issues

2.2.1 Change of system

There are three key aspects that we will need to consider regarding the systems changes implemented during the year.

- The operating effectiveness of the old system

  As this is our first year as auditors we will need to document the old system and gain an understanding of the way in which it operated including an understanding of internal control. The fact that the system has been changed suggests that there may have been particular problems with the old system which we should identify. We should review systems files and interview IT personnel regarding specific deficiencies in the old system that the introduction of the new system has attempted to address.

- The development of the new system including the changeover

  A key risk is the potential loss or corruption of financial information. We will need to establish whether appropriate security for the previous systems was maintained during the development and installation of the new systems. This might have included for example appropriate access controls and confidentiality relating to the new system developers and installers. We also need to obtain details of the way in which data was transferred, details of the controls implemented over the change-over and the extent and results of testing performed on the new system to determine whether it is operating effectively.

- The operating effectiveness of the new system

Systems notes will need to be updated and we will need to ensure that we have an good understanding of the way in which the new system operates including the internal controls implemented by management. We will need to evaluate controls to determine our detailed audit approach. However increased substantive testing of payables and receivables is likely to be necessary due to the increased audit risk resulting from the fact that it is the first year of the audit and systems changes have taken place.

2.2.2 Provision of other servicesThe proposed project commencing in July 20X8 does not affect the current audit but does have implications for future audits. Even if our staff members are not involved in development, as auditors we should be consulted during it and carry out the following procedures:

- At the design stage, ascertain whether the systems specification appears to include appropriate data security and authorisation processes;

- At the design stage, review plans to establish whether there are any obvious problems with data collection, input, processing and output;

- Determine whether all aspects of the systems have been tested, and testing has been carried out by users as well as developers;

- Either by carrying out procedures ourselves, or reviewing the results of internal tests, confirm that controls over security and accuracy of data have been satisfactorily tested;

- Ascertain whether there is a full information trail for the design and development process;

- Confirm that new systems have been approved by management and users;

- Confirm that staff have been fully trained and user documentation is complete.

2.3 Financial reporting issues

Hardware costs recognised as part of plant and equipment will include the purchase price plus the costs directly attributable to bringing the assets to the location and condition necessary to be capable of operating as intended. Installation costs would therefore be capitalised. Related revenue expenditure eg ongoing maintenance costs must not be capitalised but must be recognised in profit or loss. The hardware should be depreciated over its estimated useful economic life from the point that it is available for use.

The computer software should be recognised as an intangible non-current asset in accordance with IAS 38 *Intangible Assets*. It is both identifiable as it is separable and under the control of Lyght. As the software has been provided by an external contractor it should also be possible to measure the software reliably based on the amounts invoiced and paid by Lyght in respect of this. Capitalised costs may include the costs of testing the software prior to use on the basis that these costs are directly attributable. The software should be amortised over its useful economic life commencing when it is available for use.

3 Inventories

3.1 Audit issues

Inventories at around £20 million are clearly material both in their impact on profit and on net assets. Verifying inventories is therefore clearly necessary. If we can obtain sufficient evidence by alternative procedures, then we may be able to give an unmodified audit report in spite of the fact that we have not attended year end inventory counts.

Alternative procedures may include:

- Attendance at physical inventory counts performed after the year-end with a review of the 'roll-back' reconciliation performed by management

- Assess the effectiveness of internal controls and other management controls over inventory amounts and movements;

- Undertake analytical procedures to assess the reasonableness of inventory amounts given the levels of sales and purchases prior to year-end. (This is most valid for sales of large numbers of identical, small items – such as clothing and small appliances – where patterns in sales may be more discernable than for large one-off sales);

- Inspect purchase documentation and ultimate sales and receipt of cash documentation for dates that straddle year-end. (This is most valid for sales of large items – such as medical equipment and military vehicles – where there may be third-party documented verification of dates);

If we are unable to obtain sufficient appropriate evidence regarding the existence of inventory we will need to consider issuing a modified audit opinion due to the limitation on scope of the work we have been able to perform.

This issue of exchange rate volatility gives additional audit concerns. The dates of transactions in foreign currencies need to be established in order to verify the amounts in the functional and presentation currencies. The specific details are considered below under financial reporting issues.

3.2 Financial reporting issues

3.2.1 Foreign currency

According to IAS 21 an entity is required to translate foreign currency items and transactions into its functional currency.

Lyght's functional currency "is the currency of the primary economic environment in which it operates". The primary economic environment "is normally the one in which it primarily generates and expends cash". It is assumed that Lyght's functional currency is sterling as it operates from the UK.

Inventories are a non-monetary asset. Lyght therefore initially records both the inventory and the associated liability at the exchange rate at the date of purchase (perhaps the £/€ rate if acquired within the EU).

The inventory needs no further translating. Thus, while the exchange rates in customers' countries may vary substantially, this will not directly affect inventory values stated at cost. (Any outstanding liability is a monetary item and should be retranslated at the reporting date. Exchange gains and losses should be recognised in profit or loss.)

If however the exchange rate moves substantially post year-end, then the recoverable amounts of inventories may fall in sterling terms, and thus an impairment review may be required.

3.2.2 Other issues

In accordance with IAS 2 Inventories inventories must be valued at the lower of cost and net realisable value. Net realisable value may be a particular issue here due to the 'pre-used' nature of the items sold. Audit procedures should include a review of after date sales with a comparison to cost.

Revenue recognition may also be an issue. Further details are required regarding the point at which revenue is recognised and therefore inventory derecognised, particularly in respect of the high value items where there is an identified buyer prior to the inventory being purchased.

4 Sale of tyres

4.1 Financial reporting issues

4.1.1 The purchase

Lyght bought a batch of tyres from a depot managed by Leslie Moore's cousin. IAS 24 identifies key management personnel which includes directors, and 'close family members' of key management personnel as related parties of an entity. Cousins are not specifically identified in IAS 24 as 'close family members' but the depot manager may fall within the more general description of 'those family members who may be expected to influence, or be influenced by, that individual in their dealings with the company'. The provision of gifts to the depot manager could be a factor which indicates that the depot manager is influenced by Leslie Moore or vice versa. Whether the purchase of the tyres represents a related party transaction requires further investigation. If it is a related party transaction disclosure will be required in the financial statements.

4.1.2 The sale

As an associate company of VenRisk Lyght is a related party of VenRisk. Hott is also an associate of VenRisk and therefore they are related parties, however, Hott is unlikely to be a related party of Lyght, as the possibility of exercising significant influence, or having significant influence exercised upon it, by another associate of VenRisk seems unlikely. More information on governance structures and contractual rights would clarify this situation. The sale of the tyres is thus not a related party transaction.

4.2 Audit issues

4.2.1 Related party transactions

Establishment of whether related party relationships exist is a key issue. Given that the directors do not appear to have made all relevant information available in the first instance there may be a high risk of further undisclosed transactions. Audit procedures need to be designed in this context. The under-disclosure may be due to a lack of knowledge/awareness of the transactions' nature or it may be deliberate concealment.

Audit procedures need to establish and evaluate the controls that exist to identify and approve such transactions.

Audit procedures that may indicate the effectiveness of controls and reveal RPTs include:

- Review the board minutes for transactions with other parties and evidence of influence;
- Review disclosures in previous year's financial statements;
- Review RPT disclosures in the financial statements of entities suspected of being related parties;
- Review large transactions, particularly loans and other financial transactions, for evidence that they may not be on an arm's length basis;
- Review legal correspondence for guarantees and other undertakings where no monetary amount has been transferred;
- Examine shareholder records of group entities and, where possible, of entities suspected of being related parties;
- Enquire of the directors the nature of the controls to identify and record RPTs.

4.2.2 Unethical behaviour

There may have been fraudulent behaviour by Lyght and Leslie Moore. There is a risk that the purchase of tyres by Lyght may be at a price significantly below their fair value. This may be either as a favour to a cousin, or in return for a financial inducement from Lyght. Alternatively, it may be that the purchase price is legitimate. The army may have wished to dispose of the tyres even at a nominal price as it had no other means of distribution. As bulky items, the purchase cost may have been small by comparison to the transport costs to be incurred, making the eventual sale price reasonable. An explanation should however be obtained from Leslie Moore.

The invoice of £3,487 also requires further investigation. The gifts and entertainment may have been provided in order to secure a reduced purchase price. Not only would this represent unethical behaviour but could also be seen as a payment of a bribe in contravention of the Bribery Act. This would be an offence for both the giver and receiver of the bribe. Reasonable and proportionate hospitality would not be considered a bribe however. Further information is required to determine whether illegal acts may have taken place which we, as auditors, may be permitted or required to disclose.

If unethical or illegal behaviour has taken place this also has implications for our assessment of the integrity of management and may affect the extent to which we rely on responses provided by them to other issues.

5 Leased building

5.1 Financial reporting issues

On the basis of the information regarding the length of the lease term, the lease appears to have been misclassified as a finance lease when it should have been classified as an operating lease. If the lease is an operating lease, in accordance with IAS 17 the asset and corresponding liability would not be recognised and the payments under the lease would be recognised in profit or loss on a straight line basis. The classification of the lease for accounting purposes depends on its economic substance rather than legal ownership. Therefore where the risks and rewards of ownership are transferred to the lessee, a lease is classified as a finance lease. More information is required to determine the appropriate treatment.

The lease was initially capitalised at £1.1 million, which is material in the context of the statement of financial position. However the misclassification has not led to profits being materially misstated. The annual lease payment of £150,000 is 1.25% of pre-tax profits of £12 million, which would not normally be regarded as material. In addition the impact of not charging the £150,000 lease payments is mitigated by the fact that £110,000 depreciation (£1.1 million/10) will be recognised in profit or loss.

5.2 Audit issues

We would carry out the following audit procedures in connection with the lease:

- Review the lease agreement and assess whether the terms appear to show that the risks and rewards have been transferred to Lyght (for example is Lyght allowed to sublet the office space?);

- Assess the significance of arrangements at the end of the finance lease (in particular whether legal title transfers to Lyght or whether Lyght has been granted an option to extend the lease so that it could occupy the premises for all or a substantial part of its economic life);

- Examine invoices and other documents related to maintenance, insurance and other office costs to assess the economic substance of the lease terms;

- Inspect the premises to confirm their existence and that they are used by Lyght;

If we conclude that the treatment as a finance lease is correct the following procedures would be required:

- Recalculate the present value of lease payments, confirming that the calculation is taken from the start of the lease date, and that the finance cost is being spread over the lease term in a method that accords with IAS 17;

- Agree payment figures and implicit interest rate used to lease agreement

- Recalculate the depreciation charge and agree the calculation basis to the accounting policy note

- Check that disclosures of liabilities under the lease are in accordance with IAS 17

If we decide that the lease has been misclassified we would discuss the matter with management. If management were to refuse to revise the financial statements a qualified audit opinion would be given on the grounds of material misstatement (disagreement) in respect of non-compliance with IAS 17.

6 Asset treated as available for sale

6.1 Financial reporting issues

Lyght has classified its head office as available for sale from 1 January 20X8 on the basis that management made the decision to dispose of this asset on that date. However in accordance with IFRS 5 certain conditions must be met in order for this classification to be made. These are as follows:

- The asset must be available for immediate sale in its present condition
- Its sale must be highly probable

For the sale to be highly probable:

- Management must be committed to the plan

- There must be an active programme to locate a buyer

- The asset must be marketed for sale at a price that is reasonable in relation to its current fair value

- The sale should be expected to take place within one year from the date of classification

- It is unlikely that any significant changes to the plan will be made or that the plan will be withdrawn.

On the basis that Lyght is not planning to market the property until May 20X8 and there is no current active programme to locate a buyer, all of the above conditions are not met. The asset should not therefore be classified as held for resale but should be retained within property, plant and equipment and should be depreciated for the remainder of the year. This would result in an additional depreciation charge of approximately £33,000 (2,000,000/20 × 4/12).

On the basis that Lyght has treated the asset as held for sale the following adjustments would have been reflected in the draft financial statements:

	£000	£000
DR Assets held for sale (1,600 –20)		1,580
DR Profit or loss	20	
DR Revaluation surplus	400	
CR Property, plant and equipment		2,000

These entries should be reversed on the basis that the treatment of the asset as held for sale is not in accordance with IFRS 5.

Impairment of the asset should also be considered if its recoverable amount is less than the carrying amount. See audit issues below.

6.2 Audit issues

- Confirm with management that marketing is only going to commence on 1 May 20X8 ie the asset does not qualify as available for sale at the period end.

- Consider materiality. The treatment of the property as held for sale has resulted in a reduction in net assets of 1.2% (420/36,000). However if the property is deemed to have suffered an impairment the difference in the financial effect of the two treatments may be negligible. Further investigation is required. In this instance materiality also needs to be considered from the qualitative aspect as well as the quantitative aspect. The classification adopted in the draft financial statements results in the property being removed from non-current assets and being disclosed separately immediately below current assets. This impacts on the perception of the company's liquidity.

- Check that the asset has been included in property plant and equipment and that it has been depreciated for the full year. The net impact of correcting the treatment of £13,000 (33,000 additional depreciation – 20,000 estimated costs of disposal) is unlikely to be material however the additional depreciation is consistent with continued recognition of the asset as part of property, plant and equipment.

- Consider whether the property has suffered an impairment. Its fair value is currently below its carrying value. An assessment of the value in use of the asset should be made to determine whether an adjustment is required. If the recoverable amount (higher of fair value less costs of disposal and value in use in accordance with IAS 36) is less than the carrying amount the asset will be impaired and should be written down to its recoverable amount. Any loss would initially be treated as a revaluation decrease.

7 Receivables

7.1 Financial reporting issues

7.1.1 IAS 39 requirements

IAS 39 classifies trade receivables as financial assets, under the heading of loans and receivables.

IAS 39 requires that loans and receivables should be measured at amortised cost using the effective interest rate method. However it allows short-term receivables with no stated interest rates to be measured at the original invoiced amount, if the effect of discounting is not material.

IAS 39 also requires an annual exercise, in order to assess, at each reporting date, whether there is any objective evidence that the receivable is impaired. If so, then the carrying amount of the trade receivable must be compared with the present value of the estimated future cash flows.

Lyght has calculated the impairment partly using a formulaic approach. This is only acceptable if it produces an estimate sufficiently close to that produced by the IAS 39 method. The general allowance of 5% is not acceptable, because it is not based on past experience and is unlikely to be an accurate estimate of the cash flows that will be received.

7.1.2 Cristina

Where it is probable that payment will not be received in full for a significant balance, an allowance for impairment must be made. It looks as if Cristina will pay in full plus a penalty. However, the payment will be in a year's time, and so discounting should be used to calculate its present value and hence any impairment. The receivable should be recorded at 30 April 20X8 as £1,944,444 (2,100,000 × 1/(1.08)

As the receivable is not due to be paid until 1 May 20X9 the asset is recoverable after more than one year from the date of the statement of financial position. However in accordance with IAS 1 it will still be classified as a current asset as current assets include assets that are sold, consumed and realised as part of the normal operating cycle even where they are not expected to be realised within 12 months.

7.1.3 Foreign exchange translation

As with inventories, there is also the issue of translating foreign currency items in accordance with the requirements of IAS 21. The receivables balance due from Boulogne SA is a monetary item, so must be shown in the statement of financial position translated at the exchange rate at the reporting date. Any exchange gain or loss on retranslation will be recognised in profit or loss.

7.2 Audit issues

We would carry out the following audit procedures in connection with the allowance:

- Review correspondence with the Cristina government and assess whether its commitment appears legally binding;

- Consider whether external factors may result in the monies owed by Cristina not being paid, such as a likely change of government in the next year;

- Determine the basis on which the 8% effective interest rate has been calculated (In accordance with IAS 39 the effective interest rate is the rate that exactly discounts estimated future cash payments or receipts through the expected life of the financial instrument to the net carrying amount of the financial asset);

- For other receivables, examine customer files on overdue debts, and assess whether additional allowances are required;

- Ensure that the allowance made in the accounts relates to specific receivables, and does not include any general allowance;

- Confirm that all other receivables (apart from Boulogne SA) are denominated in sterling;

- Assess the need to recognise any impairment of the value of material balances if the exchange rate weakens materially between the date of the year-end and the audit;

- Review any significant changes in circumstances occurring between the interim audit and the final audit.

22 Minnex

Note:

The solutions provided are more detailed than would be expected from even a very well prepared candidate. They reflect a range of points that could be raised by candidates generally.

Background comments

The scenario in this question concerns a listed company, Minnex, which operates a chain of department stores located throughout the world, but with a concentration in the UK. The company has been struggling in recent years and, as a consequence, the board was replaced about a year ago. The new board has begun to implement a reorganisation including the raising of new finance. The candidate is placed in the position of an audit senior at the interim audit. A number of issues have arisen concerning: a reorganisation, management remuneration, and financing.

Candidates are required to set out and explain the correct financial reporting treatment for each of these issues and to redraft the financial statements to include any adjustments arising from the matters raised. Also, with respect to each of the matters raised, the audit manager has identified specific auditing and advisory issues that the candidate is required to address.

The solution below provides significant detail, but it is sufficient for a good quality answer, that would obtain a clear pass mark, to provide concise explanations/calculations relating to the following:

- The reorganisation issue should clearly identify the relevant IFRS 5 criteria and apply them to the two stores, noting uncertainties. The audit tests should question the assertions made by the director including the values provided and should consider the impact of future decisions, including those before the year end.

- The remuneration section should apply the relevant IFRS 2 criteria, with clear supporting calculations. The auditing considerations should include an identification of the factors affecting the fair value of the options in this scenario.

- The financing section should include the correct identification of the swap as a fair value hedge and set out the relevant entries. The auditing section should explain the risk management issues and the nature of the supporting documentation required to substantiate hedge effectiveness. The loan stock and the bank loan should also be compared qualitatively and quantitatively. A clear explanation of the assurance issues for the bank loan should also be provided.

- The adjustments should be incorporated into revised financial statements and the necessary EPS variants should be computed.

Memorandum

To: Eddie Futch (audit manager)
From: T.I. Senior
Date: 1 December 20X6
Subject: Minnex audit

1   The reorganisation

Financial reporting

IFRS 5 requires that a non-current asset, such as one of Minnex's retail stores (or disposal group of assets eg including the stores' fixtures and fittings), should be classified as 'held for sale' when the company does not intend to utilise the asset as part of its on-going business but instead intends to sell it. The two Scottish stores identified in the Minnex Strategic Review are therefore potentially in this category.

To be classified as 'held for sale' the stores should be available for immediate sale. The likelihood of a sale taking place should also be considered to be highly probable and normally completed within one year of the date of its classification. Also, the stores must be actively marketed for sale by Minnex at a price that is reasonable in relation to its current fair value (which appears to be the case for the Edinburgh store where the expected sales price is £24 million and the fair value is £25 million). For a sale to be considered as highly probable there should be a committed plan and Minnex management should be actively trying to find a buyer. The commitment by Minnex's management that a sale will take place should be such that withdrawal from the plan is unlikely.

The conditions for sale should be met before the end of the reporting period if the stores are to be recognised as 'held for sale' assets in Minnex's statement of financial position at 31 December 20X6. If the conditions are only met after the end of the reporting period, there should be full disclosure in the notes to the financial statements. Depreciation should cease when the held for sale criteria are satisfied.

Edinburgh store – It would appear that this store should probably be treated as 'held for sale' if a contract is drawn up with a specific buyer and if completion is due only three months after the year end. However, if the company did not wish to have the asset treated as held for sale, it would need to delay signing the contract until after 31 December 20X6, but even this may not be sufficient, as there would need to be significant uncertainty regarding the sale and contract completion before the asset would not be treated as held for sale.

Glasgow store – As the decision has not yet been made it would appear unlikely that there is currently a committed plan, even though a potential buyer has been found. On the basis of current evidence therefore, this store is not 'held for sale' in accordance with IFRS 5. This situation must be reviewed, however, up to 31 December 20X6 in case such conditions are fulfilled before the year end.

Accounting treatment

A non-current asset, or disposal group, that meets the recognition criteria to be classified as 'held for sale' should be measured at the lower of its carrying amount and its fair value less costs to sell at the date that they are deemed as held for sale. The current values will therefore need to be reassessed at this date.

Separate disclosure in the statement of profit or loss and other comprehensive income as 'discontinued operations' is also required when a company discontinues a 'component' of its activities, which should have been a cash generating unit while held for use. The definition of a discontinued operation is when it is classified as 'held for sale' or when it is sold and according to IFRS 5 para 32:

(a) Represents a separate major line of the business or geographical area of operations

(b) Is part of a single co-ordinated plan to dispose of a separate major line of the business or geographical area of operations; **or**

(c) Is a subsidiary acquired exclusively with a view to resale

Thus, in this case, IFRS 5 para 32(b) probably applies as the closures are part of the single co-ordinated plan to withdraw from the Scottish market as part of the strategic review.

A component of an entity comprises operations and cash flows that can be clearly distinguished operationally, and for financial reporting purposes, from the rest of the entity and this seems likely to include each individual Minnex store given their size and discrete nature. The question of whether the two closures are 'major' is, however, a question of judgement. However, from the redrafted financial statements (see below) the profit after tax from continuing operations is £7.66 million while the profit after tax of discontinued operations is around £1.54 million (which is just the Edinburgh store). Thus discontinued profit is 20% of continuing profit, which would normally be judged to be 'major'. As the disposal is to be made under multiple contracts to different purchasers it does not constitute a disposal group.

Edinburgh store – Given that the carrying amount (£2m) is significantly less than the fair value and the estimated sales proceeds, no adjustment would be made to the asset's value upon classification as a 'held for sale' asset. These values should be re-estimated at their year end values, but on reclassification as held for sale there should be no further depreciation.

Assuming classification as 'held for sale' before the year-end, the profit relating to the Edinburgh store should be disclosed separately as discontinued operations in the statement of profit or loss. If revenue is £14 million, then cost of sales is 66% of this amount at approximately £9.2m. Operating profit is £2m, leaving £2.8m for other operating costs. These figures should be backed out of the continuing activities net of tax.

Glasgow store – While the Glasgow store should not be classified as 'held for sale,' its fair value (£8m) is less than the carrying amount (£12m).

At the year end, there is a requirement to consider whether there is indicative evidence of impairment in accordance with IAS 36. The difference identified above is an indicator of impairment. Given that the Glasgow store is to be sold, and does not appear to be making any profit, its value-in-use does not appear to be significant. There should therefore be an impairment charge of £4m in respect of the Glasgow store. The 31 December values should be used for impairment so the valuations need to be reviewed at the year end for any major changes from those existing at 30 November.

The impairment charge may affect the deferred tax charge/balance as it has no effect on the tax base but it will change the carrying amount. More information will be required to consider the deferred tax adjustment further.

Specific audit and advisory issues

Establishing fair values

The fair value assertions made by Minnex's management in respect of the two properties planned for disposal need to be evidenced by third party valuations. This may be evidence provided by management's experts, independent third parties used by the client (eg valuers) or, where there is doubt, it may be necessary to commission our own expert independent valuations, especially if the sales of the properties have not been completed by the time we conduct the audit.

Audit tests may include scrutiny of: board minutes; strategic plans; legal contracts and correspondence; valuations; budgets; performance reports. If we use evidence provided by management's experts we will need to perform audit procedures to evaluate the competence, capabilities and objectivity of that expert, obtain an understanding of the work of that expert; and evaluate the appropriateness of that expert's work as audit evidence.

2   **Managerial remuneration**

Financial reporting

The share option issue is an equity-settled share-based payment transaction in accordance with IFRS 2.

The three years of service required by the option contract is a non-market vesting condition which should be taken into account (per IFRS 2, para 19) when estimating the number of options which will vest at the end of each period. The proportion of directors and senior managers retained is therefore relevant in determining the remuneration charge arising from the options.

The retention rate is not, however, relevant in determining the fair value of the options which are measured at their fair value at the grant date (per IFRS 2 para 11). It is thus the fair value at 1 December 20X6 that is used in determining the remuneration expense (ie £3).

The cumulative remuneration expense in respect of the options is thus:

(The number of managers expected to be retained for three years) × (the number of options granted) × (fair value of options at the grant date) × (the proportion of the vesting period elapsed).

As there was no brought forward amount in respect of the options, the remuneration expense for the year ended 31 December 20X6 is:

(120,000 × 75) × (80%) × £3 × 1/36 months = £600,000

The expected number of options to be issued will depend on management's estimates at 31 December 20X6 about retention. In this illustration the expectation at the date of grant has been used. The change is unlikely to be material in such a short period of time.

In 20X7 however there will be a full year's charge of:

(120,000 × 75) × (80%) × £3 × 1/3 years = £7.2 million.

This assumes that there is no change in the estimated retention rate.

This would be a substantial amount in relation to the current profit before tax. (It would however be moderated by the deferred tax effect in terms of profit after tax – see below.)

The financial reporting expense charged to profit or loss in respect of equity-settled share-based payments does not normally correspond to the tax charge. A tax allowable expense in connection with a share-based scheme is available at the date of exercise, measured on the basis of the option's intrinsic value at that date.

As a result, there is a deferred tax impact, as a deductible temporary difference arises between the tax base of the remuneration expense recognised in the profit or loss and its carrying amount of nil in the statement of financial position (as the credit is to equity). This generates a deferred tax asset.

A further difficulty in the calculation of the deferred tax asset is that the share price for tax purposes is determined at the exercise date which is unknown at Minnex's current year end. It therefore needs to be based on the best available information which is normally the value at the year end.

Therefore if the intrinsic value of an option is £3.33 (ie £6 – £2.67) at 31 December 20X6:

Then the tax deduction per share is £3.33

The total tax deduction is therefore £3.33 × (120,000 × 75) × 80% = £24m

The deductible temporary difference relating to the expense recognised to date is:

is therefore:

£24m × 1/3 × 1/12 × 23% = £153,000

This will be recognised as a deferred tax credit in the statement of profit or loss and other comprehensive income and a deferred tax asset in the statement of financial position.

Notes:

1 IAS 12 requires the use of the liability method, which means that we use the tax rate in force when the liability reverses. This may not be 23%; however, given that the tax rate is not expected to change at present, it is reasonable to assume a rate of 23%.

2 This deferred tax adjustment is rounded to £0.05m in the adjustments to the financial statements in the appendix below.

Specific audit and advisory issues

Valuing of options

The fair value of the options depends on a number of variables and these need to be judged in an option pricing model (eg Black-Scholes-Merton model, Binomial Lattice, Monte Carlo simulation). The key date to judge fair value is the proposed grant date for Minnex which is 1 December 20X6.

The following variables are relevant to the fair value of Minnex's share options:

The underlying share price – as Minnex is a listed company the share price is observable. While it may change from its current estimated value before granting this is likely to be insignificant given the short time span.

Exercise price – this is determined by the terms of the arrangement and is thus known and verifiable.

Dividend – given that the option holders are not normally entitled to a dividend, the greater the dividend the lower the share price and thus the lower the option price. Any uncertainty in dividend policy will therefore impact upon the fair value of the options. The past dividend history of Minnex would indicate future dividends but a review of board minutes may indicate any change in intended dividend policy.

Volatility – there are a number of different measures of volatility but, in general, the greater the volatility in the underlying share price the greater the value of the option. This is because option holders have downside protection from large falls in share price but have upside potential for increases in share price. The historic share price of Minnex appears to have been volatile but the key issue is future volatility, which is difficult to ascertain and verify as it depends upon market expectations.

Interest rates – if interest rates increase then the present value at the exercise date decreases.

The intrinsic value of the option is used if estimates are unreliable but given that Minnex is a listed company this is unlikely. The intrinsic value is, however, an initial lower boundary guide price for the fair value of the option before considering other variables such as the time to exercising and volatility.

Matters to discuss with the audit committee

The basis upon which the company determines the fair value of the options will have to be discussed. It is unlikely that any of the instruments has a comparable financial instrument that is actively traded on the open market. As discussed above, the values should be based upon one of the recognised valuation models provided in finance theory, maximising the use of observable inputs as required by IFRS 13. These are combined with a number of inputs such as whether the options are 'in the money' or not, the remaining life of the options and the volatility of the underlying shares.

Provided the company is using an orthodox valuation model and calculated the estimated fair values using historical observations of the associated parameters, it should be relatively straightforward for us to check that the resulting figures are defensible. We might consider

The numb
conditions
options or
informatic

The assum
audit com
assumptic
company
This is, ho

3   Financinc

3.1 Bond anc

Financial r

Assuming

Assuming
the adjust

The swap

Dr   D
Cr   C

The swap
value:

Dr   D
Cr   Ir

Being the

Dr   Ir
Cr   L

Being the

Settlemer

Dr   C
Cr   D

Note: the

The draft
the hedg
impact o
at amorti
the bond
expense

Specific

Risk man

Minnex
fixed rate
moveme

While fai
more risl

The swaj
changes

IAS
esti

Thu

£45

Thu

(12

The

£9.

Dilu

£7.

Dilu
at
effe
dilu

Appenc

Forecas

Revenue
Cost of
Other e:
Financir
Profit be
Tax
Profit fr
Profit fr
   opera
Profit af

Notes –

(a) Re

(b) Im

(c) Sh

(d) Lo
     10
     ad

Forecas

ASSETS
Non-cu
        F

Current
        F
        I
        1
        C

        N
Total as

---

23   Sunnidaze

Marking guide

	Marks		
	Technical	*Skills*	
Prepare a memorandum setting out and explaining the additional audit adjustments and unresolved audit matters identified at our follow up visit together with a brief summary of any additional audit procedures required	8	13	Identify that the intangible does not seem to have been amortised since its acquisition and that this is an error
Drafting of revised financial statements			Ascertain gaps in work performed and recommend appropriate audit work
			Link inadequacy of zero provision against the £186,000 receivables with the type of customer (local builders who may be experiencing financial difficulty)
			Linking issues with audit risk eg goods delivered to the health club in June but not installed until some months later, together with delays in the payment of year end receivables suggests that revenue may be being recognised too early
			Question the verity of situations – eg query whether customers actually required the goods to be delivered pre year end and hence that revenue has been artificially accelerated into the prior year
			Identify omissions – eg need to take into account the cost of bringing the inventory back to the warehouse therefore can only determine precise entry with more information
			Appreciate that client may not agree to additional audit adjustments
			Appreciate that shareholders may not be willing or have the ability to put in more capital
			Recognise that adjustments may not be material but client unwillingness to book is concerning
			Appreciate that the cumulative effect of adjustments identified exceeds materiality
Your comments on any more general concerns including ethical issues you have in relation to the audit as a whole and what our audit response to these concerns should be	3	8	Identify the potential for manipulation by management
			Identify the implications of personal guarantees given by shareholders
			Identify no duty to disclose this to any party outside the client despite concern that wildly optimistic forecasts may be being used to attract investors
			Recognise more rigorous audit work required to satisfy concerns over manipulation of results
			Recommend that if additional audit work identified any deliberate attempt to deceive potential investors then that might be fraud and reportable under money laundering regulations – would need to consult firm's MLRO
			Identify possibility of not continuing to act as auditors

	Technical	Skills	
			Identify specific examples of potential manipulation eg inappropriate classification of bad debt provision adjustment: some indication that revenue has been accelerated; high level of unrecognised liabilities; unwillingness to agree to and recognise one of the audit adjustments
			Identify risk of Arnold's involvement in the determination of provisions and other judgmental areas
Brief notes setting out an explanation of the form of audit opinion we should give	2	6	Identify that going concern is a key issue
			Identify the importance of management taking responsibility for the conclusion about whether the entity is a going concern
			Conclude that going concern unlikely to require adjustment but emphasis of matter would be required in auditor's report
			Conclude that if disclosures not adequate then there would be a qualified or adverse opinion
Explanation of treatment of sale and leaseback transaction	2	4	Recognition of split between land and buildings
			Treatment of profit
			Treatment of subsequent lease
Total marks	15	31	
Maximum		40	

Memorandum

Additional audit adjustments and unresolved audit matters, together with additional procedures required

Credit note adjustment not posted

Although the final Jacuzzi was not delivered until after the reporting date, it must have been clear at the year end that ten were to be delivered and that a discount would therefore be given. We need to check that the discount arose from a commitment pre year end rather than a post year end decision but, assuming this to be the case, an adjustment to account for the discount on nine items should be posted:

DR   Revenue   £9,000
CR   Receivables   £9,000

This amount is not by itself material but the client's unwillingness to book it is a little concerning. We will need to reassess this along with any other unrecognised adjustments at the end of the audit.

Late adjustments made by client – health club receivable

Clearly it is appropriate to make provision for the health club receivable, because the specialist nature of the product (luxury hot tubs) means that, as per the appendix to IAS 18, point 2, revenue should not have been booked until the installation was complete. However, not so clear that this should be recorded as an exceptional item. The amount must be reversed from revenue.

Hence:

DR   Revenue   £42,000
CR   Exceptional item   £42,000

In addition, we need to consider the entry for inventory that is expected to be returned. We can only record this at the lower of cost and net realisable value and will need to take into account the cost of bringing the inventory back to the warehouse. Hence, we can only determine the precise entry with more information.

Assuming appropriate to record at cost and average margin made, likely entry is:

DR   Inventory   £22,260   (assumes margin of approx 47% as per statement of profit or loss and
                                    other comprehensive income)

CR   Cost of sales   £22,260

However also it is likely some provision is required against the inventory as this will not be in pristine condition, and therefore the net realisable value is likely to fall below cost.

> ## Tutorial note:
>
> Reasonable estimates of this were accepted.

Late adjustments made by client – broader implications of delay in installation

Concerning the goods which were delivered to the health club in June but not installed until some months later – this together with delays in the payment of year end receivables suggests that revenue may be being recognised too early. We will need further audit procedures to consider:

- Extent of revenue recognised for goods delivered pre year end but installed afterwards

- Whether installation is optional or required for all sales in which case it could be argued that the installation cannot be separated from the supply of goods and no revenue should be recognised until installation is complete

- Whether there is a separate charge for installation and if so, when is that element invoiced

- Does some installation revenue need to be deferred at year end or is a cost accrual more appropriate. Has such an accrual been made?

- Whether customers actually required the goods to be delivered pre year end. Possible that revenue has been artificially accelerated into the prior year especially as post year end sales are quite low. Need to look at customer order information re required date of delivery and consider circularising customers. Particular attention should also be given to invoices still not paid or paid some time after year end.

Bonus accrual

The entry seems reasonable as the bonus clearly relates to performance for the financial year which draft accounts show has met the target.

It is unclear whether the related social security taxes have been accrued – we need to check this.

In addition, adjustments may mean that the target operating profit has not in fact been met, in which case the bonus would need to be reversed.

Dividend

This should not be accrued unless actually declared pre year end which seems unlikely. We may well have been a similar error in prior year as brought forward retained earnings nil so will need to check this.

Intangible assets

Intangible assets do not seem to have been amortised since its acquisition which is an error. Total amortisation to the reporting date should be £250,000 on a straight line basis of which £200,000 should have been booked in prior years (see consideration under general matters below of potential implications of this). Hence adjustment required:

DR   Operating expenses   £50,000
DR   Retained earnings at 30 June 20X5   £200,000
CR   Intangible asset   £250,000

We need to consider whether the remaining balance of £250,000 is impaired, given reducing sales of the DupaSpa product. If sales are expected to continue at the 20X6 level then the asset is probably not impaired as £400,000 @ 47% = £188,000 of margin generated in one year. However we need to look in more detail at forecast sales for the DupaSpa product and the cash flows arising and perform sensitivity analysis.

Cash after date – recoverability of receivables

We are now four months after the year end so we would expect all balances outstanding at the reporting date to have paid. It seems unlikely that a nil provision against the £186,000 outstanding is adequate, especially as some debts are due from local builders who may be experiencing financial difficulty. Again much more analysis is required to determine the level of allowance required – we need to look at each customer in turn and analyse the reasons for non-payment.

We should also consider days sales outstanding (DSO) at the year end and on average when considering whether receipts have been received within the anticipated time period or whether there is any indication of extended payment terms being offered.

Bank loan

The instalment of £400,000 due on 31 December 20X6 should be classified within current liabilities not long term creditors.

It is not clear how loan arrangement fee has been treated – it may have been expensed, or recognised within other current assets. Should be spread over term of loan in proportion to outstanding balance giving rise to a charge to profit or loss.

For year ended 30 June 20X6, a crucial measure for the covenant is an operating profit of no lower than £280,000.

Draft financial statements show £467,000, adjusted to £388,000 (467–9–42+22–50) by the above adjustments. However there are also potentially significant adjustments re loan fee, bad debts, intangible impairment and revenue recognition which could reduce this below £280,000. In this case the bonus accrual might also be reversed. Hence finalisation of accounts is crucial in determining whether there has been any breach.

It seems odd that there are no restrictions in respect of dividends and major transactions (including sale of shares) in the agreement – there needs to be a review by more senior personnel to ensure that all relevant factors have been summarised and taken into account. In addition need to check whether there is any obligation for the auditor to report direct to bank as this would require a separate engagement.

Review of post year end results

The key issue to be considered here is going concern. Results are not in line with budget and operating profits at this level are insufficient to meet the covenant going forward (which requires £280,000 profit for the year). The inability to comply with loan agreements is a key factor which may cast doubt on the application of the going concern assumption. The cash balance will be seriously depleted once the loan repayment and dividend paid, although movement for the post year end period is not out of line with operating profit.

It is important that management takes responsibility for the conclusion about whether the entity is a going concern and produces forecasts and arguments to support this, which are then audited. We will need detailed cash flow forecasts for at least a 12 month period (from date of signing) to consider going concern and these should include modelling to ensure that covenants will be met. The budget should be used as a starting point but will need a critical review and sensitivity analysis, as there is an indication that it may be far too optimistic – we need to make sure specifically that factors such as declining sales are taken into account. In addition, ongoing changes to accounting policies in respect of revenue recognition and intangible amortisation need to be taken into account when modelling the covenant compliance as these may affect operating profit in future.

Another factor to consider is the willingness and ability of shareholders to put in more capital. This seems unlikely as they are actually planning to sell. However they are already at risk over bank borrowing and finding a buyer may be difficult.

Maisie's view of forecasts must be considered when planning our work.

Revised summary financial information

	Per draft financial statements £'000	Adjustments £000	Revised balances £000
		(9) (42) (50 amortisation)	
Operating profit	467	22	388
Exceptional items	(42)	42	–
Interest payable	(100)		(100)
Profit before taxation	325		288
Taxation	(125)		(125)
Profit after taxation	200		163
Assets			
Property, plant and equipment	392		392
Intangible assets	500	(250)	250
Inventories	1,392	(22)	1,414
Trade receivables	1,587	(9)	1,578
Other current assets	40		40
Cash and cash equivalents	555		555
	4,466		4,229
Equity and liabilities			
Share capital	1,000		1,000
Retained earnings (from P/L)	200	(37)	163
Long-term borrowings	2,000	(400) 1,600	
Trade and other payables	1,141		1,141
Loan		400	400
Tax payable	125		125
	4,466		4,229

Comments on more general concerns

Ethical considerations and fraud risk

Knowledge of Maisie's view of the forecasts needs further consideration. There is no duty to disclose this to any party outside the client despite concern that wildly optimistic forecasts may be being used to attract investors, unless there is the possibility that there is misconduct by a member of the Institute or reportable fraud.

Discussion of concerns with the directors is possible but would need to be done sensitively and without quoting Maisie's view. The most appropriate way to address this is to plan very rigorous work on the forecasts as part of the going concern review, challenging assumptions and subjecting them to sensitivity analysis.

If this work identified any deliberate attempt to deceive potential investors then that might be fraud and reportable under money laundering regulations – we would need to consult the firm's MLRO.

We might also want, at that point, to reconsider whether we wanted to continue to act as auditors.

Potential investment has raised the risk associated with audit conclusions and it may be necessary to revisit risk considerations and/or allocate additional reviews.

Fraud risk

All three directors have a strong incentive to ensure that operating profit is stated at a certain level either because of bonus arrangements or personal guarantees and a desire to sell the company at the best price.

Inappropriate classification of the adjustment to the allowance for receivables and some indication that revenue has been accelerated may suggest that they are prepared to manipulate the results to meet this target as might the high level of unrecognised liabilities identified by our earlier work and their unwillingness to agree to and recognise one of the audit adjustments.

Arnold has potentially been involved in the determination of provisions and other judgmental areas. We need to ensure that our procedures throughout the audit take into account this risk of fraud and that we revisit any areas where we have relied on written representations from management. We may also enlist the use of a specialist to assist the audit team.

Time-scales and need for appropriate focus on audit completion

The financial statements need to be delivered to the bank before the end of November so time is tight. A meeting with the bank is also clearly very important and it is crucial that directors understand fully the status of the audit, further work that is required and final review processes necessary to close down the audit completely. Time must be allowed for audit completion and necessary quality control procedures.

Opening balances

Prior year accounts were unaudited and work on intangibles and dividends suggests that they may include a number of misstatements. We need to ensure that sufficient work has been performed on all opening balances. Areas of particular focus might include:

Revenue recognition and cut-off
Purchases
Capitalisation policy and existence of property, plant and equipment
Adequacy of provisions
Classification of items within the financial statements

If there is any indication of accounting irregularity or a deliberate intention to mislead tax authorities or bank in the past, then we should reconsider whether we want to act for this client at all. It may, however, just be due to ignorance about accounting standards or lack of clarity about the GAAP being followed.

We have full responsibility for comparative figures in the accounts even though no opinion is given on them.

Materiality

Materiality was initially set at £30,000 based on a profit before tax of £551,000. This in itself may be a little high as it is slightly above normal benchmarks, especially given that this is a first year audit.

Profit is likely to be much lower and headroom compared to the bank covenant could be very tight. We need to revisit this level of materiality and consider if it should be lower which might well require additional audit procedures.

Another factor relevant to this is the very high level of adjustments identified to date – this far exceeds materiality and presumably estimation of likely mis-statements. Again this could require some re-assessment of performance materiality as applied to each balance tested and to the sample sizes used during our audit procedures. Again additional work may well be necessary.

Consideration of form of audit opinion

Key factors for consideration here are:

- Whether client will agree to additional audit adjustments – if not then there may be a qualified audit opinion setting out the matters on which we have been unable to agree. Such a paragraph would depend entirely on the reasons for the disagreement and the nature of the items involved. Opinion might even be adverse if matters are of such significance that this is justified.

- Whether we believe we can gain sufficient audit evidence to give an opinion. There is no evidence that we cannot in this case, although reliance on written representations from management could become an issue if further work uncovers evidence of fraud.

- Seems unlikely that things are so bad that the going concern assumption will be inappropriate although this could be the case if the bank calls in the loan. However, there may well be significant uncertainty over the entity's ability to continue as a going concern or possible insufficient disclosure by the directors of the relevant factors. Assuming disclosures are sufficient, we would not modify our opinion but would include an emphasis of matter drawing attention to the uncertainty and the key factors underlying it. In this case, it would be continued compliance with the covenant and cash flows sufficient to repay the loan and interest as they fall due while meeting all other obligations. If disclosures are not adequate then there would be a qualified or adverse opinion. If management will not provide an adequate review for a long enough period then might possibly be a need to modify report due to inadequate audit evidence.

We will also need a reference in auditor's report to fact that prior year comparatives are unaudited, although we still have responsibility to perform appropriate procedures in respect of opening balances and to ensure that adequate disclosures are made.

We should also consider the use of the Bannerman clause in respect of duty of care.

Sale and leaseback transaction

- IAS 17 requires the land element of the sale and leaseback transaction to be classified as an operating lease

- The treatment of the lease over the building depends on the terms of the lease

- In accordance with IAS 17 there are five factors which would normally indicate that a lease is a finance lease:

    - The lease transfers ownership of the asset at the end of the lease term;

    - The lessee has the option to purchase the asset at a price sufficiently below fair value at the option exercise date, that it is reasonable certain the option will be exercised;

    - The lease term is for the major part of the asset's economic life even if title is not transferred;

    - Present value of the minimum lease payments amounts to substantially all of the asset's fair value at inception;

    - The leased asset is so specialised that it could only be used by the lessee without major modifications being made.

- More details are required regarding the terms of the lease but based on the information provided:

    - The lease term of 20 years is inconclusive as the asset is a building (buildings may have a useful life well in excess of 20 years)

    - The present value of the minimum lease payments does appear to amount to substantially all of the asset's fair value at inception. The present value of the minimum lease payments in respect of the warehouse building is £204,326 (32,000 × ¾ × 8.5136). This is 97.2% of the fair value of the warehouse building 204,326/(3/4 × 280,000). On this basis it is likely that the lease will be treated as a finance lease.

- As a sale and operating leaseback transaction, the land should be derecognised and the profit on sale should be recognised immediately (as the original cost of the property and the land was £75,000 it is highly probable that a profit will be made on sale).

    The operating lease element will then be recognised over the lease term. In this case this would result in an annual charge of £8,000 (1/4 × £32,000).

- Assuming the lease of the property is a finance lease any profit would be deferred and amortised over the lease term.

- The asset and finance lease liability will initially be recognised as £204,326 (see above). This is the lower of the present value of the minimum lease payments and the fair value of £210,000 (3/4 × £280,000).

24 Tydaway

		Technical	Skills	
		Marks		
(i)	Follow up work from inventory count	5	7	Identify gaps in work performed
				Recognise inadequacies in count procedures
				Identify need for roll forward
				Identify directional testing for understatement in mezzanine area
				Recognise cut off error possible from inadequate counting in dispatch area
				Recommend additional tests for the audit senior to complete
(ii)	Audit work arising from concerns and need to address financial statement assertions	5	8	Recognise assertions relevant to scenario
				Identify that different methods of valuation require two different audit approaches
				Recognise relevant financial reporting adjustments arising from the scenario
				Relate price variance to year end valuation
				Appropriate financial data analysis to support audit assertions
				Identify need for additional work required on Woodtydy opening balances
				Recognise no work done on provision
				Eliminate double counting from intercompany sales
				Recommend additional procedures to support audit assertions
(iii)	Financial reporting effects of four hedging options		10	Assimilate the relevant information and apply relevant regulations to demonstrate the impact of foreign currency exposure and related hedging on the financial statements
(iv)	Explanation and comparison of the alternative financial reporting treatments	2	3	Assimilate information and draw valid comparisons highlighting key differences
(v)	Documentation required for audit purposes	3	2	
Total marks		<u>15</u>	<u>30</u>	
Maximum		<u>40</u>		

(i)   **Questions and follow up work on inventory count attendance notes**

Counting procedures

It appears that counters had access to the quantities shown on the system as they counted. This is not best practice and can lead to a tendency to 'count' what should be there, as possibly illustrated in the mezzanine area discrepancies.

You need to determine whether this was in fact the case and then to evaluate whether we can still rely on the count. If they did have access to quantities then you will need to raise a management letter point in this area.

In addition, investigating only differences greater than 10% tolerance level may be insufficient given the level of materiality and significance of the inventory balances.

Overall count difference

No mention in your notes of what the overall count difference was – important to know this both to evaluate accuracy of count and to assess what work is necessary on roll-forward of count quantities to year end.

Audit sample count sizes

How were audit sample sizes for both raw materials and WIP determined? Important to know this so we can assess adequacy of work done and also understand how to evaluate the potential impact of errors identified. If errors are to be extrapolated into the population as a whole then we need to make sure a representative sample has been chosen.

Whether this is the case is not clear from documentation at present. WIP sample size is very low at only five and unlikely to be representative unless number of WIP items is very low. You need to find out and clarify this.

Weigh counting method for WIP

What value of total inventory was counted using weigh counting? 5% error rate is only acceptable if this is clearly immaterial when applied to the whole relevant population.

You need to clarify whether weigh counting differences noted all went in one direction or whether there were unders and overs as would be expected. 5% error rate does seem quite high unless value of items involved is clearly immaterial.

Inventory controller – discussion on paint and chemicals

We cannot rely on discussion with controller to evaluate whether the approach taken on paint and chemicals is reasonable. Again you need to determine the total value of such items and to estimate what total possible mis-statement could be from the approach taken. If potentially significant then additional work and analysis will be necessary at the year end.

Errors in mezzanine area – need for additional year end procedures

Although specific differences noted in the mezzanine area have been corrected, the fact that two differences were noted in the same area may be indicative that counters in that area were not accurate enough. You should ideally have performed additional counts in the areas that team had counted to determine whether errors were indeed isolated or whether the whole area should be checked and recounted. However you cannot now do that but, depending on the significance of inventory counted by that team, we will need to consider additional procedures at year end, possibly including a year-end inventory count.

It is important to understand fully the nature of the errors and inventory items on which they arose as it may be possible to isolate the risk of similar errors to part of the population and thus either determine that any misstatement cannot be material or limit additional procedures to the relevant part of the overall population. As the errors went in both directions this suggests that there is both overstatement and understatement risk. You need to determine the nature of the errors and the inventory items which were miscounted.

No work on finished goods

No work appears to have been performed on finished goods quantities – were there any at inventory count date? We might have expected some from the management accounts analysis which showed goods made for Swishman.

Old or damaged inventory

Was any old or clearly damaged inventory noted during the count? We need details of this to ensure adequately provided at year end.

Consignment inventory

Do you have any further details of how inventory sent on consignment to subcontractors is accounted for? We would expect it to remain within inventory records but notes from count imply that it is booked out and then booked back in again when it is received back. This might result in under-recognition of inventory and a grossing up of revenue and cost of sales entries.

You need to understand and document fully the arrangements with the subcontractors and to review all accounting entries. There may also be more inventory at the subcontractor which we need to consider. In addition there is a question as to how inventory received back should be accounted for – as raw materials or as WIP. It is also important to understand and document where subcontractor costs are recorded in profit or loss so appropriate amount is inventorised but there is no double counting.

Cut off at count date

There is no evidence that you have tested the accuracy of cut-off entries at the inventory count date. You need to do this so that the comparison of book to physical quantities is accurate as books have been updated for all physical transactions before the count and post count transactions are not included.

(ii) **Financial statement assertions – concerns or issues and key audit procedures**

Introduction

Inventory is a material debit balance and audit work would be expected therefore to focus on the assertions of *existence, valuation and ownership*. Each of these is considered below.

Within the statement of profit or loss and other comprehensive income the inventory balance is a credit element of cost of sales and so it is also important to ensure that it is not understated.

Work on existence of inventory

Roll forward – work on book inventory

The count at the South London factory was on 30 June, one month before year end; we will need to perform work on inventory movements over the last month to ensure that the year-end inventory at that factory exists and has been accurately recorded. This might include test counts and cut off work at year end or detailed work on completeness and accuracy of movements recorded within the book stock records.

Also need to make sure that the count data tested at the inventory count has been tied into the system and that the physical inventory count (including any book to physical adjustment) has been recorded accurately in the accounting records.

Woodtydy – not included in count?

Inventory at Woodtydy does not appear to have been included in the 30 June count – we will need to make arrangements to attend a count at this site and to perform appropriate audit tests of the accuracy and completeness of this count. If the count is not at year end then we will also need to roll-forward procedures as above. Will also need to address risk of incorrect cut-off on inventory transferred between the two sites.

Work on valuation of inventory

The fact that differing methods are used to value inventory at the two sites is not necessarily an issue, providing both result in a reasonable approximation to actual cost of inventory held. However the different approaches mean that there will be two separate populations for audit testing and that the testing will need to be tailored for each site.

Purchase price variance

Tydaway's inventory is valued at standard cost which has proved to be a reasonable approximation to actual cost in the past. However purchase price variances are much higher in the 10 months to 31 May 20X1 than in the equivalent prior year period and might well need to be taken into account in determining the actual cost of inventory held at year end.

- Audit work should include testing a sample of individual raw material costs, comparing the actual cost to the standard cost and ensuring that the difference has been posted accurately to the purchase price variance account.

- Purchase price variances (PPV) should then be reviewed for any significant one-off items such as that already identified in the commentary on the management accounts. Such items should be excluded from any adjustment made to inventory if, like the £25,000 in the commentary, they relate to purchases of inventory which has been sold prior to year end.

- We will then need to determine whether any adjustment has been made by management to include a proportion of PPV in inventory and thus adjust the raw material inventory valuation to a closer approximation to actual cost. An independent assessment of the reasonableness of this adjustment should then be made. Calculations to assess the appropriateness of the PPV add back could include:

  - Extrapolating the difference between actual and standard costs noted in the sample testing and comparing this to the add back made;

  - Calculating the ratio of PPV to raw material purchases (excluding in both cases the one off items identified above);

  - Applying this percentage to the raw material element of inventory; and

  - Considering PPV over the period of average inventory turn and ensuring after adjustment for one off items that the amount added back is equivalent to PPV over the period in which inventory was acquired.

The change between old and new standard costs may have been posted to PPV when standard costs were changed on the first day of the financial year. If it was, then this would need to be excluded from the PPV add back calculation.

- No PPV add back should be applied to £60,000 of components which were purchased in the previous year. However, we will need to look at whether the standard cost for these was increased at the beginning of year and to reverse that entry as the correct cost is cost components that were actually purchased in prior year.

Freight costs

Freight is added to standard cost at 1.5% whereas actual costs are running at around 3.2% of raw materials (£77,000/£2,431,000). It is not clear where the variance has been accounted for. It may have been taken into account in variances already considered. In any case the amounts which might potentially be included in inventory are not material so are not considered further. However should note that % in 20X0 was 1.4% so may be exceptionally high costs in 20X1 which should not be included within inventory valuation.

Overheads

Overheads included in inventory need consideration as these are based on May figures and could well be material. You should obtain client calculation of the amount to be included in year-end inventory and perform the following procedures:

- Consider whether the assumption that WIP is on average 50% complete is reasonable – this may involve an inspection of the WIP on site at year end.

- Verify accuracy of calculations and agree amounts to expenses tested in statement of profit or loss and other comprehensive income testing or other supporting evidence.

- Agree overheads included are all items that can be included within inventory valuations. As they appear to include delivery costs this may well not be the case as such costs are selling costs and should not be inventorised.

- Consider whether levels of activity through the factory have been normal as it would be inappropriate to include in inventory excess levels of overhead arising from idle time or inefficient production. There are some indications that this may have arisen as sales are at around 75% of prior year level and direct production costs are also lower (despite higher unit costs for materials) but overheads have remained at around the same level.

- Ensure both finished goods and WIP are included in the calculation.

Woodtydy's inventory

Work will also be necessary on Woodtydy's inventory valuation. In designing this work we will need to consider the extent to which audit work has been completed in the past as Woodtydy was only a division. Work may also be required on opening balances.

- In addition, the description of the inventory records implies that they may be manual in which case additional work may be needed to ensure internal consistency and clerical accuracy.

- Raw materials are valued at the latest invoice price and the accuracy of this can be tested by taking a sample and agreeing the value to an invoice for the last transaction.

- We also need to consider whether latest invoice price is appropriate as this may result in inventory which was purchased earlier in the year being included in inventory at a price which is higher or lower than actual cost. If differences are significant then additional testing may be necessary to determine error over whole population. It would normally be more appropriate to use FIFO pricing and although latest invoice can be an estimate of this, it is not always an accurate one.

- To test overheads we will need to look at actual hourly rates and compare to the £30 rate used to include overhead in inventory. Also we need to ensure that hours included on each job card appear reasonable and are consistent between similar jobs. Information available to test this is not clear at present so further investigation will be necessary. As for Tydaway we need to look at the nature of costs included and whether overheads are for normal level of production.

- No obvious freight costs are included in the value at Woodtydy so we need to discuss whether freight and other purchasing costs are included and if not, whether the effect could be material.

- Woodtydy's inventory is also likely to include components purchased from Tydaway as there are sales between the factories. We will need to ensure that any interdivisional profit is eliminated in the company accounts.

- To the extent that any issues are noted with valuation of Woodtydy inventory, we will need to consider whether there is any impact on fair values recorded at the time of Woodtydy acquisition. In addition, we need to consider any pre-existing supply contract between Tydaway and Woodtydy and assess whether the fair value of this needs to be taken into account.

Provisions

We will need to do work on inventory provisions at both sites. The provision at Tydaway appears not to have been reassessed since the last year end and looks very low compared to the level of inventory, the slower stock turn and the provision made by Woodtydy which is in a similar business.

It seems likely that a specific provision will be required against the finished goods made for Swishman as the margin (11%) possible on any sales is unlikely to cover the rework costs and may also only be able to sell repainted units at a lower price.

We also need to consider whether any contingent asset should be recognised re claim against Swishman. Swishman has agreed to pay an immaterial amount £6,000, which prima facie can be shown as an asset – however financial position of Swishman means it is unlikely to be able to pay. The same consideration applies to any further amounts claimed from Swishman and we would need to be virtually certain that the additional claim would be upheld to meet the criteria for recognition of a contingent asset.

- We need to consider whether there is any risk of further order cancellations from other customers.

- Old components still in stock but purchased in a prior year may also need a provision as they are clearly very slow moving. Need to discuss this with management.

- Work done should include understanding and assessing the appropriateness of the provisions that have been made but also considering whether the provisions are complete. This will mean following up on potentially obsolete items noted at stock count; considering data available which will allow us to identify slow moving items; and looking at the margins made on individual product sales (including post year-end sales of WIP held at year end) to determine whether there are low margin items or items sold at a loss where a provision may be necessary.

Overhead costs which are not included in standard costs at Tydaway, selling costs and any rework costs should all be considered in this analysis. In addition a sample of high value items should be reviewed to ensure that there are no NRV issues, that the items are being used in current production and that there is no excess inventory.

Ownership of inventory

- Testing of value will ensure agreement to valid purchase invoices. However testing is also required around cut-off to ensure that inventory is only included where either it has been paid for or a creditor recorded and where the delivery was received before the year end.

This will involve testing the last few deliveries before year end to ensure both inventory and creditor included and the first few post year end to ensure that goods not delivered until after year end have not been booked into year-end inventory.

- We will also need to test sales cut-off to ensure that goods shipped to a customer before the year end are not also included in inventory. This will involve detailed testing but also enquiry as to any goods held at year end on behalf of customers.

Consignment stock sent to subcontractors will need more consideration as highlighted under stock count queries as this may well be owned stock not included at present.

Understatement of inventory

Much of the work outlined above will be two directional – for example the detailed sample testing of valuation. In addition, cut-off testing will test for understatement as well as overstatement, as will stock count work.

Work on PPV add back and freight will involve an expectation/calculation which is also two-directional. Work on provisions will need to be extended to ensure that provisions made are on a valid basis and not overstated.

(iii) **Impact of Chinese transaction on the financial statements**

No hedging

In the absence of hedging there is no recognition of the purchase of the metal in the financial statements for the year ending 31 July 20X1 as there has been no physical delivery of the inventory, so it is unlikely that risks and rewards would have passed from the seller to Tydaway. The firm commitment would not therefore be recognised.

On 15 December 20X1, the purchase takes place and the transaction would be recognised at the exchange rate on that day at a value of £354,409 ($500,000/1.4108) as follows:

Dr Inventory	£354,409	
Cr Cash		£354,409

This cost of inventory (which is £44,004 greater than at the time the contract was made) would then be recognised in cost of sales and impact on profit in the year ending 31 July 20X2.

Hedging with forward contract – but no hedge accounting

At 31 July 20X1:

Dr Forward contract – financial asset	£20,544	
Cr Profit or loss		£20,544

To recognise the increase in the fair value of the forward contract (ie a derivative financial asset) and to recognise the gain on the forward contract in profit or loss.

At15 December 20X1:

Dr Forward contract – financial asset	£23,450	
Cr Profit or loss		£23,450

To recognise the further increase in the fair value of the forward contract (ie a derivative financial asset) and to recognise the gain on the forward contract in profit or loss.

Dr Cash	£43,994	
Cr Forward contract		£43,994

To recognise the settlement of the forward contract by receipt of cash from the counterparty.

Dr Inventory	£354,409	
Cr Cash		£354,409

Being the settlement of the firm commitment (ie the purchase of inventory) at the contracted at the spot rate on 15 December 20X1 ($500,000/1.4108).

Fair value hedge

A hedge of a foreign currency firm commitment may be accounted for as a fair value hedge or as a cash flow hedge (IAS 39 para 87) at the choice of the entity.

If the hedged risk is identified as the forward exchange rate, rather than the spot rate, then it could be assumed to be perfectly effective.

The value of the transactions are as follows:

At 15 July 20X1

$500,000/1.6108 = £310,405$

At 31 July 20X1

$500,000/1.5108 = £330,950$

Difference = £20,545 is almost identical to the movement in the fair value of the forward at £20,544 and is clearly therefore highly effective:

Similarly, at 15 December 20X1

$500,000/1.4108 = £354,409$

Difference = £23,459 which is almost identical to the movement in the fair value of the forward at £23,450 and therefore remains highly effective.

At 15 July 20X1:

No entries are required at this date as the firm commitment is unrecognised. The forward contract is potentially recognised, but it has a zero fair value and there is no related cash transaction to record.

However the existence of the contract and associated risk would be disclosed form this date in accordance with IFRS 7.

At 31 July 20X1:

Dr Forward contract – financial asset	£20,544	
Cr Profit or loss		£20,544

To recognise the increase in the fair value of the hedging instrument (which is the forward contract, being a derivative financial asset) and to recognise the gain on the forward contract in profit or loss.

Dr Profit or loss	£20,545	
Cr Firm commitment		£20,545

To recognise the increase in fair value of the hedged item liability (ie the previously unrecognised firm commitment) in relation to changes in forward exchange rates and to recognise a debit entry in profit or loss, which offsets the profit previously recognised in respect of the gain on the derivative financial asset. (IAS 39 para 89)

At 15 December 20X1:

Dr Forward contract – financial asset	£23,450	
Cr Profit or loss		£23,450

To recognise the increase in the fair value of the hedging instrument (which is the forward contract, being a derivative financial asset) and to recognise the gain on the forward contract in profit or loss.

Dr Profit or loss	£23,459	
Cr Firm commitment		£23,459

To recognise the increase in the fair value of the hedged item liability (ie the firm commitment) and to recognise a debit entry in profit or loss, which offsets the profit previously recognised in respect of the gain on the derivative financial asset (IAS 39 para 89).

Dr Cash	£43,994	
Cr Forward contract		£43,994

To recognise the settlement of the forward contract by receipt of cash from the counterparty.

Dr Inventory	£354,409	
Cr Cash		£354,409

Being the settlement of the firm commitment (ie the purchase of inventory) at the contracted price of $500,000 at the spot rate on 15 December 20X1 ($500,000/1.4108).

Dr Firm commitment	£44,004	
Cr Inventory		£44,004

To remove the firm commitment from the statement of financial position and adjust the carrying amount of the inventory resulting from the firm commitment.

Cash flow hedge

At 15 July 20X1:

No entries are required at this date as the firm commitment is unrecognised. The forward contract is potentially recognised, but it has a zero fair value and there is no related cash transaction to record.

At 31 July 20X1:

The increase in the fair value of the future cash flows (the hedged item) of £20,545 is not recognised in the financial statements. However, as it exceeds the change in the fair value of the forward (the hedge instrument) it is fully effective (IAS 39 paras 95–96).

Dr Forward contract – financial asset	£20,544	
Cr Other comprehensive income		£20,544

To recognise the increase in the fair value of the forward contract (ie a derivative financial asset) and to recognise the gain on the forward contract in other comprehensive income.

At 15 December 20X1:

Dr Forward contract – financial asset	£23,450	
Cr Other comprehensive income		£23,450

To recognise the increase in the fair value of the forward contract financial asset and to recognise the gain on the forward contract in other comprehensive income. It is recognised in its entirety in other comprehensive income (ie no part is recognised in profit or loss) as there is no ineffectiveness as the increase in the fair value of the forward contract (the hedging instrument) is less than the change in the fair value of the future cash flows (the hedged item) (IAS 39 paras 95–96).

Dr Cash	£43,994	
Cr Forward contract		£43,994

To recognise the settlement of the forward contract at its fair value by receipt of cash from the counterparty.

Dr	Purchases	£354,409
Cr	Cash	£354,409

Being the settlement of the firm commitment (inventory purchase) at the contracted price of $500,000 at the spot rate on 15 December 20X1 ($500,000/1.4108).

Dr	Other comprehensive income	£43,994
Cr	Purchases	£43,994

To remove the firm commitment from other comprehensive income and adjust the carrying amount of the inventory resulting from the hedged transaction.

(iv) **Discussion of financial reporting differences**

Year ending 31 July 20X1

	No hedge £	No hedge accounting £ £ £	Fair value hedge	Cash flow hedge
SPLOCI				
Profit or loss	–	20,544	20,544 (20,545)	–
Other comprehensive income	–	–	–	20,544
SOFP				
Financial asset	–	20,544	20,544	20,544
Inventory	–	–	–	–
Cash	–	–	–	–
Retained earnings	–	20,544	–	–
Hedging reserve	–	–	–	20,544
Firm commitment	–	–	20,545	–

Year ending 31 July 20X2

	No hedge £	No hedge accounting £ £ £	Fair value hedge	Cash flow hedge
SPLOCI				
Profit or loss	–	23,450	23,450 (23,459)	–
Other comprehensive income	–	–	–	Note (2)
SOFP				
Financial asset	–	Note (1)	Note (1)	Note (1)
Inventory	354,409	354,409	354,409 (44,004)	354,409 (43,994)
Cash	(354,409)	(354,409)	(354,409) 43,994	(354,409) 43,994
		43,994		
Retained earnings	–	43,994	–	–
Hedging reserve	–	–	–	Note (2)
Firm commitment	–	–	44,004 (44,004)	–

Note (1) the financial asset increases to £43,994 before being settled for cash.

Note (2) other comprehensive income and the hedging reserve each increase to £43,994 before being recycled into inventory.

Tutorial notes:

The notes below are more detailed than would be expected from even the best candidates.

The purpose of hedging is to enter into a transaction (eg buying a derivative) where the derivative's cash flows or fair value (*the hedging instrument*) are expected to move wholly or partly, in an inverse direction to the cash flows or fair value of the position being hedged (*the hedged*

item). The two elements of the hedge (the hedged item and the hedging instrument) are therefore matched and are interrelated with each other in economic terms.

Overall, the impact of hedge accounting is to reflect this underlying intention of the matched nature of the hedge agreement in the financial statements. Hedge accounting therefore aims that the two elements of the hedge should be treated symmetrically and offsetting gains and losses (of the hedge item and the hedging instrument) are reported in profit or loss in the same periods. Normal accounting treatment rules of recognition and measurement may not achieve this and hence may result in an accounting mismatch and earnings volatility, which would not reflect the underlying commercial intention or effects of linking the two hedge elements which offset and mitigate risks. For example, typically, derivatives are measured at fair value through profit or loss; whereas the items they hedge are measured at cost or are not measured at all (eg a firm commitment in the case of the Chinese contract).

Hedge accounting rules are therefore required, subject to satisfying hedge accounting conditions.

In the case of the Chinese contract, the forward rate hedge attempts to lock Tydaway into the contractual price of £310,405 ($500,000/1.6108). This reflects the US$ price at the exchange rate at the time of the contract at the spot rate at the original contract date.

In the absence of hedging, the inventory cost would be higher at £354,409 ($500,000/1.4108) reflecting the movement in the spot rate by the settlement date (according to the scenario in the working assumptions). This would be reflected in a higher cost of sales in the year ended 31 July 20X2 and therefore lower reported profit, due to the exchange loss, than would have been the case with hedging.

With hedging, but without hedge accounting, the inventory would still be recognised at £354,409, but there would now be a gain on the forward contract derivative. This overall gain of £43,994 would be recognised through profit or loss entirely separately from the inventory purchase contract without trying to match the two elements of the hedge transaction in the same period. The gain on the derivative is split between the two accounting periods according to when the gain arose (£20,544 in the year ending 31 July 20X1; and £23,450 in the year ending 31 July 20X2). The earnings therefore would be inflated in the year ended 31 July 20X1 by the £20,544 gain. Earnings would be deflated in the year ended 31 July 20X2 as the higher inventory cost of £44,004 in cost of sales would only be partially offset by the derivative gain of £23,450, resulting in earnings volatility.

Fair value hedge accounting attempts to reflect the use of the forward rate derivative (the hedging instrument) to hedge against fair value movements in inventories arising from foreign exchange movements (the hedged item). To do this, movements in the derivative, in the year ending 31 July 20X1, go through profit or loss and are recognised in the statement of financial position as a financial asset. The treatment of the firm commitment (the hedged item), in order to match the treatment of the hedging instrument, is also recognised through profit or loss and as a liability in the SOFP in order to avoid a mismatch. (A firm commitment would not, in the absence of hedge accounting, satisfy normal recognition criteria and so would not normally be recognised.) The small ineffective element for Tydaway represents the net difference in the movements of the fair values of the hedged item and the hedging instrument and is recognised through profit or loss in accordance with IAS 39 para 89. On settlement, the firm commitment is offset against the inventory cost to reflect the inventory price that the futures contract originally tried to lock in.

Cash flow hedge accounting attempts to reflect the use of the forward rate derivative to hedge against future cash flow movements from inventory purchases arising from foreign exchange movements. To do this, movements in the derivative, in the year ending 31 July 20X1, which would normally go through profit or loss, are recognised in other comprehensive income. The other comprehensive income balance (including further movements in 20X2 in the forward exchange derivative) is recycled to profit or loss in the same period in which the hedged firm commitment (the Chinese contract) affects profit or loss. (This may be regarded as superior to fair value hedge accounting as it avoids the need to recognise a firm commitment, which would not be recognised in any other circumstances.) In this case, this is in the year ending 31 July 20X2 when the contract is settled and the hedging gain is recognised as part of the inventory assets (basis adjustment) which in turn affects cost of sales and profit in the period. The offset against the carrying amount of the inventory resulting from the hedged transaction is to reflect the inventory price and ultimate cash flows that the futures contract originally tried to lock into.

Note that under cash flow hedge accounting, the increase in the fair value of the future cash flows (the hedged item) of £20,545 is not recognised in the financial statements. However, as it exceeds the change in the fair value of the forward (the hedging instrument) it is *fully effective* (IAS 39 paras 95–96). This is because the separate component of equity associated with the hedged item is limited to the *lesser* of: (i) the gain/loss on the hedging instrument; and (ii) the change in fair value of the hedged item (IAS 39 para 96).

(v) **Documentation**

For audit purposes and to meet the requirements of IAS 39, we would expect the following documentation to be available:

- Details of the risk management objectives and the strategy for undertaking the hedge
- Identification and description of the hedging instrument (forward contract)
- Details of the hedged item or transaction (payable settled in $)
- Nature of the risk being hedged (exchange rate changes £:$)
- Description of how Tydaway will assess the hedging instrument's effectiveness

25 Wadi Investments

Marking guide

	Technical	Skills	Marks
Report describing, explaining and quantifying required accounting treatment of:			
(a) Acquisition of Strobosch	3	4	
(b) Additional audit procedures	1	4	
(c) Change of use of asset	3	3	
(d) Audit procedures	2	3	
(e) Points for instruction letter	4	4	
(f) Loan to Strobosch	2	2	
(g) Hedging of net investment	4	4	
Total marks	19	24	
Maximum			40

For more guidance on how skills are tested and rewarded, please refer to the section at the start of this question bank.

Report

To: T Flode
From: A Perdan
Date: 30 July 20X9
Subject: Audit of Wadi Investment Group

1 Audit of parent company

1.1 Acquisition of Strobosch

We need to consider whether Strobosch is a subsidiary. The acquisition of an 80% stake in the equity of Strobosch strongly suggests that Wadi has control of the entity, and provided there are no indications to the contrary as listed in IFRS 10 *Consolidated Financial Statements* the investment should be treated as a subsidiary. On this basis the purchase consideration will be accounted for in accordance with IFRS 3 *Business Combinations*.

1.2 Cost of investment in the books of Wadi

The cost of the investment does not appear to have been calculated correctly. IFRS 3 requires that the initial investment in the subsidiary is recorded in Wadi's statement of financial position at the fair value of the consideration transferred.

- Under IFRS 3 **costs relating to the acquisition must be recognised as an expense** at the time of the acquisition. They are not regarded as an asset. The RR 23m legal costs and the £2m internal costs incurred by Wadi's M&A team must therefore both be expensed. The RR 23m should be translated at the rate ruling at the date of acquisition.

- IFRS 3 requires that costs of issuing debt or equity are to be accounted for under the rules of IAS 39. The £6m transaction costs associated with the issue of the debentures must therefore be written off against the carrying amount of the debentures and expensed over the life of the debentures using the IRR%.

Based on the above the investment should initially have been accounted for as follows:

		£m	£m
DR	Consideration transferred (675 + 360)	1,035	
DR	Profit or loss for the year (2 + (23 × 0.45))	12	
CR	Cash (675 + 2 + 6 + (23 x 0.45)		693
CR	Non-current liability: Debentures (360 – 6)		355

The following journal is therefore required to correct the investment:

		£m	£m
DR	Profit or loss for the year	12	
DR	Non-current liability: Debentures	6	
CR	Investment in Strobosch		18

At the year end, the debentures must be measured at amortised cost (Working 1).

- The interest expense of £16m, determined by the IRR of 4.42%, should be charged to profit or loss for the year.

- The coupon of 4% for the six month period is the amount actually paid.

- The debenture is therefore recognised at £356m.

The following adjustment is required:

		£m	£m
DR	Interest expense	16	
CR	Cash		14
CR	Debenture		2

1.3 Audit procedures

The following additional procedures are required:

- Details of the consideration paid for the investment should be agreed to the purchase agreement

- The purchase agreement should also be reviewed to determine that there is no additional consideration to be paid

- The number of shares purchased should be agreed to the sale agreement to confirm the 80% holding and the details should be reviewed to determine that Wadi does have control of Strobosch

- Ownership of the shares should be checked by examination of share certificates

- Confirm the nature of costs detailed as issue costs of the debenture to ensure that they should not be written off to profit or loss

- Confirm where the IRR of 4.42% has been obtained from and the basis on which it has been calculated

- Discuss with management the way in which the costs of the internal team have been allocated to the acquisition

- Agree legal costs to invoices

- Discuss adjustments required to the investment and the debenture with management to determine whether they will be made

1.4 Change of use of non-current asset

IAS 40 *Investment Property* requires that property that is held to earn rental or capital appreciation or both, rather than for ordinary use by the business, must be recognised as investment property. Hence the head office in London must be reclassified from Property, plant and equipment to Investment property in the statement of financial position.

The asset must be accounted for under IAS 16 *Property, Plant and Equipment* up to the date of change in use, and any difference between its carrying amount and its fair value at this date must be dealt with as a revaluation in accordance with this same standard.

The carrying amount of the asset at 15 March 20X9, the date of change in use, was £108m (Working 2a), hence the £16m uplift to its fair value of £124m at this date should have been recognised in OCI and as a revaluation surplus.

The accounting treatment of the asset from this date is governed by IAS 40 and, as the company applies a fair value policy to its investment property, no further depreciation should have been charged on this asset from 15 March 20X9. At the year end, the £4m uplift to the new fair value of £128m (Working 2a) should have been credited to profit or loss for the year.

By continuing to record the asset in Property, plant and equipment, the asset has continued to be depreciated and hence excess depreciation of £1m (Working 2b) must be added back to the group's profits. The revaluation surplus of £21m (128m – 107m, Working 2b) has been recognised in the revaluation reserve, meaning that profit for the year is understated by £5m (21m – 16m). A further adjustment must be made to recognise the gain on remeasurement of £4m.

1.5 Audit procedures

- Agree original cost and confirm depreciation policy

- Check that fair values have been calculated in accordance with IFRS 13

- Check basis on which the fair values have been calculated. Current prices in an active market should be available for this type of asset

- Agree valuations to valuer's certificates

- Confirm the date that the office was vacated

- Review details of the rental agreement to confirm terms ie occupier is not a company connected to Wadi and rent has been negotiated at arm's length

- Reperform calculations to confirm the net book value at the date of change of use

- Discuss adjustments required to remove the asset from property, plant and equipment with management to determine whether management is willing to make these

- Confirm that disclosure is adequate ie disclosure of the policy and a reconciliation of the carrying amount of the investment property at the beginning and end of the period

2 Audit of the consolidation

2.1 Points to be included in the letter of instruction

The following points should be included:

Matters that are relevant to the planning of the work of Kale & Co

- A request that the component auditor will co-operate with our firm

- Timetable for completing the audit

- Dates of planned visits by group management and our team, and dates of planned meetings with Strobosch's management and Kale & Co

- The work to be performed by Kale & Co, the use to be made of that work and arrangements for co-ordinating efforts

- Ethical requirements relevant to the group audit, particularly regarding independence

- Component materiality and the threshold above which misstatements cannot be regarded as clearly trivial

- A list of related parties

- Work to be performed on intra-group transactions and balances

- Guidance on other statutory reporting responsibilities

Matters relevant to the conduct of the work of Kale & Co

- The findings of our tests of control of a processing system that is common for all components, and tests of controls to be performed by Kale & Co

- Identified risks of material misstatement of the group financial statements, due to fraud or error, that are relevant to Kale & Co's work, and a request that Kale & Co communicates on a timely basis any other significant risks of material misstatement of the group financial statements, due to fraud or error, identified in Strobosch and Kale & Co's response to such risks

- The findings of internal audit

- A request for timely communication of audit evidence obtained from performing work on the financial information of Strobosch that contradicts the audit evidence on which the team originally based the risk assessment performed at group level

- A request for a written representation on Strobosch's management's compliance with the applicable financial reporting framework

- Matters to be documented by Kale & Co

Other matters

- A request that the following be communicated on a timely basis:

  - Significant accounting, financial reporting and auditing matters

  - Matters relating to going concern

  - Matters relating to litigation and claims

  - Significant deficiencies in internal control and information that indicates the existence of fraud

We should also request that Kale & Co communicate matters relevant to our conclusion with regard to the group audit when they have completed their work on Strobosch.

2.2 Loan to Strobosch

The loan to Strobosch represents an intra-group item. On consolidation the non-current liability must be cancelled against the matching financial asset of Wadi. The inter company loan of £200m must be translated into RR at the spot rate. It has been recorded as a non-current liability in the books of Strobosch at RR 444m (£200m/0.45). As a monetary liability, retranslation to the closing rate at the year end is required to give a liability of RR 426m (£200m/0.47) and an exchange gain in the books of Strobosch of RR 18m.

We must confirm that the financial statements of Strobosch included in the consolidation schedule reflect the adjustments above. We should confirm that the inter-company balances agree and that the cancellation has been reflected in the adjustments column of the consolidation schedule.

2.3 Hedging of net investment

There is a risk that hedging provisions have been adopted inappropriately. IAS 39 *Financial Instruments: Recognition and Measurement* states that the use of a foreign currency loan to hedge an overseas investment can only be used where strict conditions are met:

(i) The hedge has been designated and documented at inception.

   We would need to confirm that the hedge has been formally designated as such and check that the following have been documented:

   - Identification of the hedging instrument ie the loans

- The hedged item ie the net investment in Strobosch

- Details of how hedge effectiveness is to be calculated

- Statement of the entity's risk management objective and strategy for undertaking the hedge

(ii) The hedge must be highly effective. We would need to confirm that the exchange difference on retranslation of the net investment in the subsidiary compared to that of the loan falls in the 80%–125% band. Based on the information available this does appear to be the case.

(a) The gain on the translation of the net investment in Strobosch is 80% × 41m = £33m (Working 3).

(b) The exchange loss on the hedging loans is £36m.

Hence the hedge is 91.7% effective and hedge accounting rules may be applied provided that the first condition has also been met.

Assuming the conditions have been met we must confirm that the following accounting treatment has been adopted:

- The portion of loss on the loans that is determined to be an effective hedge, £33m, should be recognised directly in equity to offset the gain on the translation of the subsidiary.

- The ineffective portion of the exchange difference on the loans, a loss of £3m, should be recognised in profit or loss for the year.

If we conclude that the hedging provisions of IAS 39 have not been met an audit adjustment will be required. The exchange loss on the loans would be charged to profit or loss for the year and the gain on the subsidiary to the foreign currency reserve.

Workings

W1 Debenture

	£m
Initial measurement (360 – 6)	354
Interest for 6 months @ 4.42%	16
Coupon paid (8% × 360 × 6/12)	(14)
Year end balance	356

W2 Correction of investment property

(a) **Correct treatment**

Date		£m
3 April 20X6	Initial measurement	90
30 June 20X7	Depreciation (90 × 15/600)	(2.250)
30 June 20X7	Carrying amount	87.750
	Revaluation to FV	112
30 June 20X8	Depreciation (112 × 12/585)	(2.297)
15 March 20X9	Depreciation (112 × 8/585)	(1.532)
15 March 20X9	Carrying amount	108.171
	Gain on revaluation (OCI and revaluation surplus)	15.829
15 March 20X9	Revaluation to FV	124
	Gain on remeasurement (profit or loss)	4
30 June 20X9	Revaluation to FV	128

(b) **Current treatment**

Date		£m
15 March 20X9	Carrying amount	108
30 June 20X9	Depreciation (112 ÷ 4/485)	(1)
30 June 20X9	Carrying amount	107
	Gain on revaluation (to revaluation reserve)	21
30 June 20X9	Revaluation to FV	128

W3 Foreign currency reserve

			£m
Opening net assets:	RR 1,865m	@ Closing rate 0.47	877
		@ Opening rate 0.45	839
			38
Retained earnings:			
280 + gain on loan 18 =	RR 298m	@ Closing rate 0.47	140
		@ Average rate 0.46	137
			3
Gain on retranslation of Strobosch			41

26 Poe, Whitman and Co

Commedia Group

Background comments

The scenario in this question considers an independent television production company. At the beginning of the period the company had two subsidiaries but it disposed of its majority shareholding in one of these companies during the current year for an amount which included a contingent consideration element. Other issues raised include: taking over from the previous auditor who had resigned late into the relevant accounting period; changes in the funding basis for commissioned productions; a provision in the company which is the subject of the partial disposal; and possible impairment in the other subsidiary.

Candidates were required to identify audit risks and draft the audit procedures to mitigate these events. They were also required to advise on financial reporting matters raised by a director.

The solution below provides significant detail, but it is sufficient for a good quality answer, that would obtain a clear pass mark, to provide concise explanations of the following:

- Clear identification of the ethical issues of taking over from a resigning auditor and the practical issues of late appointment, including the possible inability to obtain sufficient appropriate audit evidence (limitation of scope) that may arise as a consequence of not being in office for the entire accounting period

- Identification of the risk and implications of the shift from a 'funded commission' to a 'licensed commission' basis and an explanation of the associated audit work

- Regarding the Scherzo subsidiary, there should be a clear identification of the valuation and financial reporting risks associated with partial disposal. There should be particular emphasis on the incentives given to directors to creatively account given the nature of the contingent consideration contractual terms. The risks arising from the provision should also be identified and explained together with the associated audit work

- Regarding the Riso subsidiary, the key issue of impairment should be identified, quantified and explained. This should include the appropriate financial reporting treatment

---

Client: Commedia Group

1 Practical and ethical issues arising from late appointment

The unexpected resignation of the previous auditor could be as a result of an ethical or other professional issue identified by that auditor. We must have already ensured that there were no such issues preventing us from accepting the appointment as we have already been appointed.

We must have checked, prior to accepting the appointment, that adequate professional clearance has been obtained from the previous auditor and that there are no matters of which we should be aware.

We need to discuss the late resignation with the directors of Commedia to ensure there are no matters such as a disagreement with the auditors that would have adverse implications for our firm's audit.

Before carrying out any work for Commedia we must ensure that satisfactory client identification procedures have been performed (money laundering regulations).

We were not appointed as auditor until after the year end. Therefore, we may not be able to assess adequately the stage of completion of the various commissions at 28 February 20X7 and the value of work in progress at that date. If there are no other audit procedures that we can carry out to gain sufficient audit evidence as to the value of work in progress at the year end, we may conclude that the audit opinion will have to be modified. If the possible errors are considered to be material, this may result in a qualified opinion ('except for'). If the potential effect is pervasive, we may have to issue a 'disclaimer' of opinion.

As the auditors of Scherzo, we will have access to confidential information which would be of use to Commedia in assessing the probability of contingent consideration. This presents us with a conflict of interest. We need to ensure that there are adequate procedures in place within our firm to ensure that confidential information cannot be passed from one company to the other. Staffing a separate team for the Scherzo audit is probably not feasible as we remain responsible for the Commedia group audit and Scherzo probably remains as an associate company. The potential conflict of interest must be disclosed to Commedia's audit committee. It may be necessary to arrange independent partner reviews of the Commedia group and Scherzo audit files.

2   **Auditor's responsibilities for initial engagements**

The auditor must obtain sufficient, appropriate audit evidence that the opening balances do not contain misstatements that materially affect the current period's financial statements. The auditor must obtain evidence that the prior period's closing balances have been brought forward correctly to the current period or have been restated, if appropriate. The auditor should also obtain sufficient, appropriate audit evidence that appropriate accounting policies are consistently applied or changes in accounting policies have been properly accounted for and adequately disclosed.

If this evidence cannot be obtained, the auditor's report should include a modified opinion (inability to obtain sufficient appropriate audit evidence) or a disclaimer of opinion.

If the opening balances contain misstatements that could materially affect the current period's financial statements, the auditor should inform the client's management and the predecessor auditor. If the effect of the misstatement is not properly accounted for and disclosed, a qualified or adverse opinion will be expressed.

If the current period's accounting policies have not been consistently applied to the opening balances and the change not accounted for properly and disclosed, a qualified or adverse opinion will be expressed.

If the prior period's auditor's report was modified, the auditor should consider the effect of this on the current period's accounts. If the modification remains relevant and material to the current period's accounts then the current period's auditor's report should also be modified.

The auditor must obtain sufficient appropriate audit evidence that the **comparative information** meets the requirements of the applicable financial reporting framework. Auditors must assess whether:

*   The accounting policies used for the comparative information are consistent with those of the current period or whether appropriate adjustments and/or disclosures have been made.

*   The comparative information agrees with the amounts and other disclosures presented in the prior period or whether appropriate adjustments and/or disclosures have been made. In the UK and Ireland this will include checking whether related opening balances in the accounting records were brought forward correctly.

If the auditor becomes aware of a possible material misstatement in the comparative information while performing the current period audit, then additional audit procedures should be performed to obtain sufficient appropriate audit evidence to determine whether a material misstatement exists.

An Other Matter paragraph should be included in the auditor's report in the case of the prior period financial statements not having been audited at all, or having been audited by another auditor. This is irrespective of whether or not they are materially misstated, and does not relieve the auditor of the need to obtain sufficient appropriate audit evidence on opening balances.

3 Audit risks arising from specific events during the year

3.1 Commedia Limited

3.1.1 Changes from a funded to a licensed basis

During the year ended 28 February 20X7 a number of the company's commissions changed from a funded to a licensed basis. This has the following implications for our audit:

- A funded commission entitled Commedia to invoice their customer in instalments as the production progressed. Under the terms of a licensed commission, Commedia must wait until the programme is delivered before they can invoice. This may cause cash flow shortages for the company which, if not addressed through the securing of alternative funding, may cause going concern issues. Licensed commissions generally attract a lower fee from the commissioning broadcaster (due to the smaller bundle of rights attached to them). The costs of making the programmes are, however, likely to remain the same, which again will have a probable negative impact on company cash flow and profitability in the short term.

- The cost of making a licensed commission sometimes exceeds the value of the invoice to the broadcaster. If future revenues from the residual rights are not forthcoming, this may result in excess costs needing to be written off as incurred in the financial statements rather than being carried forward. The estimation of future revenues from residual rights is an area of uncertainty with which Commedia's management may not be familiar.

- We will need to examine work in progress carefully as this is likely to be a material area. We will need to examine the contracts with broadcasters to ensure the correct valuation of work in progress. According to IAS 18 we will need to be able to measure the outcome reliably in order to be able to recognise any excess costs as an asset at the year end.

Audit procedures

With respect to licensed commissions, where the costs exceed the initial fee from the originating broadcaster we should consider the following:

- Examine a sample of the new licensed commission contracts to ensure the company is accounting in accordance with their terms

- Discuss with management the rationale for carrying costs forward where they exceed the value of the broadcaster's payment under the terms of the licensed commission

- We need to examine management's estimates of future revenues for a sample of such contracts to ensure these exceed the costs carried forward

- We should obtain documentation supporting the estimates of future income where possible. This will include sales programmes.

  - Any sales contracts for the exploitation of the rights to the programmes made to other broadcasters

  - Agreements to make sales or the progress of negotiations to sell programmes

  - Any evidence of the popularity of the programme with the originating broadcaster

Reviews of these factors should continue up to the date the financial statements are authorised for issue.

We should review Commedia's cash flow forecasts to identify the new funding requirements, if any, arising from the change from funded to licensed commissions. This change in production funding should be discussed with management to assess their view on its impact on the company's cash flow. Where gaps in funding are identified, discuss with management to assess what steps they have taken to fill them. We also need to ensure management have considered the going concern status of the company for the foreseeable future.

3.1.2 Disposal of Scherzo

The disposal by Commedia of part of its investment in Scherzo during the year also has audit risk implications. The sales proceeds should include any contingent consideration payable even if, at the date of acquisition, it is not deemed probable that it will be paid. Bob Kerouac of Commedia has requested advice on the accounting treatment of the disposal in the financial statements. This shows he is unfamiliar with such items and so increases the audit risk as this may have been accounted for incorrectly. We need to examine the sale and purchase agreement for the disposal of the shares in Scherzo to ensure that the disposal has been accounted for in accordance with its specific terms, particularly to ensure that the transaction results in a loss of control. We should also:

- Review management's calculation of the profit or loss on disposal of the shares.

- Review Scherzo forecasts as prepared prior to sale to support contingent consideration element.

- Review management's calculation of the fair value of the remaining investment in Scherzo and check that any revaluation gain is included in the calculation of the gain or loss on disposal.

- Review Scherzo year end financial statements (as provided by Commedia only and not as obtained in our capacity as auditor of Scherzo) and assess whether the amount of contingent consideration recognised is appropriate.

- Ensure this figure is included in the calculation of the profit or loss on disposal.

- Consider the need to discount the future consideration, but given the short time period involved the effect of this is not likely to be material.

A key issue with respect to the audit of the disposal of Scherzo is the audit of the net assets at the date of disposal. Given that our firm was not appointed at this date, attesting the net assets retrospectively is potentially a major problem where the information is no longer attestable and there is thus a limitation of scope issue.

A related problem is ascertaining the pre disposal results. Time apportionment is unlikely to be applicable in a business that is dependent on concerts and events that do not accrue evenly over the year.

There is also an issue of auditing the relevant disclosures relating to the disposal under IFRS 5 *Non-Current Assets Held for Sale and Discontinued Operations*. This might include attestation in the parent and the group financial statements of:

- The date assets became held for sale
- Impairment
- Discontinued operations

3.2 Scherzo Limited

3.2.1 Audit risks and contingent consideration

£5 million of the total possible £20 million share sale consideration payable by management is contingent upon the results of the company for the year ended 28 February 20X7. Management therefore have an incentive in this year to

- Suppress profits
- Overstate costs
- Understate income

in order to reduce the contingent sum payable. Management will want the profit for the year to be below £3 million. Below this level, no further sums will be payable.

Every £1 of pre-tax profit for the year between £3 million and £5 million will result in £2.50 additional contingent consideration which increases the risk of management manipulation of the figures. This also increases our audit risk because a misstated profit figure may have a multiplied direct impact on the sum receivable by Commedia for the shares in respect of the contingent consideration element. Indeed, for every extra £1 profit earned between £3 million and £5 million there will be net loss to Scherzo of £1.50.

Moreover, as the nature of the incentives for the new management of Scherzo is to engage in undue prudence, this may be more difficult to argue against as auditors, given the inherently prudent nature of many accounting principles.

In addition to excessive prudence concerning measurement, there are also incentives for the new management of Scherzo to manipulate presentation, particularly in the classification of costs. The contingent consideration contract terms suggest that exceptional items should be excluded. This gives the incentive to classify any unusual income as exceptional but any unusual costs to be presented as normal items (ie not exceptional).

It should, however, be noted that the incentives may become redundant if Scherzo is making a profit below £3 million. Any further downward manipulation would be pointless as it would give rise to no further benefit as the contingent consideration would already be zero. Similarly, if the profit before tax is significantly in excess of £5 million there is no benefit from small amounts of profit reduction. At the audit planning stage, an assessment of the likely profit before tax (eg from management accounts) would help identify the key inherent risks with respect to managerial incentives to account creatively.

Specific areas where management may seek to manipulate profits are as follows:

Collapsed stage

Provisions in connection with the collapsed stage. This is likely to be treated as an exceptional item and therefore excluded from the calculation of pre-tax profit for these purposes. However, management have an incentive to:

(i)   Classify some of the costs associated with the incident as 'normal' operating expenses and so suppress the pre-tax profit figure used in the calculation of contingent consideration.

(ii)   Overstate any elements of the provision which are not to be classified as exceptional or understate any that would be classified as exceptional.

Aside from the issue of the contingent consideration, the issue of the collapsed stage itself represents an audit risk in that the provision for costs associated with the incident may be misstated at the year end, particularly the provision for any potential litigation from members of the crew and general public. If the company is found to have been negligent, this may result in criminal implications for the company which may have going concern implications for the financial statements. The incident will have no doubt caused adverse publicity for the company which may adversely affect attendance at future events staged by the company.

A key issue is the role of Highstand to whom Scherzo subcontracted the erection of the stage. There may be a contingent asset in respect of Scherzo taking litigation against Highstand. This would, however, be an issue of disclosure rather than recognition. There should be no set-off between the potential provision and the contingent asset.

The question of the probability of success of the litigation against Scherzo needs to be considered. If it is possible, rather than probable, then this needs to be disclosed as a contingent liability rather than recognised as a provision. This is a question of fact but also some legal judgement may be needed.

No provision can be made in respect of anticipated future operating losses arising from the reputational effects of the accident.

Audit procedures

- Request management provide you with a reconciliation of costs incurred on this exceptional item, reconciling the charge in profit or loss with the closing provision in the statement of financial position. This will enable you to ensure all costs have been appropriately recognised and measured

- Review legal documentation for the claims being made and the possibility of a counter claim against Highstand

- Check insurance documentation to assess the extent that any liability may be covered by insurance

- Review any correspondence with insurers over whether any claims would be fully covered

- Review any correspondence with the injured parties directly regarding any evidence of the fact, nature and amount of any claims. Examine the level of complaints from customers and request to see any additional undisclosed correspondence threatening litigation

- Review any correspondence with Highstand directly regarding any evidence of the fact, nature and amount of any claims and the ability of Highstand to pay any claim (eg whether they have insurance cover)

- Consider speaking or corresponding directly with the company lawyers to assess the extent, and the probability of success, of legal proceedings

- Ensure that we obtain written representations from management on the level of claims included within the financial statements and review any payments made in respect of the incident both before and after the year end

- Assess impact on company's reputation from a review of reports in the media

Directors' emoluments

Directors' emoluments exceeding £350,000 are to be excluded from the calculation. Management may seek to report a lower emoluments figure by excluding benefits in kind or use share based payments according to IFRS 2. Only those emoluments over £350,000 are to be excluded, therefore management may defer payment of a portion of their salary below this figure until the following year in order to reduce pre-tax profit. Similarly, any bonuses to which the directors are entitled may not be provided for by management, or may be deferred or waived for this year.

Audit procedures

The major issue with respect to the directors' emoluments is their impact on the contingent consideration. The key risk therefore is the extent to which directors' emoluments are understated below the benchmark of £350,000 in year to 28 February 20X7. Audit tests should therefore focus on this shortfall risk and may include:

- Assess whether there is a clear definition of 'directors' emoluments' in the contingent consideration contract. Areas of doubt may be:

  - Whether they are determined for the purposes of the contract on a normal IAS 19 accruals basis

  - Whether bonuses are included

  - Whether share-based payments are included and if so whether they are measured for the purposes of the contract on an IFRS 2 basis

  - Assess the treatment under the contract of any other payments to directors (eg pension payments)

  - Whether any actions by the new Scherzo directors are forbidden under the contract (eg waiving or deferring emoluments)

- Obtain a list of all directors and verify that both executive and non-executive directors are included in the contract

- Ascertain from the contract that all directors are included (ie anyone who was a director at any time during the year)

- Attest all payments made and owing to directors at any time during the year

- Ensure that payments to the directors in the pre disposal period are included

- Review the contract for any other terms relevant to the determination of directors' emoluments for the purposes of determining the contingent consideration

- Compare the level of emoluments with prior years to review whether they are likely to be understated, particularly benefits in kind

- Examine directors' service contracts to ensure emoluments are in line with these and that any bonus entitlements have been provided appropriately

Other audit procedures

We need to pay particular attention to revenue and purchases cut-off in Scherzo to ensure profits are not understated. Any new provisions should be examined in detail to ensure they are fairly stated and presented. Similar tests should be carried out with respect to impairments.

The purchase by management is likely to have been funded by external debt or equity coming into Scherzo. If they are made available to us, examine the agreements for any such funding to ensure appropriate treatment in the financial statements. We need to assess the ability of management to fund any contingent consideration element, as any issues here could have implications for Scherzo's future activities. The debt element of any external funding introduced into Scherzo will need to be serviced. This will place a cash flow strain upon the company and therefore we need to assess both short and medium term serviceability of this debt (eg from review of cash flow forecasts) to ensure there are no adverse going concern implications for the company.

3.3 Riso Limited

The company has lost a major customer accounting for approximately 35% of its revenue. It has not as yet been able to find a suitable replacement customer for this lost studio time. This is partly due to a surplus of studio space within the UK which is likely to make it harder for Riso to fill the spare capacity within the studio. This gives rise to a going concern risk for Riso if its losses continue.

The loss during the year ended 28 February 20X7 and forecast cash outflows for the next two years indicate that the value of the television production equipment may be impaired at 28 February 20X7. Its carrying amount at that date was £5.6 million (£8m – (£8m – £2m) × 4/10) which was well in excess of its fair value at that date of £4 million. It is therefore necessary to carry out an impairment review to determine whether the value of the equipment needs to be written down. If this is not adequately done, there is a risk of overstatement of non-current assets in the financial statements.

Audit procedures

Given the loss of a major customer during the year, we should assess the reasonableness of the preparation of the financial statements on a going concern basis. This will include discussions with management, review of profit and cash flow forecasts, and examination of new contracts to ascertain whether the surplus capacity in the studio has been filled post year end.

We need to carry out a review of the client's impairment review on the television studio equipment. This will include the following procedures:

- Obtaining a copy of the recent valuation of equipment and agree to the review

- Review the estimate of future cash flows prepared by management, ensuring they are based upon reasonable assumptions

- Check the calculations of the possible impairment, including an assessment of whether the pre-tax discount factor used is reasonable

- Ensure any impairment identified is appropriately accounted for and disclosed in the financial statements

Notes in response to Bob Kerouac's email

Disposal of shares in Scherzo Limited

On disposal the assets and liabilities of Scherzo (including the goodwill) should be derecognised and the fair value of the consideration recorded. The remaining investment in Scherzo should be recognised at its fair value on the date the control was lost (30 April 20X6). Where there are any assets held at fair value with movements as part of other comprehensive income then these other comprehensive income amounts need to be transferred to retained earnings or profit or loss (for instance in the case of available for sale financial assets). Any resulting difference is recorded in profit or loss and would be likely to be recognised as an exceptional item.

After the disposal, Scherzo is no longer a subsidiary but rather an associate company of Commedia. It will need to be accounted for in the consolidated financial statements under the equity method of accounting. This involves including the fair value of the 30% retained interest in Scherzo on the date control was lost plus 30% of its retained earnings since that date in the group's consolidated statement of financial position.

Television production equipment in Riso Limited

The company's loss in the year ended 28 February 20X7 and anticipated future losses indicate that the television production equipment may be impaired under IAS 36. An impairment review therefore needs to be carried out. This involves a comparison of the carrying amount of the television production equipment in the financial statements (net book value) at 28 February 20X7 with its recoverable amount. For these purposes, recoverable amount is defined as the higher of (i) the fair value less costs to sell and (ii) the value in use. The fair value less costs to sell is (per IFRS 13) the price that would be received to sell the equipment and other net assets (£4m plus £0.25m) in an orderly transaction between market participants at the measurement date' trade of, and value in use equals the present value of expected future cash flows from the cash generating unit ('CGU') where the impaired assets exist. These cash flows should be discounted at a rate the market would expect for an equally risky investment. If the carrying amount is higher than the recoverable amount, the difference should be written off in profit or loss for the year.

Because Riso's sole activity is the operation of the television studio, it can be considered a CGU in itself. From the information given to us by management the calculation will be as follows:

At 28 February 20X7

Carrying amount of net assets	–	Equipment £5.6m (£8m cost less £2m estimated disposal proceeds = £6m. Depreciation for four years is therefore £2.4m on the depreciable amount of £6m)	
	–	Other net assets	£0.25m
	–	Total	£5.85m
Fair value less costs to sell	–	Equipment	£4.0m
	–	Other net assets (assumed)	£0.25m
	–	Total	£4.25m

Value in use – cash flows	Before discount £m	After discount £m
Year 1	(0.1)	(0.091)
Year 2	(0.05)	(0.041)
Year 3	0.9	0.676
Year 4	1.375	0.939
Year 5	1.495	0.928
Year 6	2+1.695	2.086
Total discounted value in use		4.497m

It is assumed all cash flows occur at year ends.

IAS 36.33(b) requires a justification of a period of over five years for value in use to be disclosed. The validity of the disclosed explanation would need to be reviewed as part of the audit to ensure compliance with IAS 36.

The value in use is higher than the fair value less costs to sell and therefore it is the former that needs to be compared with the carrying amount to determine whether an impairment is necessary. Comparing the two, there is a shortfall of £1.353m that needs to be recognised (£5.85m less £4.497m). This figure should be taken off the carrying amount of the television production equipment.

27 Pottington Printers

Internal Memorandum

To: Alice Kumar, Partner
From: A Senior
Date: 9 April 20X3
Subject: Pottington Printers audit

(a) **Meeting with finance director**

The meeting with the finance director highlighted a number of concerns. The key points appear to arise from the business strategy being pursued by Pottington Printers Ltd (hereafter PP). If some, or all, of the above business risks are realised the company's ability to continue as a going concern may be in question.

Lack of diversification

PP appears to be dependent on selling a single product acquired from a single supplier.

Finite contract

PP is three years into a five year contract which gives them a UK monopoly. There does not appear to be any clear strategy as to what will happen if the contract is not renewed on such favourable terms, or indeed, if it is not renewed at all. In particular, there may not be sole supplier status given that other firms are already entering the market in contravention of the existing contract.

Future financing

PP is to seek an AIM listing in future. Reported profits will be significant in determining the share price. Any accounting misstatement thus has significant potential for subscribers to suffer loss. This also generates significant engagement risk for our firm.

Expansion

There has been very significant expansion of sales and major investment in current assets, specifically inventory. This creates a risk of overtrading, given the additional financing that is proving necessary.

Management reliability

There are strong incentives for management to overstate profit. Some of the evidence to date suggests they are doing so (see below). The reliability of assertions from management may therefore be questionable and a degree of professional scepticism needs to be applied.

Unreliability

The sole product is unreliable which may damage the reputation of the business.

Guarantees

Significant long-term guarantees have been given, which may lead to material future costs, given the unreliability of the product.

Company stockpiling activity

The company's decision to stockpile the Mitzuki product exposes the company to the very real risk of obsolescence given the fast-moving nature of the technology industry.

Currency risks

PP may be exposed to currency risks for the duration of the contract. We should assess whether steps taken to manage risks appear reasonable, and whether the company appears to be bearing the risks of significant losses.

Audit procedures

The future business and financial strategy needs to be discussed with the directors. We need to assess the probability of the Mitzuki contract being renewed (eg by inspecting correspondence to see if negotiations have begun, and the progress of any such negotiations).

The key point here is that, given the dependence of the current business strategy upon the relationship with Mitzuki, it is implausible that PP should attempt to obtain an AIM listing if the new contract is not actually signed by that time.

Ethical issues

The client is putting pressure on us to guarantee a clean audit report. This situation may give rise to an intimidation threat. It is possible that this is the reason behind the recent change of auditor although this should have come to light in our quality control procedures regarding acceptance of a new client. We must remain independent in spite of this threat and should not provide management with any kind of guarantee regarding the audit opinion. This must be made clear to the client before we progress any further with the audit. If the threat is significant such that we cannot conduct our work in an objective manner we will need to consider whether we can continue.

(b) **Audit issues from junior staff**

Based upon the first week's work at the client a number of issues have arisen. These are summarised as follows.

Faulty machines in inventory

There are 5,000 machines in inventory, which have been returned from customers by repair engineers who have been unable to fix them.

They are measured at £320 each, which gives a total value of £1,600,000.

Once repaired, these machines will be sold on to new customers. They are therefore inventory and should be measured at the lower of cost and net realisable value (NRV) as required by IAS 2.

In the absence of a contractually agreed selling price, the best estimate of NRV must be the likely selling price, less appropriate deductions. In this case this would be £280 (460-180). This assumes that the machines will be able to be sold at the £460 and that the repair costs estimated are reasonable based on the work which is required. Total NRV of the machines amounts to £1,400,000 (5,000 x 280). An adjustment of £200,000 would be required to write down the inventory. The materiality of this adjustment should be considered. At 1.8% of profit before tax based on the draft accounts provided by the client it does not appear material however it should be considered in the light of other adjustments that may be required due to these faults (see below) and other adjustments identified during the course of the audit.

If the faults are systematic or likely to reoccur then consideration should be given to making a provision on the basis of sales already made, which are likely to incur future repair costs not covered by the Mitzuki guarantee.

One problem is that the nature of the fault is likely to be different in each case (unless there is a common design fault) so that it is impracticable to ascertain the precise NRV of every single machine.

Audit procedures

- Obtain from the client an explanation of how the figure of £180 for repairs was arrived at;

- Examine a random sample of machines to ascertain the cause and nature of the problem and likely repair costs, if indeed they can be repaired;

- Confirm the basis on which management has calculated the resale price of the repaired machines;

- Consider what has happened to faulty machines in the past, whether they have ultimately been sold and if so for how much;

- Ascertain whether the problem is likely to continue in the future or whether the causes have been identified and resolved (in order to assess the need for a provision against future repair costs on past sales);

- Ascertain the typical age of the sample of faulty machines, and where they are less than a year old whether they are covered by the Mitzuki guarantee. Consider in this context, not only the legality of any claim, but also its commerciality (eg who pays for the return transport costs?); and

- Ascertain how long the faulty machines have been in inventory.

Training costs

It seems inappropriate to capitalise ongoing training costs where there is little certainty that under IAS 38 an asset has been created.

For an intangible asset to be determined as identifiable it must be either:

- Separable; or
- Arise from contractual or other legal rights.

An asset is separable if it can be sold, licensed, or rented to another party on its own, rather than as part of the business. IAS 38 points out that the skills of staff do not normally fall within this definition, since a company cannot exercise control over the future economic benefits derived from these (the staff may leave).

Training costs are therefore normally revenue expenditure and the £5m training costs should not have been capitalised at the start of 20X1. On the basis of the current information available it appears likely that a prior year error adjustment of £4m arising from costs capitalised and relating to previous years needs to be made to reserves brought forward in the statement of changes in equity for the year ending 31 March 20X2 , and no training cost asset or related depreciation recognised in this year's financial statements or in the comparatives.

Audit procedures

- Verify the total amount of training costs incurred (eg review major external invoices making up the initial expenditure of £5 million; review internal training cost allocations)

- Confirm basis for amortisation and recalculate amortisation in the year

- Obtain agreement from the client that no training cost asset or related depreciation will be recognised in this year's financial statements or in the comparatives.

- On the basis that training costs have been capitalised in the previous year, obtain client's agreement to restate comparatives;

- On the basis that training costs have been capitalised in the year ended 31 March 20X1, obtain client's agreement to a prior year adjustment.

Litigation

PP is suing another company. PP has received legal advice that the claim will be successful and PP will receive £4 million. Credit has been taken for £2 million as an exceptional item in the current year.

Under IAS 37 a contingent asset is a possible asset that arises from past events, but whose existence can only be confirmed by the outcome of future events not wholly within the entity's control. A contingent asset should be disclosed (not recognised in the statement of financial position) when the expected inflow of economic benefits is probable.

Audit procedures

- Obtain the client's agreement that the item will be reversed and thus the revenue will not be recognised in the current period

- Inspect the correspondence and evidence for the legal opinion that the claim will be successful and that it will yield £4 million

- If, on the basis of legal opinion, the claim appears to have a probable chance of success, then disclosure should be made in the financial statements as a contingent asset

- The progress of the case should be re-assessed immediately prior to audit completion

Loan

PP took out a loan with deferred interest payable and therefore did not recognise any interest in profit or loss.

This treatment is not in accordance with IAS 39 which requires the loan to be measured at amortised cost. An implicit interest rate should be calculated and charged over the period of the entire loan, irrespective of when the charges fall due or are paid in individual years (the effective interest rate method).

The implicit rate is calculated over four years, but with interest being paid only in the final two years. An initial estimate of the average implicit interest rate is:

$(1.0 \times 1.0 \times 1.12 \times 1.12)^{\frac{1}{4}} = 1.0583 = 5.83\%$

Interest for the year of £1,166,000 (20,000,000 × 5.83%) should be recognised in profit or loss.

Audit procedures

- Verify the terms of the loan agreement, including the date of the interest payments (it is assumed in the calculations that they are paid annually in arrears in the years when payment is made)

- Ensure that any security on the loan is disclosed

(c) **Review of the draft financial statements**

The following is a selection of some of the key areas in the draft financial statements that appear to raise questions and have not already been discussed.

Revenue

The revenue figure of £72 million is consistent with the figures given by the finance director, ie 150,000 machines at £480 each.

The potential problem in this instance is that the sale relates not only to the supply of a machine in the current year but also the provision of a service to repair the machine that occurs over three years.

It would be unreasonable to recognise the full amount of revenue in the year of sale, as the sale is likely to lead to future repair costs. This is an example of a bundled contract under IAS 18; part of the revenue is earned from the sale of the machine and partly from a repair service. The timing of these events is different and thus they need to be unbundled and recognised separately.

Most obviously the repair service could be valued at the external arm's length rate of £50 per machine per year and two years per machine, recognised over the two years following the one-year guarantee period.

Thus if a machine is sold on 1 April 20X2, revenue would be recognised in the years to 31 March as

	£
20X3	380
20X4	50
20X5	50

This approach means that revenue would be reduced by £15 million in the current year.

However, on average, we would expect sales to be made half way through the year. Thus the average revenue per machine of £355 [(£480 - £150) + (£50 × 6/12)] should be recognised in respect of the current year's sales. However, there should be recognition of revenue of £50 in 20X3 from warranty income in respect of 20X2 and 20X1 sales. Based on the Financial Director's statement that 125,000 machines were sold in 20X2 and 80,000 machines were sold in 20X1, total revenue should be:

150,000 × 355	53,250,000
125,000 × 50	6,250,000
80,000 × 50	4,000,000
	63,500,000

Revenue should therefore be reduced by £8,500,000 (72 – 63.5) and recognised as deferred income.

A similar adjustment is also likely to be required for the previous year's comparative revenue figure. A prior period adjustment would be required in respect of excess revenue recognised in the year ended 31 March 20X1. This would be recorded as an adjustment to the brought forward retained earnings at 1 April 20X1.

Tutorial note:

An alternative view is that the company is making a guarantee rather than selling a service as the service is not needed unless the machine actually breaks down. If this view is taken, the company has a constructive obligation to repair faulty machines (the sale of a machine is the obligating event). As some outflow of economic benefit is virtually certain IAS 37 requires a provision to be recognised. The provision should be measured at the best estimate of the expenditure required to settle the obligation. The probability of an outflow and the expenditure required are assessed for the warranty obligations as a whole.

Audit procedures

- Discuss the approach with management and the need for separate recognition of sales revenue and repair service revenue;

- Confirm duration of guarantee to sales agreement;

- Once available review calculations to ensure that current period revenue includes repair service revenue on sales made in previous year;

- Select a sample of sales invoices and ensure that the appropriate proportion of revenue is deferred at the year end;

- Verify value of repair service eg obtain confirmation of cost charged by a competitor.

Audit procedures (alternative view)

- Ascertain the terms of the warranty;

- Estimate the direct costs and incidence of repairs on the basis of historic evidence;

- Ascertain whether any provision has been made already in the draft financial statements and consider whether an additional provision should be made.

Gross profit margin

The cost and selling price per machine seem inconsistent with the ratio of cost of sales to revenue.

If total revenue is £72 million, then cost of sales should be expected to be at least £48 million (£72 million × 320/480) whereas it is only £45 million (indeed with items such as transport costs, the cost of sales may be expected to be higher than £48 million). Warranty costs incurred would also need to be considered.

This may indicate that sales are overstated or cost of sales is understated.

Audit procedures

- Seek an explanation from the FD of the differences between the individual and overall margins;

- Obtain an analysis of the sales and cost of sales amounts (eg using monthly management accounts to determine whether there is a systematic difference each month between expected and actual gross profit margins);

- Consider other costs and write-offs that may have been included;

- Consider whether there is an inventory cut-off problem, given the physical distance over which the goods are transported from the Far East.

Operating costs

Operating costs have risen less in percentage terms than revenue (6% compared with 20%).

Audit procedures

- Obtain an analysis of all costs making up operating costs (eg from monthly management accounts);

- Seek explanations of changes and verify these to documentation as appropriate according to the explanations received;

- Consider the validity of non-cash costs in particular (eg provisions, write-offs, depreciation);

- Review post year-end payments to see if any significant costs should have been put through during year ended 31 March 20X3.

Inventories

Inventories have risen substantially. The reason, however, may be commercially defensible if, when the existing contract expires, the price of the machines is likely to increase. Stockpiling thus makes commercial sense and is likely to increase over the next few months.

Nevertheless, the high inventory levels increases the risks of damage and obsolescence. They also carry high stockpiling costs and opportunity costs (the money spent on buying inventory early could be put to better use) – see the Financing section below.

Audit procedures

- Discuss with directors for how long stockpiling will continue and maximum levels that inventory is likely to reach. Calculate how long, based on current sales levels, it will take to sell inventory stockpiled, and consider evidence casting doubts about whether all the items purchased can be sold (for example competitor plans to introduce a smaller model)

- Ensure that stockpiling does not breach the terms of the contract with Mitzuki

- Review post year end inventory levels to see whether they are consistent with the policy of stockpiling

- Ascertain what controls exist over inventories. In particular, assess whether controls over security of inventories are adequate, and the steps taken to avoid conditions causing loss of inventory value

Financing

Clearly stockpiling needs to be financed. The increased overdraft, loan and trade payables are likely to be caused by increased inventories.

Audit procedures

- Inspect cash budgets and inventory purchase budgets for predicted cash outflows over the next few months

- Review overdraft facility at the bank and ascertain whether PP has breached terms, or is likely to breach terms in the near future

- Examine correspondence with the bank for evidence of possible modification or withdrawal of overdraft facility

Conclusion

A number of significant audit adjustments have been suggested, almost all of which are likely to reduce profit. If implemented, these will take the client from a profit to a substantial loss for the current year (see below).

We therefore need to communicate with the directors urgently.

(d) **Revised financial statements**

Statement of profit or loss and other comprehensive income for year ended 31 March 20X3

	Draft 20X3 £m	Adjustments £m	Revised 20X3 £m
Revenue	72	(8.5)	63.5
Cost of sales	(45)	(0.2)	(45.2)
Gross profit	27		18.3
Operating costs	(17)	(1)	(18)
Litigation claim	2	(2)	–
Operating profit/loss	12		(0.3)
Interest payable	(1)	(1.166)	(2.166)
Profit/loss before taxation	11		(1.866)
Taxation	(2)	–	(2)
Profit for the year	9		(3.866)

Statement of financial position as at 31 March 20X3

	£m	£m	Adjustments £m	Revised £m
Non-current assets				
Land and buildings		10		10
Training costs		2	(2)	–
Inventories	67		(0.2)	66.8
Receivables	10		(2)	8
		77		
Total assets		89		84.8
Share capital: £1		5		5
Retained earnings		14	(3), 1, (0.2), (2), (1.166), (8.5)	(0.134)
		19		4.866
Non-current liabilities		32	1.166	33.166
Current liabilities				
Trade payables	15			15
Overdraft	23			23
Deferred income	–		8.5	8.5
		38		
Total equity and liabilities		89		84.8

28 Precision Garage Access

		Technical	Skills	
			Marks	
1	Carry out revised analytical procedures identifying any unusual patterns and trends in the data which may require further investigation	8	10	Comparison of actual and imputed figures based on data provided. Use of judgement in interpreting data and offering potential reasons for variances. Correct analysis and treatment of staff bonus. Appropriate calculation and interpretation of working capital ratios
2	Outline the audit risks that arise from the patterns and trends identified in the analytical procedures and set out the audit procedures you would carry out	4	4	Structuring of presentation of audit work to link into each analysis for each audit area. Use of data to identify risks and identification of appropriate audit tests
3	Set out the financial reporting issues that arise from the above audit work	4	4	Identification of key financial reporting issues. Specify correct financial reporting treatment
4	Outline impact on profit of share option schemes and explain reasons for differences	4	4	
	Total marks	20	22	
	Maximum		30	

To: Gary Megg, Audit Manager
From: A. Senior
Date: 26 July 20X6
Subject: PGA audit

1. Analytical procedures

1.1 Statement of profit or loss and other comprehensive income (in £'000)

	9m to 30/6/20X6	9m to 30/6/20X5	
Revenue:			Note 1
Monty	7,500	9,600	
Gold	14,000	28,800	
Cost of sales:			Note 2
Monty	(6,700)	(7,800)	
Gold	(15,500)	(23,400)	
Gross (loss)/profit	(700)	7,200	
Fixed administrative and distribution costs	(1,200)	(1,200)	
Exceptional items			
Staff bonus scheme	(450)	–	Note 3
(Loss)/Profit before tax	(2,350)	6,000	
Income tax expense	–	(1,680)	
(Loss)/profit for the period	(2,350)	4,320	

Note 1 – Revenues

Revenue of the Monty has declined by 22%.

Revenue of the Gold has declined by 51%.

The predicted values of revenue for each of the products for the nine months to 30 June 20X6 are as calculated below. These are based on actual volumes sold (from the inventory records) × list prices.

Monty

9,000 units × £840 = £7.56m

The actual revenue for sales of Monty is £7.5m which is extremely close to the predicted level and therefore provides some assurance.

Gold

6,000 units × £2,520 = £15.12m

The actual revenue for sales of Gold is £14m which is a difference of 7% and may represent a risk of material understatement of sales (eg through significant and inappropriate discounting of sales, or errors in recording of sales.)

Audit work

- Verify the data provided by Claire which was used to make the predictions in the analytical procedures.

- Agree standard prices to price lists and time of price change.

- Test standard prices against sample of invoices.

- Review inventory records against inventory count information or continuous inventory records.

- Enquire whether significant discounts have been given which may explain the shortfall. Determine conditions for discounting and relevant authorisation enquiries from invoice sample.

- 70% of sales are overseas and denominated in euro. The standard price is fixed in euro at the beginning of the year as equivalent to the £, but exchange rate movements during the year may have caused a change. As a consequence, the actual revenue may have moved out of line with the predicted revenue based in £s. Review exchange rate movements and examine whether the translation is at the actual or average £/euro exchange rate. (This test also applies to each category of cost.)

Note 2 – Cost of sales

Cost of sales of the Monty declined by 14%.
Cost of sales of the Gold declined by 34%.

Using the quantity data provided by Claire, a significant fall in cost of sales would have been anticipated due to reductions in total variable costs. The reduction in cost of sales would however be expected to be smaller in percentage terms than the reduction in revenues as this is a manufacturing company and hence some costs are fixed. This fixed element of costs does not change despite the fall in volumes.

The predicted values of cost of sales are:

Monty

(£4m × 9/12) + (9,000 units × £840 × 50%) = £6.78m

The actual cost of sales of Monty is £6.7m which is extremely close to the predicted level and therefore provides some assurance.

Gold

(£12m × 9/12) + (6,000 units × £2,520 × 50%) = £16.56m

The actual cost of sales of Gold is £15.5m which is a difference of 6.4% and may represent a risk of material understatement of cost of sales if the understatement is due to errors and omissions. It is not clear from the data whether the cost saving arises from lower variable cost per unit or fixed costs savings but this requires further investigation.

Audit work

While the percentage difference is smaller for cost of sales than for revenue it may be more concerning as exchange rates do not appear to be an explanatory factor as manufacturing is in the UK. However installation costs and the sales network are incurred in euro so the exchange rate effect is not entirely to be ignored. As cost of sales and revenues are both lower than anticipated this may be a consistent explanation.

- Agree the total fixed costs being incurred against budget assumptions.

- Review the method of allocation of fixed production costs as given the seasonal nature of the business then if the allocation is on a time basis, rather than a normal usage basis, this may distort the costs allocated to cost of sales and inventory.

- Similarly, the large fall in volumes compared to previous years may not represent a normal usage basis in allocating fixed production costs to units of output.

- An alternative explanation for the difference in costs may be that there are fewer economies of scale arising from the smaller production runs from the lower volumes. Variable cost per unit may therefore have risen.

- As we are relying on budget data, review of the budgeting process and its historic accuracy.

A key audit concern is that the analysis implies there is a risk that revenue and cost of sales of the Gold may both be materially understated.

Gold based on results for nine months to 30.6.X6

	£'000
Actual gross loss	(1,500)
Revenue difference	1,120
COS difference	(1,060)
Imputed loss from analysis	(1,440)

Overall the possible indicated misstatement in overall profit or loss is quite small at £60,000 as the two differences are largely compensatory. Nevertheless individually they are of concern and need investigating.

Summary analysis

There has been a 25% reduction in sales volumes of Monty and a 50% reduction in sales volumes of Gold compared to the nine month period last year. Given the high fixed costs, the cost of sales has not fallen in line with revenues and a gross loss has been made.

As the business is seasonal, further losses are anticipated in the fourth quarter as revenues will be low and fixed costs will be high, being recognised on a time basis.

Note 3 – Staff bonus

The full year bonus is potentially £600,000. An accrual of 9/12 of this amount (ie £450,000) appears to have been made for the three quarters interim accounts. However this is not appropriate as the business is seasonal as: 'Sales volumes in the final quarter of the year ending 30 September 20X6 are expected to be the same as the final quarter of the year ended 30 September 20X5.'

On this basis revenue will be:

	£'000
Y/e 30 Sept 20X5 (10,400 + 31,200)	41,600
9 months to 30 June 20X5 (9,600 + 28,800)	(38,400)
Final quarter y/e 30 Sept 20X5	3,200
Final quarter revenue adjusted for 5% Price increase	3,360
9 months to 30 June 20X6	21,500
Projected revenue y/e 30.9.20X6	24,860

This is lower than the £26 million threshold thus the bonus should not be recognised. (See financial reporting below.)

Tutorial note:

The forecast revenue for the final quarter to 30 Sept 20X6 can also be calculated as follows:

Sales volumes expected in the quarter to 30 Sept 20X6 (in units)

Monty (13,000 – 12,000) 1,000

Gold (13,000 – 12,000)   1,000

Total revenue expected in the final quarter = (1,000 × £840) + (1,000 × £2,520) = £3,360,000

Audit work

Review the sales budgets for the final quarter up to the year end to assess whether the threshold level of sales to trigger the bonus has been achieved. For the final audit this figure will be known but for the purpose of reviewing the interim financial statements a combination of the latest actuals and the budget would be needed.

Examine the terms of the bonus agreement and of any announcement or other undertakings with staff regarding the possible payment of the bonus.

1.2 Statement of financial position

1.2.1 Receivables

9 months to 30 June 20X6

Receivables days =   (2,400/21,500) × 270 days

=   30 days

9 months to 30 June 20X5

Receivables days =   (4,300/38,400) × 270 days

=   30 days

Y/e 30 Sept 20X5

Receivables days =   (1,000/41,600) × 360 days

=   8.7 days

Superficially it may seem that receivables have fallen substantially from June 20X5 to June 20X6, from £4.3m to £2.4m. On closer inspection however the reduction is in line with the fall in sales and the receivables days are more or less the same.

Conversely, it may seem that receivables at 30 September 20X5 are very low using the calculation of 8.7 days. However receivables reflect sales in the most recent month(s) before the statement of financial position is drawn up, rather than the average for the year. Given the seasonality of PGA, the final quarter sales are low and therefore the year end receivables are expected to be low.

1.2.2 Inventories

Superficially it may seem there has been little movement in inventories and thus it is low risk. However, the inventory days show significant movement:

9 months to 30 June 20X6

Inventories days $=$ (3,500/22,200) × 270 days

$=$ 43 days

9 months to 30 June 20X5

Inventories days $=$ (3,500/31,200) × 270 days

$=$ 30 days

The significant increase in inventory days shows that inventory remained constant but the expectation was that it should have fallen as the cost of sales has reduced through a lower level of commercial activity.

Audit work

Analytical procedures show a low level of risk for receivables as the receivables days (30 days) is consistent both with the previous period and with the credit terms extended.

Inventories are more concerning as we would have expected them to fall and they have not. The key tests are to look at older inventory to see if there is a problem with quality, settlement or ability to sell.

It may also be worth looking at whether there has been a large increase in finished goods (eg cancelled orders in a recession). If this is the case, then a write-down of such inventories should be considered.

Financial reporting issues

Revenue

There is a risk from the revenue recognition policy as it may not be appropriate to record the sale of garage doors until the installation is complete unless the two elements are separable.

Foreign currency translation

According to IAS 21 sales should be translated at the date of the transaction (or the average rate as an approximation). Given that sales are seasonal in the full year then there is a risk that the average rate may not be at an appropriate rate.

Staff bonus

The bonus should only be recognised according to IAS 37 and 34 when there is a constructive or legal obligation to make a payment. In this case, the full year's revenue on which the bonus is based is expected to fall below £26m in the full year (see note 3 above) thus no bonus should be recognised in the interim or the final full year financial statements.

Impairments of PPE

The Gold product looks to be performing poorly in making losses and the estimate is that "Sales of Gold doors are not expected to increase in the foreseeable future."

Gold doors production seems likely to be a cash generating unit as the assets to make the Gold doors are separately identifiable from the Monty assets. Similarly, the revenue streams are also separately identifiable.

As a consequence the value in use of the PPE used on the Gold production line (and other PPE specifically associated with the Gold product) seems likely to be low.

Also the fair value less costs of disposal also seem to be low as the "Production equipment is specialised and highly specific to each of the separate production processes".

In such circumstances the sharp downturn in Gold sales could represent an impairment event and therefore an impairment review of the Gold assets should be carried out.

Receivables

The amount for receivables is a monetary asset and so should be translated at the year end exchange rate.

If in the recession bad debts are increasing then an impairment charge should be considered.

2 Response to David May's request

Proposal A – equity settled

Scheme commencing	Computation of annual expense for each scheme	Expense each year £	Equity impact each year £
1/10/20X6	600 × £8 × 1/3 × (80 – [3 × 10])	80,000	80,000
1/10/20X7	600 × £10 × 1/3 × 50	100,000	100,000
1/10/20X8	600 × £12 × 1/3 × 50	120,000	120,000

Scheme commencing	Year ending 30/09/20X7 £	Year ending 30/09/20X8 £	Year ending 30/09/20X9 £
1/10/20X6	80,000	80,000	80,000
1/10/20X7		100,000	100,000
1/10/20X8			120,000
Total expense	80,000	180,000	300,000

Proposal B – cash settled

Scheme commencing 1/10/20X6

Year ending 30 September		Expense £	Liability £
20X7	(600 × £10 × 1/3 × 50)	100,000	100,000
20X8	(600 × £12 × 2/3 × 50) – £100,000	140,000	240,000
20X9	(600 × £14.4 × 3/3 × 50) – £240,000	192,000	432,000

Scheme commencing 1/10/20X7

Year ending 30 September		Expense £	Liability £
20X8	(600 × £12 × 1/3 × 50)	120,000	120,000
20X9	(600 × £14.4 × 2/3 × 50) – £120,000	168,000	288,000

Scheme commencing 1/10/20X8

Year ending 30 September		Expense £	Liability £
20X9	(600 × £14.4 × 1/3 × 50)	144,000	144,000

Scheme commencing	Year ending 30/09/20X7 £	Year ending 30/09/20X8 £	Year ending 30/09/20X9 £
1/10/20X6	100,000	140,000	192,000
1/10/20X7		120,000	168,000
1/10/20X8			144,000
Total expense	100,000	260,000	504,000

Comparison – charge to profit or loss

	Year ending 30/09/20X7 £	Year ending 30/09/20X8 £	Year ending 30/09/20X9 £
Proposal A	80,000	180,000	300,000
Proposal B	100,000	260,000	504,000

Variation in profit

With the equity settled proposal the charge for each yearly tranche is constant over its life, as the fair value is determined at the grant date and then apportioned evenly over the life of the scheme.

The total charge to profit or loss does however increase over the period with the equity settled proposal for two reasons:

- The share price is projected to increase so the annual cost of later schemes is greater than earlier schemes

- There is a cumulative effect as in 20X7 there is only one scheme in operation, in 20X8 there are two schemes and in 20X9 there are three schemes. In 20Y0 and beyond the cost will not however continue to increase due to this cumulative effect, as there will only ever be three schemes in operation in steady state.

The annual expense under the cash settled proposal will also increase due to the above effects but, in addition, there is an annual increase for each individual scheme as the liability is recalculated each year. Thus, as share prices rise, the charge will increase for this proposal and will include the cumulative shortfall from previous years in respect of the increase. As a consequence, with rising share prices the cash settled proposal will result in a higher charge to profit or loss than an equivalent equity settled scheme.

In both cases there will, in reality, be volatility in the charge to profit or loss due to the actual number of managers who leave and join in each year. This factor is not evident above due to the simplifying assumption that ten managers leave and join in each year. In addition the actual share prices at the time of granting the cash settled items could vary significantly and this would be a further cause of volatility.

29 Tawkcom

Marking guide

	Marks		
	Technical	Skills	
Explanation of financial reporting and auditing issues arising from Jo's work.	9	8	Key skills assessed here are those of interpreting and analysing data from a variety of sources to enable a critical analysis of the control information presented
Identification of additional steps required to complete audit procedures and to support opinion on financial statements	5	5	Key skill assessed here is the application of technical advice to a given scenario and a given audience
Summarise where group audit team may provide useful information	3	3	Key skill here is the application of technical skills to a given scenario and the selection of audit techniques most appropriate to the given situation. Efficiency is key given the time constraints and this should influence the candidate's choice of tests

	Technical	Skills
Ethical points re potential for manipulation of the financial statements		2
	—	—
Total marks	17	18
Maximum		30

(i) **Explanation of financial reporting and auditing issues**

Prior year adjustment for repairs and maintenance costs

- Need to understand whether prior period audit adjustment of £1.3 million has been recognised through pack in current year. If not then will give rise to an adjustment which, whilst not material, is above the scope and should be reported to group.

- Also need to consider whether there are similar items which have been wrongly capitalised in the current year. Procedures performed on additions to network assets are probably insufficient to identify such items at present.

Sample sizes

- Unclear from work sent for review whether sample sizes for detailed testing have been calculated correctly. Documentation on additions states that Jo has used group materiality rather than the tolerable mis-statement for PPE. Hence need to consider carefully whether adequate samples tested for all areas.

Head office lease

- Although presumably tested in prior years, may be a question over whether lease of head office building is really an operating lease, given length of term. Cannot tell without further information. Need to start with prior year work papers/manager's own knowledge.

Leasehold improvements

- Given that lease of head office expires in 20Z5, should be depreciating leasehold improvements over remaining 16/17 years. The depreciation charge for the year seems ow and work on depreciation and figures suggests that a life of 20 years is still being used even for additions in the year. Unlikely to be material for group but is a clear error and could well be above reporting scope, depending on timing of additions. Hence this needs to be evaluated and posted to the schedule of adjustments. In addition, need to make sure that improvements are being depreciated over no longer than their actual useful life, which may be shorter than lease term.

- Given major refurbishment of building, would expect much more significant disposals of improvements capitalised in previous years (or perhaps significant expensing of expenditure if it is not a true improvement).

Network asset additions

Appears from comments on additions that certain of the network assets are specific to particular customers. If this is the case need to consider carefully the terms under which customers use them and whether they are in substance leased to customer and, if so, how that lease should be accounted for. Even if correct to continue to include the assets in PPE, the depreciation periods should not exceed the expected life of the relationship with the particular customer which may well be less than the 22 year depreciation period. Cannot at present evaluate the extent of this potential issue but could be material given the size of the network assets.

Appears that rates used to capitalise labour and overhead may be inconsistent with prior year, include an element of profit (as they are based on day rates for external customers) and were increased at the request of group management. Effect is material and will affect both PPE and statement of profit or loss and other comprehensive income.

Disposal of computer and office equipment

- Disposals of fixtures and equipment include a disposal of office equipment to a company owned by friends of the FD. Whilst not a RPT for FR purposes, this transaction is large and clearly raises questions of propriety, especially as the equipment was relatively new (since low accumulated depreciation) and no proceeds were received. Need also to check on whether authority limits for disposals followed.

Sale and leaseback

- Sale and leaseback transaction has been accounted for as a disposal of Glasgow House and a profit of £1.295 million recognised. This is only the correct treatment if the lease is an operating lease and the disposal proceeds represent fair value. Option to extend lease to up to 50 years and fact that the lessor is a finance company and not a property company are both indications that the lease may be a finance lease. However further details are required. Transaction was also concluded very close to year-end which may be indicative of window dressing. Transaction increases cash (ie reduces net borrowings) and decreases PPE so may have had an effect on critical ratio for covenants.

Sale of land

- It appears that the sale of land has been treated as an adjusting event after the reporting period. Sale and profit have been recognised despite the fact that the sale was not completed at 30 September 20X9. This treatment is not correct in accordance with IAS 10 *Events after the Reporting Period* as the sale in October does not provide evidence of circumstances which existed at the reporting date as the contract was still conditional at that time. The profit on disposal should therefore be reversed and the cost of land added back to PPE. If considered material to the users the transaction could be disclosed as a non-adjusting event after the reporting period.

- Consideration should be given as to whether the land meets the criteria to be classed as 'held for sale' in accordance with *IFRS 5 Non-current Assets Held for Sale and Discontinued Operations*. If this were the case the asset would be measured at the lower of its carrying amount and its fair value less costs to sell at 30 September 20X9. In this case the valuation would be at carrying amount.

Valuation of freehold property

Last valuation of freehold properties was at 30 September 20X7. Given recent movements in property market, that may be out of date. The client appears to have provided no documentation to support keeping the valuation unchanged. Even if they can support the valuation remaining unchanged, a depreciation charge should be made to profit or loss and a revaluation recognised separately. The way they have accounted for it at present overstates profit which may affect bonus. Revaluation entries should also result in reversal of accumulated depreciation. Amount is not material to group but is above level which should be reported and is a clear error.

Investment property

- Investment property has been shown within PPE which is incorrect as it should be shown in a separate asset category (as should related revaluation reserve). In addition, need to determine group policy for investment properties and whether using cost or fair value model. Neither applied at present as property is held at an out of date valuation. Given that sale fell through and company has decided to postpone sale, seems likely that current market value has fallen and reduction in value may be necessary.

- Also question as to whether the property is really an investment property at all as Tawkcom is offering services as well as accommodation to the lessees. This would preclude classification as an investment property unless such services are insignificant to the arrangement as a whole which seems unlikely in the case of serviced offices. If classification is incorrect then depreciation should be charged. However depreciation amount unlikely to be above scope for reporting to group. Classification question and impairment question potentially more significant.

Useful life increase

- Increase in useful life by two years does not explain fully the very low depreciation charge for network assets. A charge of around £7-8 million would have been expected based on a rough calculation. It appears that an error has been made, perhaps by adjusting prior years' depreciation through the current year charge. This is incorrect as any change in useful life should be accounted for prospectively and the carrying value at the time of the change simply depreciated over the remaining revised useful life. Initial indicators are that effect is material and an adjustment will be required even if longer life can be justified.

- Will need input from head office team to determine whether longer useful life is reasonable for core network assets. In addition, may well need input from auditor's expert/specialist audit team to consider evidence for the longer useful life and whether it is representative of reality.

(ii) **Additional steps required to complete audit procedures**

Group scope not entity level procedures performed

- Indication from additions testing in particular that procedures to date have been completed to group scope only – procedures will need to be updated to take into account materiality for individual statutory entity.

Procedures on impairment

- At present there is no consideration as to whether there are indications of impairment. Carrying value of network assets in particular continues to grow and is very material to both group and company figures. There will need to be consideration of whether impairment indicators exist before we sign off to group. (Important to consider each asset separately for impairment). Likely to be the case given the general economic downturn. If indicators do exist then the recoverable amount of the assets will need to be considered and evidence of external value or cash flow projections obtained as necessary. As network supports all of company's business, overall cash flow projections obtained for going concern purposes will also be relevant here. However this work may not yet have been completed as typically left until statutory accounts sign off for subsidiary. Given that Tawkcom is a significant trading subsidiary of the group, procedures performed on going concern at group level may be relevant.

Procedures on brought forward position

- No procedures appear to have been performed to verify the existence/ownership of brought forward PPE balances and so test the completeness of disposals. Need to determine what work the company/internal audit have done on this and to consider the extent to which such work can be relied on as audit evidence. Will also need to do own testing. This is an important step given the materiality of the balances involved.

Physical verification

- Physical verification of property should be possible, as should agreement to deeds or land registry.

- Physical verification of fixtures and equipment should be possible although might be possible to leave this for statutory work as balance (excluding additions in year which have been tested) is not material for group purposes.

- Physical existence vouching should be possible for leasehold improvements although potential issue has already been raised above. Therefore important that procedures done in this area reflect the high risk of unrecorded disposals and consider specifically whether any previous improvements have been disposed of or rendered redundant as a result of the work done in the last two years.

- Physical existence procedures for network assets much more challenging as already highlighted by procedures on additions. Need to look for evidence that network is still being used – perhaps by review of sales/operational data; discuss with personnel outside of accounts whether there are stretches of cabling which are redundant/little used or superseded by alternative routing; consider whether additional cabling laid in year has rendered any existing cabling redundant. May well need to involve a specialist. This review should consider additions in the year as well as brought forward assets as work on additions has not been completed. Additional review of customer specific assets also relevant – see below.

Capital/revenue?

- Need to look much more critically at nature of additions to network assets and consider carefully whether there is evidence that any of the capitalised projects represent expense items such as repairs and maintenance. This can be done through discussion of the nature of the projects with the project managers or other personnel outside accounts. Also need to review procedures performed on repairs and maintenance expense in the consolidated statement of profit or loss to ensure that there is no evidence that this is lower than would be expected and therefore potentially incomplete.

- Need to evaluate extent to which network assets relate to particular customers and compare depreciation period to the life of the relevant customer relationship.

- Need to understand in much more detail the costs and any mark up included within the day rates used to capitalise labour and overhead incurred on the creation of network assets. Important that only the direct cost of bringing assets to working condition should be capitalised and this should not include an allocation of administrative cost or a profit element. Costs should be vouched and the hours/days incurred tied in to time reports (nature of projects already covered in proposed work above). Material elements of additions should be vouched in the normal way – not clear that this has been done.

Disposal to AR Hughes

- Need to understand rationale for disposal of assets to AR Hughes – ie were assets surplus to requirements? Why was their useful life so much shorter than that assumed in setting the depreciation rate? Were other potential buyers considered? What was market value of similar assets at time of sale?

Glasgow property

- Obtain evidence of fair value of Glasgow property at time of sale and leaseback transaction, having liaised first with group audit team to see what procedures can be done/have already been done at group level. Review leaseback agreement and conclude as to whether it is a finance or operating lease.

- Need to obtain further support from client to support valuations of freehold property and investment property at year-end. This might include external valuations, or use of indices which show how values for similar properties have moved since last formal valuation on 30 September 20X7.

- Obtain details of terms of rental agreement to tenants of the investment property to determine whether services offered are significant to the overall arrangement.

Sale of land

- Confirm details of the sale agreement to determine whether classification as held for sale is appropriate.

Areas where group audit team may provide useful evidence

- Understanding extent to which procedures performed on going concern or impairment of investments at group level may assist Tawkcom team in assessing impairment of PPE.

- Enquire as to procedures done on day rates for capitalisation of employees' time as this has been driven by a head office project. Would be useful to understand fully group policy and the procedures performed at head office to validate the way in which rates are calculated.

- Discuss with group FD the disposal of assets to AR Hughes and his rationale for approving this.

- Obtain further information re Glasgow House transaction and consider fully the impact of this transaction on compliance with the bank covenant.

- Understanding of group policy for investment properties.

- Background to and support for the group decision to increase the useful life for network assets.

30 Expando Ltd

			Marks
	Technical	*Skills*	
Explain FR treatment and audit procedures for the outstanding issues			
Revaluation	2	3	
Debenture loan	2	3	
Acquisition of Minnisculio	2	2	
Disposal of premises	2	3	
Acquisition of Titch		3	
Comment on procedures performed by the auditors of Titch	1	2	
Provision of temporary staff	2	2	
Complete the draft statement of profit or loss and other comprehensive income, statement of changes in equity and statement of financial position	3	4	
Total marks	14	22	
Maximum			30

For more guidance on how skills are tested and rewarded, please refer to the section at the start of this question bank.

Revaluation of land

Accounting treatment

The basic treatment of the land adopted in the draft financial statements is correct. In accordance with IAS 16 *Property, Plant and Equipment* there is no requirement to depreciate land. In addition, the revaluation has been correctly recognised in the revaluation surplus and as other comprehensive income. This gain is recognised but not realised therefore it will not be distributable.

Audit procedures

Verify valuation to valuation certificate.

Consider reasonableness of the valuation by reviewing:

- Competence, capabilities and objectivity of valuer
- The scope of their work and obtaining an understanding of it
- Methods and assumptions used
- Valuation basis is in line with IAS 16, as amended by IFRS 13 (market-based evidence of fair value)

Ensure that all assets within the same class as the land have been revalued (in accordance with IAS 16 if an asset is revalued the entire class to which it belongs must be revalued).

Check that disclosures are adequate in accordance with IAS 16 and IFRS 13. These should include:

- Effective date of revaluation

- Whether an independent valuer was involved

- The methods and significant assumptions applied in estimating fair value

- The extent to which fair values were determined by reference to market transactions or other valuation techniques

- The carrying amount that would have been recognised had the land not been revalued

- The change for the period in the revaluation surplus and the restrictions on the distribution of the balance to shareholders.

Debenture loan

Accounting treatment

In accordance with IAS 39 *Financial Instruments: Recognition and Measurement* a debenture initially should be measured in the financial statements at the fair value of the consideration received net of issue costs. (The exception to this is where the financial instrument is designated as at fair value through profit or loss.) The initial treatment in Expando's financial statements in this respect appears to be correct as the liability shows an amount of £1,850,000 (£2,000,000 – £150,000).

However, the subsequent treatment of the debenture does not appear to be correct. Interest recognised in profit or loss of £60,000 has been based on the coupon rate of 3% (£2,000,000 × 3%). (The interest recognised in profit or loss is made up of this charge of £60,000 and the interest on the 6% bank loan of £200,000 (£3,333,333 × 6%)). The debenture should be measured at amortised cost using the effective interest method. This means that the amount recognised in profit or loss should have been based on the effective interest on the debenture of 7% amounting to £129,500 (7% × £1,850,000). The difference between the actual interest paid (£60,000) and the interest charged (£129,500) represents a proportion of the premium at which the debenture will be redeemed. It is therefore rolled up into the liability in the statement of financial position.

Audit procedures

- Agree the details of the debenture to the debenture documentation, ie issue date, coupon rate, premium

- Agree the receipt of cash to the cash book/bank statement

- Check the nature of the costs and confirm that they are directly attributable to the issue of the debenture

- Check calculation of effective interest rate ie it should be the rate that exactly discounts estimated future cash payments or receipts through the expected life of the debenture to the net carrying amount of the financial liability

- Agree the change in the accounting treatment of the interest charge and the liability in the statement of financial position with the client

- Check the financial liability is adequately presented and disclosed in accordance with IAS 32 *Financial Instruments: Presentation* and IFRS 7 *Financial Instruments: Disclosures,* eg qualitative and quantitative disclosures about exposure to risk, carrying amount of the liability by IAS 39 category, interest recognised in profit or loss.

Acquisition of Minnisculio

Accounting treatment

The purchase of the trade and assets of Minnisculio is currently represented as an investment at cost of £250,000. This should be shown in the statement of financial position as inventories of £20,000 and an intangible asset of goodwill £230,000 as it is these assets which have been purchased as a result of the business combination. In accordance with IFRS 3 *Business Combinations* the goodwill should not be amortised, but should be subject to an impairment review. Whilst the basic provision of IAS 36 *Impairment of Assets* is that an impairment review only needs to be conducted where there is an indication that an asset may be impaired, goodwill acquired in a business combination is an exception to this rule. In this instance IAS 36 requires an annual test for impairment irrespective of whether there is any indication of impairment therefore the management of Expando must address this. Provided that we are satisfied with the impairment review subsequently performed no further adjustment will be required.

Audit procedures

- Agree the purchase price of Minnisculio to the purchase documentation

- Establish the basis on which the value of £20,000 has been attributed to the inventories (and therefore the £230,000 to goodwill)

- Confirm that goodwill does not include any non-purchased goodwill or any identifiable intangible assets

- Discuss with the directors the need to perform an impairment review

Assuming this is carried out determine the means by which the goodwill impairment review has been conducted, eg in accordance with IAS 36 has goodwill been allocated to the cash-generating units expected to benefit from the synergies of the combination?

Disposal of premises

Accounting treatment

The premises would appear to be an asset held for sale in accordance with IFRS 5 *Non-current Assets Held for Sale and Discontinued Operations* as its carrying amount is to be recovered principally through a sale transaction rather than through continuing use. For this to be the case the asset must be available for immediate sale in its present condition and the sale must be highly probable. For the sale to be highly probable the following conditions must be met:

- Management must be committed to the plan

- An active programme to locate a buyer and complete the plan must have been initiated

- The asset must be actively marketed for sale at a price that is reasonable in relation to its current fair value

- Management should expect the sale to be completed within one year from the date of classification

- It should be unlikely that significant changes will be made to the plan or that the plan will be withdrawn

Assuming that these conditions are satisfied the asset should be classified as held for sale and disclosed separately, in the statement of financial position. It should be measured at the lower of its carrying amount and fair value less costs to sell. An impairment loss should be recognised where fair value less costs to sell is lower than the carrying amount. Until the date of reclassification the asset should be depreciated as normal. An additional charge of £3,125 (£125,000/20 × 6/12) is therefore required. The asset would no longer be depreciated from the date of reclassification even if the asset remained in use.

Assuming that the asset does meet the criteria to be classified as held for sale the following adjustment would be required:

	£
Carrying amount at date of reclassification (125,000 – 125,000/20 × 6/12)	121,875
Fair value less costs to sell	115,000
Impairment	6,875

Audit procedures

Confirm that the asset is held for sale by ensuring that the IFRS 5 conditions above are satisfied:

- Discuss with management their plans for the sale and marketing of the asset

- Obtain evidence of management commitment eg proposed sale should be minuted

- Obtain evidence of an active programme for sale eg property agents being appointed

- Assess the market to determine the likelihood of the sale being completed within the one year time frame

- Recalculate current book value of the asset

- Assess the means by which the fair value of the asset has been established and determine whether this is reasonable

- Obtain information about costs to sell to assess whether they relate directly to the disposal of the asset

- Confirm that separate disclosure of the asset has been made in accordance with IFRS 5.

Acquisition of 25% of Titch

Accounting treatment

Assuming that the 25% owned by Expando allows it to exert significant influence Titch will be treated as an associate. As such the investment will be equity accounted as follows:

In the statement of profit or loss and other comprehensive income the group's share of profit/loss after tax is added to consolidated profit. This is normally achieved by adding the group share of the associate's profit/loss before tax and the group's share of tax. In this case the tax has already been dealt with. Therefore the adjustment required is as follows:

Share of loss of associate ($350,000 \times 9/12 \times 25\%$) = £65,625

The group's share of any other comprehensive income would also be included if relevant.

In the statement of financial position the group share of net assets is shown as a single item. This is represented by the initial cost of the investment increased or decreased each year by the amount of the group's share of the associated company's profit or loss for the year less any impairments in the investment to date. In this case, the 'Investment in associates' will be £334,000 (£400,000 - £66,000) to the nearest thousand.

Audit procedures

The audit of the financial statements of Titch is the responsibility of the auditors of Titch. We do not have any direct responsibility for this. However, we are responsible for the audit opinion of Expando even though the results will include information not directly audited by us. The amount of work we will need to do depends on the extent to which we can rely on the component auditors and whether Titch represents a significant component. At the planning stage we will have assessed the competence of the component auditors and will have requested a summary of the audit procedures conducted. Therefore the following additional work needs to be performed:

- Review the summary of the audit procedures and assess whether the work is comprehensive enough for our purposes

- Identify any areas requiring special consideration and/or additional procedures

- Consider the impact of any significant findings made by the component auditors

If the component is not significant, analytical procedures at the group level may be sufficient for the purposes of the group audit.

Once we have sufficient confidence in the individual financial statements of the associated company audit work will be concentrated on the mechanics of the equity accounting as follows:

- Confirm the date of acquisition and that the shareholding is 25%

- Check the shareholder agreement to verify that the relationship with Titch is that of 'significant influence' – it could also be an interest in a joint arrangement, in which case we would see evidence of 'joint control' as defined in IFRS 11 *Joint Arrangements*

- Agree the purchase cost of the investment to the purchase documentation

- Recalculate the group's share of the loss of the associate ensuring that only post acquisition losses have been consolidated

- Recalculate the statement of financial position balance to confirm that the cost has been reduced by the appropriate share of losses

- Confirm that any intra-group transactions have been identified and dealt with appropriately.

Provision of temporary staff

As Expando is a private company ES5 does allow the provision of accounting services by the audit firm. However, this is on the basis that:

- The services do not involve us undertaking part of the role of management

- The services do not involve us initiating transactions or taking management decisions and are of a technical, mechanical or an informative nature.

The specific nature of the role and the accounting work to be performed by the individual would have to be assessed.

In addition, steps would have to be taken to reduce the potential self-review threat to an acceptable level. The individual involved should not take part in any future audits and steps should be taken to ensure that other members of the audit team do not place too much reliance on the work performed by their colleague.

There are also practical issues to consider including whether we have sufficient staff available who can be seconded and whether they have the relevant experience and expertise. There is a potential for our reputation to be damaged if an unsuitable individual is sent.

Revised draft financial statements

Statement of profit or loss and other comprehensive income

Year ended	30/06/20X7 (draft) £'000	30/06/20X6 (audited) £'000
Revenue	4,430	3,660
Less: Operating expenses (3,620 + 3)	(3,623)	(2,990)
Operating profit	807	670
Interest payable (260 + 70)	(330)	(200)
Impairment loss on reclassification of non-current asset as held for sale	(7)	–
Share of loss of associate	(66)	–
Profit before tax	404	470
Taxation	(91)	(141)
Profit for the year	313	329
Other comprehensive income:		
Gain on property revaluation	1,000	–
Total comprehensive income for the year	1,313	329

Statement of changes in equity 30 June 20X7 (extract)

	Retained earnings £'000	Revaluation surplus £'000
Balance at 1 July 20X6	713	–
Total comprehensive income for the year	313	1,000
Balance at 30 June 20X7	1,026	1,000

Statement of financial position

Period end date	30/06/20X7 (draft) £'000	30/06/20X6 (audited) £'000
Non-current assets		
Land	5,000	4,000
Plant and machinery	2	2
Intangible assets: goodwill	230	–
Investment in Titch (400-66)	334	–
Current assets (2,155 + 20)	2,175	520
Asset held for sale	115	–
Current liabilities		
Taxation	(91)	(141)
Other	(300)	(149)
Non-current liabilities		
6% bank loan	(3,333)	(3,333)
3% debenture (1,850 – 60 + 130)	(1,920)	–
	2,212	899
Share capital	86	86
Share premium	100	100
Revaluation surplus	1,000	–
Retained earnings	1,026	713
	2,212	899

31 Netus UK Ltd

		Marks		
		Technical	*Skills*	
(1)	Comments on design of payroll controls	2	6	Interpret and analyse data from a variety of sources to enable a critical analysis of the control information presented.
				Identify gaps in the control information.
				Apply technical advice to a given scenario and a given audience.
(2)	FR advice	1	3	Identify accounting issues for pension fund.
				Specify appropriate audit tests.
				Identify need for expert in assessing pension assumptions.
				Use of efficient and appropriate reporting style.
(3)	Summary of proposed audit work	2	13	Select audit techniques most appropriate to the given situation. Efficiency is key given the time constraints and this should influence the candidate's choice of tests.
				Identify need for expert in assessing pension assumptions.
				Use of efficient and appropriate reporting style.
(4)	Other comments – ethical issues		6	This requirement tests both ethical awareness and the ability to determine when items noted from one area of audit work might have a more pervasive impact.
				Identify potential pressure from management.
				Determine ethical issue.
				Link information from other areas of the audit.
Total marks		5	28	
Maximum		30		

1 Comments on design of payroll controls

Overall comments

Objectives identified by the company do not cover all of the relevant financial statement assertions – in particular assertions about classification, presentation and disclosure are not really covered at all.

Controls identified by the company do not cover all of the staff cost balances we need to audit. Pension costs are not covered at all and neither are payments to temporary staff. In addition there are no explicit controls relating to employee expenses, bonus payments or commission or to the related accruals.

The company's assessment includes no consideration of systems or IT controls. Access controls are likely to be very important in an area such as this and the company is also relying on the system to calculate the payroll, PAYE, NI etc. As a result IT controls are likely to be key.

Departmental heads have very extensive responsibilities, giving rise to concern about lack of segregation of duties. They can authorise new joiners and changes to salary levels and are also responsible for the only detailed review of costs. Although the CFO authorises the payroll and reviews the monthly management accounts these are very high level controls of a large balance and might not identify all mis-statements. This is especially true in a department which includes up to 400 staff. It is likely that departmental controls are very inconsistent across departments and may not be wholly effective in the largest ones or wholly adequate in terms of segregation in the smallest ones. It is also unclear who approves the salary etc for departmental heads.

Specific comments

The payroll summary is authorised by the CFO but there is no indication of what level of review takes place or of what level of detail is presented. Ideally the CFO should be given a summary by department and a reconciliation explaining significant differences from the prior month's payroll.

There are likely to be sundry manual adjustments for corrections to payroll, leavers etc but controls over these are not mentioned at all.

Controls over joiners are identified but there are no controls listed which will ensure that leavers are removed from the payroll on a timely basis.

Controls over joiners/numbers of employees include no reconciliation with data held by HR. Such a control would make it more difficult to include fictitious employees or for leavers to be paid after employment has ceased.

If payroll is prepared five days before the month end, how are hours for the last five days captured for hourly paid staff? This seems to indicate that an accrual may be necessary.

No controls are listed relating to the calculation of NI, PAYE or pension contributions. All of these are relevant in ensuring that payroll costs are calculated accurately.

Controls do not cover all changes to master files used as a source of data. We would expect there to be a report of changes made to pay rates, bank account details etc so that this can be reviewed by the CFO/head of HR. At present the payroll clerk could make unauthorised changes and these might not be picked up.

2 FR advice

Pension should be accounted for in accordance with IAS 19. This means that the net surplus/deficit on the pension plan will be recognised in the financial statements.

Harry needs to obtain details of the scheme assets and liabilities from the actuary and to record entries in the financial statements to:

- Record the opening balance on the scheme as shown in the prior year statutory accounts (gross of deferred tax).

- Using details provided by the actuary, analyse the movement in assets and liabilities in the year into the following and make the entries indicated below:

  - Current service cost (as calculated by actuary). Will need to split between departments and allocate between various statement of profit or loss and other comprehensive income captions. Charge to operating profit.

  - Interest on obligation (as calculated by the actuary). Forms part of finance cost in financial statements.

  - Interest on plan assets (as calculated by the actuary). Forms part of finance cost/income in statement of profit or loss and other comprehensive income. It is netted off against the interest on obligation to show 'net interest on net defined benefit asset/liability'

  - Contributions paid – this will be the contributions paid in the year by employer and employee. Employee contributions reduce current service cost (unless already netted off). Employer contributions are what have already been charged to profit or loss. That entry needs to be reversed so that profit or loss charge is only as specified above and amounts paid form part of movement on deficit within statement of financial position.

  - Remeasurement gains and losses (actuarial gains and losses) should be recognised immediately in other comprehensive income

- Closing deficit should then agree to amount advised by the actuary.

3   **Schedule of audit procedures**

Interim work

Tests of controls – overview:

- Need to resolve design issues identified above by identifying, where possible, controls which eliminate gaps and deficiencies in controls and in the objectives which the controls address.

- Key controls sufficient to meet each objective should then be identified and tested.

- Tests of controls will include discussion, observation, re-performance and examination of relevant documentation. Work done on each control should be sufficient to ensure that it has operated throughout the nine months to June 20X9 and so should cover the whole period.

- Where a control is not operating effectively then a mitigating control should be sought or additional substantive procedures planned.

- Work by computer audit specialists on the systems based controls should take place at this interim visit.

Substantive procedures:

- Even if all controls testing is satisfactory, there is still a minimum level of substantive procedures which must be performed. For the statement of profit or loss and other comprehensive income items, much of this can be done at interim with only roll forwards/updates at final. Sample sizes will be smaller but all balances need to be covered.

Substantive analytical procedures are likely to be the most efficient and effective way to audit the main payroll balances as headcount figures and details of pay increases are available. Such procedures can also be used for commission as that would be expected to move in line with revenue. Procedures for the first nine months should be:

- Completed and expectations for annual figures established during the interim visit. Pension contributions can also be audited this way as the relationship to main payroll cost is known.

- Sample of temporary staff costs should be agreed to invoices, timesheets and contracts for rates of pay. Position re tax status of temporary staff should be considered, to address risk of underpayment of income tax and NI via PAYE. Creditor balance should be discussed and basis for calculation reviewed as creditor for temporary staff looks very low.

- Sample of employee expenses should be vouched to receipts/other documentation. Analytical procedures should be performed for completeness of expense claims.

- Procedures should be performed to ensure that it is possible to audit year end pension figures on a timely basis. We will need to ensure client understands entries to make and has made arrangements with actuary/investment managers to get information in time (challenging given deadline). Discussions must be held with the actuary at interim and assumptions to be used in valuation of liabilities can be reviewed at this stage and discussed with management's experts as appropriate. Circularisation letters can be sent to investment managers and actuaries, backed up by discussions on how quickly information can be provided. We must ensure Harry understands the entries he must make and where the information can be sourced from. Entries to record correct opening position in the statement of financial position can be determined at interim visit.

- Liaise with auditors of parent company with respect to opening balances relating to pensions.

- Basis for bonus provision should be discussed, rules of bonus scheme reviewed and expectation established for year-end accrual.

- Discuss with client why there is no holiday pay provision as would be expected.

Final work

Tests of controls:

- Roll forward controls work, ensuring by discussion/review that the controls continued to operate for the last three months of the year.

Substantive procedures:

- Compare annual costs with expectations established at interim and investigate any significant fluctuations. Complete sample testing by including samples from last three months of the year.

- Perform overall analytical procedures on balances, investigating unexpected fluctuations and key ratios etc.

- Obtain summary of pension balances to be included in the accounts from the actuary. Ensure assumptions used to calculate actuarial liabilities are in line with those discussed at interim and there are no market conditions which would make amended assumptions re discount rates etc more appropriate. Ensure contributions shown by actuary agree to those in the accounting records and tie in investment values to investment manager returns. Consider procedures required on any other assets and liabilities within scheme and ensure that balances owed by company to scheme are correctly eliminated when scheme deficit is included in the accounts.

- Obtain support for year-end holiday pay and bonus provisions if not in line with expectations set up at interim.

- Perform work to check all payroll disclosures including those for pension scheme and directors' remuneration.

4   **Other comments**

- Need to consider whether Mary Fox should be on the team given that her boyfriend, Mark Young is the new financial controller. If he were considered a close family member then she should be removed from the team as his role is likely to give him influence over the financial information submitted for audit. the fact that he used to work for the audit firm is not relevant unless he were a partner of the firm in which case the audit appointment should not be accepted.

- Level of temporary staff used in admin area may indicate issues with staffing and controls over the course of the year – needs further investigation.

- CFO's attitude to controls is concerning – the tone at the top is a crucial element of entity level control and it is difficult to rely on controls if his is not appropriate. This may also increase the risk of mis-statement/fraud more generally.

- Full compliance with IFRS is required this year whereas some items were handled centrally last year – may be other areas where this applies – need to consider more generally.

- Help in calculating entries for pensions – need to ensure that the threat of self-review – ie auditor auditing their own work is safeguarded. May do this by using people from outside the audit team to assist, suggesting that parent company staff rather than audit firm provide assistance, ensuring that CFO and his team take full managerial responsibility for all assumptions made, including in particular judgmental assumptions for actuarial calculations and volatility assumptions etc in share option valuation models. It is very important that these are not suggested by the audit firm.

- CFO's general lack of expertise is concerning for such a large subsidiary. We need to be alert for other more complex areas where he may not have the necessary financial accounting knowledge.

32   Dormro

Scenario

The candidate has recently assumed responsibility for the audit of Dormro Ltd and its consolidated financial statements. Dormro heads a group of companies which supply security surveillance systems. An assistant has completed work on the parent company and consolidation. The candidate is asked to brief the audit manager on the status of the audit work, and potential issues arising and additional information required from the client. An overseas subsidiary company has been acquired during the year, audited by another firm overseas which raises technical audit issues regarding the audit approach and the application of ISA 600. In addition, the candidate is required to prepare a revised statement of financial position incorporating the new subsidiary.

The candidate is required to review the junior assistant's work papers identifying potential audit adjustments. The financial reporting requirement is therefore embedded within the exhibits. The candidate must identify potential financial reporting errors, including the correction of an accounting error (incorrect treatment of intercompany balances), incorrect application of a financial reporting standard (treatment of loan under IAS 39) and the identification of embedded potential financial reporting adjustments arising from the scenario (understatement of provisions for warranty and inventory). There is also the potential non-compliance with IFRS with respect to the recognition of fair value adjustments on the acquisition of CAM. The candidate needs to identify whether there is sufficient information to propose an adjustment or whether further enquiries are required to determine the appropriate accounting treatment.

A successful candidate will understand fully the principles and mechanics of a consolidation and be able to identify issues from the information provided. The scenario also tests the candidate's ability to determine what is significant to a group (as opposed to an individual subsidiary) audit and to consider wider implications across the group of issues identified at a particular subsidiary.

Work paper for the attention of audit engagement manager

Introduction

The purpose of this work paper is to identify and explain the issues which may give rise to an adjustment or an indication of a significant audit risk in the group accounts and additional audit procedures to enable FG to sign off the Dormro group accounts. The work paper also includes a revised consolidated statement of financial position at Appendix 1, reflecting an adjustment for the accounting treatment of the £8 million loan and the acquisition of Klip.

Investments (Notes 1 and 2)

Issues and potential adjustments

- The work of the audit senior is inadequate and this in itself presents a risk for the firm. The insufficient audit procedures performed has a direct impact on the audit opinion. Agreeing a £10 million investment to bank statement alone is clearly inadequate.

- The audit senior has failed to identify a subsidiary requiring consolidation and this will require adjustment – see below.

- CAM appears to have an investment which has not been considered further. The amount is immaterial (£15,000) but it should be determined whether this is a trade investment or an investment in a subsidiary or associate whose results should be included in the group accounts. Further information on the nature of this investment and a determination of subsidiary / associate treatment are required so that the need for, and materiality of, any adjustment can be fully assessed.

- The consolidation entries for the acquisition of CAM seem very simplistic and may not comply with IFRS. No fair value exercise appears to have been carried out at the date of acquisition and the difference between the net assets in CAM and the acquisition price has been posted to goodwill. There may be elements which should be allocated to intangibles. There may be consequential effects on performance for the year because of amortisation of the identified intangibles.

- In addition, costs and revenues for CAM have been assumed to occur evenly throughout the year which may not be the case, especially as CAM is clearly a growing company. Given materiality of CAM's results and goodwill balance, adjustments here could clearly be material. Further enquiries are required.

Additional audit procedures

Detailed reviews of the audit senior's work should be carried out by an appropriate member of the audit team to ensure no further inadequacies in the senior's work.

The sale and purchase agreement for CAM and for Klip should be reviewed to ensure there is no additional consideration payable, or adjustments required (for example, in respect of inventories and warranties). Also evidence of ownership of shares through examination of share certificates must be confirmed in particular it is important to check that ownership of CAM is 100% as has been assumed in consolidation entries.

Need to enquire as to how any costs related to the acquisition of CAM have been treated as these do not appear to have been included within the investment value.

Audit work on the acquisition of CAM should be performed to substantiate that no fair value adjustments are required and to identify separate intangible assets, if any. An expert valuer may be required to assess this, unless an exercise was carried out at the time of the acquisition. Also, consideration should be given to whether adjustments should be made at the acquisition date for the application of group policies.

Need to obtain management accounts or other evidence which give a more precise analysis of the split between pre and post-acquisition results. Likely to be significant additional work to do in auditing this once this information is available.

Consolidation schedules are at summarised level. Work should be performed on the detailed disclosures within group accounts.

Work done on consolidation adjustments comprises largely a description of the adjustment. Need to ensure that the amounts of the adjustments and the accounts to which they have been posted have been substantiated by agreement to individual company results or other supporting documentation.

Need to confirm that Dormro has not issued any shares in year through reviewing Board meeting minutes and documents filed at Companies House. Review of Board minutes and legal correspondence for the holding company are important tests which do not appear to have been performed/documented.

Intercompany balances and transactions (Note 3)

Issues and potential adjustments

- There is a difference on the intercompany balances which has been written off to profit or loss. Need to investigate further the difference on intercompany balances as the current treatment may be incorrect.

- There does not appear to be any consolidation entries to eliminate intercompany sales and purchases. Given that all group companies operate in similar sectors, it seems unlikely that the only intercompany trading is management recharges so consolidation entries may well be incomplete.

Additional audit procedures

FG needs to enquire further into the nature of intercompany trading to ascertain whether further adjustment to eliminate intercompany sales and purchases is required.

Also need to ensure that completeness of the consolidation entries has been considered by comparison to prior year and our knowledge of the way the companies trade and interact.

Loan (Note 4)

Issues and potential adjustments

No loan interest has been accrued on the long-term loan and the loan arrangement fee of £200,000 appears to have been treated incorrectly as an administrative expense. Under IAS 39, it should instead have been deducted from the loan balance outstanding and charged over the loan period in proportion to the outstanding balance on the loan. The adjustment proposed by the junior to charge accrued interest of £480,000 to profit or loss is incorrect. Interest should be calculated using the effective interest rate which would give a charge for the year of £521,040 not £480,000 as proposed. The accrued interest payable should be recognised in current liabilities and deducted from the loan term loan. The loan should also be split between current liabilities, £956,219, and long term borrowings £6,884,821 as follows:

£8,000,000 – £200,000 = £7,800,000

	£	Finance charge £	Interest payable £	Instalment paid £	£
Year 1	7,800,000	521,040	(480,000)		7,841,040
Year 2	7,841,040	523,781	(480,000)	(1,000,000)	6,884,821

Journals required

	£'000	£'000
Dr Loan	200	
Cr Admin expenses		200
Dr Loan	480	
Cr Accrued interest		480
Dr Finance costs	521	
Cr Loan		521
Dr Loan – long term borrowings	956	
Cr Loan – current liabilities		956

Additional audit procedures

Need to consider carefully cash flow forecasts and ability of Dormro to repay its debts as they fall due. In addition, terms of the loan agreement need to be reviewed and covenant compliance assessed both now and over the next year as any breach of covenant might render the entire debt repayable immediately.

Outstanding audit work

Issues and potential adjustments

- Going concern sign off is not required on each individual company for the sign off of group accounts. However, the overall cash position of the group is relevant and this looks poor, especially given that first instalment of £1 million on long-term debt is due in four months-time on 1 November 20X2 and both Secure and CAM have very high trade payables. Although companies are profitable, there are also signs that trading is difficult.

- The group policy on the obsolescence provision is potentially concerning. The potential adjustment identified in CAM is not material but should be considered along with any other unbooked adjustments at subsidiary or group level. An overall group adjustment schedule should be maintained.

- If a similar error rate which is identified in CAM is applied to the provision in the other group companies, then the total error could be material. The Klip auditors have not raised this as an issue but that may be because their audit work has not gone beyond ensuring compliance with group policies (see below). However, the same issue could apply to Klip, particularly as a fair value adjustment on acquisition required a significant adjustment to inventory.

- Warranty provision – Although the balance is not material, the key audit consideration here will be whether it is complete. An understatement could be material.

- The tax position of Secure looks incorrect as no tax credit has been recognised at present. This requires further investigation and explanation to ensure that tax losses have been claimed appropriately.

- There is also no deferred tax balance separately identified on the SOFP of all three companies and this needs to be followed up to ensure compliance with IFRS.

Additional audit procedures

The bank letters should be obtained as these also provide details of any loan accounts and other arrangements and are important audit evidence.

Confirmations of all intercompany balances are not required, providing the balances eliminate on consolidation – there is in fact a difference and this is discussed above. The difference requires further investigation and possible adjustment.

The nature of inventories in each entity should be considered and to evaluate further any potential error which may arise.

In respect of the potential understatement of the inventory provision, discussion is required with management and the other audit teams to determine the extent to which additional analysis is required based on actual post year-end sales and sales forecasts rather than historic data.

The warranty provision should be assessed based on the number of months for which warranty is given, historic experience of warranty claims and any known issues or problems with security equipment supplied.

The tax position of Secure should be discussed with management to determine whether an adjustment is appropriate. The tax computation should be reviewed and discussed with a tax expert.

Overseas subsidiary – Klip

Issues and potential adjustments

- Control is established when a parent owns more than 50% of the voting power of an entity. A 90% shareholding in Klip would therefore signify that control exists unless Dormro management can identify reasons why the ownership of the shares does not constitute control. Therefore, an adjustment is required to include the results from the date of acquisition and the assets and liabilities of Klip – see Appendix 1.

- No assessment appears to have been made at the planning stage of whether Klip is a significant component.

- FG has placed reliance on other auditors to audit this entity. There appears to be no evidence, however, that FG has obtained an understanding of the component auditor as required by ISA 600, or confirmed that the component auditor meets the relevant independence requirements. Furthermore, confirmation appears to have been addressed to Dormro FD and not to FG.

- The audit of Klip has been conducted under Harwanian Standards of Auditing, which may not be equivalent to the ISA.

- Klip has prepared financial statements under group accounting policies supplied by group financial controller. Local policies have been used where group policies are silent. There is a risk that these are not compliant with IFRS or that they are incomplete.

Additional audit procedures

To determine whether Klip is a significant component, FG will need to assess whether Klip has financial significance, is significant by nature of its circumstances or a significant material risk of misstatement to the group. Depending on the outcome of this assessment will determine the nature of the audit approach; full audit, audit of specific balances, specified procedures based on specified risks.

ISA 600 requires FG to evaluate the reliability of the component auditor and the work performed. A formal confirmation of the independence of the Harwanian auditors will be required as this is not covered in the clearance supplied. FG will need to assess their competence by reviewing size, reputation, experience, client base of the firm.

FG will need to assess adequacy of the audit procedures performed by the Harwanian auditors. This could be achieved by asking them to complete a questionnaire confirming their compliance with the ethical and independence requirements of the group audit, their professional competence, and the level of involvement the group auditor is able to have in the component auditor's work.

If the component auditor does not meet the independence requirements, their work must not be relied upon, and FG must perform additional risk assessment or further audit procedures on the financial information of the component.

If there are less serious concerns about the component auditor's competency, FG should be able to overcome the problems by being involved in the component auditor's work. In particular, FG will to conduct a very detailed review of completeness and appropriateness of policies supplied. As Klip is in a different business (manufacturing) to the UK entities, there may well be omissions and differences in the accounting policies adopted.

Appendix 1 – Dormro: Revised consolidated statement of financial position

ASSETS	Group
Non-current assets	£'000
Property, plant and equipment (3,014 + 462)	3,476
Goodwill (6,251 + 52)	6,303
Investments	15
Current assets	
Inventories (6,327 + 262)	6,589
Trade receivables (9,141 + 143)	9,284
Cash and cash equivalents (243+10)	253
Total assets	**25,920**
EQUITY AND LIABILITIES	
Equity	
Share capital	200
Retained earnings (working 4)	5,766
Foreign exchange reserve (working 6 and 7)	52
Non-controlling interests	22
Non-current liabilities	
Long-term borrowings (6,885 (see above) + 333)	7,218
Current liabilities	
Loan	956
Trade and other payables (10,252 + 329+ 480)	11,061
*Current tax payable	645
Total equity and liabilities	**25,920**

*Further adjustments may be required to taxation

WORKINGS

1 Translation of the statement of financial position of Klip

	H$'000	H$'000	Rate	£'000
ASSETS				
Non-current assets				
Property, plant and equipment		1,940	4.2 CR	462
Current assets				
Inventories	2,100			
Less write down at acquisition	1,000	1,100	4.2 CR	262
Trade receivables		600	4.2 CR	143
Cash and cash equivalents		40	4.2 CR	10
Total assets		3,680		877
EQUITY AND LIABILITIES				
Equity				
Share capital		200	5.4 HR	37
Pre-acquisition reserves		575	5.4HR	107
Post-acquisition reserves Including exchange differences to date)		125	Balance	71
Non-current liabilities				
Long-term borrowings		1,400	4.2 CR	333
Current liabilities				
Trade and other payables		1,380	4.2 CR	329
Total equity and liabilities		3,680		877

2 Pre-acquisition reserves

	H$'000
Balance at 30 April 20X2	1,700
Less: Earnings post acquisition	125
Reserves at 31 January 20X2	1,575
Less: Inventory write down	1,000
Pre-acquisition reserves	575

3 Goodwill

			H$'000		£'000
Consideration transferred			918		
Non-controlling interest	775 ×	10%	77		
			995		
Less net assets of acquiree			775		£'000
Goodwill			220	HR 5.4	41
Exchange gain					11
Retranslated at closing rate			220	CR 4.2	52

4 Consolidated retained earnings

	£'000
Dormro (see below)	5,743
Adjustments	
Share of Klip post-acquisition profits	
3 months × 90% of Klip H$500,000	
= 112.5 @AR 4.8	23
	5,766

Dormro	£'000
Retained earnings at 1 May 20X1	5,496
Add Profit for the year	568
Add write back of arrangement fee on loan	200
Less: Finance charge on loan	(521)
Revised retained earnings at 30 April 20X2	5,743

5 Non-controlling interest

		£'000
Closing net assets (37 + 107 + 71)	215,000 × 10%	22

6 Exchange difference on retranslation of subsidiary

	H$'000		£'000
Net assets at acquisition	775	HR 5.4	144
	775	CR 4.2	185
Gain			41
Retained profits since acquisition			
500 × 3/12	125	AV 4.8	26
	125	CR 4.2	30
			4
Total gain (41 + 4)			45
Group share 90%			41

7 Foreign exchange reserve

	£'000
Exchange gain on Goodwill	11
Exchange difference on retranslation of subsidiary	41
	52

33 Kime

The candidate has been appointed to assist an FD for a property company, in the preparation of the financial statements. The auditors are due to start their work and the FD would like to be aware of any contentious issue in advance of their arrival. The candidate is required to determine whether the accounting treatment applied is correct and determine the appropriate treatment given director's instructions to maximise the profit in the current period. The adjustments in respect of current tax and deferred taxation are to be completed given the assumptions in the scenario. The financial reporting issues include IAS 16 (recognition of appropriate costs and depreciation). IAS 11 *Construction contracts*, lessor accounting, asset held for sale and foreign currency adjustment in respect of a receivable, and a cash flow hedge. The candidate is required to prepare a summary Statement of financial position and statement of profit or loss and other comprehensive income.

Email

From:	Jo Ng
To:	FD
Sent:	xx July 20X2
Subject:	Draft financial statements

Please find attached a draft statement of financial position and statement of profit or loss and other comprehensive income (Attachment 1). I have also attached an explanation of my adjustments and a determination of their impact and proposed alternative accounting treatments.

Regards

Jo

Attachment 1

Draft statement of profit or loss and other comprehensive income for the year ended 30 June 20X2

	£m
Revenue (549.8 + 10.2)	560.0
Cost of sales (322.4 + 18)	340.4
Gross profit	219.6
Distribution costs	60.3
Administrative expenses (80.7– 21.5 + 8)	67.2
Finance costs (4.8 + 2.0 – 1.3 +0.2 + 1.3)	7.0
Finance Income	(1.0)
Profit before tax	86.1

	£m
Income tax expense (20.7 + 3.4)	(24.1)
PROFIT FOR THE YEAR	62.0
Cash flow hedge	1.3
Reclassification of cash flow hedge (W5)	–1.3
TOTAL COMPREHENSIVE INCOME FOR THE YEAR	62.0

Draft statement of financial position as at 30 June 20X2

	£m
ASSETS	
Non-current assets	
Property, plant and equipment	
(80.7 – 18 + 120 – 22.8)	159.9
Current assets	
Finance lease receivable	20.5
Gross amounts due from customers	10.2
Trade receivables (174.5 – 10 + 1.3)	165.8
Cash and cash equivalents	183.1
	379.6
Non-current assets classified as held for sale	2.0
Total assets	541.5
EQUITY AND LIABILITIES	
Equity	
Share capital	100
Share premium	84
Retained earnings b/f 102 Profit for year 62.0	164.0
Non-current liabilities	
Long-term borrowings	80.0
Deferred tax liability (33 + 3.4)	36.4
Current liabilities	
Trade and other payables	75.6
Financial liabilities	1.5
Total equity and liabilities	541.5

Attachment 2

1   Freehold land and buildings

1.1   Additions

Renovation of Ferris Street property – allocation of costs

The basis on which the renovation costs have been allocated between repairs and maintenance and capital appears somewhat arbitrary and has not been supported by adequate analysis.

IAS 16 requires that only direct expenditure on property improvements should be capitalised and that maintenance costs should be written off to profit or loss. The 80:20 split was based on budgeted costs but has been used to allocate actual spend to date.

It is possible that the expenditure to date may include a higher or lower proportion of maintenance than that expected for the project as a whole. As repairs should be expensed as the work is performed, this could affect the result for the period. Hence it is important to review a breakdown of the costs actually incurred for the period.

For costs which are capital in nature, we need to evaluate whether any could more appropriately be recorded as plant and machinery rather than included within building costs. The asset lives and depreciation rates would then differ if the asset is not treated as a single composite property asset. I need much more information on the nature of the project to do this.

No disposals have been recorded in the year for any previous renovation or construction work on the Ferris Street building which has been replaced by the work done in the year. In a major project of this type it is likely that there will be elements of the original cost or of previous renovation projects which should be written off. I need to ascertain the nature of building and previous work on it in order to determine what element of the carrying amount, if any, should be written off. For example there may be partition walls which have been demolished and replaced.

I need to review the budget and the basis of the 80:20 split proposed by the project manager. The project manager may not understand the requirements of accounting standards and in particular of IAS 16 and may have been motivated by capital budget constraints or other funding/approval limits than by an analysis of the true nature of the costs to be incurred.

The allocation of costs on a project which includes both types of cost is open to manipulation and can be judgmental and be challenged by our auditors.

Adjustments required?

I cannot at present quantify whether any adjustment is required without further analysis being performed on the additions accounts in the general ledger.

Construction of a sports stadium

The cost of £18 million has been incorrectly treated as an addition to PPE and I have therefore corrected this as follows:

Kime as the contractor should account for the construction of the sports stadium in accordance with IAS 11. This appears to be a contract specifically negotiated for the construction of an asset for which a fixed contract price has been agreed.

IAS 11 requires revenue and costs to be recognised as contract activity progresses. There is a significant amount of judgement required in determining the appropriate accounting policy and in the assessment of progress to date.

Contract costs were predicted to be £16 million. However the estimated total costs to complete the project have now increased to £22.5 million. The project is still expected to make a profit of £11.5 million.

This is a fixed price contract and therefore there is reasonable reliability in respect of the measurement of contract revenue but there is less certainty regarding the costs to be incurred. However the surveyor has determined that these can now be reliably determined.

Using the *contract costs* as a method of accounting for this contract, the contract is ((£18 m / £22.5 m) × 100 =) 80% complete. Therefore £27.2 million representing 80% of the contract revenue would be recognised.

Using the *certified sales method*, the contract is 70% complete ((£23.8/34.0) x 100). Revenue of £23.8 million would therefore be recognised.

In the statement of financial position gross amounts due from customers should be presented as contract costs incurred plus recognised profits less invoices raised to customers. Trade receivables should include the amounts invoiced less amounts received from the local authority.

A comparison of the two methods (assuming costs are recognised on an incurred basis) is as follows:

Statement of profit or loss

	Contract cost basis £m	Work certified basis £m
Revenue	27.2	23.8
Cost of sales	(18.0)	(18.0)
Profit	9.2	5.8

Statement of financial position

	Contract costs £m	Work certified £m
Gross amounts from customers		
Costs incurred	18.0	18.0
Recognised profit	9.2	5.8
	27.2	23.8
Progress billings	(17.0)	(17.0)
	10.2	6.8
Trade receivables (£17.0m – 17.0 m)	0	0

An alternative presentation for the work certified method is to include the costs on the basis of the work certified. This would result in an increase in the amount of profit recognised under this method.

	Work certified £m
Revenue	23.80
Costs 70% × 22.5 m	15.75
Profit	8.05

	Work certified £m
Gross amounts from customers	
Costs	18.00
Recognised profit	8.05
	26.05
Progress billings	(17.00)
	9.05

Implication for the financial statements

Using the work certified to date method results in a lower profit, although this method is also less subjective since it does not rely on estimations of future costs to calculate the % complete. To maximise the amount of profit recognised the directors could select the contract cost method. Ultimately the profit recognised overall on the contract is the same over time, but the allocation to accounting periods is affected by the choice of presentation.

As £17 million of revenue has already been recognised, the following adjustment to the financial statements is required if the maximum amount of profit is to be recognised:

Dr Gross amounts from customers	£10.2 million
Cr Revenue	£10.2 million

Also I have reversed the additions to property plant and equipment as follows:

Dr Cost of sales	£18 million
Cr PPE	£18 million

The assumption has been made that this has been classified as an asset under construction and no depreciation has been charged.

1.2 Disposals

FX House

The lease does appear to be a finance lease given the transfer to the lessee at the end of the contract; this appears to be the case for both the buildings and the land.

As the lease to the third party is a finance lease it is correct to treat the property sale as a disposal. However the junior assistant has failed to account correctly for the disposal and the new finance lease following the guidance for lessor accounting as set out in IAS17. As title to both land and buildings transfer to the lessor at the end of the lease period, the lease should be accounted for as a single lease comprising both land and building elements. Assuming that the new lease is at fair market rates, Kime should realise a gain on the asset disposal and show a new lease receivable equal to the net investment in the lease. This will be equal to the minimum lease payments discounted at the rate implicit in the lease.

Correcting journal entries

Hence entries required to correct the accounting are:

At inception of lease on 1 January 20X2:

Dr Non-current assets – net investment in lease	£21.5 million	
Cr Gain/loss on non-current asset disposals		£21.5 million

Dr Gain/loss on non-current asset disposal	£5.8 million	
Cr administrative expenses		£5.8 million

Thus giving rise to a gain on disposal of £21.5 million less carrying amount at date of disposal of £5.8 million = £15.7 million

As this is material it will require disclosure.

To record correctly the receipt of annual rental payment on 1 January 20X2:

Dr Finance costs	£2 m	
(reversing incorrect entry made by the assistant)		
Cr Non-current assets – net investment in lease		£2m

To record interest income for 6 months to 30 June 20X2:

Dr Non-current assets – net investment in lease	£975,000	
(6/12 of interest income at 10% on (£21.5 million less £2 million)		
Cr Interest income		£975,000

Therefore the net investment in the finance lease receivable will be £20.475 million (£21.5 – £2 + £0.975)

To confirm that these are the correct entries, I need to see evidence that £21.5 million is the fair value of the property at its disposal date.

Estate agency buildings

As the properties were not sold at the year end, it is incorrect to derecognise the assets and recognise a gain in profit or loss. IFRS 5 requires that a non-current asset should be classified as 'held for sale' when the company does not intend to utilise the asset as part of its on-going business but intends to sell it. The Estate agency buildings, having been closed, potentially fall in this category. To be held in this category, the likelihood of a sale taking place should be highly probable. As the sale is to be completed within 12 months of the year end, then this categorisation would appear to be appropriate. Therefore the following adjustment has been made:

Dr Assets held for sale	£10 million	
Cr trade receivables		£10 million

Dr Admin expenses (Gain on disposal)	8 million	
Cr Assets held for sale		£8 million

Discontinued operations

Separate disclosure in the statement of profit orl loss as 'discontinued operations' may also be required.

The question of whether the closures are a withdrawal from the market is a question of judgment as the business is now operated entirely on-line.

There is insufficient information in the summarised trial balance to determine this issue but it will be required before the auditors can commence their work next week.

Depreciation

The depreciation charge suggests a cost of £295 million based upon the accounting policy of the company (£5.9 million × 50 years).

This is significantly greater than the cost in the financial statements and is an issue which should be investigated.

2 Foreign currency receivables and forward contract

	£m
Receivable originally recorded (R$60.48m/5.6)	10.8
Receivable at year end (R$60.48/5.0)	12.1
Exchange gain	1.3

	£m	£m
Dr Trade receivables	1.3	
Cr Profit or loss (other income)		1.3

Forward contract:

This is a cash flow hedge:

Dr Equity – (Other comprehensive income)	1.3	
Dr Finance cost	0.2	
Cr Financial liability		1.5

As the change in cash flow affects profit or loss in the current period, a reclassification adjustment is required:

Dr Profit or loss	1.3	
Cr Equity – (Other comprehensive income)		1.3

Foreign currency and financial instruments gains and losses are taxed on the same basis as IFRS profits. As the finance cost and the exchange gain are both in profit or loss

There are also no further current or deferred tax implications.

The scenario states that 'the arrangement satisfies the necessary criteria to be accounted for as a hedge.' This transaction could be treated as either a fair value or cash flow hedge. However as a receivable is created there is no need for hedge accounting as the exchange difference on the receivable and the future are both recognised through profit or loss.

Therefore an alternative accounting treatment would be not to apply hedge accounting.

3 Taxation

The following journal is required to adjust for current and deferred tax as noted in the assumptions:

Dr Income tax expense	£20.7 million	
Cr Current tax obligation		£20.7 million
Being current tax adjustment – revised profit × 24%		

Dr Income tax expense		
£14 m × 24%	£3.4 million	
Cr Deferred tax obligation		£3.4 million

Being adjustment for temporary timing differences

Deferred tax summary

	£m
Deferred tax liability brought forward	33.0
Increase in taxable temporary differences	
Temporary differences at 30 June 20X2 (£14 million × 30%)	3.4
	36.4

34 Thyme

The candidate is asked to review the analytical procedures prepared by a member of the audit team in the context of the planning of the audit. The scenario covers payroll and payroll controls and financial reporting topics of share based payment (IFRS 2) and pensions and bonuses (IAS 19). The financial reporting is both interpretative; i.e. the candidate identifies that there is a potential error in respect of the pension costs but the question does not provide sufficient information to enable an adjustment; and technical in that the candidate has to propose adjustments. Financial statement analysis forms part of both the analytical review procedures and determining the technical adjustment to the financial statements. The question also includes an ethical issue regarding the employment of a former employee at a client.

Subject: Thyme Ltd – Audit planning document – Staff costs and staff costs payables and accruals
Prepared by: Audit senior
Date: August 20X2

1 Explanation of the correct financial reporting treatment for employee incentive schemes set out in Jon's email

1.1 Staff Bonus

The full year bonus is potentially £600,000. An accrual of 9/12 of this amount (i.e. £450,000) appears to have been made for the three-quarters interim accounts. However this is not appropriate as the business is seasonal as: "This is a quiet time in the industry and revenue is expected to be the same in the final quarter to 30 September 20X2 as it was in the quarter to 30 September 20X1"

On this basis revenue will be:

9 months to 30 June 20X1	28,400
Y/e 30 Sept 20X1	31,600
Final quarter y/e 30 Sept 20X1	3,200
9 months to 30 June 20X2	21,500
Projected revenue y/e 30.9.20X2	24,700

This is lower than £26 million threshold, thus the bonus should not be recognised.

The bonus should only be recognised according to IAS 19 when there is a constructive or legal obligation to make a payment. In this case, the full year's revenue on which the bonus is based is expected to fall below £26m in the full year, so no bonus should be recognised in the interim or the final full year financial statements.

The bonus should therefore be reversed as follows

Dr Bonus accrual – staff payables	£450,000	
Cr Payroll costs		£450,000

1.2 Share appreciation rights

These are deemed to be cash-settled share-appreciation rights because they do not involve the issue of shares. The vesting conditions are not market-based, because they relate only to continued employment.

A liability is created in the statement of financial position and an expense recognised in profit or loss. The fair value of the liability is remeasured at each reporting date, and also takes into consideration the expected number of employees in the scheme at the vesting date.

The charge is therefore £1,368,000 (£2.28 × 4,000 × 450 × 1/3), with an equal increase in liability.

Therefore an adjustment is required to:

Dr Staff costs – income statement	£1,368,000	
Cr Staff costs – payables		£1,368,000

1.3 Other Financial reporting issues – Director's bonus and pension

There may also be further adjustments regarding the pension scheme which will have an impact on operating profit.

The pension should be accounted for in accordance with IAS 19. This means that the net surplus/deficit on the pension plan will be recorded in the financial statements.

We need to obtain details of the scheme assets and liabilities from the actuary in order to:

- Record the opening balance on the scheme

- Analyse the movement in assets and liabilities in the year into the following and make the entries indicated below:

  - Current service cost (as calculated by actuary). Will need to split between departments and allocate between various captions in the statement of profit or loss and other comprehensive income. Charge to operating profit.

  - Interest cost (as calculated by actuary). Forms part of finance cost in financial statements.

  - Return on plan assets excluding amounts in net interest (as advised by actuary). Forms part of finance cost/income in statement of profit or loss and other comprehensive income.

  - Contributions paid – this will be the contributions paid in the year by the employer and employees. Employer contributions have already been charged to statement of profit or loss and other comprehensive income. That entry needs to be reversed so that statement of profit or loss and other comprehensive income charge is only as specified above and amounts paid form part of movement on net pension liability/asset within statement of financial position.

- Closing remeasurement (actuarial) gain/loss should then agree to amount advised by the actuary. The directors will need to determine the accounting policy regarding the treatment of this in the financial statements.

Clearly the above entries will have an impact on profit or loss. Therefore, it is not possible to determine whether the directors' bonus of £100,000 will be paid. This should be reversed as follows:

Dr Accruals – staff payables –	£100,000	
Cr Profit or loss		£100,000

2   Analytical procedures for staff costs identifying any unusual patterns and trends and outlining the audit risks:

	Revised 9 months to 30 June 20X2 £'000	9 months to 30 June 20X1 £'000	Year ended 30 September 20X2 £'000
Revenue	21,500	28,400	31,600
Cost of sales	(1,505)	(2,700)	(2,920)
Gross profit	19,995	25,700	28,680
Operating expenses	(520)	(520)	(690)
Staff costs			
Directors' salaries (Note 1)	(600)	(600)	(800)
Payroll (Note 2)	(14,850)	(14,150)	(18,860)
Pension costs (Note 3)	(2,050)		
Temporary staff (Note 4)	(815)	(105)	(110)
Employee expenses	(270)	(240)	(250)
Share options costs	(1,368)		
Operating (loss) profit revised	(478)	10,085	7,970

Notes

1   The directors bonus has been reversed – see above note 1.3

2   Payroll costs

	£'000
As originally stated	15,300
Less bonus accrual	(450)
As revised above	14,850
Add 10% 14850 × 100/90	16,500
9 months to 30 June 20X1	14,150
Increase	2,350

After adjustment for the 10% pay reduction and removing the bonus accrual, the payroll cost has increased by £2,350,000. Assuming that average employee cost in nine months to 30 June 20X1 was £28,300 (£14,150,000/500 = £28,300). The expected cost for the nine months to 30 June 20X2 before the 10% reduction in pay would be 525 × £28,300 = £14,857,500. Therefore the difference of £16,500,000 – 14,857,500 = £1,642,500 represents an unusual trend and requires explanation as payroll appears to be overstated.

The payroll cost must be disaggregated to determine which elements of cost have increased or decreased. The movements could be due to an increase in employer payroll taxes or staff promotions. Without further information, this cannot be determined and currently presents a significant audit risk of misstatement exceeding the planning materiality level.

3   Pension costs appear to be incorrectly recorded – see above 1.3 – This is a major area of audit risk and will require experienced audit staff to be allocated to audit the pension costs recorded in the financial statements. There may also be need to appoint an auditor expert to determine the risk of potential misstatement arising from the adjustments.

4   The explanation of the increase in temporary staff costs given by the junior is inadequate and given that there are no apparent controls over these costs (see below section 3) this represents a significant audit risk of misstatement. Although this is below the materiality level but due to the nature of the payments is an audit risk requires further investigation.

Other points

No explanation of the increase in employee expenses has been obtained. Further information is required.

3   Payroll controls

3.1   Evaluation of the summary of key internal payroll controls

The objectives identified by the company do not cover all of the relevant financial statement assertions – in particular, assertions about classification, presentation and disclosure, including the disclosure and presentation of share-based payments, are not really covered at all.

Controls identified by the company do not cover all of the staff cost balances we need to audit. Staff bonus payments and share based payments are not covered at all, and neither are payments to temporary staff. In addition, there are no explicit controls relating to employee expenses, bonus payments or commission or to the related accruals.

The summary includes no consideration of systems or IT controls. Access controls are likely to be very important in an area such as this and the company is also relying on the system to calculate the payroll, PAYE, NI etc. As a result, IT controls are likely to be key.

Departmental heads have very extensive responsibilities, giving rise to concerns about the lack of segregation of duties. They can authorise new joiners and changes to salary levels and are also responsible for the only detailed review of costs. Although the financial controller authorises the payroll and reviews the monthly management accounts, these are very high level controls for a large balance and might not identify all misstatements. This is especially true in a department which includes up to 100 staff. It is likely that departmental controls are very inconsistent across the business and may not be wholly effective in the largest ones or wholly adequate in terms of segregation in smallest ones. It is also unclear who approves the salary for departmental head.

Payroll summary is authorised by financial controller but there is no indication of the level of review that takes place or of the level of detail presented. Ideally, there should be a summary by department and a reconciliation explaining significant differences from the prior month's payroll.

There are likely to be sundry manual payments for corrections. Controls over these are not mentioned at all.

Controls over joiners are identified, but there are no controls listed which will ensure that leavers are removed from the payroll on a timely basis.

Controls over joiners/leavers/numbers of employees include no reconciliation with data held by HR. Such a control would make it more difficult to include fictitious employees or for leavers to be paid after employment has ceased.

If payroll is prepared five days before the month end, how are the hours for the last five days captured for hourly paid staff? This seems to indicate that an accrual may be necessary.

No controls are listed relating to the calculation of NI, PAYE or pension contributions. All of these are relevant in ensuring that payroll costs are calculated accurately.

There are also no controls over payments to temporary staff and staff expenses noted on the schedule.

Controls do not cover all changes to master files used as source of data. A report of changes made to pay rates would be expected, bank account details for example so that this can be reviewed by the financial controller/head of HR. At present, the payroll clerk could make unauthorised changes and these might not be picked up.

3.2 Determination of reliance to be placed on these controls in reducing, to an acceptable level, the risk that the financial statements will be materially misstated.

There are significant gaps in the documentation of controls before reliance can be placed on the controls. In particular:

- Need to resolve design issues above by identifying, where possible, controls which eliminate gaps and deficiencies in controls and in the objectives which the controls address.

- Key controls sufficient to meet each objective should then be identified and tested.

- Tests of controls will include discussion, observation, re-performance and examination of relevant documentation. Work done on each control should be sufficient to ensure that it has operated throughout the nine months to June 20X2 and so should cover the whole period.

- Where a control is not operating effectively, a mitigating control should be sought or additional substantive work planned.

- Work by computer audit specialists on the systems based controls should take place.

4 **Ethical concerns**

Our firm should consider whether Tina Jie should be on the team given that her boyfriend is the financial controller. If he were considered a close family member, she should be removed from the team as his role is likely to give him influence over the financial information submitted for audit. The fact he used to work for the audit firm is not relevant unless he were a partner of the firm in which case the audit appointment should not be accepted.

There appears to be no current FD in place and the financial controller is under pressure to produce good results as his promotion may depend upon a reduction in the audit fee.

The financial controller's attitude to controls is concerning – the importance management places on controls is a crucial element of entity level control and it is difficult to rely on controls if this is not appropriate. May also increase the risk of misstatement or fraud more generally.

The financial statements are currently not in compliance with IFRS in respect of pension costs. There may be other areas of non-compliance.

The financial controller has asked for assistance in calculating entries for pensions. Our firm needs to ensure that any threat of self-review can be mitigated. We may do this by using people from outside the audit team to assist, suggesting that parent company staff rather than audit firm provide assistance, ensuring that financial controller and the directors take full managerial responsibility for all assumptions made, including in particular judgmental assumptions for actuarial calculations and volatility assumptions in share option valuation models. Very important that these are not suggested by audit firm.

Financial controller's general lack of expertise is concerning for such a large subsidiary. Need to be alert for other more complex areas where he may not have the necessary financial accounting knowledge.

Tutor marking guidance – Corporate Reporting (Sample paper)

32 Dormro

MARKS WITH HEADROOM (Maximum available marks shown in brackets)		Technical		Skills
(a) Identifies and explains any known and potential issues which you believe may give rise to material audit adjustments or significant audit risks in the group financial statements.	7	Calculate effective interest £521,040 and deduct £200,000 – 1 Determine adjustments for loan – 3 Going concern sign off not required on all companies – 1 Klip's status as a significant component – may have changed significantly audit approach – 2	13 (Max 11)	Identifying inadequate work by senior is a risk for quality • omission of Klip from consolidation, failure to determine nature of investment held by CAM, simplistic consolidation adjustments not investigated – 3 Identify lack of fair value adjustment and implications for financial statements – 2 Determine that entries may be missing in respect of intercompany balances. – 1 Identify incorrect treatment of loan – 1 Appreciate going concern as a potential risk. – 1 Apply concept of materiality to potential audit adjustments for obsolescence and warranty. – 2 Identify the need for tax expert to determine adjustment to the group accounts. – 1 Identify potential risk from use of overseas auditors. – 1 Appreciate potential difference between Ruritanian accounting standards and IFRS and impact on group accounts. – 1
(b) Outlines, for each issue, the additional audit procedures, if any, required to enable us to sign our audit opinion on the group financial statements			10 (Max 9)	Ascertain gaps in work performed and recommend appropriate audit work for: • Investments – 2 • Intercompany balances – 1 • Loan – 1 • Outstanding audit work – 3 • Overseas subsidiary – 3

MARKS WITH HEADROOM (Maximum available marks shown in brackets)	Technical		Skills
(c) A revised consolidated statement of financial position for the year ended 30 April 2012, which includes the overseas subsidiary, Klip	10 (Max 9)	Net assets of Klip at acquisition H$775,000 (1) Goodwill H$ 220,000 (1) Exchange gain on Goodwill (1) Adjust retained earnings for loan (1.5) Consolidated Retained earnings (1.5) NCI (1) Exchange gain on retranslation of subsidiary (3)	4	Apply technical knowledge to use appropriate exchange rates. Assimilate information to produce adjusted consolidated SOFP.
	17 (Max 16)		27 (Max 24)	
Total marks	44			
Maximum available marks	40			

33 Kime

MARKS WITH HEADROOM (Maximum available marks shown in brackets)		Technical		Skills
(a) Explain the potentially contentious financial reporting issues. Determine any adjustments you consider necessary and explain the impact of your adjustments on the financial statements, identifying any alternative accounting treatments				
• Renovation of Ferris street	1	IAS 16 – capitalise direct costs only not an arbitrary split write off revenue costs	2	Distinguish between accounting treatment of revenue and capital expenditure in accordance with IAS 16.
				Appreciate that judgement is required and the allocation is open to manipulation.
				Understand that project manager may not have appropriate accounting technical knowledge to determine the split of 80:20.
				Query why no disposal noted for Oxford project.
• IAS 11	4	Contract cost basis – 2 Work certified basis – 2	2	Identify incorrect treatment in PPE.
				Identify potential alternative accounting treatments and the implications for financial statements.
				Determine contract is still profitable and the significance of this in terms of recognition.
				Appreciate why judgement is required in application of IAS 11.
				Conclude on implications for financial statements.

		Technical		Skills
• FX House disposal	3	21.5 million – net investment in lease – 1 Gain in IS now £15.7 million – 2 Reverse rental income of £2m and charge interest of £975,000 – 2	2	Identify interest cost not capitalised in accordance with IAS 23. Identify incorrect treatment of finance lease.
• Estate agency buildings	2	Journal adjustment for IFRS 5	2	Apply technical knowledge of IFRS 5 to the scenario. Determine insufficient information to conclude on treatment of discontinued operations. Recognise depreciation requires investigation.
• Foreign currency receivable and forward contract	2	Journal adjustments Retranslation of receivable	2	Identify no deferred tax adjustment required. Recognises that no real need for hedge accounting to apply.
• Taxation	3	Journal adjustments Current tax – 1 Deferred tax – 2		
	15 *(Max13)*		10 *(Max 9)*	
(b) After making adjustments for matters arising from your review of the outstanding issues, prepare a draft statement of financial position and statement of comprehensive income.			8	Assimilate adjustments and produce financial statements.
	15 *(Max13)*		18 *(Max 17)*	
Total marks	**33**			
Maximum available marks	*30*			

34 Thyme

MARKS WITH HEADROOM (Maximum available marks shown in brackets)		Technical		Skills
(a) Explain the correct financial reporting treatment for employee incentive schemes set out in Jon's email showing, where appropriate, calculations and correcting journal adjustments				
• Staff bonus	1	Application of IAS 19 and journal adjustment.	3	Link information from different parts of the scenario. – 1 Financial statement analysis to determine revenue target not achieved. – 2
• SAR	2	Application of IFRS 2 and journal adjustment – 1 £1.368 m – 1	2	Recognition of share-based payment as cash settled and the impact on financial statements. – 1 Apply technical knowledge to the scenario to arrive at charge and payable. – 1
• Pension			4	Determination that the cash payment is not the correct income statement charge for pension. Appreciate need for actuary in identifying the information required to recognise the net pension obligation in the financial statements.
• Directors Bonus	1	Journal adjustment to remove directors' bonus	1	Assimilate information and adjustments to determine bonus accrual is not appropriate.
	4 (Max 3)		10 (Max 8)	

MARKS WITH HEADROOM (Maximum available marks shown in brackets)		Technical		Skills
(b) Perform relevant analytical procedures for staff costs based on the information available, identifying any unusual patterns and trends and outlining the audit risks which arise from your work	2	Relevant calculations to determine overstatement – 2	6 *(Max 5)*	Assimilate information and adjustments. Analyse date to identify potential overstatement. Recognise that overstatement represents significant audit risk. Apply concept of materiality to determine significant of potential adjustment and need for further audit work. Appreciate that the explanations offered by the junior are inadequate and require further investigation. Recommend the use of experienced audit staff to investigate staff costs and pension. Identify that the pension adjustment will be a significant area of audit risk and an auditors' expert will be required to review the assumptions of the actuary.
(c) Evaluate the summary of key internal payroll controls prepared by Jon Dillan. Identify any areas where controls appear inadequate and any further risks associated with staff costs not covered by these controls. Determine the extent of reliance that can be placed on these controls in reducing the risk that the financial statements will be materially misstated.			8 *(Max 6)*	Interpret and analyse data from a variety of sources to enable a critical analysis of the control information presented. Identify gaps in the control information (eg employee expenses, bonus payments, share based payments, IT controls). Identify risks arising from lack of segregation of duties, relative size of departments, joiners and leavers. Apply technical advice to a given scenario and a given audience. Identify the need for documentation of controls before reliance possible. Recommend use of computer audit specialist.

MARKS WITH HEADROOM (Maximum available marks shown in brackets)	Technical	Skills
(d) Your comments on any ethical issues or concerns you have arising from the information you have received."	7 (Max 6)	Determine the ethical issues arising from the relationship between Tina and the financial controller and explain the audit risks.
		Appreciate the impact on the audit of the pressure placed upon the FD by the client.
		Identify the self-review threat arising from the FD's request for assistance.
		Relate FD's lack of expertise to potential audit risks arising from other complex areas.
	6 (Max 5)	31 (Max 25)
Total marks	37	
Maximum available marks	30	

REVIEW FORM – CORPORATE REPORTING QUESTION BANK

Your ratings, comments and suggestions would be appreciated on the following areas of this Question Bank

	Very useful	Useful	Not useful
Number of questions in each section	☐	☐	☐
Standard of answers	☐	☐	☐
Amount of guidance on exam technique	☐	☐	☐
Quality of marking guides	☐	☐	☐

	Excellent	Good	Adequate	Poor
Overall opinion of this Question Bank	☐	☐	☐	☐

Please return completed form to:

The Learning Team
Learning and Professional Department
ICAEW
Metropolitan House
321 Avebury Boulevard
Milton Keynes
MK9 2FZ
E learning@icaew.com

For space to add further comments please see overleaf.

REVIEW FORM (continued)

TELL US WHAT YOU THINK

Please note any further comments and suggestions/errors below.